THE HIDDEN PLACES OF

YORKSHIRE

Including The Yorkshire Dales, Moors and Coast

By David Gerrard

Published by: Travel Publishing Ltd, Airport Business Centre,
10 Thornbury Road, Estover, Plymouth, Devon PL6 7PP

ISBN13 9781904434764

© Travel Publishing Ltd

First published 1990, second edition 1993,
third edition 1995, fourth edition 1998,
fifth edition 2000, sixth edition 2002,
seventh edition 2004, eighth edition 2006,
ninth edition 2008

Printing by: Latimer Trend, Plymouth

Maps by: ©MAPS IN MINUTES ™ (2008)
©Collins Bartholomew 2008 All rights reserved.

Editor: David Gerrard

Cover Design: Lines and Words, Aldermaston

Cover Photograph: Rhodesfield Lock, Ripon Canal,
North Yorkshire © www.picturesofbritain.co.uk

Text Photographs: © www.picturesofbritain.co.uk
and © Bob Brooks, Weston super Mare
www.britainhistoricsites.co.uk

Foreword

This is the 9th edition of the *Hidden Places of Yorkshire*. The guide has been been fully updated and in this respect we would like to thank the Tourist Information Centres in Yorkshire for helping us update the editorial content. The guide is packed with information on the many interesting places to visit in the area. In addition, you will find details of places of interest and advertisers of places to stay, eat and drink included under each village, town or city, which are cross referenced to more detailed information contained in a separate, easy-to-use section to the rear of the book. This section is also available as a free supplement from the local Tourist Information Offices.

The county of Yorkshire is full of scenic, historical and cultural diversity. In the northwest are the picturesque Dales with their varied scenery of peat moorland, green pastureland and scattered woods intersected by the numerous brooks, streams and rivers. To the northeast are the imposing Yorkshire Moors, the rich agricultural Vale of York, the chalky hills of the Wolds and the dramatic storm-tossed coastline. In the south are the industrial and commercial cities and towns, which have made such a major contribution to our industrial and cultural heritage

The Hidden Places of Yorkshire contains a wealth of interesting information on the history, the countryside, the towns and villages and the more established places of interest. But it also promotes the more secluded and little known visitor attractions and places to stay, eat and drink many of which are easy to miss unless you know exactly where you are going.

We include hotels, bed & breakfasts, restaurants, pubs, bars, teashops and cafes as well as historic houses, museums, gardens and many other attractions throughout Yorkshire, all of which are comprehensively indexed. Many places are accompanied by an attractive photograph and are easily located by using the map at the beginning of each chapter. We do not award merit marks or rankings but concentrate on describing the more interesting, unusual or unique features of each place with the aim of making the reader's stay in the local area an enjoyable and stimulating experience.

Whether you are travelling around Yorkshire on business or for pleasure we do hope that you enjoy reading and using this book. We are always interested in what readers think of places covered (or not covered) in our guides so please do not hesitate to use the reader reaction form provided to give us your considered comments. We also welcome any general comments which will help us improve the guides themselves. Finally if you are planning to visit any other corner of the British Isles we would like to refer you to the list of other *Hidden Places* titles to be found to the rear of the book and to the Travel Publishing website.

Travel Publishing

Did you know that you can also search our website for details of thousands of places to see, stay, eat or drink throughout Britain and Ireland? Our site has become increasingly popular and now receives over **500,000** visits annually. Try it!

website: www.travelpublishing.co.uk

Location Map

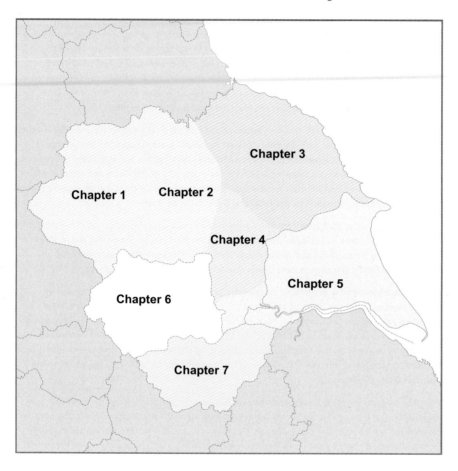

Contents

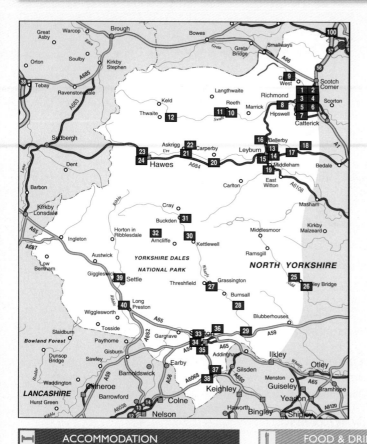

The Yorkshire Dales

The Yorkshire Dales make up one of the 11 National Parks in England and Wales. An area rich in farmland, high moorland and deep valleys, the predominant limestone found here gives rise to many of the area's interesting geological features – such as those found around Malham, the waterfalls at Aysgarth and Hardraw and White Scar Cave. Considered by many to be the most appealing and beautiful region in the country, the Yorkshire Dales have drawn increasing numbers of visitors since the arrival of the railways in the 1800s. With the large industrial areas of Yorkshire, and with Lancashire close to hand, the Dales are easily accessible – but with so much open countryside, visitors are able to avoid the more popular attractions and enjoy the beauty of the region in solitude.

The largest of the northern Dales, Swaledale is also one of the grandest and it has a rugged beauty that is in contrast to the pretty and busier Wensleydale to the south. It is this dale's sheep, the Swaledale, with their characteristic black faces, white muzzles and grey speckled legs, which have been adopted as the symbol for the National Park. The valley of the River Ure, Wensleydale, is, perhaps, the one that most people associate with the Yorkshire Dales. One of the longer dales, it is a place of green pastureland grazed by flocks of Wensleydale sheep, lines of drystone walls and, of course, this is where the famous cheese is made. Further south again, is Wharfedale, a spectacular valley that is home to one of the National Park's most famous features, the Strid, where the River Wharfe charges through a narrow gorge just to the north of Bolton Abbey. To the east lies Nidderdale, a charming valley that was dubbed 'Little Switzerland' by the Victorians as its upper reaches are steep and wooded with the River Nidd flowing through narrow gorges. To the west is Ribbledale that is overlooked by the famous Three Peaks of Whernside, Ingleborough and Pen-ghent, and that is also home to a spectacular stretch of the famous Settle-Carlisle Railway. Finally, there is Airedale, the valley of the River Aire, where, near the river's source, can be found the extraordinary limestone landscape around Malham Tarn. Further downstream lies Skipton, an ancient market town and 'Gateway to the Dales' that is often many people's first experience of this glorious region of Britain.

Easby Abbey, Swaledale

The attractive market town of Richmond, first settled by the Romans, has for many years been the major focal point of this northerly region of Yorkshire. With several interesting museums, a fine Norman castle and excellent shopping facilities, Richmond is still the key town in the northern dales.

There are several side dales to Swaledale: the small, thriving market town of Reeth lies at the junction of Arkengarthdale and the valley of the River Swale. First settled by Norsemen who preferred wild and remote countryside, the valley of Arkle Beck was not considered important enough to gain an entry in the *Domesday Book*. There is much evidence of the old lead-mining days although the dale is now chiefly populated by hardy Swaledale sheep. At the head of this rather bleak and barren dale lies England's highest inn, Tan Hill. Though only a short section of the River Tees flows through Yorkshire, the section of Teesdale around Piercebridge is particularly charming and well worth a visit.

RICHMOND

The British Architectural Society acclaimed Richmond as one of England's "35 most precious towns"; the architectural guru Nikolaus Pevsner commended it as 'one of the most visually enjoyable small towns in England'. Another visitor described it as "a town to savour like old wine".

The former county of Richmondshire (which still survives

SWALEDALE

For many, Swaledale is the loveliest of the Yorkshire Dales. From historic Richmond it runs westwards through countryside that ranges from the dramatic lower dale with its steep-sided wooded hills to austere upper reaches – a terrain where your nearest neighbour could be several miles away. Its rugged beauty makes quite a contrast to pretty and busier Wensleydale just to the south. There are several other noticeable differences: the villages in Swaledale all have harsher, Nordic sounding names, the dale is much less populated, and the rivers and becks are fast-flowing mountain streams.

At one time Swaledale was a hive of activity and enjoyed a prosperous century and more when the lead-mining industry flourished here. The valley of the River Swale still bears many of the scars left behind since the mining declined and the dale once again became a remote and under-populated place.

1 SEASONS

Richmond

Outstanding café/restaurant occupying former railway station and serving Mediterranean-influenced cuisine.

🍴 see page 206

2 THE HOLLY HILL INN & IVY RESTAURANT

Richmond

A medieval style inn with a warm atmosphere offering home-cooked meals in the Ivy Restaurant and spacious en-suite accommodation.

🍴 🛏 see page 207

4

as a parliamentary constituency) once occupied a third of the North Riding of Yorkshire. Today, Richmond is an appealing small town with a cobbled Market Place, surrounded by fine Georgian buildings, which is said to be one of the largest in England. It has even been compared (by the Prince of Wales) to the sweeping market area in Siena. The outdoor market takes place on Saturdays and is joined on the 3rd Saturday of the month by a Farmer's Market.

Dominating the town centre is the mighty Keep of **Richmond Castle** (English Heritage), built by Alan Rufus, the 1st Earl of Richmond, in 1071. He selected an impregnable site, 100 feet up on a rocky promontory with the River Swale passing below. The keep rises to 109 feet with walls 11 feet thick, while the other side is afforded an unassailable defence by means of the cliff and the river. Richmond Castle was the first Norman castle in the country to be built, right

from the foundations, in stone. Additions were made over subsequent years but it reached its final form in the 14th century. Since then it has fallen into ruin though a considerable amount of the original Norman stonework remains intact.

With such an inspiring setting, it is hardly surprising that there is a legend suggesting that King Arthur himself is buried here, reputedly in a cave beneath the castle. The story goes that a simple potter called Thompson stumbled across an underground passage which led to a chamber where he discovered the king and his knights lying in an enchanted sleep, surrounded by priceless treasures. A voice warned him not to disturb the sleepers and he fled. Predictably, he was unable to locate the passage again.

Another legend associated with the castle tells how a drummer boy was sent down the passageway. Beating his drum as he walked, the boy's progress was followed by the

3 THE TALBOT HOTEL

Richmond

Overlooking Richmond's cobbled market place, the Talbot Hotel offers a warm welcome, good food and comfortable en suite rooms.

see *page 208*

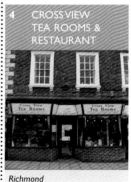

4 CROSS VIEW TEA ROOMS & RESTAURANT

Richmond

Well-established town centre tea rooms serving excellent home-cooked fare.

see *page 209*

5 SIP COFFEE

Richmond

Popular town centre café with excellent choice of coffees, teas and light meals.

see *page 210*

Green Howards Museum, Richmond

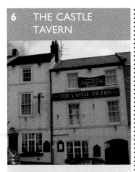

6 THE CASTLE TAVERN

Richmond

Former coaching inn in town centre offering quality food, real ales and accommodation.

‖ ⊨ see page 210

7 ARCHER'S JERSEY ICE CREAM

Walworth Gate, nr Darlington

Creamy, delicious ice creams in a wide variety of tempting flavours are sold in an ice cream parlour on a farm not far from Darlington.

‖ see page 211

soldiers on the surface until, suddenly, the drumming stopped. Though the passageway was searched the boy was never seen again but, it is said, his drumming can still be heard. The mile-long **Drummer Boy Walk** takes a scenic route along the banks of the River Swale to Easby Abbey.

The **Green Howards Museum**, the regimental museum of the North Riding's infantry, is based in the former Holy Trinity Church in the centre of the cobbled market square. The regiment dates back to 1688 and the displays and collections illustrate its history with war relics, weapons, uniforms, medals, and regimental silver. Also housed in the museum is the town's silver. The church itself was founded in 1135 and, though it has been altered and rebuilt on more than one occasion, the original Norman tower and some other masonry have survived.

Just a few yards from the museum, the **Town Hall,** built in 1756, has a superbly restored Georgian Court which is open to the public on weekday mornings.

The **Richmondshire Museum** traces the history of this ancient place and its county. There is also a reconstruction of James Herriot's veterinary surgery taken from the popular television series *All Creatures Great and Small,* as well as other period costumes and displays.

One of the grandest buildings in the town is the **Culloden Tower,** just off the town green. It was erected in 1747 by the Yorke

family, one of whose members had fought at the Battle of Culloden the previous year. Unlike most follies, the interior of the three storey tower is elaborately decorated in the rococo style and since it is now in the care of the Landmark Trust it is possible to stay there.

Richmond is also home to England's oldest theatre, the **Georgian Theatre Royal,** which originally formed part of a circuit that included Northallerton, Ripon, and Harrogate. Built in 1788 by the actor and manager Samuel Butler, it had at that time an audience capacity of 400. The connection with the theatrical Butler family ended in 1830 and from then until 1848 it was used, infrequently, by travelling companies. After the mid-19th century and right up until the 1960s, the theatre saw a variety of uses, as a wine cellar and a corn chandler's among others, and it did not re-open as a theatre until 1963 and only then after much restoration work had been carried out. Guided tours are available. The **Georgian Theatre Royal Museum** was also opened and it contains a unique collection of original playbills as well as the oldest and largest complete set of painted scenery in Britain.

A few yards from the museum **The Friary Tower and Gardens,** with its picturesque ruined Franciscan bell tower, provides a pleasant setting in which to relax.

A fairly recent addition to the town's amenities is the former **Richmond Railway Station,** a fine old Victorian building which now contains two cinema screens, a café/restaurant, craft bakery, microbrewery and heritage centre.

AROUND RICHMOND

HUDSWELL

2 miles W of Richmond off the A6136

This ancient village, which was well established by the time it was recorded in the *Domesday Book*, stands high above the River Swale and over the years the village has gravitated to a more sheltered spot. The present St Michael's Church was built in the late 19th century on the site of an older building and the view from the churchyard is considered to be one of the finest in Richmondshire.

The walk from the village down to the river leads through pleasant woodland and also takes in some 365 steps. About half way down, below a path leading off to an old lime kiln, can be found **King Arthur's Oven**, a horizontal crack in the limestone which, it is claimed, has connections with Richmond Castle and the legend of King Arthur.

KIRBY HILL

4 miles NW of Richmond off the A66

This quiet hamlet lies midway between London and Edinburgh on the old Great North Road and in the days of the stagecoach it was a busy stopping place. The cellar of the Blue Bell Inn still retains the rings to which prisoners travelling between the two capitals were tethered overnight.

FORCETT

8 miles N of Richmond on the B6274

Forcett Park, which is privately owned, is a particularly outstanding example of an early Georgian house, complete with stables, lodges, and a fine dovecote. The dovecote and the splendid east gate can be seen from the road leading to the park from the village.

REETH

Considered the capital of Upper Swaledale, this popular hill-top town is scattered around a spacious village green above the junction of the River Swale and its main tributary, Arkle Beck. The town was recorded in the *Domesday Book*, while everything else in the area was written off as untaxable wasteland.

Along the top of the green is High Row, with its inns and shops and outstanding Georgian architecture, reflecting the affluence of the town in the 18th century when the trade in wool and lead was booming. The recently refurbished **Swaledale Folk Museum** (see panel), housed in what was once the old Methodist Sunday School, contains more than 500 exhibits of local farming methods, crafts, and mining skills, as well as displays on local pastimes, the impact of Wesleyan Methodism, and the exodus of the population to the industrial areas of the south Pennines and America when the lead mines closed.

This little town is noted for its variety of craft shops. There's a

8 THE GEORGE & DRAGON

Hudswell

A popular country pub with friendly family hosts, a good choice of real ales and menus to suit appetites large and small

see page 211

9 THE ANGEL INN

Gilling West

Popular hostelry in pretty village serving outstanding food and real ales.

see page 212

10 SWALEDALE FOLK MUSEUM

Reeth

The **Swaledale Folk Museum** was opened in 1974, and is based in the old Methodist School, which took its first pupils in 1836.

see page 213

11 THE KINGS ARMS HOTEL

Reeth

18th century former coaching inn with good, wholesome cuisine, real ales and recently refurbished en suite rooms

see page 214

cluster of them at the **Reeth Craft Workshops** near the green. Here you'll find a cabinet maker, a furniture maker, a guitar maker, a pottery shop, a clock maker and restorer, a sculptor, a silversmith, a photographer and Stef's Models where visitors can see the production of beautifully crafted animal models. Paintings are also on sale here.

A good time to visit Reeth is on the last Wednesday in August when the town hosts the annual **Agricultural Show** which attracts not just tourists but working farmers from the length of the dale. Entertainments, trade stands and a chance to see some of the best livestock on display make the event a great day out for the family.

AROUND REETH

GRINTON

1 mile S of Reeth on the B6270

Just to the south of Reeth is the quiet village of Grinton whose fine parish **Church of St Andrew** served the whole of the dale for centuries. The building dates back to the 13th and 15th centuries, though there are still some Norman remains as well as a Leper's Squint (a small hole through which those afflicted by the disease could follow the service within). For those people living in the upper reaches of Swaledale who died, there was a long journey down the track to Grinton which became known as the **Corpse Way**.

HEALAUGH

2 miles W of Reeth on the B6270

In the 12th century an Augustinian Priory was founded here but none of the remaining fragments date from earlier than the 15th century. However, the village Church of St Helen and St John, which dates from around 1150, not only has outstanding views over the dale to the Pennines but also has a bullet hole which, it is alleged, was made by a Cromwellian trooper on his way to Marsden Moor.

LANGTHWAITE

3 miles NW of Reeth off the B6270

Langthwaite, the main village of Arkengarthdale, will seem familiar to many who have never been here before as its bridge featured in the title sequence of the popular television series *All Creatures Great and Small*. Just outside this beautiful place stands the cryptically named CB Hotel – named after Charles Bathurst, an 18th-century lord of the manor who was responsible for the development of the lead-mining industry in the dale. His grandfather, Dr John Bathurst, physician to Oliver Cromwell, had purchased the land here in 1659 with the exploitation of its mineral wealth in mind.

In a field just up the hill from Langthwaite, where the Barnard Castle road goes off to the right, stands a curious 6-sided building, very solidly constructed. It needed to be since it served as a **Powderhouse** providing storage for the gunpowder used to blast tunnels through the hillsides for the lead mines.

LOW ROW

4 miles W of Reeth on the B6270

In medieval times the track along the hillside above Low Row formed part of the Corpse Way along which relays of bearers would carry the deceased in a large wicker basket on journeys that could take two days to complete. Along their route, you can still see the large stone slabs where they rested their burden. Even more convenient was the 'Dead Barn' above Low Row where the carriers could deposit the body and scramble downhill for a convivial evening at the Punch Bowl Inn.

GUNNERSIDE

6 miles W of Reeth on the B6270

This charming Dales village in the heart of Swaledale was, until the late 19th century, a thriving lead-mining village. Gunnerside became known as the Klondyke of Swaledale and, although the boom centred around lead rather than gold, the Old Gang Mines are the most famous in Yorkshire. The paths and trackways here are mainly those trodden by the many successions of miners travelling to their work and the valley's sides still show the signs of the mine workings. In the village, one can visit tearooms that offer such delights as 'Lead Miners' Bait' and the delicious 'Gunnerside Cheese Cake' made from a recipe handed down from mining days.

Hazel Brow Farm, Low Row

After the closure of the mines, many families left the village to find work elsewhere in northern England while others emigrated to America and even as far afield as Australia. For many years afterwards one of the village's most important days was Midsummer Sunday when those who had left would, if able, return and catch up with their families and friends.

Gunnerside's most impressive building is its **Methodist Chapel,** a classically elegant building, wonderfully light and airy. The indefatigable John Wesley visited Gunnerside in 1761 and found the local congregation 'earnest, loving and simple people'.

What makes **The Old Working Smithy & Museum** rather special is the fact that nothing has been bought in – all the artefacts on show are from the smithy itself, indeed many of them were actually made here. The smithy was established in 1795 and over the years little has been thrown away. Cartwheels, cobblers'

•

Located on the edge of the village of Low Row, Hazel Brow Organic Farm & Visitor Centre provides a popular family day out. Set in glorious Swaledale scenery the 200-acre traditional family-run farm offers children the opportunity of bottle feeding lambs, riding a pony or helping to feed the calves, sheep and pigs. The farm also has a tea room, children's play area and gift shop, and hosts various demonstrations of farming activities throughout the year.

•

Packhorse Bridge, Ivelet

tools, horseshoes, fireside implements and a miner's 'tub' (railway wagon) from a lead mine are just some of the vintage articles on show. This is still a working smithy. Stephen Calvert is the 6th generation of his family to pursue the trade of blacksmith and he still uses the original forge and hand bellows to create a wide range of wrought ironwork.

Gunnerside's picturesque hump-backed bridge over the Swale is reputed to be haunted by a headless ghost. Oddly, no gruesome tale has grown up around this unfortunate spirit.

IVELET

7 miles W of Reeth off the B6270

Just a few hundred yards off the B6270, the 14th-century **Packhorse bridge** at Ivelet is regarded as one of the finest in Yorkshire. It's a very picturesque spot and you can also join a delightful riverside walk here.

MUKER

8 miles W of Reeth on the B6270

An old stone bridge leads into this engaging village which consists of a collection of beige-coloured stone cottages overlooked by the **Church of St Mary** which dates back to the time of Elizabeth I – one of the very few to be built in England during her reign. Most church builders until that time had spared no expense in glorifying the house of God. At Muker they were more economical: the church roof was covered in thatch, its floor in rushes. No seating was provided. Despite such penny-pinching measures, the new church of 1580 was warmly welcomed since it brought to an end the tedious journey for bereaved relatives along the Corpse Way to the dale's mother church at Grinton, some eight miles further to the east.

On the gravestones in the churchyard local family names, such as Harker, Alderson, and Fawcett feature prominently as they do among the villagers still living here.

Close by the church is a quaint little building identified as the Literary Institute from whence you may hear the strains of a brass band rehearsing. In Victorian times, most of the Dales villages had their own brass band – Muker's is the only survivor and is in great demand at various events throughout the year.

Swaledale cuisine is equally durable: specialities on offer in the local tearooms include Swaledale Curd Tart, Yorkshire Rarebit, and

Deep Apple Pie with Wensleydale cheese. And the main crafts still revolve around the wool provided by the hardy Swaledale sheep, in great demand by carpet manufacturers and for jumpers worn by fell walkers, climbers, and anyone else trying to defeat the British weather.

You'll find many of these items on sale at **Swaledale Woollens** (see panel opposite) which was founded in Muker in Swaledale more than 30 years ago by villagers reviving the old cottage industry of knitting. The shop stocks a wide range of high quality knitwear, including sweaters, cardigans, hats, gloves, rugs, hangings, shawls, scarves, slippers and socks. It also stocks sheepskin slippers, gloves and rugs.

THWAITE

10 miles W of Reeth on the B6270

Surrounded by dramatic countryside which includes Kisdon Hill, Great Shunnor, High Seat, and Lovely Seat, this is a tiny village of ancient origins. Like so many places in the area the name comes from the Nordic language, in this case *thveit*, meaning a clearing in the wood. The woodlands which once provided shelter and fuel for the Viking settlers have long since gone.

But the surrounding gills and moors are rich in wildlife, it's easy to understand why the brothers Richard and Cherry Kearton, who were born at Thwaite in the late 1800s, developed an early enthusiasm for studying nature. They went on to become the David

Attenboroughs of their day. Pioneers in wildlife photography, their work took them all over the world. The small house where they were born, set back from the main road, has a stone lintel decorated with carvings of birds and animals, together with the initials RK and CK and their dates of birth.

To the southwest of the village runs **Buttertubs Pass**, one of the highest and most forbidding mountain passes in the county. **The Buttertubs** themselves are a curious natural feature of closely packed vertical stone stacks rising from some unseen, underground base to the level of the road. A local Victorian guide to the Buttertubs, perhaps aware that the view from above was not all that impressive, solemnly assured his client that 'some of the Buttertubs had no bottom, and some were deeper than that'. No one is quite sure where the Buttertubs name came from. The most plausible explanation is that farmers used its deep-chilled shelves as a convenient refrigerator for the butter they couldn't sell immediately. Unusually, these potholes are not linked by a series of passages as most are, but are free-standing and bear only a slight resemblance to the objects after which they are named.

The narrow road from Thwaite across the

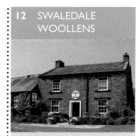

12 SWALEDALE WOOLLENS

Muker in Swaledale

Fascinating shop selling beautiful and distinctive high quality hand-made knitwear, woollen and sheepskin items.

🏛 see page 215

The Buttertubs

On the last Thursday in May is when the Tan Hill Sheep Fair takes place and, if only for a day, Tan Hill Inn becomes the centre of agricultural Yorkshire. 'It's the Royal Show for Swaledale Sheep is Tan Hill,' said one proud farmer scrutinising his flock, 'and I've got some princes and princesses here.' In cash terms the value of the prizes awarded at the Fair is negligible – just a few pounds for even a first class rosette. But at the auction that follows it's a different story. In 1990 one particularly prized Tupp Hogg (a young ram) was sold for £30,000.

Buttertubs Pass is not for the faint-hearted driver. Only a flimsy post and wire fence separates the road from a sheer drop of Alpine proportions. In any case, it's much more satisfying to cross the pass from the other direction, from Hawes: from the south, as you crest the summit you will be rewarded with a stupendous view of Swaledale stretching for miles.

KELD

10 miles W of Reeth on the B6270

The little cluster of stone buildings that make up this village stand beside the early stages of the River Swale. The place is alive with the sound of rushing water and it comes as no surprise that the word *keld* is Nordic for 'spring'.

Wain Wath Force, with rugged Cotterby Scar providing a fine backdrop, can be found alongside the Birkdale road. Catrake Force, with its stepped formation, can be reached from the cottages on the left at the bottom of the street in the village. Though on private land the falls and, beside them, the entrance to an old lead mine can still be seen. For less adventurous pedestrians Kisdon Force, the most impressive waterfall in Swaledale, can be reached by a gentle stroll of less than a mile from the village along a well-trodden path.

TAN HILL

10 miles NW of Reeth off the B6270

Standing at the head of Arkengarthdale on the border with County Durham, 1732 feet above sea level, stands England's highest pub, the **Tan Hill Inn**. Why on earth should there be a pub here, in one of the most remote and barren stretches of the north Pennines, frequently cut off and often in total isolation during the winter? A century ago, the inn's patrons didn't need to ask. Most of them were workers from the Tan Hill coal mines; others were drivers waiting for their horse-drawn carts to be filled with coal. The coal mines have long since closed but an open coal fire still burns in the inn 365 days a year and some 50,000 visitors a year still find their way to Tan Hill. Many of them are walkers who stagger in from one of the most gruelling stretches of the Pennine Way Walk and, clutching a pint of Theakston's 'Old Peculier', collapse on the nearest settle.

Before the present series of mild winters, the moorland roads often disappeared under 12-feet deep snowdrifts. Despite cellar walls three feet thick, the pub's beer-pumps have frozen, and trade tends to fall off a bit.

WENSLEYDALE

Wensleydale, perhaps above all the others, is the dale most people associate with the Yorkshire Dales. Charles Kingsley once described it as 'the richest spot in all England … a beautiful oasis in the mountains'. At some 40 miles long it is certainly the longest dale and it is also softer and greener than many of its neighbours. The pasture land, grazed by flocks of Wensleydale sheep, is only broken by the long lines of dry stone walls and the occasional field barn. The dale is, of course, famous for its cheese whose fortunes were given an additional boost by Wallace and Gromit who have declared it to be their favourite!

Wensleydale is the only major dale not to be named after its river, the Ure, although until fairly recent years most locals still referred to the area as Yoredale, or Uredale. The dale's name comes from the once important town of Wensley where the lucrative trade in cheese began in the 13th century. Wensley prospered for many years until 1563 when the Black Death annihilated most of its people and Leyburn became the trading centre of the lower dale.

At the western end of the dale is Hawes, derived from the Norse word *hals* meaning neck and, indeed, the town does lies on a neck of land between two hills. Home of the Dales Countryside Museum and the Wensleydale Creamery, Hawes is an ideal starting point for exploring the dale. It is widely believed that the medieval monks of Jervaulx Abbey were responsible for introducing the manufacture of cheese to the dale some 700 years ago (they were of French origin). It was first made from ewe's milk but by the 1600s the milk of shorthorn cows was used instead since the sheep were becoming increasingly important for their wool and mutton. Originally just a summer occupation and mainly the task of the farmer's wife, the production of Wensleydale cheese was put on a commercial footing when the first cheese factory was established at Gayle Beck, near Hawes, in 1897.

As it flows down the dale, the Ure is fed by a series of smaller rivers and becks, many of which have their own charming dale. Among the better-known are Coverdale, the home of some of England's finest racehorse stables, and peaceful Bishopdale with its ancient farmhouses. Remote Cotterdale, with its striking waterfall, and the narrow valley of the River Waldern are also well worth exploring.

LEYBURN

The main market town and trading centre of mid-Wensleydale, Leyburn is an attractive town with a broad cobbled marketplace (plus two other squares) lined by handsome late-Georgian and Victorian stone buildings. Friday is market day when the little town is even busier than usual. There's an

13 THE BOLTON ARMS

Leyburn
Impressive 18th century inn noted for its home-made cooking and real ales; flower-filled patio and spacious function room.

🍴 see page 216

14 MRS PUMPHREYS

Leyburn
Popular coffee shop with extensive menu of wholesome fare; also available to take away.

🍴 see page 217

Leyburn Market Square

13

15 THE GOLDEN LION HOTEL

Leyburn

Superb traditional inn with a good reputation for excellent food, drink and accommodation, in the heart of Leyburn overlooking the Market Square.

see page 218

The town of Leyburn has several interesting connections with famous people. Lord Nelson's surgeon, Peter Goldsmith, once lived in the Secret Garden House on Grove Square (and is buried in Wensley church, just a mile up the road). Flight Lieutenant Alan Broadley DSO, DFC, DFM, of Dam Busters fame, is named on the War Memorial in the main square, and just a few yards away is the birthplace of the 'Sweet Lass' of Richmond Hill. Many believe that the popular song refers to Richmond Hill in Surrey rather than Richmond, North Yorkshire. Not so. Frances I'Anson was born in her grandfather's house on Leyburn High Street and his initials, WIA, can still be seen above the door of what is now an interior decorator's shop. It was her husband-to-be, Leonard McNally, who composed the immortal song.

---

interesting mix of traditional family-run shops and surprisingly large supermarkets behind deceptively small frontages. Leyburn also boasts the only cinema, The Elite, to be found in Wensleydale.

A fairly recent addition to Leyburn's attractions is **Beech End Model Village** in Commercial Square. Unique among model villages, this one is indoors. The scenery is finely detailed and there's plenty of hands-on fun to be had controlling the working models.

On the eastern edge of the town is Leyburn Station. Until recently you would have had a long wait here for a train – the last passenger train left in 1954. But an energetic group of railway enthusiasts have laboured for years to get the line re-opened and on July 4th, 2003 their efforts were finally successful. The **Wensleydale Railway** now offers regular services to Bedale and Leeming Bar, a 12-mile route through pretty countryside. Normally, the train is driven by a vintage diesel locomotive but there are special steam train days. Passengers can connect with a vintage bus at Redmire station to travel on to Hawes. The Wensleydale Railway Company hopes to extend the service to the main line station at Northallerton and, even more ambitiously, to extend westwards to meet up with the Settle and Carlisle railway.

The Shawl, to the west of the town, is a mile-long limestone scarp along which runs a footpath offering lovely panoramic views of the dale. A popular legend suggests that it gained its unusual name when Mary, Queen of Scots dropped her shawl here during her unsuccessful attempt to escape from nearby Bolton Castle. However, a more likely explanation is that Shawl is a corruption of the Nordic name given to the ancient settlement here.

Leyburn Business Park is home to **The Violin Making Workshop**. Little has changed in the art of violin making over the centuries and the traditional tools and methods used by such master craftsmen as Stradivari are still employed today. Repairs and commissions are undertaken.

Close by, at **The Teapottery**, you can see other craftspeople at work – in this case creating a whole range of witty and unusual teapots, anything from a grand piano to a bathtub complete with yellow duck. The finished pots can be purchased in the showroom where there's also a tea room where your tea is served, naturally, in one of the astonishing teapots produced here.

Within the same business park are Tennant's of Yorkshire, the only major provincial auction house in England which holds regular auctions throughout the year, and the **Little Chocolate Shop** where visitors can watch hand-made chocolates being crafted and choose from more than 200 varieties of chocolates and confectionery.

About two miles east of Leyburn, off the A684, the

Longwool Sheepshop at Cross Lanes Farm in Garriston is a treat for anyone who appreciates good knitwear. Garments can be specially knitted to the customer's requirements. You can see the raw material grazing in the surrounding fields – rare Wensleydale longwool sheep. The Sheepshop also stocks an extensive range of hand knitting yarns and patterns for the enthusiast.

AROUND LEYBURN

CONSTABLE BURTON

4 miles E of Leyburn on the A684

Surrounded by walled and wooded parkland **Constable Burton Hall** is famous for its gardens (open March to October) and in particular its spacious, romantic terraces. The house itself, designed by John Carr, is not open to the public but its stately Georgian architecture provides a magnificent backdrop to the fine gardens, noble trees and colourful borders.

SPENNITHORNE

2 miles SE of Leyburn off the A684

This pleasant little village dates back many years. The present Church of St Michael and All Angels stands on the site of a Saxon church although the only remains of the ancient building to be seen are two ornamental stones set into the walls of the chancels and a Saxon monument in the vestry.

Two of Spennithorne's earlier residents are worth mentioning. John Hutchinson was born here in 1675 and went on to become steward to the 6th Duke of

Somerset – and a rather controversial philosopher. He vehemently disagreed with Sir Isaac Newton's theory of gravity and was equally ardent in asserting that the earth was neither flat, nor a sphere, but a cube. Though there are no records mentioning that Hutchinson was ever considered as of unsound mind, another resident of Spennithorne, Richard Hatfield, was officially declared insane after he fired a gun at George III.

MIDDLEHAM

2 miles SE of Leyburn on the A6108

Middleham is an enchanting little town which, despite having a population of fewer than 800, boasts its own Mayor, Corporation and quaint Town Hall. It is also the site of one of Yorkshire's most historic castles, 12 of England's most successful racing stables and not just one, but two, marketplaces. It is almost totally unspoilt, with a wealth of handsome Georgian houses and hostelries huddled together in perfect architectural harmony.

Rising high above the town are the magnificent ruins of **Middleham Castle** (English Heritage), a once-mighty fortress whose most glorious days came in the 15th century when most of northern England was ruled from here by the Neville family. The castle's most famous resident was the 'evil' Richard III who was sent here as a lad of 13 to be trained in the 'arts of nobilitie'. Whatever crimes he committed later down in London, Richard was popular

16 THE CROSS KEYS

Bellerby

Traditional 18th century family-friendly village inn with great food, real ales, en suite accommodation and regular entertainment events.

see page 219

17 THE WYVILL ARMS

Constable Burton

Traditional village hostelry serving outstanding food and real ales. Lovely beer garden and en suite rooms.

see page 220

18 THE COUNTRYMAN'S INN

Hunton

Traditional village inn serving outstanding food and real ales; quality en suite rooms are available

see page 221

15

Middleham Castle

19 THE BLACK SWAN HOTEL

Middleham

Quality cuisine and accommodation in delightful 17th century Grade II listed building.

see page 222

locally, ensuring the town's prosperity by granting it a fair and a twice-yearly market. The people of Middleham had good reason to mourn his death at the Battle of Bosworth in 1485.

Middleham is often referred to as the "Newmarket of the North", a term you'll understand when you see the strings of thoroughbred racehorses clip-clopping through the town on their way to the training runs on Low Moor. It was the monks of Jervaulx Abbey who founded this key industry. By the late 18th century, races were being run across the moorland and the first stables established. Since then the local stables have produced a succession of classic race winners with one local trainer, Neville Crump, having three Grand National winners to his credit within the space of 12 years.

EAST WITTON

4 miles SE of Leyburn on the A6108

An attractive village set beside the confluence of the rivers Cover and Ure, East Witton was almost entirely rebuilt after a great fire in 1796. The new buildings included the well-proportioned Church of St John although the old churchyard with its many interesting gravestones remains. Some two decades after that conflagration the village was struck by another calamity. In 1820, 20 miners perished in a coal mine accident at Witton Fell. They were all buried together in one grave in the new churchyard.

Just to the west of the village is **Jervaulx Abbey**, one of the great Cistercian sister houses to Fountains Abbey. The name Jervaulx is a French derivation of Yore (or Ure), and Vale, just as Rievaulx is of Rye Vale. Before the Dissolution, the monks of Jervaulx Abbey owned huge tracts of Wensleydale and this now-solitary spot was once a busy trading and administrative centre. Despite its ruination, Jervaulx is among the most evocative of Yorkshire's many fine abbeys. The grounds have been transformed into beautiful gardens with the crumbling walls providing interesting backdrops for the sculptured trees and colourful plants and shrubs.

COVERHAM

4 miles S of Leyburn off the A6108

Lying beside the River Cover in little-visited Coverdale, this village is perhaps best known for the remains of **Coverham Abbey** (private). Built in the late 1200s, only some decorated arches remain, along with a Norman gateway. The nearby 17th-century manor house, Braithwaite Hall (National Trust), as well as other surrounding buildings, have clearly used the Abbey's stones in their construction – in some of the walls effigies from the old building can clearly be seen. The Hall can be visited by prior arrangement.

WENSLEY

1 mile W of Leyburn on the A684

This peaceful little village beside the River Ure was once the main settlement in mid-Wensleydale and such was its importance it gave its name to the dale. However, in 1563, the town was struck by plague and those whom the pestilence had not struck down fled up the hill to Leyburn which was thought to be a healthier place.

The stately **Church of the Holy Trinity** is one of only two surviving medieval structures in Wensley (the other is the graceful bridge nearby) and it is thought to have been built on the site of an earlier Saxon church. Inside can be seen the unusual Bolton family pews which are actually a pair of opera boxes that were brought here from London during the 1700s when a theatre was being refurbished.

The Bolton family still live at nearby Bolton Hall, a massive 18th-century house which is closed to the public although its splendid gardens are occasionally open during the summer months.

'Purveyors to the Military, Colonies, Overseas Missions, Churches and the Cinematograph Industries' runs the proud claim in the brochure for **White Rose Candles Workshop**. 'Patronised by the Nobility and Gentry' it continues; 'Cathedrals supplied include Ripon and Norwich'. One of Wensleydale's most popular attractions, the workshop is housed in a 19th-century water mill – the water wheel still exists and mills have been recorded on this site since 1203.

WEST WITTON

4 miles W of Leyburn on the A684

Recorded in the *Domesday Book* as 'Witun', this village was then the largest in Wensleydale and exceptional in having stone rather than wooden houses. West Witton is well known for its annual feast of St Bartholomew, patron saint of the parish church. The festival takes place on August 24th when an effigy of a man, known as the Bartle, is carried through the village. According to legend, Bartle was an 18th-century swine that was hunted over the surrounding fells before being captured and killed. The culmination of the three days of celebration is the burning of the effigy at Grassgill End.

CARLTON-IN-COVERDALE

4 miles SW of Leyburn off the A684

Unspoilt Coverdale is known as the 'Forgotten Dale'. Carlton is the dale's principal village – with a population of less than 100. Nevertheless, it has its own pub and provides a wonderfully peaceful

•

Just outside the village of Coverham, on the Tupgill Park Estate is the delightful walled Forbidden Garden, a series of follies created by Colin Armstrong, an eccentric millionaire and former ambassador to Ecuador. Strange and exotic buildings are scattered around the park, including a grotto with an underground labyrinth of chambers and passages. Visitors are given a list and then discover these fantastic constructions by themselves. "In parts you might find your heart's delight" says the brochure, "In others you'll tremble with fear". There's also a shop and refreshment room. Admission is by pre-booked tickets only which can be obtained from the Leyburn Tourist Information Centre.

•

Bolton Castle, Castle Bolton

base for walking, hiking, fishing or touring the Dales National Park.

REDMIRE

4 miles W of Leyburn off the A684

Throughout its long history this village is thought to have occupied several sites in the vicinity. However, Redmire has been at its present location for many years. On the village green stands an old oak tree, supported by props, which is estimated to be at least 300 years old. When John Wesley preached in the village during his two visits in 1744 and 1774 it is believed that he stood in the shade of this very tree.

CASTLE BOLTON

5 miles W of Leyburn off the A684

Bolton Castle has dominated mid-Wensleydale for more than six centuries and is one of the major tourist attractions of the area. In 1379 the lord of the manor, Richard le Scrope, Lord Chancellor of England in the reign of Richard II, was granted permission to fortify his manor house and, using

stone from a nearby quarry and oak beams from Lake District forests, the building was completed some 18 years later. The 14th century state-of-the-art garde-robes (lavatories) were constructed with such sophistication that they were still in use some 500 years later. Today, this fortified manor house remains an impressive sight with its four-square towers acting as a local landmark. The halls and galleries are remarkably well-preserved as are some of the private apartments used by Mary, Queen of Scots when she was a reluctant visitor here for six months between 1568-69. Indeed, modern day visitors can take tea in the grand room where she spent many melancholy days.

Vivid tableaux help bring history to life – the castle chaplain, the miller at work, the blacksmith at his forge – and there are regular living history events during the summer. If you climb to the battlements you will be rewarded with some breathtaking views along the dale.

The owner, Lord Bolton, has recently restored two of the castle gardens as they would have been in medieval times – a Herb Garden and a Walled Garden.

THORALBY

8 miles W of Leyburn off the A684

Situated on the north slope of Bishopdale, opposite its sister village Newbiggin, Thoralby was once a centre for lead-mining and although lead is no longer extracted here the mine can still be found on maps of the area. A side dale of Wensleydale,

Bishopdale was once covered by a glacial lake that has given rise to its distinctive wide valley base. Here can be found many of Wensleydale's oldest houses.

NEWBIGGIN-IN-BISHOPDALE

9 miles SW of Leyburn on the B6160

As might be supposed, the name of this Bishopdale village means 'new buildings' and it is indeed a relatively new settlement having been first mentioned in 1230! There is only one road along Bishopdale, a beautiful unspoilt valley with hay meadows, stone barns, traditional Dales long houses and a fine old coaching inn.

WEST BURTON

7 miles SW of Leyburn off the B6160

One of the most picturesque villages in Wensleydale, West Burton developed around its large central green where a busy weekly market used to take place. A distinctive feature of the green is its market 'cross'- actually a modestly sized pyramid erected here in 1820. Just to the east of the village a path leads across a small packhorse bridge to **Mill Force**, perhaps the most photogenic of the Wensleydale waterfalls.

Cat lovers will enjoy the wide variety of felines on display at the **Cat Pottery**, overlooking the village green. The Nichols family have been making their Moorside Cats since 1982 and their original collection of cats in ceramics and metallic or granite resin includes life-size stone cats for house or garden.

CARPERBY

7 miles W of Leyburn off the A684

This ancient village reflects its typical Danish layout with a long straggling street and a small green at one end. In some of the nearby fields, grassy terraces indicate the old ploughed strips left by both pre-Norman Conquest and medieval farming methods. Carperby was one of the first villages to have a market - the charter was granted in 1305. The village's market cross dates from 1674 and it was from its steps that George Fox, the founder of the Quaker Movement, preached in the 17th century.

AYSGARTH

7 miles W of Leyburn on the A684

The village is famous for the spectacular **Aysgarth Falls** where the River Ure thunders through a rocky gorge and drops some 200 feet over three huge slabs of limestone which divide this

West Burton lies at the bottom of Walden, a narrow, steep-sided valley that provides a complete contrast to neighbouring Bishopdale. Secluded and with a minimal scattering of houses and farms, Walden was one of the last places in Yorkshire where wild red deer were seen.

Carperby Market Cross

wonderful natural feature into the Upper, Middle and Lower Falls. So cinematic are they that they were deemed to be the perfect location for the battle between Robin Hood and Little John in Kevin Costner's film *Robin Hood, Prince of Thieves*.

Close to the falls stands the **Church of St Andrew**, home of the Jervaulx Treasures – a vicar's stall that is made from the beautifully carved bench ends salvaged from Jervaulx Abbey. During the Middle Ages, Aysgarth enjoyed the distinction of being the largest parish in England though the parish has since been subdivided into more manageable areas. But it still has the largest churchyard in England.

The Dales National Park has a Visitor Information Centre here, with a spacious car park and café located close to the Church and Falls.

The **Aysgarth Edwardian Rock Garden,** originally designed by James Backhouse in 1906 and restored in 2003, is one of the few examples of a Backhouse rock garden remaining in the UK. The garden is visited and admired by many alpine gardeners each year and has recently been the subject of many magazine articles. Guided tours are available by arrangement.

ASKRIGG

10½ miles W of Leyburn off the A684

Recorded in the *Domesday Book* as 'Ascric', this once-important market town became better known to TV viewers as Darrowby, a major location for the long-running series *All Creatures Great and Small*. The 18th-century Kings Arms Hotel often featured as 'The Drovers Arms', and Cringley House doubled as 'Skeldale House', the fictional home of the TV vets.

During the 18th century Askrigg was a thriving town with several prosperous industries. Cotton was spun in a nearby mill, dyeing and brewing took place here and it was also a centre for hand-knitting. However, the town is particularly famous for clock-making, introduced by John Ogden in 1681.

The village has been popular with tourists since the days of Turner and Wordsworth when the chief attractions here were the two waterfalls, Whitfield Force and Mill Gill. Despite its olde worlde atmosphere Askrigg was one of the first places in the dales to be supplied with electricity. That was in 1908 when the local miller harnessed the power of Mill Gill Beck.

Askrigg is bountifully supplied with footpaths radiating out to other villages, river crossings and farmsteads. One of the most scenic takes little more than an hour and takes in the two impressive waterfalls. The route is waymarked from Mill Lane alongside the church.

BAINBRIDGE

11½ miles W of Leyburn on the A684

Back in the Middle Ages this area of Upper Wensleydale was a hunting forest, known as the Forest and Manor of Bainbridge. The village itself was established around the 12th century as a home for the foresters. One of their duties was to show travellers the way through the forest. If anyone was still out by nightfall, a horn was blown to guide them home. The custom is still continued between the Feast of Holy Rood (September 27th) and Shrove Tuesday when the present horn is blown at 10pm. The horn is kept on display in the Rose & Crown pub.

Ancient stocks are still in place on the spacious village green and on the eastern edge of the village, the River Bain, officially the shortest river in England at less than 2 miles long, rushes over a small waterfall as it makes its way down from Semer Water.

Just to the east of Bainbridge is **Brough Hill** (private) where the Romans built a succession of forts known collectively as *Virosidum*. First excavated in the late 1920s, they now appear as overgrown grassy hummocks. Much easier to see is the Roman road that strikes south-westwards from Bainbridge, part of the trans-Pennine route to Lancaster. It passes close to the isolated lake of **Semer Water**, one of Yorkshire's only two natural lakes. (The other is Lake Gormire, near Thirsk.) Semer Water stretches half a mile in length and teems with wild fowl.

GAYLE

15½ miles W of Leyburn off the A684

Set beside the Gayle Beck, the village has some pleasant riverside walks that pass close to **Gayle Mill,**

a late 18th century structure built originally to support cotton spinning but then changing to wool to supply local hand-knitters. In 1870 the old waterwheel was replaced by a turbine. This, in turn, gave the village electric street lights as early as 1917. The Mill eventually fell into disuse in the 1980s but thanks to its appearance in the television series *Restoration* in 2004 has been renovated, its water-power systems reinstated and the Victorian wood-working machinery returned to working order. Tickets must be bought in advance at the Dales Countryside Museum in Hawes.

HAWES

15½ miles W of Leyburn off the A684

At 850 feet above sea level, Hawes is the highest market town in Yorkshire. The present town expanded greatly in the 1870s after the arrival of the railways but there's still plenty of evidence of the earlier settlement in street names relating to ancient trades: Dyer's Garth, Hatter's Yard and Printer's Square. Now the commercial and market centre of the upper dale, Hawes offers a good range of shops, inns, accommodation and visitor attractions.

The most picturesque corner of the town is by the bridge over Gayle Beck where the stream tumbles over a sheer drop by the old mill. It's just a short step from the bridge to the **Dales Countryside Museum** (see panel), housed in the former railway

An enduring legend claims that a town lies beneath the depths of Semer Water, cast under water by a curse. A poor traveller once sought shelter in the town but was turned away by the affluent inhabitants. The next day he stood on the hill above the town, pronounced a curse, and a great flood engulfed the town immediately. There's an intriguing postscript to this tale. During a severe drought, the level of the lake dropped to reveal the remains of a Bronze Age town.

23 DALES COUNTRYSIDE MUSEUM

Hawes

Award winning museum where the past of the Yorkshire Dales is brought to life.

see page 225

24 THE WHITE HART INN

Hawes

Popular town centre tavern noted for its excellent food and real ales; comfortable accommodation also available.

see page 225

station. The museum tells the story of how man's activities have helped to shape the Dales' landscape. Providing fascinating historical details on domestic life, the lead-mining industry, hand-knitting and other trades as well as archaeological material, the museum covers many aspects of Dales' life from as far back as 10,000 BC. Children visit free.

One of those local industries was rope-making and at **The Hawes Ropeworkers** (free), adjacent to the museum, visitors can still see it in operation, with experienced ropers twisting cotton and man-made fibres to make halters, hawsers, picture cords, dog leads, clothes lines and other 'rope' items. The gift shop here stocks a comprehensive range of rope-related items along with an extensive choice of other souvenirs of the dale.

Wensleydale's most famous product (after its sheep), is its soft, mild cheese, and at the **Wensleydale Creamery**, on the western edge of the town, you can sample this delicacy and also learn about its history through a series of interesting displays. With a museum, viewing gallery of the production area, cheese shop, gift shop and licensed restaurant, there's plenty here for the cheese lover to enjoy.

HARDRAW

15½ miles W of Leyburn off the A684

Located in a natural amphitheatre of limestone crags, **Hardraw Force** is the highest, unbroken waterfall in England above ground, a breathtaking cascade 98 feet high. The top ledge of hard rock projects so far beyond the softer stone beneath that it used to be possible to walk behind the falling water as JMW Turner and Wordsworth did. Sadly, for safety reasons this is no longer possible. The waterfall shows at its best after heavy rain as, generally, the quantity of water tumbling over the rocks is not great. On two separate occasions, in 1739 and 1881, the falls froze solid into a 100-feet icicle. In the 1870s, the French stuntman Blondin astounded spectators when, not content with crossing the falls on a tightrope, he paused halfway to cook an omelette.

The amphitheatre here provides superb acoustics, a feature which has been put to great effect in the annual brass band competitions which began here in 1885 and have recently resumed. Access to Hardraw Force is through the Green Dragon pub where a small fee is payable. The inn itself is pretty venerable with records of a hostelry on this site since at least the mid-13th century. At that time the land here was a grange belonging to the monks of Fountains Abbey who grazed their sheep nearby.

COTTERDALE

18 miles W of Leyburn off the A684

The small valley of Cotter Beck lies below the vast bulk of Great Shunner Fell which separates the head of Wensleydale from

Swaledale. **Cotter Force**, although smaller than Hardraw, is extremely attractive though often neglected in favour of its more famous neighbour.

NIDDERDALE

This typical Yorkshire dale with its dry stone walls, green fields, and pretty stone villages was christened 'Little Switzerland' by the Victorians. Indeed, the upper reaches of the valley of the River Nidd are steep and wooded, with the river running through gorges, and with a covering of snow in winter it is easy to see the resemblance. It is this natural beauty that draws many people to the dale and there are also several remarkable features that are well worth exploring.

The history of the dale is similar to that of its neighbours. The Romans and Norsemen both settled here and there are also reminders that the dale was populated in prehistoric times. It was the all powerful Cistercian monks of Fountains and Byland Abbeys who began the business-like cultivation of the countryside to provide grazing for cattle and sheep and the space to grow food. This great farming tradition has survived and, though prosperity came and went with the lead-mining, a few of the textile mills established in the golden age of the Industrial Revolution can still be found.

Best explored from Pateley Bridge, keen walkers will delight in

Scar House Reservoir, Nidderdale

the wide variety of landscape that can be covered within a reasonable amount of time. High up on the moorland, famed for its brilliant colour in late summer, there are several reservoirs, built to provide water for the growing population and industry in Bradford. This area is a must for bird watchers as there are excellent opportunities for spotting a number of species of duck as well as brent geese and whooper swans. Further down the valley, in the rich woodland, wildlife again abounds and the well-signposted footpaths help visitors reach the most spectacular sights.

PATELEY BRIDGE

Considered one of the prettiest towns in the Dales, Pateley Bridge straggles up the hillside from its elegant 18th-century bridge over the Nidd. Considering its compact size, the town is remarkably well connected by roads which have been here since the monastic orders

25 WILDINGS OF PATELEY BRIDGE

Pateley Bridge
Popular riverside traditional tea room serving huge choice of appetising food.

see page 226

The Nidderdale Museum, a winner of the National Heritage Museum of the Year award, is housed in one of Pateley Bridge's original Victorian workhouses and presents a fascinating record of local folk history. The exhibits include a complete cobbler's shop, general store, Victorian parlour, kitchen and schoolroom, chemist's, haberdasher's, joiner's shop, solicitor's office as well as an agricultural, transport and industrial display.

26   THE BIRCH TREE INN

Willsill

Fine old country inn in lovely rural location offering excellent food, real ales and en suite rooms.

🍴 🛏 see page 226

established trade routes through the town for transporting their goods. A street market, whose charter was granted in the 14th century, has however, been abandoned for some time although sheep fairs and agricultural shows still take place here.

Pateley Bridge is more than just a market centre – the nearby lead mines, spinning and hand-loom weaving also provided employment for the local community. The construction of the turnpike road to Ripon in 1751, followed by the opening of a road to Knaresborough in 1756, gave the town a further economic boost. In the early 19th century, the brothers George and John Metcalfe moved their flax-spinning business to nearby Glasshouses, where the business expanded rapidly. The lead mines, too, were expanding, due to the introduction of new machinery, and the town saw a real boom. The arrival of the railway in 1862 maintained this flourishing economy, making the transportation of heavy goods cheaper and the carriage of perishable foods quicker.

Much of the Pateley Bridge seen today was built in those prosperous years. A town of quaint and pretty buildings, the oldest is St Mary's Church, a lovely ruin dating from 1320 from which there are some fine panoramic views. Another excellent vista can be viewed from the aptly named **Panorama Walk**, part of the main medieval route from Ripon to Skipton.

AROUND PATELEY BRIDGE

WILSILL

1 mile E of Pateley Bridge on the B6165

About two miles east of Wilsill are **Brimham Rocks** (National Trust), an extraordinary natural sculpture park. Formed into fantastic shapes by years of erosion, these great millstone grit boulders lie atop a steep hill amidst some 400 acres of heathland. Some of the shapes really do resemble their names – the 'Dancing Bear' in particular, but perhaps the most awe-inspiring is 'Idol Rock', a huge boulder weighing several tons which rests on a base just a foot in diameter.

The National Trust has provided large scale maps showing suggested itineraries and the positions and names of the major formations.

BEWERLEY

1 mile SW of Pateley Bridge on the B6265

Recorded as *Bevrelie* (a clearing inhabited by badgers) in the *Domesday Book*, this is Nidderdale's oldest settlement. It was also the

Brimham Rocks, nr Wilsill

site of the earliest and most important of Fountains Abbey's many granges. Not only were they farming here but lead was being extracted from the nearby moor. The recently restored Chapel, built here by one of the last abbots, Marmaduke Huby, acted for many years as the village school.

In the 17th century the Yorke family moved to the embellished hall at Bewerley following their purchase of the former lands of Byland Abbey in Nidderdale. During the subsequent years, the family laid out the parkland as well as rebuilding some of the village and, though the estate was sold in the 1920s and the hall demolished, the park remains and plays host to the annual Nidderdale Show. The name of the village's most influential family, however, is not lost to the village as Yorke's Folly, two stone stoops, still stand on the hillside overlooking Bewerley.

RAMSGILL

5 miles NW of Pateley Bridge off the B6265

This pleasant village, clustered around its well kept green, was the birthplace of Eugene Aram in 1704. The son of a gardener at Newby Hall, Aram was arrested in 1758 in Kings Lynn for the murder of Daniel Clark in Knaresborough 13 years before. The trial took place in York and Aram caused a stir by conducting his own defence. However, he was convicted and later executed before his body was taken to Knaresborough where it was hung from a gibbet. The gruesome story has been the centre of many tales and songs including a very romantic version by Sir Bulwer Lytton.

LOFTHOUSE

7 miles NW of Pateley Bridge off the B6265

This is a small dales' village lying in the upper valley of the River Nidd and, unlike neighbouring Wharfedale, the stone walls and rocky outcrops are of millstone grit though the valley bottom consists of limestone. As a result, only in excessive weather is there water under the bridge here as, in normal conditions, the river drops down two sumps: Manchester Hole and Goydon Pot.

MIDDLESMOOR

8 miles NW of Pateley Bridge off the B6265

This tucked away village of stone built cottages and houses lies at the head of Upper Nidderdale and is reached by a single, winding road. The existence of ancient settlers can be seen in the present 19th-century Church of St Chad where an early 10th- or 11th-century preaching cross, bearing the inscription *Cross of St Ceadda* can be seen.

WHARFEDALE

The valley of the River Wharfe, Wharfedale is the longest of the Yorkshire Dales following the river from its origins on Cam Fell for more than 70 miles to Cawood, where it joins the River Ouse. At its source, almost 2000 feet above sea level, the river is nothing more than a moorland stream and, even in

•

How Stean Gorge, in the heart of Nidderdale near Lofthouse, is often called Yorkshire's Little Switzerland and for good reason. This spectacular limestone gorge, which is up to 80 feet deep in places, through which the Stean Beck flows, is a popular tourist attraction. A narrow path with footbridges guide the visitor along the gorge where the waters rush over the large boulders below. However, there are also many sheltered areas of calm water where fish hide under the rocks. As well as taking a stroll up this fascinating path, visitors can also step inside Tom Taylor's Cave and, along the walk, marvel at the wide variety of plant life that grows in this steep ravine.

•

27 THE YORKSHIRE LASS CAFÉ

Grassington

Hearty home cooking, internet access and the chance to decorate a pot, mug or plate.

🍴 🏛 see page 227

The Upper Wharfedale Folk Museum is housed in two 18th-century lead miners' cottages in Grassington. Containing many exhibits and displays relating to the lives of those who have lived in the dale, the museum is open (afternoons only) at the weekend during the winter and daily throughout the summer. In October, the museum hosts the Feast Sports. Among the many traditional events it features is a teacake eating race in which children have to eat a teacake then race to the other end of the field. The winner is the first child to then whistle a tune.

mid-Wharfedale, it is little more than a mountain river, broad, shallow, and peat brown in colour. The Romans named a local Goddess, *Verbeia*, after the river, and those who visit will understand why, since the goddess was known for her treachery as well as her beauty. Wharfedale is one of the most spectacular and most varied of the Yorkshire dales. No one who sees the river charging through the narrow gorge at The Strid, near Bolton Abbey, will deny that the power of the river is to be respected.

Over the years, Wharfedale has inspired many poets, writers and painters. Colderidge and Wordsworth were captivated by its beauty and, in Wordsworth's case, with the local stories and legends. Ruskin enthused about its contrasts and Turner painted several scenes that capture the dale's history and mystery.

GRASSINGTON

One of the best loved villages within the Yorkshire Dales National Park, Grassington in many ways typifies the dales' settlement with its characteristic market square. Known as the capital of Upper Wharfedale, the historically important valley roads meet here and the ancient monastic route from Malham to Fountains Abbey passes through the village.

Grassington's origins are rooted in ancient history; there was certainly a Bronze Age settlement here, the remains of an Iron Age village have been found, a Celtic

field system can be seen on nearby Lea Green, and the village was mentioned in the *Domesday Book*. However, the settlement seen today is Anglian and, having passed through various families, is now part of the estate of the Dukes of Devonshire. With its narrow streets lined with attractive Georgian buildings, Grassington is a delightful place to wander around. It is also home to the National Park Dale Visitor Centre.

Although often described as a village, Grassington is actually a town, and was granted a charter in 1282 to hold a fair and market. Both were regular events until the 1860s, but nowadays only a farmers' market is held on the third Sunday of each month.

Two annual events which attract many visitors are the **Grassington Festival of Music and Arts**, which is held over the last two weeks of June, and the **Grassington Dickensian Festival** - a lively market, with street entertainment, dancing and music - held before Christmas.

AROUND GRASSINGTON

HEBDEN

3 miles E of Grassington on the B6265

From this quiet hamlet it is only a short distance to the wonderful 500,000-year-old cave at **Stump Cross Caverns**. Discovered in 1860 by miners looking for lead, the large show cave holds a fantastic collection of stalactites and stalagmites which make it one of the most visited underground attractions in the area. During excavations, remains of wolverines, a giant member of the weasel family have been discovered at Stump Cross. It is thought that these animals entered the caves looking for food such as reindeer and bison, the remains of which have also been found. The wolverine remains are on display in the visitor's centre where there is also a gift shop and tea room.

THORPE

2 miles SE of Grassington off the B6160

This small hamlet, the full name of which is Thorpe-sub-Montem (meaning 'below the hill'), lies in a secluded hollow between drumlins – long, low alluvial mounds. As well as taking advantage of its hidden position, ideal for secreting valuables and family members during Scots' raids, the village was also known for its cobblers. Their fame was such that the monks of Fountains Abbey were among their regular customers.

BURNSALL

2 miles SE of Grassington on the B6160

Claimed to be the most photographed village in England, Burnsall is very dramatically situated on a bend in the River Wharfe with the slopes of Burnsall Fell as a backdrop. It is thought that, sometime prior to the 8th century, Wilfrid Bishop of York, founded a wooden church here. Its site is now occupied by the village's 12th-century church. The only remnant of Wilfrid's building is the font which can still be seen at the back of **St Wilfrid's Church**. The churchyard is entered via a unique lychgate and here can be seen two hogback tombstones and various other fragments which date back to the times of the Anglo-Saxons and the Danes.

Burnsall was the site of the quintessential village fête featured in the 2003 film *Calendar Girls*.

APPLETREEWICK

4 miles SE of Grassington off the B6160

This peaceful village, which is known locally as Aptrick, lies between the banks of the River Wharfe and the bleak moorland and is overlooked by the craggy expanse of **Simon's Seat**, one of Wharfedale's best-loved hilltops. The village was once the home of William Craven, a Lord Mayor of London, who returned to spend much of his amassed wealth on improvements and additions to Appletreewick's fine old buildings. Known as the Dick Whittington of the Dale, William Craven was born in 1548 and moved to London when he became apprenticed to a mercer (a dealer in textiles and fine fabrics).

A little further down river is the stately ruin of **Barden Tower**, a former residence of Lord Henry Clifford, owner of Skipton Castle. It was built in the 15th century but allowed to fall into decay and, despite repair in 1657, it is once more a ruin. Nearby is the attractive Barden Bridge, a 17th-century arch now designated as an ancient monument.

It is not this sturdy dales' church which draws visitors to Burnsall but its bridge. Today, this typical dales' bridge of five stone arches is the start of the annual Classic Fell Race which takes place on a Saturday towards the end of August. Over the years, the flood waters of the River Wharfe have washed away the arches on several occasions but the villagers have always replaced them as this is the only crossing point for three miles in each direction.

28 THE CRAVEN ARMS & CRUCK BARN

Appletreewick

Outstanding traditional Dales hostelry with excellent restaurant in authentic replica of a Tudor Cruck Barn.

see page 228

Bardon Tower, Appletreewick

29 BOLTON ABBEY

Bolton Abbey, Skipton

Visitors flock to the
Yorkshire Estate of the
Duke and Duchess of
Devonshire, to enjoy the
magnificent scenery and
superb facilities.

🏛 see page 229

Just to the north of
Appletreewick lie **Parcevall Hall
Gardens,** a wonderful woodland
garden which contains many
varieties of unusual plants and
shrubs. Though the 16-acre
gardens are high above sea level -
which provides the visitor with
some splendid views - many plants
still flourish. The gardens have a
special quality of peace and
tranquillity - appropriately enough
since the lovely old Hall is now a
Bradford Diocesan Retreat and
Conference Centre.

BOLTON ABBEY

7 miles SE of Grassington on the B6160

The village is actually a collection
of small hamlets which have all
been part of the estate of the
Dukes of Devonshire since 1748.
Bolton Abbey itself stands on the
banks of the River Wharfe while
the hamlets of Storiths, Hazelwood,
Deerstones, and Halton East lie
higher up.

The main attraction in the
village is the substantial ruin of

Bolton Priory, an Augustinian
house that was founded in 1155 by
monks from Embsay. Occupying an
idyllic situation on the banks of the
River Wharfe, the ruins are well
preserved while the nave of the
priory church, first built in 1220, is
now incorporated into the parish
church.

After the Dissolution of the
Monasteries the priory was sold to
the 2nd Earl of Cumberland,
Henry Clifford, and it has since
passed into the hands of the Dukes
of Devonshire, the Cavendish
family. The 14th-century priory
gatehouse, Bolton Hall, is the
present duke's shooting lodge.
Visitors walking to the priory ruins
from the village pass through a hole
in the wall which frames one of the
most splendid views of the
romantic ruins. An attractive option
when visiting the priory is to travel
on the Embsay and Bolton Abbey
Steam Railway whose station is
about half a mile away, reached by a
pleasant riverside footpath.

In and around this beautiful
village there are some 80 miles of
footpaths and nature trails, skirting
the riverbanks and climbing up
onto the high moorland. Upstream
from the priory lies one of the
most visited natural features in
Wharfedale, a point where the wide
river suddenly narrows into a
confined channel of black rock
through which the water thunders.
This spectacular gorge is known as
The Strid because, over the
centuries, many heroic (or
foolhardy) types have attempted to
leap across it as a test of bravery.

Located within the Bolton Abbey estate, **Hesketh Farm Park** is a 600-acre working beef and sheep farm. Voted National Farm Attraction of the Year, 2006, the farm encourages visitors to interact with the many animals within the site. Tractor and trailer tours are available, there are outdoor and indoor play areas, and a pedal go-kart course.

LINTON
1 mile SW of Grassington off the B6160

This delightful and unspoilt village, that is more correctly called Linton-in-Craven, has grown up around its village green through which runs a small beck. This flat area of land was once a lake and around its edge was grown flax which the villagers spun into linen.

The **Church of St Michael and All Angels** is a fine example of rural medieval architecture. Believed to have been built on the site of a pagan shrine, the church lies some way from the village centre though its handsome bell-cote is a suitable landmark. Among the 14th-century roof bosses can be seen the Green Man, an ancient fertility symbol of a man's head protruding through foliage which was adopted by the Christian church.

Spanning Linton Beck is a graceful 14th-century packhorse bridge that was repaired by Dame Elizabeth Redmayne in the late 17th century. During the repair work, Dame Elizabeth had a narrow parapet added to the bridge to prevent carts from crossing

Bolton Abbey

because, so it is said, the local farmers refused to contribute to the cost of the repairs.

CRACOE
3 miles SW of Grassington on the B6265

The village contains several 17th-century houses that are typical examples of the building style of the day. Constructed from stone quarried on nearby Cracoe and Rylstone Fell, the cavity between

Packhorse Bridge, Linton

29

Above the village of Cracoe, on top of the fell, is a cairn built in memory of local men who died during the First World War. Construction of the cairn began in the early 1920s but the professional masons experienced great difficulty as high winds tore down their work over night. Eventually, a local man was hired for the task and, instead of coming down from the fell each night, he pitched his tent close to the cairn and remained on-site until it was completed.

the 3feet thick walls was filled with rubble.

RYLSTONE

4 miles SW of Grassington on the B6265

On Rylstone Fell, above this Pennine village, stands **Rylstone Cross** which was, originally, a large stone that looked rather like a man. In 1885, a wooden cross was erected on top of the stone to commemorate peace with France and the initials DD and TB, carved on the back of the cross, refer to the Duke of Devonshire and his land agent, Mr T Broughton.

In the early 1800s, when Wordsworth was touring the area, he heard a local legend which became the basis for his poem *The White Doe of Rylstone,* published in 1815. The story is set in the 16th century and concerns the local Norton family. Francis Norton gave his sister Emily a white doe before he went off to battle. He survived the conflict but after his return to Rylstone was murdered in Norton Tower. Emily was inconsolable but found some comfort from the same white doe which had returned from the wild. It used to accompany Emily when she visited her brother's grave and long after her death, a white doe was often seen lying on Francis's grave.

THRESHFIELD

1 mile W of Grassington on the B6160

Across the river from Grassington, Threshfield has at its heart a small village green called the Park, complete with the original village stocks and surrounded by charming 17th-century houses. Perhaps the most striking building is the Free Grammar School built in 1674. According to local people its porch is haunted by a fairy known as Old Pam the Fiddler. Threshfield was once famed for the production of *besoms* (birch brooms) but the last family to make them, the Ibbotsons, died out in the 1920s.

CONISTONE

2½ miles NW of Grassington off the B6160

This ancient settlement, whose name suggests that it once belonged to a king, is clustered around its maypole and village green. The village Church of St Mary is thought to have been founded in Saxon times and there are certainly two well-preserved Norman arches to be seen. The land surrounding Conistone is unusually flat as it was once the bottom of a lake formed by the melt water from the glacier that carved out Kilnsey Crag.

KILNSEY

3 miles NW of Grassington on the B6160

This small hamlet, on the opposite bank of the River Wharfe from Conistone, is a great place from which many anglers fly fish and the Kilnsey Angling Club has its home in the village pub. This quiet and peaceful place is overlooked by the now uninhabited Old Hall which was originally built as a grange for the monks of Fountains Abbey.

Kilnsey Park and Trout Farm is a popular place for family outings. Under-12s can enjoy their first experience of trout fishing, with all the tackle provided. Pony trekking is available, there's an estate shop selling dales' produce and fresh Kilnsey trout, a restaurant and children's adventure centre. Visitors can also wander around the farm. Fly fishing, for those who like to indulge, is available in two well-stocked lakes.

The striking outline of **Kilnsey Crag** is unmistakable as one side of this limestone hill was gouged out by a passing glacier during the Ice Age. One of the most spectacular natural features in the dales, the crag has a huge 'lip' or overhang which presents an irresistible challenge to adventurous climbers.

KETTLEWELL

Surrounded by the beautiful countryside of Upper Wharfedale, Kettlewell is a popular centre for tourists and walkers. At the meeting point of several old packhorse routes, which now serve as footpaths and bridleways, the village was a busy market centre and, at one time, the home of 13 public houses which catered to the needs of the crowds. The market charter, granted in the 13th century, is evidence that Kettlewell was once a more important place than it is today and the various local religious houses of Bolton Priory, Coverham Abbey, and Fountains Abbey all owned land in the area.

Today, however, Kettlewell is a conservation area, a charming place of chiefly 17th- and 18th-century houses and cottages. Keen cinemagoers will know that

Kettlewell provided almost all the locations for the enormously successful 2003 film *Calendar Girls* based on the true story of a local Women's Institute that produced a calendar of discreetly naked ladies to raise funds for leukaemia research.

AROUND KETTLEWELL

STARBOTTON

2 miles N of Kettlewell on the B6160

This quiet little Wharfedale village was the scene in 1686 of a disastrous flood when a huge head of water descended from the surrounding fells and swept away many of the houses and cottages. The damage was such that a national appeal was started and aid, in the form of money, was sent from as far afield as Cambridgeshire.

BUCKDEN

4 miles N of Kettlewell on the B6160

Marking the beginning of Wharfedale proper, Buckden is the first full-sized village of the dale and proudly boasts that it is also home to Wharfedale's first shop. Unusually for this area, the village was not settled by the Anglo-Saxons but, later, by the Normans and it was the headquarters of the officers hunting in the forest of Langstrothdale. As the forest was cleared to make way for agriculture, Buckden became an important market town serving a large part of the surrounding area. Wool was one

30 BLUE BELL INN

Kettlewell

Lovely old hostelry offering tasty home-cooked food, real ales and en suite rooms.

see page 229

31 THE BUCK INN

Buckden

Impressive Georgian coaching inn in a lovely setting, acclaimed for its cuisine and offering top quality en suite accommodation.

see page 230

32 THE QUEENS ARMS INN

Litton

Authentic rural free house in the heart of Littondale; excellent cuisine, comfortable en suite rooms and real ales from its own micro-brewery.

¶ ⊨ *see page 231*

of the important sources of income for the dalesfolk and the local inn here still has some of the old weighing equipment from the days when the trade was conducted on the premises. The village is an excellent starting point for those wanting to climb Buckden Pike (2,302 feet), which lies to the east. The route to the summit takes in not only superb views but also several waterfalls.

Designated in Norman times as one of the feudal hunting forests, **Langstrothdale Chase** was governed by the strict forest laws. Just to the south of the village, which lies on the edge of the Chase, can be seen an old stone cross which was used to mark the forest boundary. Buckden's name means the 'valley of the bucks' but its last deer was hunted and killed here in the 17th century.

HUBBERHOLME

5 miles N of Kettlewell off the B6160

This small village was originally two places: Hubberholme proper and Kirkgill, which takes its name from the nearby Church of St Michael and All Angels that was, at one time, a forest chapel. Each year, on New Year's Day, the villagers gather at the local pub for the **Hubberholme Parliament**. For that night, the public bar becomes the House of Commons, where the farmers congregate, while the room where the vicar and churchwardens meet is the House of Lords. Bidding then takes place between the farmers for the rent of a field behind the church and, encouraged by the vicar, the highest bidder gains the lease for the coming year.

LITTON

5 miles NW of Kettlewell off the B6160

This pretty village lends it name to the dale, **Littondale**, which is actually the valley of the River Skirfare. Once part of a Norman hunting forest, the dale was originally called Amerdale (meaning 'deep fork') and this ancient name is preserved in Amerdale Dub, where the River Skirfare joins the River Wharfe near Kilnsey.

YOCKENTHWAITE

6 miles NW of Kettlewell off the B6160

The unusual name of this small village is Viking in origin. Though once a prosperous place, Yockenthwaite is now a collection of old stone farms. On the surrounding fells stands a well-preserved Bronze Age stone circle and **Giant's Grave**, the remains of an Iron Age settlement.

Village of Litton, Littondale

ARNCLIFFE

3 miles W of Kettlewell off the B6160

Situated in Littondale, the village name dates back to Saxon times when the valley was referred to as Amerdale. This is a quiet, tranquil dale and life has remained the same here for many years. Many of the buildings around the central village green are listed and, in its early years, the long running TV series *Emmerdale* was filmed here. Strongly recommended is a visit to the Falcon Inn, run by the Miller family for four generations, where almost nothing has changed in more than half a century.

AIREDALE

The 'Gateway to the Dales', Skipton has long been a starting-point for any tour of the Yorkshire Dales and, though still a bustling centre for Airedale and its neighbour, Malhamdale, the town's old industries have given way, to a large degree, to tourism. The source of the River Aire lies in Malhamdale, just to the north of Malham, and it flows through both dales before finally joining the River Ouse. For some of its length, in Airedale, the river flows side-by-side with the Leeds and Liverpool Canal. The construction of a navigable waterway, linking the two great industrial areas of Lancashire and Yorkshire, changed the lives of many living in the dales and certainly played a major part in establishing the textile mills in the area.

However, the importance of farming has never been lost and market day is a key event in the daily lives of the dalesfolk. As well as the sheep, other constant features of the countryside are the dry stone walls- a familiar sight to all those visiting the Yorkshire Dales.

SKIPTON

Often called the 'Gateway to the Dales', Skipton is a busy market town that mercifully escaped the 'development' mania of the 1960s when so many old towns had their hearts ripped out. Visitors can still wander down the many alleyways, known here as 'ginnels', explore the side streets with their independent shops, bars and restaurants, or visit the canal area with its boats, footpaths and picnic areas. There are regular boat trips along the canal and motor boats can also be hired.

Skipton is also renowned for its outdoor market which received its first charter in 1204. Every Monday, Wednesday, Friday and Saturday more than 50 independent traders set up their stalls from the castle gates down both sides of the High Street.

The town's most imposing building is **Skipton Castle** (see panel on page 34), one of the best-preserved and most complete medieval castles in England, despite enduring a 3-year siege during the Civil War. Built to guard the entrance to Airedale, the powerful stone structure seen today was devised in 1310 by Robert de Clifford, the 1st Earl of Skipton.

Of the many and varied attractions in Airedale and the area surrounding Skipton, the most impressive feature is the beautiful limestone formations found to the north of Malham. The spectacular and enormous curved cliff of Malham Cove, created by glacial action during the last Ice Age, the limestone pavements above the cove, the deep gorge of Gordale Scar, and the remote natural lake, Malham Tarn, are all well worth a visit. This dramatic scenic area has been designated a Site of Special Scientific Interest and the area supports a wide range of animals, birds, and plant life. As there is a variety of terrain, from bleak, bracken-strewn moorland to coniferous plantations, there is also a wide variety of flora and fauna. Birdwatchers, particularly, will delight in the opportunity to catch sight of red grouse and short-eared owls on the moors while also having the chance to view the many wading birds which populate the lakes and reservoirs of the area.

Skipton Castle

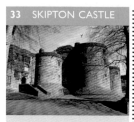

33 SKIPTON CASTLE

Skipton

Guardian of the gateway to the Yorkshire Dales for over 900 years, this unique fortress is one of the most complete and well-preserved medieval castles in England.

🏛 *see page 232*

34 THE ROYAL SHEPHERD

Skipton

Traditional hostelry in superb canalside location serving excellent food and real ales, all day, every day

🍴 *see page 232*

The Cliffords were a fighting breed and, throughout the Middle Ages, wherever there was trouble a member of the family was sure to be found. The 8th Lord Clifford, Thomas, and his son John were both killed while fighting for the House of Lancaster during the War of the Roses. Later, George Clifford, Champion to Queen Elizabeth I and a renowned sailor, fought against the Spanish Armada and, as well as participating in many voyages of his own, he also lent a ship to Sir Walter Raleigh.

It is thanks to Lady Anne Clifford that visitors to Skipton can marvel at its buildings. Following the ravages of the Civil War, Lady Anne undertook a comprehensive restoration programme. As well as an enormous banqueting hall, a series of kitchens still remain with some of their original fittings. There is also a rather unusually decorated room whose walls are lined with shells that were collected by George Clifford in the 19th century while he was travelling in the South Seas. A beautiful Tudor courtyard has survived, complete with a yew tree planted in 1659 by Lady Anne. However, the most striking feature of the castle is the impressive 14th-century gateway, which is visible from the High Street, and carries the Clifford family motto *Desormais* meaning 'Henceforth'. Visitor amenities at the castle include a licensed tea room, a bookshop and the peaceful Chapel Terrace picnic area. Throughout the year, the castle hosts a wide variety of events, including the Clog Dancing Festival in mid-July.

Many members of the Clifford family are buried in the parish **Church of the Holy Trinity** which stands adjacent to the castle. The most impressive memorial is that of the 3rd earl, George Clifford. Dating back to the 14th century, the church also suffered damage during the Civil War. Once again, Lady Anne Clifford came to the rescue, restoring the interior and rebuilding the steeple in 1655. Inside the church, among the many tombstones, is that of the Longfellow family, which included the uncle of the American poet, Henry Wadsworth Longfellow.

A good introduction to Skipton is to follow the **Millennium Walk,** a 2-hour promenade that takes you past the main sights of the town. A leaflet guide to the walk is available at the Tourist Information Centre on the High Street. Included in the walk is the Town Hall which is now also the home of the **Craven**

Museum (see panel - free). Dedicated to the surrounding area, it contains many interesting displays relating to the geological and archaeological treasures that have been found locally, including a piece of Bronze Age cloth which is considered the oldest textile fragment in the country. Closer to the present day, there are displays of furniture illustrating the fine craftsmanship that went into even the most mundane household item. Also on show are farming exhibits which reflect the changing lives of many of the people who lived off the surrounding countryside.

Almost opposite the Town Hall, on the High Street, are the premises of the **Craven Herald**, a newspaper that was established in 1874 although the publication was produced for a short time in the 1850s. The building is fortunate in having retained its late-Victorian shop front, as well as the passageway to one side. The house was first occupied by William Chippendale in the late 18th century. A trader in textiles, Chippendale made his money by buying then selling on the cloth woven by the farmers in their own homes. Close to the newspaper's offices is the **Public Library** which opened in 1910 and was funded by Andrew Carnegie. A large, ornate building, it is in contrast to the town's older buildings and stands as a reminder of the change in character which Skipton underwent in the late 19th century.

The **Leeds and Liverpool Canal**, which flows through the town, provided a cheap form of transport as well as linking Skipton with the major industrial centres of Yorkshire and Lancashire. The first of three trans-Pennine routes, the 127-mile canal has 91 locks along the full length as well as two tunnels, one of which is over a mile long. The towpath provides a number of pleasant walks, including a stretch along the cul-de-sac Spring Branch beside the castle walls.

It seems fitting that, in a town which over many years has been dedicated to trade and commerce, Thomas Spencer, co-founder of Marks and Spencer, should have been born here in 1851. Skipton, too, was the home of Sir Winston Churchill's physician, Lord Moran, who grew up here as the son of the local doctor.

AROUND SKIPTON

EMBSAY

1 mile N of Skipton off the A59

Embsay is the western terminus of the **Embsay Steam Railway** which follows a picturesque 4.5 mile route to the award-winning station at Bolton Abbey. There are more than 20 locomotives, both steam and diesel, on display together with railway carriages. During the summer months, trains run 7 days a week with 'Stately Trains' on scheduled Sundays using carriages from the historic Stately Trains collection such as those built to haul first class passengers on the Great North of Scotland Railway. Refreshments are

35 THE CRAVEN MUSEUM

Skipton
Crammed full of fascinating exhibits, the **Craven Museum** is a great place to explore the history of Skipton and the Craven Dales.

🏛 see page 233

•

As with many historic market towns, Skipton has its fair share of inns and public houses. The Black Horse Inn is one such pub and its date stone of 1676 is well worth a second look as it is carved with symbols of the butcher's trade: axes, animal heads, and twisted fleeces. Originally called The King's Head, the inn was built by, not surprisingly, a butcher, Robert Goodgion. The Black Horse commands splendid views over the canal and a mounting block for horsemen still stands outside the front door.

•

36 THE MASONS ARMS INN

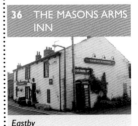

Eastby
Beautifully sited traditional Dales inn offering excellent food, real ales, en suite rooms and self-catering cottages.

🍴 🛏 see page 233

37 WHITE LION

Kildwick

Handsome hostelry in picturesque riverside village offering excellent cuisine, real ales and en suite rooms.

🍴 🛏 *see page 234*

38 THE DOG AND GUN INN

Malsis

Outstanding family-run hostelry serving excellent food and at least 5 real ales.

🍴 *see page 235*

available in the tearooms at Bolton Abbey and Embsay stations. Both have gift shops, including the famous bookshop at Embsay station. Special events are arranged throughout the year.

Those choosing to walk over the moor to the north of the village should take care as the area is peppered with old coal pits and disused shafts. However, the view from **Embsay Crag** (1217 feet high) is well worth the effort of climbing.

KILDWICK

3 miles S of Skipton off the A629

This picturesque little village, on the north bank of the River Aire, is approached over a bridge that was built in the early 14th century by the canons of Bolton Priory. The village **Church of St Andrew** was also rebuilt around the 14th and 15th centuries, though the choir was extended to its unusually long length sometime later which gives the church its local name of Lang Kirk o'Craven.

The River Aire is not the only waterway which passes through the village as it also lies on the banks of the Leeds and Liverpool Canal. Once a hive of industry with many spinning and weaving mills in the village and the surrounding area producing wool and silk yarn and cloth, the decline of the textile industry has caused many of the mills to close though some have now been converted to provide interesting accommodation or as offices for small business units. The canal, which until the 1930s was

still in commercial use, is now the preserve of pleasure craft and Kildwick is a popular overnight mooring.

LOTHERSDALE

4 miles SW of Skipton off the A629

A dramatic stretch of the Pennine Way passes through this village set in a deep valley in the heart of the moors. Charlotte Brontë knew the village well and in *Jane Eyre* the house she calls Gateshead is modelled on Lothersdale's Stonegappe, up on the hillside near the church.

THORNTON-IN-CRAVEN

5 miles SW of Skipton on the A56

This attractive village stands on the Pennine Way and from here there are magnificent views of Airedale and Pendle Forest in Lancashire. To the west of the village, **Thornton Hall Farm Country Park** promises "Animal encounters, glorious countryside and family fun come rain or shine!" Visitors can meet llamas and lambs, hens and horses, pigs and poultry, and wallabies and deer. They can also watch the sheep dogs in action, hitch a ride on the giant caterpillar, feed the friendly inhabitants, or have fun in the giant sand pit in the all-weather barn.

EARBY

6 miles SW of Skipton on the A56

Though the Yorkshire Dales are thought of as a once thriving textile producer, lead-mining was also a key industry for many centuries. Housed in an old grammar school, founded in the 1590s by Robert Windle, is the **Yorkshire Dales Mining Museum**. The large collection, as well as the substantial documentation and indexing, has been put together by several local interest groups who began their work in 1945 when the Earby Mines Research Group was formed within the Earby Pothole Club. The museum, which has limited opening times, has many excellent displays including mine tubs, photographs, mine plans, small implements, mining machinery, and miners' personal belongings.

BROUGHTON

4 miles W of Skipton on the A59

The Tempest family has been associated with this farming community for the past 800 years and their family home, **Broughton Hall** dates back to 1597, with additions made in the 18th and 19th centuries. The building itself may well seem familiar since it, as well as the grounds, have been used frequently by film crews as an historic location. The Hall is only open on Bank Holiday Mondays or by prior arrangement. However, the grounds are open on the last Sunday in June when the Broughton Hall Game Fair takes place. This well-attended event covers all manner of country sports and pursuits. The Broughton estate covers 3000 acres, part of which is home to a business park where many small businesses thrive.

GARGRAVE

5 miles NW of Skipton on the A65

This picturesque small village in Upper Airedale was once a thriving market town and it also became a busy transport centre after the Leeds and Liverpool Canal was built. Lead from the nearby mines was loaded on to the barges at the five wharves here, while other goods were unloaded ready for distribution to the surrounding area. The village also played a part in the textile boom and there were two cotton mills in the village. Now no longer in commercial use, like the canal, some of the mills have been turned into residential accommodation while the canal is very much alive with pleasure boats.

To the south of the village, at **Kirk Sink**, is the site of a Roman villa that was excavated in the 1970s. Relics recovered from the building can be seen in Skipton and Cliffe Castle Museums; the site itself has since been re-covered.

Roman Villa, Kirk Sink

To the north of the village of Malham rises the ancient glacial grandeur of Malham Cove. Access is from the Langcliffe road beyond the last buildings of the village, down a path alongside the beck that leads through a scattering of trees. The 300 feet limestone amphitheatre is the most spectacular section of the mid-Craven fault and, as recently as the 1700s, a massive waterfall that was higher than Niagara Falls cascaded over its edge. A steep path leads to the limestone pavement at the top, with its characteristic clints and grykes, where water has carved a distinctive natural sculpture through the weaknesses in the limestone. From here it is not too far to reach the equally inspiring Gordale Scar, a huge gorge carved by glacial melt water with an impressive waterfall leaping, in two stages, from a fissure in its face. Further on still is another waterfall known as Janet's Foss. Beside the waterfall is a cave which Janet, a friendly fairy, is reputed to inhabit. Three miles north of the scar is Malham Tarn, a glacial lake which by way of an underground stream is the source of the River Aire.

CONISTON COLD

7 miles NW of Skipton on the A65

Lying midway between Skipton and Settle, this small village lies on the old route to the Lake District. Like most places situated on once busy routes, the village had its share of coaching inns and one in particular was the Punch Bowl Inn which has an unusual circular indentation on the front outside wall. In days gone by the inn's patrons would stand a few yards from the wall and try to kick a ball to this mark.

AIRTON

8 miles NW of Skipton off the A65

This charming Airedale village is well known to long-distance walkers as it lies on the Pennine Way. At the beginning of the 18th century Airton became a Quaker community and the **Meeting House**, which was built on land donated by the well-known Quaker weavers William and Alice Ellis, can still be seen by the village green. Another legacy of the village's Quaker community is the absence of a public house as the drinking of alcohol was strictly forbidden by the Friends.

Also overlooking the village green is a 17th-century Squatter's Cottage – so-called because, according to the law, any person building a house and having smoke rising from the chimney within 24 hours was granted the freehold of the property including the land within a stone's throw of the front door.

MALHAM

11 miles NW of Skipton off the A65

Malham village was originally two settlements, Malham East and Malham West, which were separated by the beck. Each came under the influence of a different religious house: Bolton Priory and Fountains Abbey respectively. United after the Dissolution of the Monasteries, the focal point of Malham became the village green where the annual sheep fairs were held. This pretty village of farms and cottages is one of the most visited places in the Yorkshire Dales though it is not the charming stone built dwellings which visitors come to admire but the spectacular limestone scenery which lies just to the north. However, the two ancient stone bridges in the village centre are also worth a second glance. The New Bridge, which is also known as the Monks' Bridge, was built in the 17th century while the Wash-Dub Bridge dates from the 16th century and is of a clapper design (limestone slabs placed on stone supports).

RIBBLESDALE AND THE THREE PEAKS

The River Ribble, the source of which lies high up on bleak moorland to the northeast of Ingleton, flows through several ancient settlements before leaving the county of Yorkshire and flowing on into Lancashire. On opposite banks of the river, lie Settle and Giggleswick, which are overlooked by the towering white limestone cliffs of Castleberg Crag and Langcliffe Scar, parts of the mid-Craven fault.

Further north from these two market towns is one of the most popular tourist centres in the dales, Ingleton, and high above the village are the famous **Three Peaks** of Ingleborough, Pen-y-ghent, and Whernside. The surrounding countryside is dominated by caves, potholes, and waterfalls and it is ideal country for all those who enjoy the outdoors.

The layer of limestone which lies across this whole area was laid down around 400 million years ago, when the shells of dead sea creatures along with mud accumulated at the bottom of the warm sea that covered a huge area of northern England. Much later, the layer of sandstone, known as millstone grit, was formed over the top. Much is talked about the **Craven Fault** and, though it was formed by a series of mighty earthquakes, this all happened well over 30 million years ago so visitors need not worry about visiting the area. The line of the fault, where the land to the northwest was lifted up and the land to the southeast slipped down, is all too evident today. It was the action of water, seeping into the limestone, which froze during the Ice Age that has created the many caves and potholes of the area. Erosion, though this time on the surface, near Malham and elsewhere,

formed the magnificent limestone pavements while the Three Peaks, as they are capped by millstone grit, have stood the test of time and still stand proud.

This is farming country and the traditional agricultural methods, along with the abundance of limestone, have given this region its own distinctive appeal. The high fells, composed of grits and sandstone, support heather moorlands and here can be found the only bird unique to Britain, the red grouse, and several birds of prey. Meanwhile, the limestone areas support a much more varied plant life, though the woodlands are chiefly of ash. In these shaded places, among the wild garlic and lily of the valley, visitors might be lucky enough to come across roe deer, badgers, and foxes.

SETTLE

One of the most unspoilt market towns in the Yorkshire Dales, Settle is dominated by one of the huge viaducts from the **Settle-Carlisle Railway** as well as the towering

39 SETTLE DOWN CAFÉ

Settle

Charming eating place serving quality home cooking with a varied menu.

see page 236

Settle Carlisle Railway

Settle is probably best known as the southern terminus of the Settle to Carlisle Railway, a proudly preserved survivor of the glorious age of steam travel, although the regular daily services are now provided by diesel locomotives. The route crosses 21 viaducts, of which the Ribblehead Viaduct is the most spectacular, passes through 14 tunnels and over numerous bridges. The 72-mile line is still flanked by charming little stations and signal boxes - the station buildings at Settle are particularly appealing. This attractive railway was built amidst great controversy and even greater cost, in both money and lives, earning it the dubious title of "the line that should never have been built". In the churchyard at St Leonard's in Chapel-le-Dale, more than 100 railway workers who perished in the construction of the line are buried.

limestone cliffs of **Castleberg Crag** which offers spectacular views over the town. It can be reached by following the recently opened Tot Lord Woodland Trail.

At the heart of the town is the Market Square where each Tuesday a colourful market is held. It dates back to 1249 when Henry III granted Settle a Market Charter. In addition to the open air market, there's also an indoor market in Victoria Hall where the traders specialise in bric-à-brac and curios.

Settle's architecture is very distinctive, in the main being Victorian sandstone buildings that all look as if they are born of the railway culture. Buildings of note include the arcaded Shambles, originally butchers' slaughter houses, the French-style Town Hall and the Victorian Music Hall. The town's oldest building is the 17th-century **Preston's Folly,** described as an extravaganza of mullioned

windows and Tudor masonry. It is named after the man who created this anomalous fancy and impoverished himself in the process.

Apart from the grander structures on the main streets, there are charming little side streets, lined with Jacobean and Georgian cottages, and criss-crossed with quirky little alleyways and ginnels with hidden courtyards and workshops of a time gone by. Almost as old is **Ye Olde Naked Man** pub in the Market Place. The inn sign depicts a naked man protecting his modesty with a carpenter's plane bearing the date 1663.

Just outside the town, housed in an old cotton mill dating from the 1820s, is the **Watershed Mill Visitor Centre.** This charming place, on the banks of the River Ribble, offers a unique shopping experience.

Ye Olde Naked Man Pub, Settle

AROUND SETTLE

RATHMELL

2 miles S of Settle off the A65

From this small village, set beside the River Ribble, there are many footpaths along the riverbanks, through the nearby woods, and up to Whelpstone Crag. An ancient farming community, the oldest farm here is dated 1689 and a little row of farm cottages called Cottage Fold are from around the same period.

GIGGLESWICK

1 mile W of Settle off the A65

This ancient village, which lies below the limestone scar that is part of the Craven fault, is best known for **Giggleswick School** which was granted a Royal Charter in 1553 by Edward VI. The school's fame stems partly from its observatory which was used by the Astronomer Royal in 1927 to observe an eclipse of the sun. The school's chapel, the copper dome of which is a well-known local landmark, was built to commemorate the Diamond Jubilee of Queen Victoria.

On the edge of town is the **Yorkshire Dales Falconry Centre,** home to more than 40 birds of prey from around the world. They include eagles, owls, vultures, falcons and hawks. The centre has been careful to re-create their natural habitats, transporting 350 tons of limestone boulders to provide cliff-faced aviaries. The star attraction is Andy, the Andean condor, with a wingspan of 10 feet

6 inches. Along with other vultures, eagles and hawks, Andy takes part in the regular free-flying demonstrations. The centre has full educational facilities, an adventure playground, tea room and gift shop.

Just to the north of Giggleswick can be found the famous Ebbing and Flowing Well, one of many in the area which owe their unusual names to the porous nature of the limestone which causes there sometimes to be water and sometimes not.

FEIZOR

3 miles NW of Settle off the A65

The village dates back to monastic times when it lay on the route from Kilnsey to the Lake District which was much used by the monks of Fountains Abbey. Although both Fountains Abbey and Sawley Abbey had possessions in the area, there are few reminders of those times today. However, the **Yorkshire Dales Falconry and Conservation Centre** does bring visitors to this village. With demonstration flights held throughout the day, when the centre's wide range of birds of prey are seen flying free, and much else on offer it does make an interesting and unusual day out.

AUSTWICK

4 miles NW of Settle off the A65

This ancient village of stone cottages and crofts, dry stone walls, abandoned quarries, and patchwork hills was originally a Norse settlement: the name is Nordic for Eastern Settlement. The mostly

Rathmell is also home to the Horses Health Farm & Visitor Centre which was established in 1991 to provide a unique centre for the treatment of horses and ponies, and to put an edge on the fitness of performance animals. Within the centre are a hydrotherapy pool, solarium, an all-weather arena for schooling and a farrier's forge. The Visitor Centre was opened in 1998 in response to public interest in the work done here. Visitors can watch horses swimming in the pool and enjoying the solarium treatment, and cheer on the Racing Miniature Shetlands. The centre is only open on limited occasions - check before travelling.

40 THE BOARS HEAD HOTEL

Long Preston

Fine old hostelry offering appetising home-cooked food, real ales and quality accommodation.

see page 236

Though the existence of Ingleborough Cave was known for centuries, it was not until the 19th century that its exploration was begun. One of the explorers, geologist Adam Sedgwick, is quoted as saying, 'We were forced to use our abdominal muscles as sledges and our mouths as candlesticks', which gives an excellent indication of the conditions the early pot-holers had to endure. Those visiting the caves today see only a small part of the five miles of caverns and tunnels though, fortunately, this easily accessible portion is spectacular, with large natural passages and a veritable wonderland of stalactites and stalagmites. As well as exotic cave formations and illuminated pools there is Eldon Hall Cavern, home to a vast mushroom bed.

17th-century buildings, with their elaborately decorated stone lintels, flank what remains of the village green where the ancient cross stands as a reminder of when this was the head of a dozen neighbouring manors and the home of an annual cattle fair.

CLAPHAM

6 miles NW of Settle off the A65

By far the largest building in the village is **Ingleborough Hall**, once the home of the Farrer family and now a centre for outdoor education. One member of the family, Reginald Farrer, was an internationally renowned botanist and he was responsible for introducing many new plant species into the country. Many examples of his finds still exist in the older gardens of the village and in the hall's grounds and there is a particularly pleasant walk, the **Reginald Farrer Nature Trail**, which leads from Clapham to nearby Ingleborough Cave.

This is an area that has a great abundance of natural waterfalls but the waterfall seen near the village church is one of the very few which owes its existence to man. In the 1830s the Farrer family created a large lake, covering some seven acres of land, and the waterfall is the lake's overflow. As well as providing water for the village, a turbine was placed at the bottom of the waterfall and, with the help of the electrical power, Clapham was one of the first villages in the country to have street lighting. This is perhaps not as surprising as it

might seem as Michael Faraday, the distinguished 19th-century scientist, was the son of the village blacksmith.

The most peculiar feature of the area surrounding Clapham has to be the **Norber Boulders,** a series of black boulders that stand on limestone pedestals. Despite their contrived appearance, they are a completely natural feature. Another distinctive local feature is the clapper bridge, a medieval structure made from large slabs of rock spanning the local becks.

Also close to Clapham is the giant pot-hole known as **Gaping Gill.** Some 340 feet deep, the hole is part of the same underground limestone cave system as Ingleborough Cave. The main chamber is similar in size to York Minster. Twice a year, the public can gain access via a bosun's chair on a winch that is operated by local caving clubs.

KEASDEN

6 miles NW of Settle off the A65

Today, Keasden is a scattered farming community that is easily missed but evidence from the 17th-century church records tell a different story. At that time there were some 40 farms here (now there are around 15) as well as many associated trades and craftsmen. The name Keasden comes from the Old English for 'cheese valley' and some of the farms still retain the vast stone weights of the cheese presses though, unfortunately, the recipe for the local cheese has been lost.

NEWBY

7 miles NW of Settle off the A65

This tiny hamlet was originally situated about a mile south of its present position because in the 17th century the Great Plague decimated the village's population. The survivors moved away and rebuilt Newby and many of the buildings date from this time.

The village came under the direction of the monks of Furness Abbey and the remains of their walled garden can still be seen. By the Victorian era, Newby had become a thriving weaving community. However, the cottage industry was soon overtaken by the new factory systems and, by 1871, the village had once again returned to peace and quiet.

INGLETON

10 miles NW of Settle off the A65

Mentioned in the *Domesday Book* – the name means 'beacon town' – Ingleton is certainly one of the most visited villages in the dales. As a gateway to the Three Peaks, it is also popular with walkers. From as long ago as the late 1700s, Ingleton has been famous for the numerous caves and other splendid scenery that lie within a short distance though some are harder to find and even harder to reach. Though Ingleton is no longer served by trains, the village is still dominated by the railway viaduct that spans the River Greta. The river, which is formed here by the meeting of the Rivers Twiss and Doe, is famous for its salmon leaps. There are riverside walks or you can just relax in the Millennium Gardens.

Many thousands of years old, **White Scar Cave** was only discovered in 1923, by an adventurous student named Christopher Long. Though he saw only by the light of a torch, standing alone in the vast underground cave now known as Battlefield Cavern must have been an awesome experience. The longest Show Cave in Britain, it stretches for more than 330 feet, soaring in places to 100 feet high, with thousands of oddly-shaped stalactites dripping from its roof. The 80-minute guided tour covers one mile and passes cascading waterfalls and curious cave formations such as the Devil's Tongue, the Arum Lily and the remarkably lifelike Judge's Head. The temperature inside the cave stays constant all year round at a cool 8°c (46°f) so don't forget to bring something warm to wear.

Ingleborough which, at 2,375 feet, is the middle summit of the **Three Peaks**. For more than 2000 years, the peak has been used as a beacon and a fortress and, as a result, it is perhaps the most interesting. A distinctive feature of the horizon for miles around, it is made of several layers of rock of differing hardnesses. There are several paths to the summit most of which begin in Ingleton. On top of the peak are the remains of a tower that was built by a local mill owner, Mr Hornby Roughsedge. Though the intended use of the building is not known, its short

Discovered in 1865 by Joseph Carr, the Ingleton Waterfalls were not revealed to the public until 1885 and have been delighting visitors ever since. Along the four miles of scenic walks, the stretch of waterfalls includes those with such interesting names as Pecca Twin Falls, Holly Bush Spout, Thornton Force and Baxengill Gorge.

•

To the east of Ingleton, on the edge of the summit plateau, are the remains of several ancient hut circles and, beyond, the remains of a wall. The Romans are known to have used Ingleborough as a signal station but the wall may have been built by the Brigantes whose settlement on the mountain was called Rigodunum.

•

history is well-documented. A grand opening was arranged on the summit and the celebrations, probably helped by a supply of ale, got a little out of hand when a group of men began tearing down the structure.

At the highest point is a triangulation point while, close by, a cross-shaped shelter has been built which offers protection from the elements whatever their direction. The shelter acts as a reminder that the weather can change quickly in this area and a walk to the summit, however nice the day is at lower levels, should not be undertaken without careful thought as to suitable clothing.

LOW BENTHAM

10 miles NW of Settle on the B6480

Lying close to the county border with Lancashire and on the slopes of the Pennines, this village is pleasantly situated in the valley of the River Wenning, a tributary of the River Lune. Like many Pennine villages in the late 17th and early 18th centuries, Low Bentham was taken over by the textile industry and there was a linen mill here. After a time, the mill changed hands, and also direction, taking on the specialised task of spinning silk before that, too, ceased in the 1960s as a result of the increasing use of man-made fibres.

CHAPEL-LE-DALE

10 miles NW of Settle on the B6255

Whernside, to the north of the village, is the highest of the Three Peaks, at 2,418 feet, and also the

least popular of the mountains – consequently there are few paths to the summit. Just below the top are a number of tarns. Here, in 1917, it was noticed that they were frequented by black-headed gulls. Those walking to the top of the peak today will also see the birds, a reminder that the northwest coast is not so far away.

LANGCLIFFE

1 mile N of Settle on the B6479

As its name suggests, Langcliffe lies in the shelter of the long cliff of the Craven fault where the millstone grit sandstone meets the silver grey of the limestone. Although the majority of the houses and cottages surrounding the central village green are built from the limestone, some sandstone has also been used which gives this pretty village an added charm. The Victorian urn on the top of the **Langcliffe Fountain** was replaced by a stone cross after the First World War in memory of those villagers who died in the conflict.

STAINFORTH

2 miles N of Settle on the B6479

This sheltered sheep farming village owes its existence to the Cistercian monks who brought those animals to this area. The monks were also responsible for building the 14th-century stone packhorse bridge which carries the road over the local beck, a tributary of the River Ribble. Although the village is certainly old, there are few buildings which date beyond the days of the Civil War: during those turbulent times, much of Stainforth was destroyed.

Catrigg Force, found along a track known as Goat Scar Lane, is a fine waterfall which drops some 60 feet into a wooded pool, while to the west is **Stainforth Force** flowing over a series of rock shelves.

HORTON IN RIBBLESDALE

6 miles N of Settle on the B6479

The oldest building in Horton is the 12th-century **St Oswald's Church** which still shows signs of its Norman origins in the chevron designs over the south door. Inside, peculiarly, all the pillars lean to the south and, in the west window, there is an ancient piece of stained glass showing Thomas à Becket wearing his bishop's mitre.

This village is the ideal place from which to explore the limestone landscapes and green hills of Upper Ribblesdale. To the east lies **Pen-y-ghent** (2,273 feet high), one of the famous Three Peaks.

There are several listed buildings in the area including Lodge Hall, which was formerly known as Ingman Lodge. Before the 20th century, a judge would travel around the countryside on horseback stopping to try cases rather than villagers commuting to major towns for their trials. Here, if anyone was found guilty of a capital crime, they were brought to Ingman Lodge to be hanged.

Stainforth Force, Stainforth

RIBBLEHEAD

10 miles N of Settle on the B6479

Lying close to the source of the River Ribble is the impressive structure of the **Ribblehead Viaduct** which was built to carry the Settle-Carlisle Railway. It was opened in 1876, after taking five years to construct, its 24 arches cross Batty Moss 100 feet below. A bleak and exposed site, the viaduct is often battered by strong winds which on occasion can literally stop a train in its tracks. The viaduct is 440 yards long and shortly after it the track enters Blea Moor Tunnel, at 2629 yards long the longest tunnel on the line.

The **Ribblehead Station & Visitor Centre**, housed in former station buildings, presents an interpretive display showing the history of the line with special emphasis on the Ribblehead locality.

•

The whole of the area around Horton in Ribblesdale has been designated as being of Special Scientific Interest, mainly due to the need to conserve the swiftly eroding hillsides and paths. This is an ancient landscape, well worth the efforts to preserve its ash woodlands, primitive earthworks, and rare birdlife such as peregrine falcon, ring ouzel, curlew and golden plover. There are also a great many caves in the area, which add to the sense of romance and adventure one feels in this place.

•

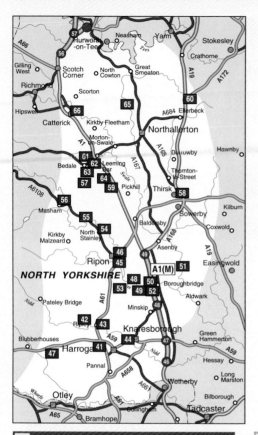

46

The Yorkshire Spa Towns

The Vale of York – or Plain, as it's sometimes called – is rich, agricultural land that stretches some 60 miles northwards from York almost to the River Tees. Although flat itself, there are almost always hills in view: the Hambleton and Cleveland Hills to the east, the Dales and the Pennines to the west. In between lies this fertile corridor of fertile farmland and low-lying meadows, a vast plain bisected by the Great North Road linking London and Edinburgh. Throughout this area the skyline is dotted with the spires and towers of churches that were built in those relatively prosperous times. The two towns of Harrogate and Knaresborough dominate the lower section of Nidderdale and though, today, Harrogate is the larger, for centuries Knaresborough was the more important of the two.

Ripon is a pleasant small city with a magnificent cathedral that dates back to Saxon times. Though the city tried to exploit the fashion for 'taking the waters', it did not have its own healing springs and so water had to be pumped in from Aldfield, near Fountains Abbey.

Many Edwardian spa buildings remain in Ripon, along with some fine Art Nouveau features and their surrounding gardens. Ripon is also home to one of the country's most beautiful racecourses; throughout the summer season there are race meetings here on what is known as Yorkshire's Garden Racecourse. Nearby, at Thirsk, is another of the country's delightful racecourses, although the town is best known as having been the home of the real-life James Herriot, Alf Wight.

Although ancient monuments abound in this area – such as the Devil's Arrows near Boroughbridge – and many of the settlements have Roman roots, it is the magnificent ruin of Fountains Abbey for which this region is best known. Set beside the River Skell, this was one of the wealthiest Cistercian houses in the country in medieval times and, today, the remains are Yorkshire's only World Heritage Site. However, there are other places of interest to see close by, including the fine stately home of Newby Hall, the Northern Horticultural Society's Harlow Carr Botanical Gardens and the two breweries at Masham.

FOOD & DRINK

PLACES OF INTEREST

HARROGATE

By the late 18th century Harrogate had become one of Europe's most fashionable spa towns serving both the needs of those with acute and chronic ailments and also members of 'good society'. Fuelled by competition from spa towns abroad, Harrogate sought to provide not only medical care for the sick but also to appeal to the needs of the fashionable. In 1858, Charles Dickens visited the town and described it as 'the queerest place, with the strangest people in it leading the oddest lives of dancing, newspaper reading, and table d'hôte.' Though its status as a spa town has declined, it is still a fashionable place, a sought after conference location, home of the annual Northern Antiques Fair, and a town with much to offer the visitor.

One of England's most attractive towns and a frequent winner of Britain in Bloom, Harrogate features acres of gardens that offer an array of colour throughout the year, open spaces, and broad tree lined boulevards. Until the 17th century Harrogate – or 'Haregate' as it was then called – was just a collection of cottages close to the thriving market town of Knaresborough. It was around 1590 that William Slingsby of Bilton Hall near Knaresborough who, while out walking his dog, discovered a spring bubbling up out of the rock that was to found the fortunes of the town. Tasting the waters, Slingsby found them to be similar to those he had tasted at the fashionable wells of Spaw, in Belgium. Expert opinion was sought and, in 1596, Dr Timothy Bright confirmed the spring to be a chalybeate well and the waters to have medicinal powers – curing a wide variety of illness and ailments from gout to vertigo.

Slingsby's well became known as **Tewit Well**, after the local name for peewits, and it can still be seen today, covered by a dome on pillars. Other wells were also found in the area, St John's Well in 1631 and the **Old Sulphur Well** which went on to become the most famous of Harrogate's springs. Though this spring had been known locally for years, it was not until 1656 that the sulphurous, vile-smelling waters, nicknamed 'the Stinking Spaw', began to attract attention.

During the mid-17th century bathing in the heated sulphurous waters became fashionable as well as a cure for various ailments and lodging houses were built around the sulphur well in Low Harrogate. Bathing took place in the evening and, each morning, the patients would drink a glass of the water with their breakfasts. The cupola over the well was erected in 1804.

In order to serve the growing number of people arriving at Harrogate seeking a cure for their ailments, the Queen's Head Hotel was built around 1680. When stagecoaches began to arrive in the 18th century the inn moved with the times and became the first at the spa to serve the needs of the coaches.

Many other hotels were built including the Crown Inn, next to the Old Sulphur Well, which became a coaching inn in 1772 and hosted a visit by Lord Byron in 1806. However, one of the town's most famous hotels, The Majestic, an Edwardian red brick building, does survive and it was the place where Elgar stayed while visiting Harrogate. But perhaps the best known Harrogate hotel is The Old Swan. It was here in 1926 that the famous crime writer Agatha Christie took refuge after staging a car accident and disappearing and sparking off the biggest man-hunt of the time with more than 1000 police and civilians called in to scour Agatha's local area. It was the first search in England to use aeroplanes.

After 10 days, Bob Tappin, a

local banjo player, recognised the author and alerted the police. Colonel Christie was informed and immediately came to collect his wife. Agatha kept her husband waiting before joining him for dinner, putting her disappearance down to total memory loss caused by the car accident. She had checked in under the name of Theresa Neele - the name of her husband's mistress! It was generally believed that his infidelity and the recent death of her mother had caused her to stage her disappearance. Two years later the couple divorced and Colonel Christie married his mistress. In 1977, the film Agatha, starring Dustin Hoffman and Vanessa Redgrave was shot on location at the Old Swan and in the Harrogate area.

The **Royal Pump Room Museum** was built in 1842 to enclose the Old Sulphur Well and this major watering place for spa visitors has been painstakingly restored to illustrate all the aspects of Harrogate's history. Beneath the building the sulphur water still rises to the surface and can be sampled.

There will be few Harrogate residents who have not heard of Betty Lupton, the almost legendary 'Queen of the Wells' who, for over 50 years, dispensed the spa waters, dishing out cupfuls to paying visitors, who were then encouraged to walk off the dubious effects of the medicine by taking a trip around the Bogs Fields, known today as **Valley Gardens**. She conducted her business in the

ostentatiously named **Royal Baths Assembly Rooms** which, in their heyday, were full of rich visitors sampling the waters. Today, the buildings have been restored to house the **Turkish Baths** where visitors can enjoy a sauna, beauty treatment and massage. The baths are open to the public daily.

Occupying the oldest of the town's surviving spa buildings, originally built in 1806, is the **Mercer Art Gallery** (see panel). The Promenade Room has been restored to its former glory and displays a superb collection of fine art along with the Kent Bequest – an archaeological collection that includes finds from both ancient Greece and Egypt.

As well as a spa, Harrogate developed into a centre for shopping for the well-to-do and the many old-fashioned shops are typified by Montpellier Parade, a crescent of shops surrounded by trees and flowerbeds. Another attractive aspect of the town is **The Stray**, which is unique to Harrogate

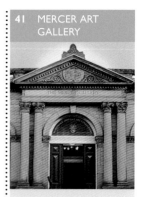

41 MERCER ART GALLERY

Harrogate

The Mercer Art Gallery is home to the district's superb collection of fine art.

🏛 see page 236

Royal Pump Room Museum, Harrogate

42 THE NEW INN

Burnt Yates

Beautifully maintained
traditional inn with
outstanding cuisine, real ales
and 4-star en suite
accommodation.

 🍴 🛏 see page 237

and virtually encircles the town centre. The 215 acres of open space are protected by ancient law to ensure that the residents of, and visitors to, the town always have access for sports, events, and walking. The spacious lawns are at their most picturesque during the spring when edged with crocus and daffodils. Originally part of the Forest of Knaresborough the land was, fortunately, not enclosed under the 1770 Act of Parliament. The large gritstone pillar beside The Stray marks the boundary of the Leeds and Ripon turnpike. On The Stray stands the Commemorative Oak Tree, planted in 1902 by Samson Fox to commemorate the ox roasting that took place here as part of the celebrations for Queen Victoria's Jubilee in 1887 and at the end of the Boer War in 1902.

One of Harrogate's major visitor attractions is the **RHS Harlow Carr Botanical Gardens,** just over a mile from the town centre. Established in 1948 by the Northern Horticultural Society and now covering some 58 acres, the gardens feature all manner of plants in a wide variety of landscapes which allows members of the public to see how they perform in the unsympathetic conditions of northern England. The society, as well as having their study centre here, has also opened a fascinating **Museum of Gardening**.

A major summer event is the **Great Yorkshire Show,** a three day event that includes top class show-jumping, displays and demonstrations of various kinds,

some 10,000 animals, miles of shopping, a flower show and much, much more.

AROUND HARROGATE

HAMPSTHWAITE

4 miles NW of Harrogate off the A59

This picturesque Nidderdale village lies on an ancient Roman way between Ilkley and Aldborough and traces of Roman tin mining have been found in the area. The village Church of St Thomas has remnants of a Saxon building in the tower and, in the churchyard, is buried Peter Barker. Known as 'Blind Peter', Barker did not let his disability hinder him: he was a skilled cabinet-maker, glazier and musician. The mysterious portrait of the bearded man hanging in the church, painted by the local vicar's daughter, may well be of Blind Peter.

BURNT YATES

4½ miles NW of Harrogate on the B6165

Located at one of the highest points in Nidderdale, Burnt Yates enjoys some fine views of the surrounding hills and moors. Its tiny village school of 1750 still stands. The original endowment provided for 30 poor boys to be taught the three Rs and for an equivalent number of poor girls to learns the skills of needlework and spinning.

BIRSTWITH

5 miles NW of Harrogate off the B6165

Evidence in the form of a Neolithic axe-head suggests that

this one-time estate village in the valley of the River Nidd was a Stone Age settlement in what was to become known as the Forest of Knaresborough. Along with both quarrying and coal-mining, Birstwith also had a cotton mill beside the river – though all that now remains is the weir that was created to ensure a good head of water for the mill-race. One notable visitor to this village was Charlotte Brontë, who stayed with the Greenwood family at Swarcliffe Hall for about six months in the 1840s, when she was governess to the children. The Hall is now a private boys' school.

RIPLEY

3 miles N of Harrogate off the A61

In the outer walls of the parish church, built around 1400, are holes said to have been caused by musket balls from Cromwell's firing squad who executed Royalist prisoners here after the battle of Marston Moor. Inside, there is a fine Rood Screen dating from the reign of King Stephen, a mid-14th-century tomb chest, and the stone base of an **Old Weeping Cross** (where one was expected to kneel in the stone grooves and weep for penance) survives in the churchyard.

Ripley, still very much an estate village, is a quiet and pretty place to explore. The unusual architecture is the legacy of Sir William Amcotts Ingilby who in 1827 began to remodel the entire village on one he had seen in Alsace-Lorraine. The original thatched cottages were

replaced with those seen today and Sir William even named the Town Hall in French style as the Hotel de Ville.

In the 1300s, a knighthood was granted to Thomas Ingilby for killing a wild boar in Knaresborough Forest that was charging at King Edward III. Ingilby's family have lived in magnificent **Ripley Castle** (see panel) for nearly 700 years. The castle is open to the public and is set in an outstanding Capability Brown landscape, with lakes, a deer park, and an avenue of tall beeches over which the attractive towers only just seem to peek. Its tranquillity belies the events that took place here after the battle at Marston Moor, when Cromwell, exhausted after his day's slaughter, camped his Roundheads here and chose to rest in the castle.

The Ingilbys, however, were Royalist and his intrusion was met with as much ill-will as possible; they offered neither food nor a bed. Jane Ingilby, aptly named 'Trooper Jane' due to her fighting skills, was the house's occupant and, having forced the self-styled Lord Protector of England to sleep on a sofa with two pistols pointing at his head, declared the next morning, 'It was well that he behaved in so peaceable a manner; had it been otherwise, he would not have left the house alive.' Cromwell, his pride severely damaged by a woman ordered the immediate

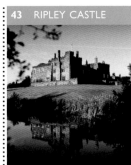

43   RIPLEY CASTLE

Ripley

For almost 700 years the Ingilby family has loved their castle and no wonder, given its fabulous treasures, and glorious grounds.

🏛 see page 238

Old Weeping Cross, Ripley

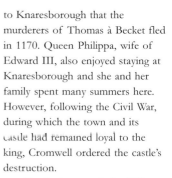

44 HANNAH'S HOUSE

Knaresborough

Superb, fully licensed restaurant serving traditional Yorkshire food and providing traditional Yorkshire value.

❙❙ *see page 238*

execution of his Royalist prisoners and left Trooper Jane regretting staying her hand during the previous night.

KNARESBOROUGH

4 miles NE of Harrogate on the A59

This ancient town of pantiled cottages and Georgian houses is precariously balanced on a hillside by the River Nidd. A stately railway viaduct, 90 feet high and 338 feet long, completed in 1851, spans the gorge. There are many unusual and attractive features in the town, among them a maze of steep stepped narrow streets leading down to the river and numerous alleyways. In addition to boating on the river, there are many enjoyable riverside walks.

The town is dominated by the ruins of **Knaresborough Castle**, built high on a crag overlooking the River Nidd by Serlo de Burgh, who had fought alongside William the Conqueror at Hastings. Throughout the Middle Ages, the castle was a favourite with the court and it was

to Knaresborough that the murderers of Thomas à Becket fled in 1170. Queen Philippa, wife of Edward III, also enjoyed staying at Knaresborough and she and her family spent many summers here. However, following the Civil War, during which the town and its castle had remained loyal to the king, Cromwell ordered the castle's destruction.

Also in the town is the **Old Courthouse Museum** which tells the history of the town and houses a rare Tudor Courtroom. The nearby Bebra Gardens are named after Knaresborough's twin town in Germany and its attractive flower beds are complemented by luxurious lawns and a paddling pool.

In the Market Square look out for Ye Oldest Chemist's Shop in England which was first recorded in 1720 although the building is probably a hundred years older. The old chemist's drawers, each marked with the scientific name of its contents, are still in place but the pungent potions have been replaced by a wide selection of quality confectionery.

Knaresborough boasts not only the oldest chemist's shop, but also the oldest tourist attraction in the UK, **Mother Shipton's Cave**, which opened in 1630. It was the birthplace of the famous prophetess and its Petrifying Well has fascinated visitors for generations. The effects that the well's lime-rich water has on objects are truly amazing and an array of paraphernalia, from old boots to bunches of grapes, are on view –

Mother Shipton's Cave, Knaresborough

seemingly turned to stone. It is little wonder that these were considered magical properties by the superstitious over the centuries or that the well was associated with witchcraft and various other interesting tales.

The foremost tale concerns Mother Shipton, who was said to have been born in the cavern situated by the well on 6th July 1488 and who has the reputation of being England's most famous fortune-teller. The story says that she was born in the midst of a terrible storm and was soon found to have a strange ability to see the future. As she grew older her prophetic visions became more widely known and feared throughout England. However, the most singular feature about Mother Shipton has to be that she died peacefully in her bed, as opposed to being burnt at the stake as most witches were at that time.

She had been threatened with burning by, among others, Cardinal Wolsey, when she had warned him on a visit to York that he might see the city again but never enter. True to her prediction Wolsey never did enter York, for he was arrested on a charge of treason at Cawood. Among her many other prophesies she reputedly foretold the invasion and defeat of the Spanish Armada in 1588 and Samuel Pepys recorded that it was Mother Shipton who prophesied the disastrous Great Fire of London in 1666.

While in Knaresborough, it is well worth taking the opportunity to visit the **House in the Rock**

hewn out of solid rock by Thomas Hill, an eccentric weaver, between 1770 and 1786. It was Hill's son who renamed the house Fort Montagu and flew a flag and fired a gun salute on special occasions. On the banks of the River Nidd there is also **St Robert's Cave** which is an ancient hermitage. St Robert was the son of a mayor of York who, at the time of his death in 1218, was so beloved that the people of Knaresborough would not allow the monks of Fountains Abbey to bury him. Instead they kept his bones and finally interred him in a place near the altar in the **Chapel of Our Lady of the Crag**. It is guarded by the statue of a larger than life-size figure of a knight in the act of drawing his sword.

Another of Knaresborough's attractive amenities is **Conyngham Hall,** a majestic old house enclosed within a loop of the River Nidd. Once the home of Lord Macintosh, the Halifax toffee magnate, the Hall itself is not open to the public but its landscaped grounds, stretching down to the river, are and provide tennis, putting and other activities.

A mile or so to the south of Knaresborough, **Plumpton Rocks** provide an ideal picnic spot. There's an idyllic lake surrounded by dramatic millstone grit rocks and woodland paths that were laid out in the 18th century. It has been declared a garden of special historic interest by English Heritage and is open every weekend, on public holidays, and daily from March to October.

In the tradition of this town's reputation for exceptional and odd characters is 'Blind Jack of Knaresborough'. Jack Metcalfe was born in 1717 and lost his sight at the age of six, but went on to achieve fame as a roadmaker. He was a remarkable person who never allowed his blindness to bar him from any normal activities – he rode, climbed trees, swam, and was often employed to guide travellers through the wild Forest of Knaresborough. He was a talented fiddle player and one of his more roguish exploits was his elopement with Dolly Benson, the daughter of the innkeeper of the Royal Oak in Harrogate, on the night before she was due to marry another man. His most memorable achievement however, was the laying of roads over the surrounding bogs and marshes which he achieved by laying a foundation of bundles of heather, a technique that had never been used before.

45 MADISON CENTRAL

Ripon

A magnet for lovers of home cooking and renowned for its range of 25 different varieties of muffins.

🍴 see page 239

46 STATION HOTEL

Ripon

Warm and friendly hostelry close to city centre and offering honest-to-goodness food, real ale and comfortable en suite rooms.

🍴 🛏 see page 240

47 THE SUN INN

Norwood

Fine old former coaching inn serving tasty home-made food and up to 10 real ales; spacious beer garden with lovely views.

🍴 see page 239

GOLDSBOROUGH

5 miles E of Harrogate off the A59

This rather special village was an estate village from the time of the Norman Conquest until the 1950s when it was sold by the Earl of Harewood to pay enormous death duties. The charming 12th-century **Church of St Mary** has some interesting features including a Norman doorhead and an effigy of a knight. It is also a 'green man church' and the image of the Celtic god of fertility, with his oak-leafed head, is well hidden on one of the many Goldsborough family tombs. In 1859, while the church was being restored, a lead casket was discovered containing Viking jewellery and coins. In the 1920s, Mary, the daughter of George V and Queen Mary, lived in the village after her marriage and her eldest son, George, was christened in the church.

SPOFFORTH

4½ miles SE of Harrogate on the A661

This ancient village, situated on the tiny River Crimple, is home to the splendid Palladian mansion, **Stockeld Park**, built between 1758 and 1763 by Paine. Containing some excellent furniture and a fine picture collection, the house is surrounded by extensive parkland which offers garden walks. Though privately owned, the house is open by appointment.

Spofforth Castle (English Heritage) is another place of note, an historic building whose sight stirs the imagination, despite its ruined state. The powerful Percy family originally built the castle here in the 16th century to replace the manor house which had been repeatedly laid to waste. The castle itself is now a crumbling ruin after it was destroyed during the Civil War. According to some accounts, the castle was the birthplace of Harry Hotspur.

BECKWITHSHAW

3 miles SW of Harrogate on the B6161

This village, as its name suggests, was once bounded by a stream and woodland though, sadly, most of the trees are now gone. It was once part of the great Forest of Knaresborough and a local legend tells how John O'Gaunt promised John Haverah, a cripple, as much land as he could hop around between sunrise and sunset. By throwing his crutch the last few yards, just as the sun was setting, John Haverah managed to secure himself seven square miles, the remainder of which is today called Haverah Park.

RIPON

This attractive cathedral city, set beside the Rivers Ure, Skell, and Laver, dates from the 7th century when Alfrich, King of Northumbria granted an area of land here, surrounding a new monastery, to the Church. Later that century, in AD672, St Wilfrid built a church on the high ground between the three rivers but, at the time of the demise of the Northern Kingdom in the mid-10th century, the monastery and church were destroyed, though the Saxon crypt survives to this day. By the time of the Norman Conquest, Ripon was a prosperous agricultural settlement under ecclesiastical rule and it was at this time that a second St Wilfrid's Church was erected on the site of the Saxon building. On Christmas Day 1132, monks from York worshipped here while they were making a journey to found Fountains Abbey and, traditionally, the people of Ripon follow this ancient route on Boxing Day.

A striking survival of the Saxon cathedral is the 1300-year-old Crypt. At its northeast corner is a narrow passage known as The Needle. According to the 17th-century antiquary Thomas Fuller, women whose chastity was suspect were made to pass through it. If they were unable to do so, their reputations were irretrievably tarnished. 'They pricked their credit', Fuller wrote 'who could not thread the Needle'.

The Crypt is all that remains of St Wilfrid's church but the magnificent **Cathedral of St Peter and St Wilfrid**, which now stands on the site, is certainly well worth visiting. Begun in the mid-12th century by Archbishop Roger of York, it was originally designed as a simple cruciform church; the west front was added in the mid-13th century and the east choir in 1286. Rebuilding work was begun in the 16th century but the disruption of the Dissolution of the Monasteries caused the work to be abandoned and it was only the intervention of

James I in the early 1600s that saved the building from ruin. Then established as a collegiate church, the diocese of Ripon was formed in 1836 and the church made a cathedral. Often referred to as the Cathedral of the Dales, the building, though one of the tallest cathedrals in England, is also the smallest. Discovered in 1976 close to the cathedral, the Ripon Jewel is the only surviving trace of the magnificence that was characteristic of the cathedral's early history. A

Ripon Cathedral

55

small gold roundel inlaid with gemstones, the jewel's design suggests that it was made to embellish a relic casket or cross ordered by St Wilfrid.

Throughout the Middle Ages, the city prospered: its market charter had been granted by King Alfred in the 9th century and, at one time, Ripon produced more woollen cloth than Halifax and Leeds. The collapse of the woollen industry saw a rise in spur manufacture in the 16th century and their fame was such that Ripon spurs were referred to in the old proverb: 'As true steel as a Ripon rowel.' As well as having three rivers, Ripon also had a canal. It was built between 1767 and 1773 to improve the navigation of the River Ure: John Smeaton, builder of the Eddystone Lighthouse, was the designer. However, by 1820 the company running the canal had fallen into debt and it was little used after that time.

Fortunately, for today's visitor, the Industrial Revolution, and all its associated implications, by-passed Ripon and it was not until the early 20th century that the town flourished, though briefly, as a spa. However, many ancient customs and festivals have

Wakeman's House, Ripon

survived down the centuries. Perhaps the most famous is the sounding of the 'Wakeman's Horn' each night at 9 p.m. in the marketplace. Dating back to the 9th century, the Wakeman was originally appointed to patrol the town after the nightly curfew had been blown and, in many ways, this was the first form of security patrol. The Wakeman was selected each year from the town's 12 aldermen and those choosing not to take office were fined heavily. Today, this old custom is revived in the Mayor-making Ceremony when the elected mayor shows great reluctance to take office and hides from his colleagues.

As might be expected, any walk around this ancient town reveals, in its buildings, its interesting and varied past. The heart of the town is the Market Place and here stands a tall obelisk which was erected in 1702 to replace the market cross. Restored in 1781, at its summit are a horn and a rowel spur, symbolizing Ripon's crafts and customs. Situated at the edge of the square are the picturesque, half-timbered 14th-century **Wakeman's House** and the attractive Georgian **Town Hall**.

The Spa Baths building, opened in 1905 by the Princess of Battenberg, is a reminder of Ripon's attempt to become a fashionable spa resort. With no spring of its own, the town had to pipe in sulphur mineral water from Aldfield near Fountains Abbey. However, the scheme failed, though the building, which now houses the city's swimming pool, is a fine example of art nouveau architecture. The **Ripon Spa Gardens** with its 18-hole putting course, flat green bowling, nine hole crazy golf, tennis courts, bandstand and café, is still a pleasant place for a stroll.

Near to the cathedral is Ripon's old **Courthouse** that was built in 1830 on the site of an earlier (17th-century) Common Hall, used for the Quarter Sessions and the Court Military. Adjacent to this fine Georgian courthouse is a Tudor building that was part of the Archbishop of York's summer palace.

Also not far from the cathedral is the House of Correction, built in 1686 which served as the local prison between 1816 and 1878 and then became the police station until the late 1950s. This austere building is now home to the **Prison and Police Museum**, established in 1984, which depicts the history of the police force as well as giving visitors a real insight into the life of a prisoner in Victorian times. Almost as unfortunate as those prisoners were the inmates of **Ripon Workhouse**, the city's newest museum. The restored vagrants' wards of 1877 provide a chilling insight into the treatment of paupers in Yorkshire workhouses and the displays include a 'Victorian Hard Times Gallery'.

Horse racing at Ripon dates back to 1713 and the present course opened in 1900. Meetings are held between April and August

and the course is widely regarded as one of the most beautiful in the country.

AROUND RIPON

SKELTON

3 miles SE of Ripon off the B6265

This charming little village has some surviving cottages, dating from 1540, which are built from small handmade bricks with pantiled roofs. A ferry used to cross the River Ure, at this point, to Bishop Monkton and, in 1869, it was the scene of a notorious hunting accident. Members of the York and Ainsty Hunt boarded the ferry in order to follow a fox that had swum across the river. Half way across the horses panicked, capsizing the boat, and the boatman, along with five hunt members, were drowned. Also here is **Newby Hall** (see panel), one of the area's finest stately homes. It was built in the 18th century and designed by Robert Adam. Much of the house is open to the public including the splendid Billiard Room with its fine portrait of Frederick Grantham Vyner; an ancestor of the family that has lived here since the mid-1800s, Frederick was murdered by Greek bandits after having been kidnapped. The house is perhaps most famous for its superb tapestries and there is also a fine collection of Chippendale furniture.

Another major attraction here is the 25 acres of award-winning gardens. It was the present owner's father who transformed a 9-hole

48 NEWBY HALL & GARDENS

Near Ripon

Newby Hall and Gardens, near Ripon in North Yorkshire, is one of England's renowned Adam Houses, and home to spectacular treasures and antiques as well as 25 acres of stunning landscaped gardens.

🏛 see page 243

49 THE CROWN INN

Roecliffe

Lovely old 16th century coaching inn serving superb food and real ales; also well-appointed en suite rooms.

see page 241

50 THE BLACK BULL INN

Boroughbridge

Former coaching inn noted for its excellent food, real ales and quality accommodation.

see page 242

51 THE GOLDEN LION

Helperby

Traditional village hostelry serving appetising home-cooked food and real ales; regular live entertainment.

see page 243

52 THE GRANTHAM ARMS HOTEL

Milby

Fine old hostelry noted for its fine ales and excellent food; well-appointed en suite rooms available.

see page 244

golf course into these delightful grounds which also contain a Woodland Discovery Walk, a miniature railway, plenty of attractions for children, a plant stall, shop and restaurant.

BOROUGHBRIDGE

2 miles SE of Ripon on the B6265

This attractive and historic town dates from the reign of William the Conqueror though it was once on a main thoroughfare used by both the Celts of Brigantia and, later, the Romans. The bridge over the River Ure, from which the village takes its name, was built in 1562 and it formed part of an important road link between Edinburgh and London. Busy throughout the coaching days with traffic passing from the West Riding of Yorkshire to the North, Boroughbridge has now returned to its former unassuming role of a small wayside town now bypassed by the A1(M) which takes most of the 21st century traffic from its streets.

The great **Devil's Arrows**, three massive Bronze Age monoliths, stand like guardians close to the new road and form Yorkshire's most famous ancient monument. Thought to date from around 2000 BC, the tallest is 30 feet high. The monoliths stand in a line running north-south and are fashioned from millstone grit which has been seriously fluted by weathering. A local legend, however, attributes the great stones to the Devil suggesting that they were, actually, crossbow bolts that he fired at nearby Aldborough which, at the time, was a Christian settlement.

ALDBOROUGH

3 mile SE of Ripon off the A59

The ancient Roman town of Isurium Brigantum, or Aldborough, as it is known today, was once the home of the 9th Legion, who wrested it from the Celtic Brigantian tribe. The modern-day focal point of the village is the tall

Devil's Arrows, Boroughbridge

maypole on the village green, around which traditional dances take place each May. At one end of the green is a raised platform which is all that remains of the Old Court House and it bears an inscription recalling that up to 150 years ago the election of members of Parliament was announced here. Below are some well-preserved stocks that are, in fact, only replicas of the originals. The **Aldborough Roman Museum** houses relics of the town's past. This was once a thriving Roman city of vital strategic importance and near the museum are some of the original walls and tessellated pavements of that city.

STUDLEY ROGER

2 miles SW of Ripon off the B6265

The magnificent **Studley Royal Gardens** were created in the early 18th century before they were merged with nearby Fountains Abbey in 1768. Started by John Aislabie, Chancellor of the Exchequer and founder of the South Sea Company that spectacularly went bust in 1720, the landscaping took some 14 years. It then took a further 10 years to complete the construction of the buildings and follies found within the gardens. With a network of paths and the River Skell flowing through the grounds, it is well worth exploring these superb gardens.

A National Trust property, like the adjoining gardens, **Fountains Abbey** is the pride of all the ecclesiastical ruins in Yorkshire and

Fountains Abbey, Studley Roger

the only World Heritage Site in Yorkshire. The Abbey was one of the wealthiest of the Cistercian houses and its remains are the most complete of any Cistercian abbey in Britain. Founded in 1132, with the help of Archbishop Thurstan of York, the first buildings housed just 12 monks of the order. The Abbey reached its peak in the 15th century with the grandiose designs of Abbot Marmaduke Huby, whose beautiful tower still stands as a reminder of just how rich and powerful Fountains became. In fact, the abbey was run on such businesslike lines that, at its height,

53 MASONS ARMS

Bishop Monkton

Fine old inn in picturesque village serving wholesome and appetising fare and real ales.

see page 244

as well as owning extensive lands throughout Yorkshire, it had an income of about £1000 a year, then a very substantial sum indeed.

The Dissolution hit the abbey as it did all the powerful religious houses. The abbot was hanged, the monks scattered, and its treasures taken off or destroyed. The stonework, however, was left largely intact, possibly due to its remote location. In 1579, Sir Stephen Proctor pulled down some outbuildings, in order to construct **Fountains Hall**, a magnificent Elizabethan mansion which still stands in the Abbey's grounds and part of which is open to the public.

WATH

4 miles N of Ripon off the A1

The stately home of **Norton Conyers**, just to the south of Wath, has been owned by the Graham family since 1624 though, undoubtedly, the house's main claim to fame is the visit made by Charlotte Brontë. During her stay here the novelist heard the story of Mad Mary, supposedly a Lady Graham. Apparently Lady Graham had been locked up in an attic room, now tantalisingly inaccessible to the public, and Charlotte eventually based the character of Mrs Rochester in her novel Jane Eyre on this unfortunate woman. Visitors to the hall will also see the famous painting of Sir Bellingham Graham on his bay horse, as Master of the Quorn hunt. It is rumoured that ownership of the painting was once decided on the throwing of a pair of dice. Other family pictures, furniture and costumes are on display and there's a lovely 18th-century walled garden within the grounds.

NORTH STAINLEY

4½ miles NW of Ripon on the A6108

Just over 100 years ago, in 1895, excavations in a field just outside the village revealed the site of a Roman villa called Castle Dykes though all that can be seen now are the grassed outlines of the foundations and the moat. However, the discovery does prove that there has been a settlement here for many centuries. The monks of Fountains Abbey also

Norton Conyers Hall, Wath

knew North Stainley. Slenningford Grange is thought to have been one of their many properties and a fishpond, dating from medieval times, is still in existence.

Just to the south of the village lies the **Lightwater Valley Theme Park** set in 175 acres of scenic grounds. The Park boasts 'Ultimate' – the biggest roller-coaster in the world (authenticated by the Guinness Book of Records), the Rat Ride, Falls of Terror, and the Viper to name just a few and there are also plenty of more appropriate activities for younger children. Also within the grounds is Lightwater Village which offers a wide variety of retail and factory shops, a garden centre, restaurant and coffee shop.

KIRKBY MALZEARD
6 miles NW of Ripon off the A6108

Dating back to the 11th century, the **Church of St Andrew** is noted for its associations with witchcraft. Apparently, the north-eastern corner of the churchyard was favoured by practitioners of the black arts for conducting their strange rituals and charms. Black magic aside, the church has been pealing its bells for more than 400 years and records show that in 1591 one of the bells was recast – the process taking place inside the church building.

This traditional Yorkshire village is also one of the few places in the country that can boast its own Sword Dance. Certainly a pagan ritual, thought to date back to prehistoric times, the

performance of the dance is supposed to make the grass grow tall and to wake the earth from her winter's sleep.

Many of the farms around the village are dairy farms and at Kirby Malzeard Dairy they still produce the traditionally made Coverdale cheese. Very much a local speciality, it is one of the few remaining Dales' cheeses still made though, at one time, each dale had its own particular variety.

WEST TANFIELD
6 miles NW of Ripon on the A6108

This attractive village on the banks of the River Ure is home to a remarkable Tudor gatehouse known as the **Marmion Tower**. Overlooking the river and with a beautiful oriel window, the tower is open to the public. For many years, West Tanfield was associated with the powerful Marmion family and the 14th-century Church of St Nicholas contains many effigies belonging to the family.

Though the purpose of the **Thornborough Circles**, which lie just outside the village, remains a mystery, these late Neolithic or early Bronze Age oval earthworks are very impressive, especially from the air.

54 STAVELEY ARMS

North Stainley
Fine old village inn with a glowing reputation for its fine food, real ales, excellent Carvery and friendly service.

🍴 🛏 see page 245

55 THE BULL INN

West Tanfield
Charming former coaching inn set beside the River Ure offering excellent cuisine, real ales and en suite rooms.

🍴 🛏 see page 246

Marmion Tower, West Tanfield

61

North of the village of Grewelthorpe are the beautiful Hackfall Woods through which the River Ure flows. During the 19th century the Victorians developed the woodland, creating waterfalls and transforming the 18th-century follies that had been built here into splendid vantage points. Following a period of neglect which began with the sale of the woodland in the 1930s, the Hackfall Woods are now in the care of the Woodland Trust and the area is being gradually restored to its 19th-century condition.

GREWELTHORPE

6½ miles NW of Ripon off the A6108

It was long thought that the Romans had a camp to the north of this leafy village and the discovery in the early 1900s of the complete skeleton of a Roman soldier confirmed the story. The remains were reburied in the churchyard at Kirkby Malzeard but the soldier's sandals are on view in the York Museum.

WELL

8 miles NW of Ripon off the B6267

This pretty village takes its name from St Michael's Well which was already being venerated long before the Romans came here and one of them built a spacious villa near the well. Part of the tessellated pavement of that villa is now on display in the parish church, which is itself a venerable building with foundations that date back to Norman times. The church's greatest treasure is a font cover dating from 1325, one of the oldest in the country. It was a gift to the church from Ralph Neville, Lord of Middleham, who also founded the line of almshouses near the church which were rebuilt by his descendants in 1758.

MASHAM

9 miles NW of Ripon on the A6108

Set beside the River Ure, Masham (pronounced Massam) is a very picturesque place with a huge marketplace at its heart. The ancient Church of St Mary stands in one corner, a school founded in 1760 in another, while at the centre is the market cross surrounded by trees and flowers. The size of the marketplace reflects Masham's historical importance as a market town and its position, between the sheep-covered hills and the corn growing lowlands, certainly helped to support its flourishing trade. The sheep fairs held in the town in the 18th and 19th centuries were among the largest in the country and in September the **Masham Sheep Fair** revives those heady days, giving visitors the chance of seeing many rare breeds of sheep and goats as well as witnessing events such as dog agility and sheep racing.

The town is famed for its beer, boasting two celebrated breweries – Theakston's and Black Sheep. **Theakston's Brewery**, noted for its Old Peculier brew, was founded in 1827 by two brothers, Thomas and Robert. Adjoining the brewery today is a modern visitor centre which illustrates the process of brewing and the art of cooperage. Those taking the tour (which must be pre-booked) should be aware that there are two flights of steep steps along the route and the tour is not suitable for children under 10. Interestingly, the name of the

Theakston's Brewery, Masham

famous brew derives from the fact that Masham in medieval times had its own Peculiar Court (meaning special rather than odd) – an ecclesiastical body with wide-ranging powers.

The **Black Sheep Brewery** (see panel) is also well worth a visit. It is owned by another Theakston, Paul, who is the 5th generation of this famous brewing family. The vessels, plants and methods employed here are from a bygone age and currently produce seven different ales, including a Monty Python Holy Grail ale which was specially commissioned to celebrate the 30th anniversary of the cult comedy series. The brewery also offers a guided tour and visitors get the chance to sample the traditionally made ales. In addition to the working brewery, the old Maltings building is home to a 'sheepy' shop and a popular bistro.

ILTON

9½ miles NW of Ripon off the A6108

This village is close to one of the area's most interesting and unusual features – the **Druid's Temple**. Though the name suggests that this was an ancient meeting place for pagan worshippers, the charming folly was built in the 1820s by William Danby of the nearby Swinton Estate. Resembling a miniature Stonehenge, the folly was inspired by a similar temple Danby saw on his travels in Europe and his building project was intended to provide work for local unemployed people. It is considered one of the best Druidic follies in the country.

From Ilton village it can be reached by following part of the long-distance footpath known as the Ripon Rowel Walk.

SNAPE

9½ miles NW of Ripon off the B6268

This quiet and unspoilt village, where the original timber-framed cottages stand side by side with their more modern neighbours, is still dominated by its castle as it has been for centuries. Reached via an avenue of lime trees, **Snape Castle** has a famous, if somewhat complicated, royal connection as it was the home of Lord Latimer of Snape (a member of the Neville family), the first husband of Catherine Parr, Henry VIII's last wife. The Nevilles owned the castle for more than 700 years and its beautiful chapel, still used by the villagers, saw the marriages of many Latimers and Nevilles.

Set in over 1000 acres of parkland, **Thorp Perrow Arboretum** is unique to Britain, if not Europe, in that it was the

56 BLACK SHEEP BREWERY BISTRO AND VISITORS CENTRE

Masham

Established in the early nineties by Paul Theakston, 6th generation of Masham's famous brewing family, the brewery has grown from strength to strength.

🏛 see page 247

Snape Castle

Thorp Perrow Arboretum

| 57 | THORP PERROW ARBORETUM, WOODLAND GARDEN AND FALCONRY CENTRE |

Thorpe Perrow

Thorp Perrow Arboretum is one of the finest private collections of trees and shrubs in the country.

🏛 *see page 247*

creation of one man, Colonel Sir Leonard Ropner (1895-1977). Sir Leonard travelled all over the world collecting rare and unusual species for Thorp Perrow and today the hundreds of trees he enthusiastically collected are in their prime. The arboretum was initially Sir Leonard's private hobby but after his death his son, Sir John Ropner, decided to open the 85-acre garden to the public and the arboretum is now one of the area's prime attractions. A treasure trove of specimen trees, woodland walks, nature trail, tree trails, a large lake, picnic area and children's play area, the arboretum also embraces the Milbank Pinetum, planted by Lady Augusta Milbank in the mid-19th century, and the medieval Spring Wood dating back to the 16th century. Thorp Perrow provides interest all year round but perhaps the most popular time is the spring when you can witness one of the finest and most extensive plantings of daffodils in the north of England, among them some old

and unusual varieties. In addition to the fascinating collection of trees, visitors will also find an information centre, a tea room and a plant sales area. An additional attraction at Thorp Perrow is **The Falcons of Thorp Perrow** (see panel), a bird-of-prey, captive-breeding and conservation centre which has been created within a large, formerly derelict walled garden. There are more than 75 birds from all continents of the world and regular flying demonstrations three times a day, weather permitting.

THIRSK

Thirsk has become famous as the home of veterinary surgeon Alf Wight, better known as James Herriot, author of *All Creatures Great and Small*, who died in 1995. In his immensely popular books, Thirsk is clearly recognisable as 'Darrowby'. A £1.4m tribute to the celebrated vet **The World of James Herriot** (see panel), is housed in the original surgery in Kirkgate and offers visitors a trip back in time to the 1940s, exploring the life and times of the world's most famous country vet. There's also the opportunity to take part in a TV production, and a Visible Farm exhibit where you can explore farm animals inside and out!

Just across the road from the surgery is the birthplace of another famous son of Thirsk. The building is now the town's museum and a plaque outside records that Thomas Lord was born here in 1755: 30 years later he was to create the famous cricket ground in Marylebone that took his name. A more recent celebrity whose home was in Thirsk was Bill Foggitt (died Sep 2004, aged 91), renowned for his weather forecasts based on precise observations of nature.

This pleasant small town of mellow brick houses has a sprawling Market Place and the magnificent 15th-century **St Mary's Church** which is generally regarded as the finest parish church in North Yorkshire. It was here that the real life 'James Herriot' married his wife, Helen. Cod Beck, a tributary of the River Swale, wanders through the town, providing some delightful – and well-signposted riverside walks.

Thirsk appeared in the Domesday Book not long after William the Conqueror had granted the Manor of Thirsk to one of his barons, Robert de Mowbray. The Mowbrays became a powerful family in the area, a fact reflected in the naming of the area to the north and west of Thirsk as the Vale of Mowbray. In the early 1100s the family received permission to hold a market at Thirsk but then blotted their copybook by rebelling against Henry II in 1173. The rebellion failed and their castle at Thirsk was burnt to the ground. Not a trace of it remains. The market however is still thriving, held twice-weekly on Mondays and Saturdays. An old market by-law used to stipulate that no butcher be allowed to kill a bull for sale in the market until the beast had been baited by the town dogs. That by-law was abandoned in the early 1800s and the bull-ring

to which the animal was tethered has also disappeared.

On the edge of Thirsk, housed in a mid-Victorian maltings, **Treske** specialises in producing bespoke furniture and designer upholstery fabrics. Among Treske's most notable commissions are some 400 chairs for the OBE chapel in St Paul's Cathedral, bedroom furniture for the College of St George's, Windsor Castle, and period replica furniture for the monks' cells at Mount Grace Priory. The showrooms are open daily and group tours of the workshop are available by arrangement.

On the outskirts of the town is **Thirsk Racecourse,** known to devotees of the turf as the 'Country Racecourse'. There are around 12 race meetings each year.

AROUND THIRSK

BOLTBY

5 miles NE of Thirsk, off the A170

Boltby is an engaging village tucked away at the foot of the Hambleton Hills, close to where the oddly-named Gurt of Beck tumbles down the hillside and, depending on how much rain has fallen on the moors, passes either under or over a little humpback bridge. On the plain below is Nevison House, reputed to be the home of the 17th-century highwayman, William Nevison, 'Swift Nick' as Charles II dubbed him. Some historians claim that it was Swift Nick, not Dick Turpin, who made the legendary ride on Black Bess from London to York to establish an alibi.

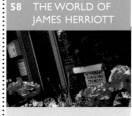

58 THE WORLD OF JAMES HERRIOTT

Thirsk

The original and cosy home of James Herriot providing a fascinating insight into his life.

see page 248

Sutton Bank used to be a graveyard for caravans because of its steep (1 in 3) climb and sharp bends. On one July Saturday in 1977, some 30 vehicles broke down on the ascent and five breakdown vehicles spent all day retrieving them. Caravans are now banned from this route. Sutton Bank may be tough on cars but its sheer-sided cliffs create powerful thermals making this a favoured spot for gliders and bright-winged hang-gliders.

59 THE WOODMAN INN

Burneston

Traditional country inn serving excellent home-made food and real ales; en suite rooms also available.

see page 248

SUTTON-UNDER-WHITESTONECLIFF

3 miles E of Thirsk on the A170

Boasting the longest place-name in England, Sutton is more famous for the precipitous cliff that towers above it, **Sutton Bank**. For one of the grandest landscape views in England, go to the top of Sutton Bank and look across the vast expanse of the Vale of York to the Pennine hills far away to the west. The real-life James Herriot called it the 'finest view in England'. He knew this area well since his large veterinary practice covered the farms from here right over to the Dales. A continuation of the Cleveland Hills, the Hambleton Hills themselves lead into the Howardian Hills: together they form the mighty southwest flank of the North York Moors.

There's a National Park Information Centre at the summit of Sutton Bank and a well-marked Nature Trail leads steeply down to, and around, **Lake Gormire,** an Ice Age lake trapped here by a landslip. Gormire is one of Yorkshire's only two natural lakes, the other being Semerwater in Wensleydale. Gormire is set in a large basin with no river running from it: any overflow disappears down a 'swallow hole' and emerges beneath White Mare Cliffs.

SOWERBY

1 mile S of Thirsk on the B1448

Georgian houses stand beneath a majestic avenue of lime trees, an old packhorse bridge crosses Cod Beck, footpaths lead across fields and the quiet stream provides a peaceful refuge. All-in-all an attractive village.

KIRBY WISKE

4 miles NW of Thirsk off the A167

Sion Hill Hall, about four miles northwest of Thirsk, is celebrated as the 'last of the great country houses'. Its light, airy and well-proportioned rooms, all facing south, are typical of the work of the celebrated Yorkshire architect, Walter Brierley – the 'Lutyens of the North'. He completed the building in 1913 for Percy Stancliffe and his wife Ethel, the wealthy daughter of a whisky distiller. The rooms haven't altered one bit since they were built, but the furniture and furnishings certainly have. In 1962, the Hall was bought by Herbert Mawer, a compulsive but highly discerning collector of antiques. During the 20 years he lived at Sion Hill, Herbert continued to add to what was already probably the best collection of Georgian, Victorian and Edwardian artefacts in the north of England. Furniture, paintings, porcelain, clocks (all working), and ephemera, crowd the 20 richly furnished rooms and make Sion Hill a delight to visit. A recent addition to the many sumptuous displays is a charming exhibition of dolls from the early 1900s.

In the Hall's Victorian Walled Garden is another major visitor attraction – **Falconry UK's Bird of Prey and Conservation Centre.** More than 80 birds from

34 different species have their home here: owls, hawks, falcons, buzzards, vultures and eagles from all around the world. At regular intervals throughout the day these fierce-eyed, sharp-beaked predators behave in a remarkably docile and co-operative way as they take part in fascinating flying demonstrations.

NORTHALLERTON

The county town of North Yorkshire, Northallerton has the broad High Street, almost half a mile long, typical of the county's market towns. (Wednesday and Saturday are the market days here.) In stage coach days the town was an important stop on the route from Newcastle to London and several old coaching inns still stand along the High Street. The most ancient is The Old Fleece, a favoured drinking haunt of Charles Dickens during his several visits to the town. It's a truly Dickensian place with great oak beams and a charming olde-worlde atmosphere. The Old Fleece recalls the great days of the stage coach which came to an abrupt end with the arrival of the railway. One day in 1847, a coach called the Wellington made the whole of the 290-mile journey from Newcastle to London, via Northallerton, completely empty. The era of this romantic – if uncomfortable and extremely expensive – mode of transport was over.

Northallerton has many old buildings of interest, including an ancient Grammar School whose history goes back to at least 1322. The school was rebuilt in 1776 at the northern end of the High Street – a building that is now a solicitors' office. By the end of the 19th century the school had 'no great reputation' and by 1902 only 13 pupils were registered. Things went from bad to worse the next year when the headmaster was convicted of being drunk and disorderly. Fortunately, the school, now **Northallerton College** and in new buildings, has recovered its reputation for academic excellence.

The town also boasts a grand medieval church, a 15th-century almshouse and, of more recent provenance, a majestic County Hall built in 1906 and designed by the famous Yorkshire architect Walter Brierley. The oldest private house in Northallerton is Porch House which bears a carved inscription with the date 1584. According to tradition, Charles I came here as a guest in 1640 and returned seven years later as a prisoner.

Two miles north of the town of Northallerton, a stone obelisk beside the A167 commemorates the **Battle of the Standard,** fought here in 1138. It was one of the countless conflicts fought between the English and the Scots, and also one of the bloodiest with more than 12,000 of the Scots, led by King David, perishing under a rain of English arrows. The battle took its name from the unusual standard raised by the English: the mast of a ship mounted on a wagon and, crowning its top, a pyx containing the consecrated Host.

Mount Grace Priory, Osmotherley

**60 MOUNT GRACE
PRIORY**

Saddlebridge

In this unusual monastery,
the best-preserved priory of
the Carthusian order in
Britain, you can see how
hermit-monks lived 600
years ago.

🏛 see page 249

AROUND NORTHALLERTON

OSMOTHERLEY

5 miles NE of Northallerton off the A19

Long-distance walkers will be
familiar with this attractive
moorland village since it is the
western starting point for the
Lyke Wake Walk which winds for
more than 40 miles over the
moors to Ravenscar on the coast.
At the centre of the village is a
heavily carved cross and, next to
it, a low stone table which was
probably once a market stall and
also served John Wesley as a
pulpit.

About a mile northeast of the
village, **Mount Grace Priory**
(English Heritage & National
Trust) is quite unique among
Yorkshire's ecclesiastical treasures.
The 14th-century building set in

tranquil surroundings was
bought in 1904 by Sir
Lothian Bell who decided
to rebuild one of the well-
preserved cells, a violation
of the building's 'integrity'
that would provoke howls
of outrage from purists if
it were proposed today.
When English Heritage
inherited the Carthusian
Priory, however, it decided
to go still further by
reconstructing other
outbuildings and filling
them with replica furniture
and artefacts to create a
vivid impression of what
life was like in a 14th-
century monastic house. The
Carthusians were an upper-class
order whose members dedicated
themselves to solitude – even their
meals were served through an
angled hatch so they would not see
the servant who brought them.
Most visitors find themselves
fascinated by Mount Grace's
sanitary arrangements which were
ingeniously designed to take full
advantage of a nearby spring and
the sloping site on which the
Priory is built. Along with
discovering what life was like for a
monk in this almost hermit-like
order, visitors can also wander
around the remains of the Great
Cloister and outer court, and see
the new monks' herb garden
designed specifically to aid
contemplation and spiritual
renewal. Mount Grace Priory is
open all year though times are
limited in the winter months.

61 THE THREE COOPERS

Bedale

Lovely 17th century village pub with wholesome home-made food, real ales and luxury accommodation.

see page 250

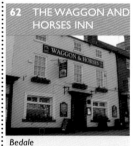

62 THE WAGGON AND HORSES INN

Bedale

Welcoming 17th century coaching inn serving superb home-cooked food; en suite rooms and charming beer garden.

see page 251

North York Moors, nr Osmotherley

BEDALE

7½ miles SW of Northallerton on the A684

This pleasant little market town with its many fine Georgian buildings and old coaching inns developed around the point where the Saxon track from Ripon joined the route from Northallerton to Wensleydale. Traders met here and in 1251 Henry III granted a charter for a weekly market every Tuesday which still flourishes today. The market cross still stands at the top of Emgate, a narrow street leading from the river to the marketplace. As commercial activity increased, water power was harnessed from the Bedale Beck for the processing of wool. Skinners and tanners worked down by the ford and the town was a lively hub of cottage industry.

The curving main street leads to the beautiful parish **Church of St Gregory** at the northern end. Recorded in the *Domesday Book* and incorporating architectural styles from the 12th to the 14th centuries, the building has a fine fortified tower and a striking medieval wall-painting of a left-handed St George. Just inside the churchyard is an old building dating from the mid-1600s which served as a school in the 18th century.

Across the road from the church is **Bedale Hall**, a Palladian-style mansion with a superb ballroom. The Hall houses the

63 THE GREEN DRAGON

Bedale

Elegant and charming this town centre inn has 6 en-suite rooms and a newly opened restaurant, serving quality food.

see page 251

64 THE GREEN DRAGON

Exelby

Early 18th century inn boasting an excellent restaurant, comfortable, well appointed accommodation and spacious beer garden

🍴 🛏 see page 252

65 THE WHITE SWAN

Danby Wiske

Friendly, family-run inn overlooking the village green and serving wholesome, home-made food and real ales.

🍴 🛏 see page 253

town library and local museum. The north front of the building is a particularly fine example of the Georgian architecture which gives Bedale its special character. Another building of interest is the 18th-century Leech House beside the beck, so called because it was once used by the local chemist to store his leeches.

CRAKEHALL

8½ miles SW of Northallerton on the A684

Crakehall has a huge village green with a small church, a 16th century pub and an enormous former country seat of the Duke of Leeds, Crakehall Hall, overlooking it. Part of the 5-acre green serves as the village's cricket pitch and is in regular use during the summer.

Sometime around AD 1090 the *Domesday Book* commissioners arrived in Crakehall and noted details of a mill on the beck that runs through this picturesque village. More than 900 years later there's still a mill on the very same spot. The present **Crakehall Water Mill** building dates from the 1600s; its mighty machinery from the 18th and 19th centuries. The Mill was still working until 2003 but at the time of writing it is not open to the public on a regular basis.

DANBY WISKE

4 miles NW of Northallerton off the A167 or B6271

This pleasant little village takes its name from the Danby family, once great landowners with huge properties across North Yorkshire, and the little River Wiske. It has a

moated former rectory and a village green overlooked by a traditional hostelry, The White Swan (see panel).

CATTERICK VILLAGE

9 miles NW of Northallerton off the A1

This is an ancient settlement with an attractive village green and a nearby race-course which, every Sunday, hosts the largest street market in England. Ever since the time of the Romans, when the settlement was known as Cataractonium, Catterick has been associated with the armed forces. Located on the Roman highway between London and Hadrian's Wall, the garrison was also close to the place where Paulinus, Bishop of York baptised 10,000 Christians in the River Swale. Today, the army garrison (the largest in Europe) is some three miles to the west. RAF Leeming lies just south of the village.

Catterick's connections with Lord Nelson are not immediately obvious but it was Alexander Scott, vicar of Catterick in 1816 who was at the admiral's side when he died at Trafalgar. Also, Nelson's sister-in-law, Lady Tyrconnell lived at nearby **Kiplin Hall,** a beautiful Jacobean country house famed for its wonderful interior plasterwork and medieval fishponds. The hall also contains many mementoes of Nelson and Lady Hamilton. On display in the Blue Room is a folding library chair from Nelson's cabin on HMS Victory. The hall also has a strong American connection since it was built by the 1st Lord Baltimore who was instrumental in founding the state of Maryland whose capital city bears his name.

MOULTON

11 miles NW of Northallerton off the A1

This small village is home to two fine 17th-century manor houses that were built by members of the Smithson family. The Manor House, in the village centre, was originally built in the late-16th century and was improved greatly in the mid-17th century. Just to the south stands **Moulton Hall**, built by George Smithson following his marriage to Eleanor Fairfax in 1654. Similar in size to the original Smithson family home and somewhat resembling it, Moulton Hall is now in the hands of the National Trust.

MIDDLETON TYAS

12 miles NW of Northallerton off the A1

Situated in a sheltered position yet close to the Great North Road, the position of the village church, away from the village centre and at the end of a long avenue of trees seems strange. However, when the Church of St Michael was built it served not only Middleton Tyas but also Moulton and Kneeton (the latter no longer in existence), between which Middleton lay. During the 18th century, the village saw a period of prosperity when

copper was found and mined from the fields near the church.

ALDBROUGH

14 miles NW of Northallerton off the B6275

To the west of the village lies the enormous complex of earthworks known as **Stanwick Camp**. The series of banks and ditches were excavated in the 1950s and their discovery also revealed that the constructions had been carried out in the 1st century. The site, open to the public, is now owned by English Heritage.

PIERCEBRIDGE

17 miles NW of Northallerton on the A67

This picturesque village in upper Teesdale was once an important Roman fort – part of a chain of forts linking the northern headquarters at York with Hadrian's Wall. (Another fort in the chain can be found to the south, at Catterick.) The Romans are thought to have originally chosen Piercebridge as a suitable river crossing back in AD 70 when Cerialis attacked the British camp at Stanwick. The extensive remains of the fort can be dated from coin evidence to around AD 270. The site is always open, though the finds from the excavations are housed in the Bowes Museum at Barnard Castle.

66 THE ANGEL HOTEL

Catterick Village

Popular hostelry close to Catterick Racecourse serving tasty home-made food and real ale; guest bedrooms also available.

see *page 254*

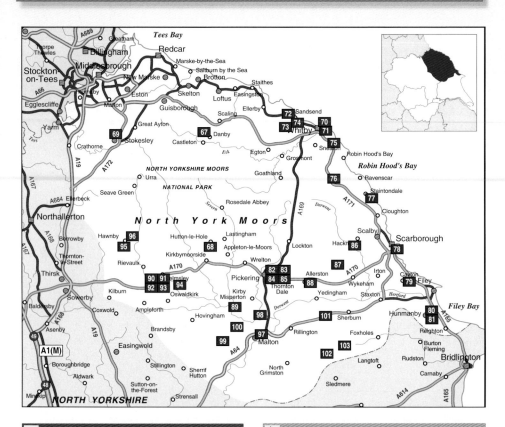

North York Moors, Heritage Coast & Vale of Pickering

Some 40 miles across and about 20 miles deep, the North York Moors National Park encompasses a remarkable diversity of scenery. There are great rolling swathes of moorland rising to 1,400 feet above sea level, stark and inhospitable in winter, still wild and romantic in summer, and softened only in early Autumn when they are mantled by a purple haze of flowering heather. Almost one-fifth of the area is woodland, most of it managed by Forest Enterprise which has established many picnic sites and forest drives. Settlements are few and far between: indeed, there may have been more people living here in the Bronze Age (1500-500 BC) than there are now to judge by the more than 3000 'howes', or burial mounds, that have been discovered.

Also scattered across these uplands is a remarkable collection of medieval stone crosses. There are more than 30 of them and one, the Lilla Cross, is reckoned to be the oldest Christian monument in northern England. Perhaps the finest example is **Ralph Cross**, high on Westerdale Moor. It stands nine feet tall at almost precisely the geographical centre of the moors and has been adopted by the North York Moors National Park as its emblem.

Wild as they look, the moors are actually cultivated land, or perhaps 'managed by fire' is the better term. Each year, gamekeepers burn off patches of the old heather in carefully limited areas called swiddens or swizzens. The new growth that soon appears is a crucial resource for the red grouse which live only in heather moorland, eat little else but heather and find these young green shoots particularly appetising.

Just as the Yorkshire Dales have large areas of moorland, so the North York Moors have many dales – Eskdale, Ryedale, Farndale, more than 100 of them in all. They cut deep into the great upland tracts and are as picturesque, soft and pastoral as anywhere in Yorkshire. To the west lies the mighty bulk of the Cleveland Hills;

Whitby Abbey

to the east the rugged cliffs of the Heritage Coast. This is marvellously unspoilt countryside, a happy state of affairs that has come about as a result of the Moors being designated a National Park in 1952, a status which severely restricts any development that would adversely affect either its natural or man-made beauty.

Between Saltburn and Filey runs some of the most striking coastal scenery in the country. Along this stretch of the Heritage Coast you'll find the highest cliffs in the country, a shoreline fretted with rocky coves, with miles of golden sandy beaches, a scattering of picture postcard fishing villages and, at its heart, the historic port of Whitby dramatically set around the mouth of the River Esk.

This glorious seaboard was designated as a Heritage Coast in 1979 in recognition of its beauty and its long history. From its small ports, fishermen have for centuries sailed out in their distinctive cobles to harvest the sea; from Whitby, sturdy whaling ships set off on their dangerous and now, thankfully, abandoned trade. It was at Whitby that one of England's greatest mariners, Captain Cook, learnt his seafaring skills and it was

from here that he departed in the tiny bark, *Endeavour*, a mere 370 tons, on his astonishing journeys of exploration.

Further down the coast are the popular resorts of Scarborough (where visitors were frolicking naked in the sea as early as 1735), and Filey, both of them offering long stretches of sandy beach and a huge variety of holiday entertainments.

Pickering Castle

ESKDALE

Eskdale is the largest, and one of the loveliest, of the dales within the National Park. It is unusual in that it runs east-west, the Esk being the only moorland river that doesn't find its way to the Humber. Instead, the river winds tortuously through the dale to join the sea beneath the picturesque cliffs at Whitby. Along the way, many smaller dales branch off to the north and south – Fryup, Danby, Glaisdale – while even narrower ones can only be explored on foot. The Esk is famed for its salmon fishing, but permits are required. These can be obtained from the local branches of the National Rivers Authority. Walkers will appreciate the Esk Valley Walk, a group of 10 linking walks which traverse the length of the valley.

DANBY
12 miles W of Whitby off the A174

A visit to **The Moors Centre** (free) at Danby Lodge provides an excellent introduction to the North York Moors National Park. Just half a mile outside the pretty village of Danby, the Centre is housed in a former shooting lodge and set in 13 acres of riverside, meadow, woodland, formal gardens and picnic areas. Visitors can either wander on their own along the waymarked woodland walks and nature trails or join one of the frequent guided walks. Inside the Lodge various exhibits interpret the natural and local history of the moors, there's a bookshop stocked with a wide range of books, maps and guides, and a tea room serving refreshments. A recent addition to the centre's amenities is "Inspired by…", a showcase for local arts and crafts. The centre is open all year round except for January.

Downstream from The Moors Centre is a superb 14th-century packhorse bridge, one of three to be found in Eskdale. This one is known as **Duck Bridge** but the name has nothing to do with aquatic birds. It was originally called Castle Bridge but re-named after an 18th-century benefactor, George Duck, a wealthy mason who paid for the bridge to be repaired. To the south of Duck Bridge are the remains of Danby Castle, now a private farmhouse and not open to the public. Built in the 14th century, and originally much larger, it was once the home of Catherine Parr, the sixth wife of Henry VIII. In Elizabethan times, the justices met here and the Danby Court Leet and Baron, which administers the common land and rights of way over the 11,000 acres of the Danby Estate, still meets here every year in the throne room. One of the court's responsibilities is issuing licences for the gathering of sphagnum moss, a material once used for stuffing mattresses but now more commonly required for flower arranging.

CASTLETON
14 miles W of Whitby off the A171

Spread across the hillside above the River Esk, Castleton is a charming village which at one time was the

67 THE MOORS TEA ROOM

Danby

Charming tea room set amidst the spectacular scenery of the North York Moors National Park.

🍴 *see page 255*

For most of the latter half of the 19th century Danby's vicar was Canon JC Atkinson, who married three times, fathered 13 children and authored one of the most fascinating books ever written about rural England in Victorian times. His **Forty Years in a Moorland Parish** *is still in print and well worth seeking out.*

On one of the stone houses in Lealholm, now a tea room and restaurant, a carved inscription reads, 'Loyal Order of Ancient Shepherds' together with the date 1873 in Roman numerals. The Loyal Order ran their lodge on the lines of a men-only London club but their annual procession through the village and the subsequent festivities were one of the highlights of the autumn.

In recent years, Lealholm has become very popular with naturalists who come to study the wealth of trees, ferns, flowers and rare plants in the deep, dramatic ravine known as Crunkley Gill. Sadly, the ravine is privately owned and not open to the public.

largest settlement in Eskdale. It still has a station on the scenic Esk Valley railway that runs between Whitby and Middlesbrough and a well-used cricket field in a lovely setting on the valley floor. The village's amber-coloured Church of St Michael and St George was built in memory of the men who fell during the First World War; inside there is some fine work by Robert Thompson, the famous 'Mouseman of Kilburn'. The benches, organ screen and panelling at each side of the altar all bear his distinctive 'signature' of a crouching mouse.

LEALHOLM
9 miles W of Whitby off the A171

From the Moors Centre at Danby a scenic minor road winds along the Esk Valley and brings you to the attractive village of Lealholm, its houses clustering around a 250-year-old bridge over the Esk. A short walk leads to some picturesque stepping stones across the river. The village was one of Canon Atkinson's favourite places – 'Elsewhere , you have to go in search of beautiful views,' he wrote, 'here, they come and offer themselves to be looked at.'

GLAISDALE
8 miles W of Whitby off the A171

From Lealholm a country lane leads to Glaisdale, another picturesque village set at the foot of a narrow dale beside the River Esk with Arncliffe Woods a short walk away. The ancient packhorse bridge here was built in 1619 by Thomas Ferris, Mayor of Hull. As an impoverished young man he had lived in Glaisdale where he fell in love with Agnes Richardson, the squire's daughter. To see Agnes, he had to wade or swim across the river and he swore that if he prospered in life he would build a bridge here. Fortunately, he joined a ship which sailed against the Spanish Armada and captured a galleon laden with gold. Tom returned to Glaisdale a rich man, married Agnes and later honoured his promise by building what has always been called the **Beggar's Bridge**.

EGTON BRIDGE
7 miles W of Whitby off the A171

This little village tucked around a bend in the River Esk plays host each year to the famous **Gooseberry Show.** Established in 1800, the show is held on the first Tuesday in August. It attracts entrants from all over the world who bring prize specimens in an attempt to beat the current record of 2.18oz for a single berry.

St Hedda's Roman Catholic Church is surprisingly large for such a small village. Inside, there are more surprises - a roof painted blue with golden stars and a flamboyant altar made in Munich in the 1860s. Outside, there's another unusual feature, the Mysteries of the Rosary set into the church walls in coloured pictures. It was at Egton Bridge that the martyr Nicholas Postgate was born in 1596. He was ordained a Roman Catholic priest in France but returned to the moors to minister to those still loyal to the outlawed faith. He travelled disguised as a jobbing gardener and eluded capture for many years. He was finally betrayed for a reward of £20. He was 81 years old when he was hung, drawn and quartered at York. A sad story to be associated with such a delightful village.

GROSMONT

6 miles SW of Whitby off the A169 or A171

Grosmont is the northern terminus of the **North Yorkshire Moors Railway**, the nation's most popular heritage railway, and houses the vintage steam locomotives that ply the 18-mile-long route. It is also on the Esk Valley line with connections to Whitby and Middlesbrough. The station itself has been restored to the British Railways style of the 1960s and contains a tea room and two shops with a wide variety of rail-related and other items on sale. In high season as many as eight trains a day in each direction are in service and there are many special events throughout the year. And if you have ever harboured the dream of driving a train, the NYMR offers a range of courses, from one day to a full week, enabling you to realise the fantasy.

CENTRAL MOORS

The area around Goathland provides some of the wildest scenery in the National Park. Murk Mire Moor, Black Rigg, Howl Moor – the very names conjure up the rigours of these upland tracts where heather reigns supreme. Even those who know the moors well treat its sudden mists and savage storms with respect. The historian of the area, Joseph Ford, recollected hearing as a child of an itinerant trader who travelled the moorland paths selling bottle corks to farmers' wives. During one particularly severe winter it was remarked that he had not paid his usual calls. The following autumn a skeleton was found on Wintergill Moor: the unfortunate victim was only 'identified by the scattered bottle corks lying nearby'. As Ford noted, 'the story was not unusual'.

It's a very different picture in the narrow dales that cleave their way down to the rivers. The sheltered villages here are as pretty as any in the better known western dales.

GOATHLAND

7 miles SW of Whitby off the A169

Goathland today is perhaps best known as 'Aidensfield' – the main location for the television series *Heartbeat*. Mostyn's Garage & Funeral Services (actually the Goathland Garage); The Aidensfield Arms (The Goathland Hotel) and the Aidensfield Stores all attract thousands of visitors each year, as does **Goathland Station** on the North Yorkshire Moors Railway whose vintage steam locomotives have often featured in the series. The station also served as Hogsmeade Station in the film *Harry Potter and the Philosopher's Stone*.

•

The Exhibition Centre in Goathland can provide you with information about the many walks in the area and guide you to one of the oldest thoroughfares in the country, Wade's Way. If you believe the legend, it was built by a giant of that name, but it is actually a remarkably well-preserved stretch of Roman road. A popular walk is the Rail Trail, a three-and-a-half mile route along the track bed of the original railway line between Goathland and Grosmont, and a return by steam train.

•

Wades Way, Goathland

final resting place marked by an enormous anchor.

In the award-winning **Goathland Exhibition Centre** you'll find a full explanation of the curious tradition of the Plough Stots Service, performed at Goathland every January. It's an ancient ritual for greeting the new year which originated with the Norsemen who settled here more than a thousand years ago. 'Stots' is the Scandinavian word for the bullocks which were used to drag a plough through the village, followed by dancers brandishing 30-inch swords. This pagan rite is still faithfully observed but with the difference that nowadays Goathland's young men have replaced the 'stots' in the plough harness.

BECK HOLE

8 miles SW of Whitby off the A169

A mile or so up the dale from Goathland is the pretty little hamlet of Beck Hole. When the North Yorkshire Moors Railway was constructed in the 1830s (designed by no less an engineer than George Stephenson himself), the trains were made up of stage coaches placed on top of simple bogies and pulled by horses. At Beck Hole, however, there was a 1-in-15 incline up to Goathland so the carriages had to be hauled by a complicated system of ropes and water-filled tanks. (Charles Dickens was an early passenger on this route and wrote a hair-raising description of his journey.) The precipitous incline caused many accidents so, in 1865,

This attractive village 500 feet up on the moors, where old stone houses are scattered randomly around spacious sheep-groomed greens, was popular long before television. Earlier visitors mostly came in order to see **Mallyan Spout**, a 70 feet high waterfall locked into a crescent of rocks and trees. They were also interested in Goathland's rugged church and the odd memorial in its graveyard to William Jefferson and his wife. The couple died in 1923 within a few days of each other, at the ages of 80 and 79, and chose to have their a 'Deviation Line' was blasted through solid rock. The gradient is still one of the steepest in the country at 1 in 49, but it opened up this route to steam trains. The original 1 in 15 incline is now a footpath, so modern walkers will understand the effort needed to get themselves to the summit, let alone a fully laden carriage.

Every year, this little village plays host to the **World Quoits Championship**. The game, which appears to have originated in Eskdale, involves throwing a small iron hoop over an iron pin set about 25 feet away. Appropriately enough, one of the houses on the green has a quoit serving as a door knocker.

On the hillside, a mile or so to the west of Beck Hole, is the curiously-named **Randy Mere**, the last place in England where leeches were gathered commercially. An elderly resident of Goathland in 1945 recalled how as a young man he had waded into the lake and emerged in minutes with the slug-like creatures firmly attached to his skin. For those interested in repeating his exploit, the leeches are still there.

LOCKTON
15 miles SW of Whitby off the A169

About three miles north of Lockton, the **Hole of Horcum** is a huge natural amphitheatre which, so the story goes, was scooped out of Levisham Moor by the giant Wade. It is now a popular centre for hang gliders. Lockton village itself is set high above a deep

ravine, boasts one of the few duck ponds to have survived in the National Park, and offers some fine walks.

LEVISHAM
15 miles SW of Whitby off the A169

Just to the west of the village, in the scenic valley of Newton Dale, is Levisham Station, one of several stops on the route of the North Yorkshire Moors Railway. This stop is the ideal location for walking with a wide variety of wildlife and flowers within a short distance of the station.

Bridestones, nr Lockton

68 RYEDALE FOLK MUSEUM

Hutton le Hole

Ryedale Folk Museum is a wonderful working museum insight into bygone eras.

🏛 see page 254

NEWTON UPON RAWCLIFFE

4 miles N of Pickering off the A169

A delightful unspoilt village on the southern fringe of the North York Moors National Park, with old stone cottages and farms clustered round the village green and duck pond. A haven of peace in delightful countryside with miles of forest and moor offer wonderful walking and touring. Just to the north of the village is the **North Riding Forest Park.** For a small toll, motorists can drive through the park.

APPLETON-LE-MOORS

5 miles NW of Pickering off the A170

Located just inside the southern boundary of the Moors National Park, Appleton-le-Moors is noted for its fine church whose tower and spire provide a landmark for miles around. It was built in Victorian times to a design by J L Pearson, the architect of Truro Cathedral, and it reflects the same Gothic style as the Cornish cathedral.

CROPTON

4 miles NW of Pickering off the A170

At this tiny village ales have been brewed from as far back as 1613 even though home-brewing was illegal in the 17th century. Despite a lapse in the intervening decades, brewing returned to the village when, in 1984, the cellars of the village pub were converted to accommodate **Cropton Brewery**, a micro-brewery with a visitors' centre, guided tours and regional dishes served in the pub, The New Inn.

HUTTON-LE-HOLE

10 miles NW of Pickering off the A170

Long regarded as one of Yorkshire's prettiest villages, Hutton-le-Hole has a character all of its own. 'It is all up and down,' wrote Arthur Mee, visiting half a century ago, 'with a hurrying stream winding among houses scattered here and there, standing at all angles'. Fifty years on, little has changed.

Facing the green is the **Ryedale Folk Museum** (see panel), an imaginative celebration of 4000 years of life in North Yorkshire. Among the 13 historic buildings is a complete Elizabethan Manor House rescued from nearby Harome and reconstructed here; a medieval crofter's cottage with a thatched, hipped roof, peat fire and garth; and the old village shop and post office fitted out as it would have looked just after Elizabeth II's coronation in 1953. Other exhibits include workshops of traditional crafts such as tinsmiths, coopers and wheelwrights, and an Edwardian photographic studio. The National Park has an Information Centre here and throughout the year there are special events such as a Rare Breeds Day and re-enactments of Civil War battles by the Sealed Knot.

Anyone interested in unusual churches should make the short trip from Hutton-le-Hole to **St Mary's Church, Lastingham**, about three miles to the east. The building of a monastery here in the

7th century was recorded by no less an authority than the Venerable Bede, who visited Lastingham not long after it was completed. That monastery was rebuilt in 1078 with a massively impressive crypt that is still in place – a claustrophobic space with heavy Norman arches rising from squat round pillars. The church above is equally atmospheric, lit only by a small window at one end.

GILLAMOOR

10 miles NW of Pickering off the A170

This pleasant little village is well worth a visit to see its very rare, and very elegant, four-faced sundial erected in 1800, and to enjoy the famous **Surprise View**. This is a ravishing panoramic vista of Farndale with the River Dove flowing through the valley far below and white dusty roads climbing the hillside to the heather-covered moors beyond.

Also of interest is the nearby village church which was once the church at Bransdale about six miles away. In the late 1700s, Bransdale Church was in good repair but little used; Gillamoor's was dilapidated but the villagers wanted a place of worship. This was achieved by commissioning a single stonemason, James Smith, to remove Bransdale church stone by stone and re-erect it at Gillamoor.

ROSEDALE ABBEY

11 miles NW of Pickering off the A170

To the east of Farndale is another lovely dale, Rosedale, a nine-mile-long steep-sided valley through

which runs the River Seven. The largest settlement in the dale is Rosedale Abbey which takes its name from the small nunnery founded here in 1158. Nothing of the old Abbey has survived although some of its stones were recycled to build the village houses. A peaceful village now, Rosedale was once crowded with workers employed in iron-ore mines on the moors. It was said that, such was the shortage of lodgings during the 1870s, 'the beds were never cold' as workers from different shifts took turns to sleep in them. The great chimney of the smelting furnace was once a striking landmark on the summit of the moor, but in 1972 it was found to be unsafe and demolished. Its former presence is still recalled at Chimney Bank where a steep and twisting road, with gradients of 1 in 3, leads up to the moor. High on these moors stands **Ralph Cross**, nine feet tall and one of more than 30 such stone crosses dotted across the moors. It was erected in medieval times as a waymark for travellers and when the North York Moors National Park was established in 1952, the Park authorities adopted Ralph Cross as its emblem.

Ralph Cross, Rosedale Abbey

CHURCH HOUSES

17 miles NW of Pickering off the A170

A few miles north of Hutton-le-Hole, the moorland road comes to

The house in Easby Lane in Great Ayton, where the Cook family lived, is sadly no longer there. In 1934 it was transported to Australia brick by brick, together with the climbing plants that covered them, and re-erected in Fitzroy Park, Melbourne. A cairn of stones is all that remains to mark the site.

Lowna, set beside the River Dove in one of the Moors most famous beauty spots, **Farndale.** In spring, some six miles of the river banks are smothered in thousands of wild daffodils, a short-stemmed variety whose colours shade from a pale buttercup yellow to a rich orange-gold. According to local tradition, the bulbs were cultivated by monks who used the petals in their medical concoctions. Yorkshire folk often refer to daffodils as Lenten Lilies because of the time of year in which they bloom. The flowers, once mercilessly plundered by visitors, are now protected by law with 2000 acres of Farndale designated as a local nature reserve.

GREAT AYTON

This appealing village, set around the River Leven, is an essential stopping point for anyone following the Captain Cook Country Tour, a 70-mile circular trip taking in all the major locations associated with the great seafarer. Cook's family moved to Great Ayton when he was eight years old and he attended the little school which is now the **Captain Cook Schoolroom Museum**, open daily from April to October. The building dates back to 1785 and was built as a school and poorhouse on the site of the original charity school that was built in 1704 by Michael Postgate, a wealthy local landowner. It was at the Postgate School that James received his early education paid for by Thomas Skottowe, his father's employer. The museum first opened in the 1920s and the exhibits here relate to Cook's life and to the 18th-century village in which he lived. The family had moved to Great Ayton in 1736, but in 1745 James moved to Staithes before finally becoming an apprentice seaman in Whitby. He joined the Royal Navy in 1755 and first surveyed the coast of Canada before being appointed 1st Lieutenant in 1768 and being given command of his most famous ship, *Endeavour*. After locating Tahiti and New Zealand in 1769, Cook went on to Australia in 1770 and, following further voyages in the Pacific, was killed by native Hawaiians in 1779.

On High Green a statue commissioned by Hambleton District Council and sculpted by Nicholas Dimbleby portrays Cook at the age of 18 when he left the village for Staithes.

An impressive monument is the 60 feet obelisk to Cook's memory erected on Easby Moor above the village by Robert Campion, a Whitby banker, in 1827. It can only be reached by a steepish climb on foot but it is well worth making the effort: from the base of the monument there are stupendous views over the Moors, the Vale of Mowbray and across to the oddly shaped hill called Roseberry Topping. The loftiest of the Cleveland Hills and sometimes called the Matterhorn of Yorkshire, Roseberry's summit towers 1000 feet above Great Ayton.

The Great Ayton of today is very different from the village that Cook would have known. The heart of the town is now a Conservation Area but in the 18th and 19th centuries it was home to much industrial activity including weaving, brewing and tile-making.

AROUND GREAT AYTON

GUISBOROUGH

5 miles NE of Great Ayton on the A171

Guisborough is a pleasant market town featuring a broad, cobble-fringed main street with some attractive buildings. A popular market is held here on Thursdays and Saturdays.

Just to the east of the town, the stark ruins of **Gisborough Priory** (English Heritage) stand on an elevated site overlooked by the Cleveland Hills. Founded by a great landowner in the region, Robert de Brus II, in 1119 the monastery became one of the most powerful in Yorkshire. It was extended in 1200 but almost a century later the whole complex was destroyed by fire. Rebuilding took several generations and was not completed until the late 1300s. A contemporary remarked that the Prior kept 'a most pompous house' and that some 500 households were dependent in some way on the priory. In 1540 the priory's estate was sold to a Thomas Chaloner who cannibalised much of the fabric to grace ornamental gardens at his mansion nearby. That mansion has since disappeared. Of the priory itself, the great arch of the east end is the most striking survival, an outstanding example of Gothic architecture. The priory

Gisborough Priory

grounds are a popular venue for picnics.

About 1 mile east of Guisborough, **Tocketts Mill** is a fully restored water-driven corn mill and a Grade II* listed building. It is one of the most complete mills in the country, with its four floors retaining the original machinery along with an extensive collection of equipment from other mills. Open Sunday afternoons in the summer; Easter Sunday and Monday; and on National Milling Day, the 2nd Sunday in May.

INGLEBY GREENHOW

3 miles S of Great Ayton off the B1257

Located on the very edge of the National Park, Ingleby Greenhow enjoys a favoured position, protected from east winds by the great mass of Ingleby Moor. The beckside church looks small and unimposing from the outside, but inside there is a wealth of rugged Norman arches and pillars, the stonework carved with fanciful figures of grotesque men and animals.

Busby Hall, nr Stokesley

69 THE QUEENS HEAD

Stokesley

Satisfying traditional hostelry service, wholesome food and well kept ales; regular karaoke nights.

see page 256

STOKESLEY

3 miles SW of Great Ayton on the A172

This attractive market town lies beneath the northern edge of the moors, its peace only troubled on market day which has taken place here every Friday since its charter was granted in 1223. Nikolaus Pevsner called Stokesley 'one of the most attractive small towns in the county'. There are rows of elegant Georgian and Regency houses reached by little bridges over the River Leven which flows through the town, and an old water wheel which marks the entrance to the town.

In the Middle Ages, Stokesley was owned by the Balliol family, one of whose scions is remembered as the founder of the Oxford college of that name.

CARLTON IN CLEVELAND

5 miles SE of Great Ayton off the A172

A pleasing little village just inside the National Park, Carlton has a haunted Manor House and a church which was destroyed by fire in 1881 just weeks after its rector had spent years helping to re-build it after an earlier one had been demolished. Another incumbent as rector was Canon John Kyle who fervently maintained the 18th century traditions of the 'squarson' - a parson who was also the village squire. Canon Kyle took the latter of these two roles much more seriously, riding to hounds, running three farms, boxing with the local lads and also running the village pub, the Fox and Hounds. The Archbishop of York was not pleased that one of his ministers owned a drinking house but the canon pointed out that his proprietorship allowed him to close the pub on Sundays.

WHITBY

The most dramatic approach to one of North Yorkshire's most historic and attractive towns is along the moorland road from Guisborough, the A171. A few miles from the town, the ruins of the great abbey perched on a huge cliff appear on the horizon. Whitby is famed as one of the earliest and most important centres of Christianity in England; as Captain James Cook's home port, and as the place where, according to Bram Stoker's famous novel, Count Dracula in the form of a large dog loped ashore from a crewless ship that had drifted into the harbour. The classic 1931 film version of the story, starring Bela Lugosi, was filmed in the original locations at Whitby and there were several reports of holidaymakers being startled by coming across the Count, cloaked and fanged, as he rested between takes. The **Dracula Experience** on Marine Parade gives a lively rendition of the enduring tale with the help of live actors and electronic special effects.

High on the cliff that towers above the old town stand the imposing and romantic ruins of **Whitby Abbey** (see panel - English Heritage). In AD 664, many of the most eminent prelates of the Christian Church were summoned here to attend the Synod of Whitby. They were charged with settling once and for all a festering dispute that had riven Christendom for generations: the precise date on which Easter should be celebrated. The complicated formula they devised to solve this problem is still in use today. Just across from the abbey, a recently opened Visitor Centre combines the best of modern technology with displays of artefacts in tracing the long history of the site.

A short walk from the abbey is **St Mary's Church**, a unique building 'not unlike a house outside and very much like a ship inside.' Indeed, the fascinating interior with its clutter of box-pews built in the 1600s and rented by families whose names were put on the sides, iron pillars and long galleries, it was reputedly fashioned by Whitby seamen during the course of the 18th century. The three-decker pulpit is from the same period; the huge ear trumpets for a rector's

deaf wife were put in place about 50 years later. Outside, a carved sandstone cross commemorates Brother Caedmon, a member of the Whitby Abbey community whose 7th-century poem, *The Song of Creation*, is the earliest known poem in English.

St Mary's stands atop the cliff: the old town clusters around the harbour mouth far below. Linking them are the famous 199 steps that wind up the hillside: many a churchgoer or visitor has been grateful for the frequent seats thoughtfully provided along the way.

The old port of Whitby developed on the slim shelf of land that runs along the east bank of the River Esk, an intricate muddle of narrow, cobbled streets and shoulder-width alleys. Grape Lane is typical, a cramped little street where ancient houses lean wearily against each other. Young James Cook lived here during his apprenticeship: the handsome house in Grape Lane where he lodged is now the **Captain Cook Memorial Museum.** The rich collection includes period rooms, models, maps and manuscripts, ships' plans, furniture, artefacts from Cook's voyages, and many original drawings, prints and paintings, including one of Cook's notorious contemporary, Captain Bligh of the *Bounty*.

By the early 19th

70 THE STATION INN

Whitby

A gem in the centre of town, hosting a minimum of 8 real ales at a time, and live bands on Friday nights

see page 256

71 WHITBY ABBEY

Whitby

The stark and magnificent ruins of Whitby Abbey are much more than a spectacular cliff-top landmark.

see page 256

Captain Cook Museum, Whitby

century, old Whitby was full to bursting and a new town began to burgeon on the West bank of the River Esk. The new Whitby, or 'West Cliff', was carefully planned with the nascent industry of tourism in mind. There was a quayside walk or 'promenade', a bandstand, luxury hotels, and a Royal Crescent of upmarket dwellings reminiscent of Buxton or Cheltenham but with the added advantage of enjoying a sea air universally acknowledged as 'invariably beneficial to the health of the most injured constitution'.

In a dominating position on West Cliff, a bronze statue of Captain Cook gazes out over the harbour he knew so well. Nearby the huge jawbone of a whale, raised as an arch, recalls those other great Whitby seafarers, the whalers.

Between 1753 and 1833, Whitby was the capital of the whaling industry, bringing home 2,761 whales in 80 years. Much of that success was due to the skills of the great whaling captains William Scoresby and his son, also named William. The elder William was celebrated for his great daring and navigational skills, as well as for the invention of the crow's nest, or masthead lookout. His son was driven by a restless, enquiring mind and occupied himself with various experiments during the long days at sea in the icy Arctic waters. He is most noted for his discoveries of the forms of snow crystals and the invention of the 'Greenland' magnet which made ships' compasses more reliable. The whaling industry is now, thankfully, long dead, but fortunately the fishing industry is not, as many of Whitby's restaurants bear witness, being famous for their seafood menus.

A popular souvenir of the town is jet stone, a lustrous black stone which enjoyed an enormous vogue in Victorian times. After the death of Prince Albert, jewellery in jet was the only ornament the Queen would allow herself to wear. The Court and the middle classes naturally followed her example and for several decades Whitby prospered greatly from the trade in jet. By 1914, workable deposits of the stone were virtually exhausted and a new generation shunned its gloomy association with death. Recent years have seen a revival of interest in the glossy stone and

HM Bark 'Endeavour', Whitby

several shops have extensive displays of jet ornaments and jewellery. The original **Victorian Jet Works**, established in 1867, are open daily and visitors can see the craftspeople at work as well as purchase jet from a wide range of interesting and contemporary jewellery designs.

On the south-eastern edge of the town the **Whitby Museum and Pannett Art Gallery**, founded in 1823, stands in the attractive setting of Pannett Park. The museum contains a nationally-important collection of Whitby jet jewellery, relics of Captain Cook and the lands he visited, displays on whaling, 60 model ships and many other items from Whitby's past.

The **Whitby Archives Heritage Centre**, which is open all year, holds an exhibition of local photographs and, along with its local history research facilities, has a shop and heritage gallery. Meanwhile, the **Museum of Victorian Whitby** has a re-creation of a 19th-century lane in the town complete with interiors and shop windows along with miniature rooms and settings.

AROUND WHITBY

SALTBURN-BY-THE-SEA

12 miles NW of Whitby on the A174

The charming seaside resort of Saltburn lies at the northern end of the Heritage Coast. It was custom-built in Victorian times and designed for affluent middle-class visitors – so much so that in the early years excursion trains were barred from calling there. Created in the 1860s by the Quaker entrepreneur Henry Pease, Saltburn is set on a cliff, high above a long sandy beach. To transport visitors from the elegant little town to the promenade and pier below, an ingenious water-balanced **Tramway** was constructed. It is still in use, the oldest such tramway to have survived in Britain. Saltburn's Victorian heritage is celebrated in mid-August each year with a full programme of events, many of them with the participants clad in appropriate costume. It seems appropriate, too, that such an olde world town should be well-known for its many shops selling antiques and collectables.

Saltburn's genteel image in Victorian times was a far cry from its notoriety in the late 18th century when it was one of the North East's busiest centres for smuggling. The 'King of the Smugglers', John Andrew, had his base here and during a long and profitable career was never apprehended. His story, and that of his partners in villainy, is colourfully recalled at **The Saltburn Smugglers Heritage Centre** next to the Ship Inn of which Andrew was landlord.

From the sea front, a miniature railway will take you to the splendid **Italian Gardens** – another Victorian contribution to the town. Here you can take tea on the lawn and explore the **Woodlands Centre** set between the formal pleasure gardens and the wild natural woodlands beyond.

•

A disused jet works has been converted to provide one of Whitby's unique attractions, the Sutcliffe Gallery in Flowergate. The gallery celebrates the great photographer Frank Sutcliffe who was born in the town in 1853. His studies of local people, places and events powerfully evoke the Whitby of late-Victorian and Edwardian times in photographs that are beautifully composed and technically immaculate. Few visitors to the gallery can resist the temptation to purchase at least one of the nostalgic prints on display.

•

A little further up the coast from Staithes rises Boulby Cliff, at 666 feet (202m) the highest point on the east coast of England. Near the village of Boulby itself is the deepest mine in Europe. From depths of between 3600 feet and 3900 feet thousands of tons of potash are mined every day - this is the only source of potash in the UK. The mining extends some 2 miles under the North Sea.

STAITHES

9 miles NW of Whitby off the A174

Visitors to this much-photographed fishing port leave their cars at the park in the modern village at the top of the cliff and then walk down the steep road to the old wharf. Take care – one of these narrow, stepped alleys is called Slippery Hill, for reasons that can become painfully clear. The old stone chapels and rather austere houses testify to the days when Staithes was a stronghold of Methodism.

The little port is proud of its associations with Captain James Cook. He came here, not as a famous mariner, but as a 17-year-old assistant in Mr William Sanderson's haberdashery shop. James didn't stay long, leaving in 1746 to begin his naval apprenticeship in Whitby with Thomas Scottowe, a friend of Sanderson. **The Captain Cook & Staithes Heritage Centre** contains a lifesize street scene of 1745 and other displays on local history.

Staithes is still a working port with one of the few fleets in England still catching crabs and lobsters. Moored in the harbour and along the river are the fishermen's distinctive boats. Known as cobles, they have an ancestry that goes back to Viking times. Nearby is a small sandy beach, popular with families (and artists), and a rocky shoreline extending north and south pitted with thousands of rock pools hiding starfish and anemones. The rocks here are also rich in fossils and you may even find ingots of 'fools gold' – actually iron pyrites and virtually worthless.

RUNSWICK BAY

6 miles NW of Whitby, off the A174

A little further down the coast, Runswick Bay is another picturesque fishing village with attractive cottages clinging to the steep sides of the cliff. This perilous position proved disastrous in 1682 when the cliff face collapsed during a violent storm and the whole of Runswick, with the exception of a single cottage, tumbled into the sea. A disaster fund was set up and a new village established.

At Runswick, as in most of Yorkshire's remote communities, superstition was once widespread. Even at the beginning of the 20th century, many still believed in witches and almost everyone would davert their gaze or cross the road to avoid someone afflicted with the 'Evil Eye'. In the late 1800s, the Revd Cooper, Vicar of Filey, visited

Staithes Old Wharf

the village and came across a 'perfectly horrible superstition'. Apparently, it was considered unlucky to save a drowning man. The Vicar was told of 'men nearly dragged ashore and then, by the advice of the elders, abandoned to their fate lest ill-fortune should result from saving them'.

GOLDSBOROUGH

5 miles NW of Whitby off the A174

Just outside this small village are the remains of one of five signal stations built by the Romans in the 4th century when Saxon pirates were continually raiding the coastal towns. The stations were all built to a similar design with a timber or stone watchtower surrounded by a wide ditch.

LYTHE

4 miles NW of Whitby off the A174

Perched on a hill top, Lythe is a small cluster of houses with a sturdy little church which is well worth a visit. Just south of the village is **Mulgrave Castle**, hereditary home of the Marquis of Normanby. The Castle grounds, which are open to the public, contain the ruins of Foss Castle built shortly after the Norman Conquest. Charles Dickens once spent a holiday at Mulgrave Castle and 'danced on its lawns in ecstasy at its beauty'. It's not known whether the great author witnessed the ancient custom of 'Firing the Stiddy'. This celebrates notable events in the Normanby family and begins with dragging the anvil from the blacksmith's shop, upturning it,

and placing a charge of gunpowder on its base. A fearless villager then approaches with a 20 feet long metal bar, its tip red hot, and detonates the powder.

In the 1850s, Mulgrave Castle was leased by an exiled Indian Maharajah, Duleep Singh. He enjoyed going hawking on the moors in full oriental dress and the story is often told of how he had the first road between Sandsend and Whitby constructed because his elephants disliked walking along the beach. Much as one would like to believe this tale, no one has yet proved it to be true.

SANDSEND

2 miles NW of Whitby on the A174

From Runswick Bay, the A174 drops down the notoriously steep Lythe Bank to Sandsend, a pretty village that grew up alongside the Mulgrave Beck as it runs into the sea at 'sands' end' – the northern tip of the long sandy beach that stretches some two-and-a-half miles from here to Whitby.

The Romans had a cement works nearby, later generations mined the surrounding hills for the elusive jet stone and for alum, and the Victorians built a scenic railway along the coast. The railway track was dismantled in the 1950s but sections of the route now form part of the **Sandsend Trail,** a pleasant and leisurely two-and-a-half hour walk around the village which is made particularly interesting if you follow it with the National Park's booklet describing the route.

72 ESTBEK HOUSE

Sandsend

Outstanding award-winning restaurant with rooms in delightful seaside village.

see page 257

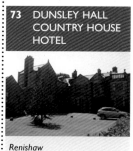

73 DUNSLEY HALL COUNTRY HOUSE HOTEL

Renishaw

Welcoming hotel offering quality food, real ales and excellent en suite rooms.

see page 258

74 RAITHWAITE HALL, LUXURY HOLIDAY COTTAGES

Renishaw

Welcoming hotel offering quality food, real ales and excellent en suite rooms.

see page 259

ROBIN HOOD'S BAY

5 miles S of Whitby off the A171

Artists never tire of painting this 'Clovelly of the North', a picturesque huddle of red-roofed houses clinging to the steep face of the cliff. Bay Town, as locals call the village, was a thriving fishing port throughout the 18th and 19th centuries. By 1920 however there were only two fishing families left in the Bay, mainly because the harbour was so dilapidated, and the industry died out. Today, small boats are once again harvesting the prolific crab grounds that lie along this stretch of the coast.

Because of the natural isolation of the bay, smuggling was quite as important as fishing to the local economy. The houses and inns in the Bay were said to have connecting cellars and cupboards,

Robin Hood's Bay

and it was claimed that 'a bale of silk could pass from the bottom of the village to the top without seeing daylight.' These were the days when press gangs from the Royal Navy were active in the area since recruits with a knowledge of the sea were highly prized. Apparently, these mariners were also highly prized by local women: they smartly despatched the press gangs by means of pans and rolling pins.

Shipwrecks in the Bay were frequent, with many a mighty vessel tossed onto its reefs by North Sea storms. On one memorable occasion in the winter of 1881, a large brig called *The Visitor* was driven onto the rocks. The seas were too rough for the lifeboat at Whitby to be launched there so it was dragged eight miles through the snow and let down the cliffside by ropes. Six men were rescued.

The same wild seas threatened the village itself, every storm eroding a little more of the chalk cliff to which it clings. Fortunately, Robin Hood's Bay is now protected by a sturdy sea wall.

The most extraordinary building in Robin Hood's Bay is undoubtedly **Fyling Hall Pigsty**. It was built in the 1880s by Squire Barry of Fyling Hall in the classical style although the pillars supporting the portico are of wood rather than marble. Here the Squire's two favourite pigs could enjoy plenty of space and a superb view over the bay. The building is now managed by the Landmark Trust who rent it out to holidaymakers.

Detailed information about the village and the Bay is on display at the **Old Coastguard Station** on The Dock. This National Trust property also houses the National Park Visitor and Education Centre. Also worth a visit are the **Robin Hood's Bay Museum**, and **Music in Miniature**, a unique exhibition of 50 dioramas at a scale of 1:12 created by a local craftswoman.

RAVENSCAR

10 miles N of Scarborough off the A171

The coastline around Ravenscar is particularly dramatic and, fortunately, most of it is under the protection of the National Trust. There are some splendid cliff-top walks and outstanding views across Robin Hood's Bay. Ravenscar is the eastern terminus of the 42-mile hike across the moors to Osmotherley known as the **Lyke Wake Walk**.

During the late 19th century there was an unsuccesful attempt to turn this scattered village, then known as Peak, into a small town and, although the roads were built, little of the land that was made available to potential buyers was ever developed. Thus, it retains a tranquil air and, along with the small church and a couple of village shops, the only building of any size here is the Raven Hall Hotel. Local legend has it that King George III visited here when it was a private house, while recovering from one of his recurring bouts of mental illness.

About three miles south of Ravenscar, at Staintondale, are two very different animal centres. At the **Staintondale Shire Horse Farm** (see panel) visitors can enjoy a 'hands-on' experience with these noble creatures, watch a video of the horses working and follow a scenic route around the area. Cart rides are also usually available. There's also a café, souvenir shop, picnic area and a play area with a variety of small farm animals to entertain the children.

At nearby **Wellington Lodge Llama Trekking**, a variety of treks with llamas is on offer, ranging from a three or four-hour journey to a whole day with a three-course meal included in the price. The llamas have many years of trekking experience and are sure-footed and friendly. They carry heavy loads of food, drink, stools and extra clothing, leaving you free to admire the splendid surroundings. Handlers and specialist guides accompany walkers.

HACKNESS

5 miles NW of Scarborough off the A170 or A171

For generations the Forge Valley has attracted sightseers – especially in autumn when the steep wooded banks of the ravine present a dazzling display of colours. There are several splendid walks along this lovely two-mile stretch of the River Derwent, a valley which takes its name from the ancient iron workings of which today not a trace remains. Nothing has survived either of the monastery established

77 STAINTONDALE SHIRE HORSE FARM

Staintondale

A fantastic day out for all the family, where you can meet horses and ponies from the largest to the smallest, and see them performing in live shows.

see page 261

SCARBOROUGH

If you happen to be visiting Scarborough on Shrove Tuesday, be prepared for the unusual sight of respectable citizens exercising their ancient right to skip along the highways. This unexpected traffic hazard is now mostly confined to the area around Foreshore Road. Another tradition maintained by local people around this time is the sounding of the Pancake Bell, a custom started by the wives of the town to alert their menfolk in the fields and in the harbour that they were about to begin cooking the pancakes.

78 CENTRAL TRAMWAY COMPANY LTD

Scarborough

The **Central Tramway Company** Scarborough Limited was created and registered in 1880 and still operates in its original corporate form.

🏛 see page 261

at Hackness in AD 681 by the first Abbess of Whitby although some of its stones were used in the building of St Peter's Church, founded in 1060. Inside the church is a fragment of an Anglo-Saxon cross with inscriptions in English, Latin and runic characters. The grandest building in the village is Hackness Hall (private), a Georgian mansion that is the home of Lord Derwent.

CLOUGHTON

4 miles N of Scarborough on the A171

Cloughton village lies less than a mile from the coast and the rocky inlet of Cloughton Wyke. Here, in 1932, a huge whale was cast, or threw itself, ashore. Press photographers and postcard publishers rushed to the scene and paid the smallest local children they could find to pose beside the stranded Leviathan. For a while, Cloughton village was busy with a steady stream of sightseers. Their numbers quickly diminished as the six tons of blubber began to rot. In Cloughton itself, residents came to dread an east wind: it reached them only after washing over the vast hulk lying on the rocks. It's surely the worst thing that has ever happened to this pleasant little village, set around a sharp kink in the A171, where the breezes now – depending on the direction of the wind – either bring a fresh tang of ozone from the sea or a soft perfume of heather from the moors.

With its two splendid bays and dramatic cliff-top castle, Scarborough was targeted by the early railway tycoons as the natural candidate for Yorkshire's first seaside resort. The railway arrived in 1846, followed by the construction of luxury hotels, elegant promenades and spacious gardens, all of which confirmed the town's claim to the title 'Queen of Watering Places'. The 'quality', people like the eccentric Earls of Londesborough, established palatial summer residences here, and an excellent train service brought thousands of excursionists from the industrial cities of the West Riding.

Even before the advent of the railway, Scarborough had been well-known to a select few. They travelled to what was then a remote little town to sample the spring water discovered by Mrs Tomyzin Farrer in 1626 and popularised in a book published by a certain Dr Wittie who named the site Scarborough Spaw. Anne Brontë came here in the hope that the spa town's invigorating air would improve her health, a hope that was not fulfilled. She died at the age of 29 and her grave lies in St Mary's churchyard at the foot of the castle.

Scarborough Castle itself can be precisely dated to the decade between 1158 and 1168 and surviving records show that construction costs totalled £650. The castle was built on the site of a Roman fort and signal station and its gaunt remains stand high on Castle Rock Headland, dominating the two sweeping bays. The spectacular ruins often provide a splendid backdrop for staged battles commemorating the invasions of the Danes, Saxons and the later incursions of Napoleon's troops. The surrounding cliffs are also well worth exploring – just follow the final part of the famous Cleveland Way.

As befits such a long-established resort, Scarborough offers a vast variety of entertainment. If you tire of the two sandy beaches, there's **Peasholm Park** to explore with its glorious gardens and regular events, among them the unique sea battle in miniature on the lake. Or you could seek out the intellectual attractions of the **Rotunda Museum,** which re-opened in May 2008 after a comprehensive redevelopment. Described as 'the finest Georgian museum in Britain', this impressive building has now returned to its original role as a Museum of Geology. A sister site to the Rotunda Museum, the **Scarborough Art Gallery** displays the borough's paintings and also has a popular programme of temporary exhibitions. **The Stephen Joseph Theatre in the Round** is well known for staging the premiere performances of comedies written by its resident director, the prolific playwright Sir Alan Ayckbourn. Rather more frivolously, you could explore the futuristic world of holograms at Jimmy Corrigans Amusement

Scarborough Castle

Arcade, one of the longest established of the amusement arcades which line the South Bay at Scarborough. And at Scalby Mills, on the northern edge of the town, the **Sea-Life & Marine Sanctuary** offers the chance of close encounters with a huge variety of marine creatures from shrimps to sharks, octopi to eels. A new addition in 2008 was the Seal Rescue Centre where visitors are invited to sample for themselves what it is like to care for these amazing creatures.

93

Just outside the village of Cayton, Playdale Farm Park is home to an array of farm animals, large and small, for visitors to pet or feed. There are also indoor and outdoor play areas, an adventure trail, pedal tractors, indoor and outdoor picnic areas or you could try the café which serves light lunches and snacks.

---

79 LINGHOLM COURT HOLIDAY COTTAGES

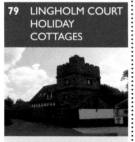

Lebberston

Marvelous award winning farm barn conversions ensure comfortable and attractive self-catering accommodation amid beautiful countryside.

see page 262

AROUND SCARBOROUGH

CAYTON

3 miles S of Scarborough on the B1261

Cayton is one of only 31 'Thankful Villages' in England. They were so named after the First World War because all of their men came back safely from that horrific conflict. Cayton had all the more reason to be grateful since 43 of its men returned – more than to any other of the Thankful Villages.

An unusual attraction here is the **Stained Glass Centre** where Valerie Green and her team produce stained glass and leaded lights for churches, hotels, restaurants, public houses and homes throughout the country. Visitors can watch the craftspeople at work, browse in the showroom, examine the exhibition of stained glass or just relax in the tearoom and lovely garden.

FILEY

7 miles S of Scarborough on the A1039

With its six-mile crescent of safe, sandy beach, Filey was one of the first Yorkshire resorts to benefit from the early 19th-century craze for sea bathing. Filey's popularity continued throughout Victorian times but the little town always prided itself on being rather more select than its brasher neighbour just up the coast, Scarborough. Inevitably, modern times have brought the usual scattering of amusement arcades, fast food outlets and, from 1939 to 1983, a Butlin's Holiday Camp capable of accommodating 10,000 visitors. But Filey has suffered less than most seaside towns and with its many public parks and gardens still retains a winning, rather genteel atmosphere.

Until the Local Government reforms of 1974, the boundary between the East and North Ridings cut right through Filey. The town lay in the East Riding, the parish church and graveyard in the North. This curious arrangement gave rise to some typically pawky Yorkshire humour. If, as a resident of Filey town, you admitted that you were feeling poorly, the response might well be, 'Aye, then tha'll straightly be off t'North Riding' – in other words, the graveyard.

Filey's parish church, the oldest

Filey Parish Church

parts of which date back to the 12th century, is appropriately dedicated to St Oswald, patron saint of fishermen, and the Fishermen's Window here commemorates men from the town who died at sea. At the **Filey Folk Museum**, housed in a lovely old building dating back to 1696, you can explore the town's long history, while the **Edwardian Festival**, held every June, re-creates the pleasures of an earlier, more innocent age. In the following month, the town hosts the Filey Regatta.

Just to the north of the town, the rocky promontory known as **Filey Brigg** strikes out into the sea, a massive mile-long breakwater protecting the town from the worst of the North Sea's winter storms. From the Brigg, there are grand views southwards along the six-mile-long bay to the cliffs that rise up to Flamborough Head and Scarborough Castle. Despite the fact that there is no harbour at Filey, it was once quite a busy fishing port and one can still occasionally see a few cobles – direct descendants of the Viking longships that arrived here more than a millennium ago – beached on the slipways.

Filey Brigg is the southern starting point for the oddly-named **Cleveland Way**, odd because only a few miles of the 110-mile footpath actually pass through Cleveland. The path follows the coast as far north as Saltburn-by-the-Sea then turns south to Roseberry Topping and the Cleveland Hills, finally ending up at Helmsley.

HUNMANBY

3 miles SW of Filey between the A165 and A1039

Here's a question worthy of Trivial Pursuit: 'On which vehicle was the wing mirror first used?' Your answer is almost certainly wrong unless you know about the grave of a 1st century British charioteer uncovered at Hunmanby in 1907. Along with his bones, those of his horses, and fragments of the chariot wheels was a rectangular strip of shiny metal: archaeologists are convinced that this was fixed to the side of the chariot as a mirror so that the driver could see the competitors behind him.

Another curiosity in Hunmanby is the village lock-up with two cells and tiny windows designed for human miscreants, and next to it a circular stone pinfold intended for straying cattle.

THE VALE OF PICKERING

Not all that long ago, the Vale of Pickering was the Lake of Pickering, an immense stretch of water far larger than any English lake today, about 32 miles long and four to eight miles wide. As the Ice Age retreated, the waters gradually drained away leaving a low-lying plain of good arable soil based on Kimmeridge clay. Much of it remained marshy however and at Star Carr, near Seamer,

80 THE HORSESHOE INN

Hunmanby

The Horseshoe Inn is the ideal place to enjoy an extensive menu and a few relaxed drinks.

see page 262

81 THE BUCK INN

Hunmanby

Traditional village inn serving quality home-made food and real ales.

see page 263

95

82 THE SUN INN

Pickering

Honest-to-goodness pub fare and real ales are served at this popular inn; Band festival in August in spacious beer garden.

see page 263

83 PICKERING CASTLE

Pickering

Set in an historic moors-edge market town, this splendid 13th century castle and royal hunting lodge make a fascinating visit for all ages.

see page 264

84 17 BURGATE

Pickering

A five star Market Town House offering individually designed and furnished en-suite accommodation for the modern traveler.

see page 264

85 THE OLD MANSE

Pickering

A fine Edwardian Hotel with a large garden and orchard, comfortable en-suite accommodation and a pleasant dining room cuisine.

see page 264

archaeologists have uncovered a late Stone Age lake community, dating back some 7500 years, where the houses were built on stilts above the water. Sadly, the remains of this fascinating excavation lie on private land and are not open to the public. It is only in comparatively recent times that the Vale has been properly drained, which explains why most of the towns and villages lie around its edge in a rough kind of horseshoe formation.

For much of its length, the Vale is watered by the River Derwent, which was also powerfully affected by the changes that occurred during the Ice Age. Originally it entered the sea near Scarborough but an Ice Age glacier blocked that outlet. The Derwent still flows to within a mile-and-a-half of Scarborough, but now turns abruptly and makes a 90-mile detour through the vale and then southwards to join the River Ouse near Howden.

The main traffic artery through the vale is the Thirsk to Scarborough road, the A170, which in summer peak periods can become very congested. But you only have to turn off this busy thoroughfare to find yourself in quiet country lanes leading to sleepy market towns and unspoilt villages. To the north rise the intricate folds of the North York Moors: to the south, the Yorkshire Wolds roll gently away towards Beverley, Hull and the River Humber.

PICKERING

This busy little town developed around the important crossroads where the Malton to Whitby, and the Thirsk to Scarborough roads intersect. It's the largest of the four market towns in Ryedale and possibly the oldest, claiming to date from 270 BC when (so it's said) it was founded by a King of the

Pickering Castle

Brigantes called Peredurus. William the Conqueror's attempts to dominate the area are recalled by Pickering's ruined **Castle** (see panel - English Heritage), and the many inns and posting houses reflect the town's prosperity during the stage coach era.

The parish church of **St Peter and St Paul** is well worth visiting for its remarkable 15th-century murals. During the glum days of Puritanism, these lively paintings were denounced as idolatrous and plastered over. They stayed forgotten for some 200 years but were rediscovered when the church was being restored in 1851. Unfortunately, the vicar at that time shared the Puritans' sentiments and, despite opposition from his parishioners and even from his bishop, had them smothered again under whitewash. A more liberal successor to the Vicar had the murals restored once again in 1878 and they now give a vivid idea of how cheerful, colourful and entertaining many English churches were before the unforgivable vandalism of the Puritan years. These superb paintings, sharp, vigorous and well-observed, happily embrace scenes from the Bible, old legends and actual history: a real insight into the medieval mind that had no difficulty in accepting both the story of St George slaying the dragon and the martyrdom of St Thomas à Becket as equally real, and inspiring, events.

Collectors of antiques can really indulge themselves at the Pickering Antique Centre where some 45 dealers display their wares in 3,500 square feet of showrooms. The goods on offer include paintings, furniture, china and porcelain, brass and copperware, postcards, books, clocks, silver and plate, old toys and collectables.

If you catch a whiff of sulphurous smoke as you wander around the town, you must be close to the railway station. Pickering is the southern terminus of the **North York Moors Railway** where you can board a steam-drawn train for an 18-mile journey along one of the oldest and most dramatically scenic railways in the country. Thanks to a grant from the heritage Lottery fund, the Booking and Parcels Office has been restored to how it was in 1937. The station's refreshment room is now a tea room and there's a shop with a wide range of gifts, books and videos.

Just up the road from the station, at the **Pickering Trout Lake,** you can hire a rod and tackle and attempt to beat the record for the largest fish ever caught here – it currently stands at a mighty 25lb 4oz (11.45 kg).

AROUND PICKERING

EAST AYTON

13 miles E of Pickering on the A170

Victorian visitors to Scarborough, occasionally tiring of its urban attractions, welcomed excursions to beauty spots such as the **Forge Valley** near East Ayton. Aeons ago,

---

• *Not to be missed in Pickering is the Beck Isle Museum housed in a gracious Regency mansion. Its 27 display areas are crammed with a 'magnificent assortment of items curious, mysterious, marvellous and commonplace from the last 200 years'. There are intriguing re-creations of typical Victorian domestic rooms, shops, workshops and even a pub. The comprehensive collection of photographs by Sydney Smith presents a remarkable picture of the Ryedale area as it was between 1909 and the 1950s. The exhibition is made even more interesting by its acquisition of the very cameras and other photographic equipment used by Sydney Smith.* •

86   THE EVERLEY COUNTRY HOTEL

Hackness

A quality converted farmhouse set in one of the most beautiful valleys of the North York Moors National Park

🛏 ❚ *see page 265*

97

Ayton Castle, East Ayton

87 THE ANVIL INN

Sawdon

Full of character, this former
blacksmiths forge offers
quality food and luxurious
self-catering cottages

🍴 🛏 see page 265

88 THE CAYLEY ARMS

Allerston

Spacious village inn serving
delicious home cooking; beer
garden and comfortable en
suite rooms.

🍴 🛏 see page 266

a sharp-edged glacier excavated the
valley; then centuries of natural
growth softened its hills, clothed
them with over-arching trees and,
quite by chance, created one of
the loveliest woodland walks in
England. For a steady walker,
going say four miles an hour, the
round trip walk from East Ayton
to the old forge from which the
valley derives its name – along one
side of the river returning on the
other, takes about 2.5 hours. A
short diversion will lead you to the
ruins of **Ayton Castle** at the edge
of the road near the junction of
the A170 and B1261. Dating from
around 1400, this is one of the
most southerly of the hundreds of
pele towers built in those turbulent
times as a protection against
invading Scottish marauders. In
more peaceful days, many of these
towers had a more comfortable
mansion added but their defensive
origins are still clearly
recognisable.

BROMPTON-BY-SAWDON

10 miles E of Pickering on the A170

It was in the medieval church of
this small village, on an autumn day
in 1802, that William Wordsworth
was married to Mary Hutchinson
whose family lived at nearby
Gallows Hill Farm. 'A perfect
woman', he wrote of Mary,

'nobly planned
To warn, to comfort, and command;
And yet a spirit still, and bright
With something of an angelic light'.

Mary's home, now the
Wordsworth Gallery, plays host to
an exhibition on the poets
Wordsworth and Coleridge, while
the medieval barn is now filled with
designer gifts, ladies clothes and
licensed tea rooms. The gallery is
open Tuesday to Saturday all year
round.

Wydale Hall (private) was the
home of the Squire of Brompton,
Sir George Cayley (1773-1857), a
pioneer aviator who achieved
successful flights with small gliders
although it was his coachman who
was actually dragooned into being
the pilot. Sir George is also credited
with inventing the caterpillar tractor.

EBBERSTON

7 miles E of Pickering on the A170

About a mile to the west of
Ebberston, in 1718, Mr William
Thompson, MP for Scarborough,
built for himself what is possibly
the smallest stately home in
England, **Ebberston Hall.** From
the front, the house appears to be
just one storey high, with a pillared
doorway approached by a grand

flight of stone steps flanked by a moderately sized room on each side. In fact, behind this modest front, there's also an extensive basement – 'deceptively spacious' as the estate agents say. The exterior can be viewed from the road or churchyard as it is now a private house.

THORNTON-LE-DALE

2 miles E of Pickering on the A170

As long ago as 1907, a *Yorkshire Post* poll of its readers acclaimed Thornton-le-Dale as the most beautiful village in Yorkshire. Despite stiff competition for that title, most visitors still find themselves in agreement.

If further proof were needed, just off the A170 near the parish church of All Saints you'll find one of the most photographed houses in Britain. The thatched cottage, set beside a sparkling beck, has appeared regularly on chocolate boxes, jigsaws and calendars. On the nearby village green there's an ancient cross and a set of wooden stocks and, across the road, are Lady Lumley's Almshouses, 12 dwellings built in 1670 and still serving their original purpose. The North York Moors National Park actually creates a special loop in its boundary to include this picture-postcard village which, somewhat confusingly, is also frequently shown on maps as 'Thornton Dale'.

About 3 miles north of Thornton-le-Dale, the Dalby Visitor Centre is the starting point for the **Dalby Forest Drive** (toll payable), a 9-miile circuit through what was once the royal hunting Forest of Pickering. The Visitor Centre can provide plentiful details of the various amenities available - way marked walks, cycle routes, picnic/barbecue sites, an orienteering course, wildlife observation hide and more. A recent addition to the forest's amenities is **Go Ape!** near the village of Low Dalby. Here visitors can take to the trees and experience an exhilarating course of rope bridges, Tarzan swings and zip slides up to 60 feet above the ground. Pre-booking is essential.

KIRBY MISPERTON

3 miles S of Pickering, off the A169

The 375 acres of wooded parkland surrounding Kirby Misperton Hall provide the setting for **Flamingo Land,** a zoo and fun park that is home to more than 1000 birds, animals and reptiles. Red-necked wallabies, meerkats, Bactrian camels, lynx, tigers, rheas, scimitar-horned oryx, bison, sea lions, baboons and guanacos (a South American relative of the camel) are just some of the many exotic creatures in residence. Beyond doubt, the most spectacular sight is that of the flock of pink flamingos gathered around the lake fringed with willow trees. With more than 100 different attractions, including a fun fair with some truly scary rides, an adventure playground and a real working farm, it's no surprise to learn that Flamingo Land is the 4th most visited theme park in the country.

89 THE GOLDEN LION INN

Great Barugh

Traditional country pub in picturesque village serving outstanding food and real ales; beer garden with stunning views.

🍴 see page 267

99

An excellent walk begins and ends at Sinnington. Covering some 7½ miles (12.1km), though it can also be done in parts, it starts at the village's fascinating Saxon and Norman church and leads along woodland paths and farm tracks towards Cropton, Rosedale and Lastingham to Lower Askew, then back through Appleton-le-Moors to the starting point. Details available from North York Moors National Park (tel. 01439 770173).

SINNINGTON

4 miles W of Pickering off the A170

At Sinnington the River Seven drops down from the moors and the valley of Rosedale into the more open country of the Vale of Pickering. The stream passes through this tiny village, running alongside a broad green in the centre of which stands a graceful old packhorse bridge. At one time this medieval bridge must have served a useful purpose but whatever old watercourse once flowed beneath it has long since disappeared – thus the bridge is known as the 'dry' bridge.

KIRKBYMOORSIDE

7 miles W of Pickering on the A170

Set quietly off the main road, this agreeable market town of fine Georgian houses, narrow twisting lanes, family-owned shops and a cobbled marketplace, straggles up the hillside. After you pass the last house on the hill, you enter the great open spaces of the North York Moors National Park, 553 square miles of outstanding natural beauty which, since they were accorded the status of a National Park in 1952, have been protected from insensitive encroachments. Within the park you don't have to worry about traffic lights – there aren't any. But you may well have to step down firmly on your brakes to avoid sheep crossing the road at their own leisurely and disdainful pace.

Of the several old coaching inns in Kirkbymoorside, the timbered Black Swan is believed to

be the most venerable – the intricately carved entrance porch bears the date 1692.

It was in another ancient inn, the King Head's Hotel, that one of the 17th century's most reviled politicians expired. In what is now Buckingham House, but was then part of the adjoining hotel, George Villiers, 2nd Duke of Buckingham died. The duke had been a favourite of Charles II and a member of the notorious 'Cabal' of the king's five most powerful ministers who colluded with him in trying to frustrate the democratic instincts of the elected Parliament. Each letter of the word 'Cabal' represented the initial of one of its five members – Buckingham being the 'B'. The duke had come to Kirkbymoorside to take part in a hunt through the nearby Forest of Pickering. In the heat of the chase he was thrown from his horse and mortally wounded. The duke's retainers carried him to the King's Head Inn where he died later that day. In the parish register for 1687 the passing of a once-mighty politician merited only a laconic, phonetic entry: *Died: April 17th George Viluas: Lord Dooke of Bookingham.*

In a secluded dale about 1½ miles west of the town, tiny **St Gregory's Minster** is a fine example of a Saxon church and is famous for its sun dial which has been dated to around AD 1055.

HELMSLEY

13 miles W of Pickering on the A170

One of North Yorkshire's most popular and attractive towns, with

Duncombe Park, Helmsley

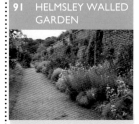

lots of specialty shops and a market every Friday, Helmsley lies on the banks of the River Rye on the edge of the North York Moors National Park. The spacious cobbled market square is typical of the area but the Gothic memorial to the 2nd Baron Feversham that stands there is not. This astonishingly ornate construction was designed by Sir Giles Gilbert Scott and looks like a smaller version of his famous memorial to Sir Walter Scott in Edinburgh.

The Earls of Feversham lived at **Duncombe Park** whose extensive grounds sweep up to within a few yards of the Market Place. Most of the original mansion, designed by Vanbrugh, was gutted by a disastrous fire in 1879: only the north wing remained habitable and that in its turn was ruined by a second fire in 1895. The Fevershams lavished a fortune on rebuilding the grand old house, largely to the original design, but the financial burden eventually forced them to lease the house and grounds as a preparatory school for girls. Happily, the Fevershams were able to return to their ancestral home in 1985 and the beautifully restored house with its 35 acres of lovely gardens and a further 400 acres of superbly landscaped grounds are now open to the public.

Before they were ennobled, the Fevershams' family name was Duncombe and it was Sir Thomas Duncombe, a wealthy London goldsmith, who established the family seat here when he bought **Helmsley Castle** (English Heritage) and its estate in 1687. Founded in the early 1100s, seriously knocked about during the Civil War, the castle was in a dilapidated state but its previous owner, the Duke of Buckingham, had continued to live there in some squalor and discomfort. Sir Thomas quickly decided to build a more suitable residence nearby, abandoning the ruins to lovers of the romantic and picturesque.

With the castle as its backdrop, **Helmsley Walled Garden** (see panel) offers five acres of lovely gardens containing many unusual varieties of flowers, vegetables and

Rievaulx Abbey, Helmsley

93 THE OLD POLICE STATION CAFÉ

Helmsley

A popular, simple café with a variety of food, drinks and snacks in the unspoilt market town of Helmsley.

🍴 see page 268

94 THE PHEASANT AT HAROME

Harome

Very comfortable country hotel with a wealth of amenities; excellent cuisine and en suite rooms.

🛏 🍴 see page 268

herbs. Originally established in the 1700s, by the late 1900s the garden had become a wilderness but has now been completely restored and work is currently under way to bring the Victorian glasshouses back into service. Plants, cut and dried flowers, vegetables and herbs are on sale; there's a café, shop and picnic area.

Just to the west of Helmsley rise the indescribably beautiful remains of **Rievaulx Abbey** (English Heritage), standing among wooded hills beside the River Rye – 'the most beautiful monastic site in Europe.' JMW Turner was enchanted by this idyllic landscape; Dorothy Wordsworth, 'spellbound'. Founded in 1131, Rievaulx was the first Cistercian abbey in Yorkshire and, with some 700 people – monks, lay brothers, servants – eventually living within its walls, became one of the largest. Like Kirkham Abbey a few years earlier, Rievaulx was endowed by Walter l'Espec, Lord of Helmsley, still mourning the loss of his only son

in a riding accident. The abbey was soon a major landowner in the county, earning a healthy income from farming and at one time owning more than 14,000 sheep. The abbey also had its own fishery at Teesmouth, and iron-ore mines at Bilsdale and near Wakefield.

Looking down on the extensive remains of the Abbey is **Rievaulx Terrace** (National Trust), a breathtaking example of landscape gardening completed in 1758. The cunningly contrived avenues draw your eyes to incomparable views of the abbey itself, to vistas along the Rye Valley and to the rolling contours of the hills beyond. At each end of the terrace is a classical temple, one of which is elaborately furnished and decorated as a dining room.

NUNNINGTON

11 miles SW of Pickering off the B1257

Nunnington Hall (National Trust) is a late 17th-century manor house in a beautiful setting beside the River Rye with a picturesque packhorse bridge within its grounds. Inside, there is a magnificent panelled hall, fine tapestries and china, and the famous Carlisle collection of miniature rooms exquisitely furnished in different period styles to one-eighth life size.

HAWNBY

16 miles W of Pickering, off the A170

Hawnby was home of the first community of Methodists in Ryedale. This caused a great scandal within the established church, and the Methodist rebels were taken before the magistrates and charged with disorderly conduct as 'lewd fellows of the baser sort'. That is why, to this day, the village of Hawnby is in two distinct parts: the original village is halfway up the hill, while down at the bottom by the bridge is the settlement the early Methodists built. Within a few years their original houses had been replaced by the ones that stand there now. The village's two chapels also no longer exist – one stands in ruins at Snilesworth on the edge of the moor; the other has been converted into business premises.

The village is close to many hiking trails including the **Cleveland Way** and **Mark Reid's Inn Way**; cycling enthusiasts will enjoy the challenging terrain with trails such as National Cycle Route 65, which passes through the village, and the MTB trails in Boltby Forest. Trout fishing is permitted on Arden Great Lake for a small fee. Other activities such as hang gliding, clay pigeon shooting, 4x4 off-road driving are available locally.

MALTON

Malton has been the historic centre of Ryedale ever since the Romans came. They built a large fort and called it Derventio after the river Derwent beside which it stands. For many years, archaeologists were puzzled by the large scale of the fort, a mystery resolved in 1970 when a building dedication was uncovered which revealed that the fort housed a cavalry regiment, the Ala Picentiana – the extra space was needed to accommodate their horses. Many fine relics from the site, showing the sophisticated lifestyles of the Roman centurions and civilians, can be seen in the **Malton Museum,** along with items from the Iron Age settlement that preceded the Roman garrison.

The River Derwent was vitally important to Malton. The river rises in the moors near Scarborough, then runs inland through the Vale of Pickering bringing an essential element for what was once a major industry in Malton – brewing. In the 19th century, there were nine breweries here, now only the Malton Brewery Company survives. It operates in a converted stable block behind Suddabys Crown Hotel in Wheelgate and welcomes visitors, but telephone them first on 01653 697580.

Charles Dickens stayed in the area with his friend, Charles Smithson, a solicitor, and is believed to have modelled Scrooge's Counting House in *A Christmas Carol* on Smithson's office in Chancery Lane.

Old Malton is located just to the north of the Roman Fort, an interesting and historic area on the edge of open countryside. Nearby villages such as Settrington and their secluded country lanes are home to many famous racehorse stables: if you are up and about early enough you will see the horses out on their daily exercises. In the

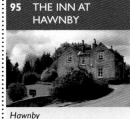

95 THE INN AT HAWNBY

Hawnby

Appealing country hotel in peaceful rural setting; outstanding food, real ales and superb en suite rooms.

see page 269

96 LASKILL GRANGE

Hawnby

Idyllic accommodation situated on an elegant Farmhouse with grounds including beautiful gardens, a lake and a summerhouse.

see page 269

97 YORKSHIRE TEA ROOMS & RESTAURANT

Malton

Family-run business serving excellent home-made food; licensed with pleasant secluded tea garden

🍴 *see page 270*

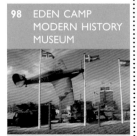

98 EDEN CAMP MODERN HISTORY MUSEUM

Malton

Eden Camp will allow you to experience the sights, sounds and even the smells of life on both the Home Front and Front Line during World War Two.

🏛 *see page 271*

centre of Old Malton stands a beautiful fragment of **St Mary's Priory**, incorporating a particularly fine Norman doorway. The Priory was built around 1155 by the only monastic order in Christendom to have originated entirely in England – the Gilbertines. The order was founded in 1148 by a Lincolnshire parish priest, St Gilbert of Sempringham.

Parts of the parish church are quite as old as the Priory but one of its most interesting features is relatively modern, the work of the 'Mouseman of Kilburn', Robert Thompson. A gifted woodcarver and furniture maker, Thompson 'signed' all his pieces with a discreetly placed carving of a mouse. There's one on the stout oak door of the church and, inside, the stalls are carved elaborately with all manner of wondrous beasts along with historical and mythical scenes.

A mile or so north of Old Malton is **Eden Camp** (see panel), a theme museum dedicated to re-creating the dramatic experiences

of ordinary people living through the Second World War. This unique museum is housed in some 30 huts of a genuine prisoner of war camp, built in 1942. Sound, lighting effects, smells, even smoke generators are deployed to make you feel that you are actually there, taking part. Visitors can find out what it was like to live through an air raid, to be a prisoner of war or a sailor in a U-boat under attack. Among the many other exhibits are displays on Fashion in the '40s, Children at War, and even one on Rationing. In 1941, one discovers, the cheese ration was down to 1oz (28 grams) per person a week! More generous portions of food are available in the café, and there's also a bar, gift shop and children's adventure playground.

AROUND MALTON

KIRKHAM

5 miles SW of Malton off the A64

In a lovely, peaceful setting beside the River Derwent, stand the remains of **Kirkham Priory**. According to legend, the priory was founded in 1125 by Walter l'Espec after his only son was thrown from his horse and killed at this very spot. (A few years later, Walter was to found another great abbey at Rievaulx). Visitors to Kirkham pass through a noble, exquisitely decorated gatehouse but one of the most memorable sights at the Priory, perhaps because it is so unexpected, is the sumptuous lavatorium in the ruined cloister. Here the monks washed their

Kirkham Priory

Castle Howard Arboretum

99 CASTLE HOWARD

Castle Howard

Castle Howard, winner of York Tourism Bureau's 'Out of Town Attraction of the Year' award, is now so much more than a magnificent 18th century house

🏛 see page 272

hands at two bays with lavishly moulded arches supported by slender pillars, each bay adorned with tracery.

CASTLE HOWARD

5 miles SW of Malton off the A64

Lying in the folds of the Howardian Hills about five miles southwest of Malton stands one of the most glorious stately homes in Britain, **Castle Howard**. Well known to TV viewers as the Brideshead of *Brideshead Revisited*, Castle Howard has astonished visitors ever since it was completed in the early 1700s.

Even that world-weary 18th-century socialite Horace Walpole was stirred to enthusiasm: 'Nobody had informed me,' he wrote, 'that at one view I should see a palace, a town, a fortified city, temples on high places ... the noblest lawn in the world fenced by half the horizon and a mausoleum that would tempt one to be buried alive: in short, I have seen gigantic places before, but never a sublime one.'

Winner of York Tourism Bureau's 'Out of Town Attraction of the Year' award, this magnificent 18th-century house with its extensive collections and breathtaking grounds, featuring temples, lakes and fountains, includes various places to stop and

Castle Howard

100 THE CRESSWELL ARMS

Appleton-le-Street

Fine old country inn serving traditional English cuisine with a twist and offering quality en suite accommodation

🍴 🛏 see page 273

101 THE DAWNAY ARMS

West Heslerton

Traditional Yorkshire Wolds village hostelry serving excellent food and real ales; patio and beer garden to the rear.

🍴 see page 274

enjoy refreshments and also a plant centre and tree nursery. A varied programme of events takes place throughout the year, including the Proms Spectacular and Archaeology Weekends.

Perhaps the most astonishing fact of all concerns the architect of Castle Howard, Sir John Vanbrugh. Vanbrugh had been a soldier and a playwright but until he began this sublime building had never yet overseen the placing of one block of masonry on another.

Castle Howard is open daily between February and November. A land-train is available to transport visitors from the car park to the house, and there is disabled access to many parts.

APPLETON-LE-STREET

4 miles W of Malton off the B1257

Appleton's Grade I listed Saxon church escaped 'improvement' by the Victorians, so it retains much original stonework and has one of the finest Anglo-Saxon towers in the North of England. Inside, effigies date from the 13th and 14th centuries and some interior woodwork dates from 1636. Outside, a statue of the Virgin and Child, defaced at the time of the Reformation, can be seen in a niche above the porch. Set high above the village, All Saints commands magnificent views over the Vale of Pickering.

HOVINGHAM

8 miles W of Malton on the B1257

'Hall, church and village gather round like a happy family', wrote Arthur Mee describing Hovingham some 70 years ago. Today the idyllic scene remains unspoilt, a lovely place boasting no fewer than three village greens. Overlooking one of them is a Victorian school, still in use and boasting an elegant oriel window.

Nearby Hovingham Hall, an imposing Georgian mansion, was built in 1760 for Sir Thomas Worsley, Surveyor General to George III, and almost exactly 200 years later, on June 8th 1961, his descendant Katherine Worsley returned here for a royal reception following her marriage to the Duke of Kent. The Worsley family still live at the Hall so it is only open to visitors for a short time in summer, but you can see its unusual entrance which leads directly off the village green. The huge archway opens, not as you would expect, into a drive leading to the Hall but to a vast riding school and stables through which visitors have to pass. Within the Hall's grounds is the village's cricket pitch, enjoying what is surely the most picturesque setting for the game.

EAST HESLERTON

7 miles NE of Malton on the A64

This little village is distinguished by one of the many churches gifted by Sir Tatton Sykes of Sledmere House in the mid-1800s. Designed in 13th-century style the church has a fine west portico, a vaulted chancel and an iron screen of very fine workmanship. The north tower has an octagonal belfry and spire, and statues of the four Latin Doctors (Ambrose, Augustine, Gregory and Jerome) originally sculpted for Bristol Cathedral.

WHARRAM PERCY

7 miles SE of Malton off the B1248

A minor road off the B1248 leads to one of the most haunting sights in the county – the deserted medieval village of **Wharram Percy** (English Heritage; free). There had been a settlement here for some 5000 years but by the late 1400s the village stood abandoned. For a while the church continued to serve the surrounding hamlets but in time, that too became a ruin. The manor house of the Percy family who gave the village its name, peasant houses dating back to the 13th century, a corn mill, a cemetery complete with exposed skeletons – these sad memorials of a once thriving community stand windswept and desolate. Until fairly recently it was assumed that the villagers had been driven from their homes by the plague but scholars are now certain that the cause was simple economics: the lords of the manor, the Percys, turned their lands from labour-intensive crop cultivation to sheep farming which needed only a handful of shepherds. Unable to find work, the villagers drifted elsewhere.

WEST LUTTON

7 miles E of Malton off the A64 or B1253

West Lutton church is yet another of the many repaired or restored by Sir Tatton Sykes in this corner of the East Riding. It stands overlooking the village green and pond, its lych gate reached by a tiny bridge.

102 THE THREE TUNS INN

West Lutton

Traditional country hostelry in picturesque village with real ales, pool room and spacious beer garden.

see page 276

103 THE BLUE BELL INN

Weaverthorpe

Handsome village inn offering outstanding cuisine, real ales and luxury en suite rooms.

see page 275

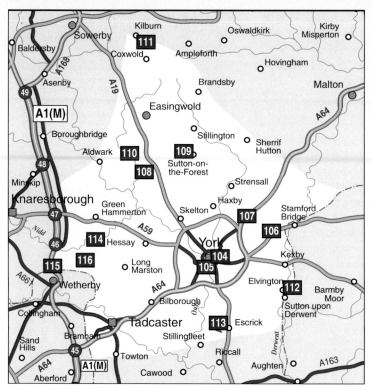

York and the Yorkshire Wolds

This region of North Yorkshire, between the North York Moors and the East Riding, between West Yorkshire and the Heritage Coast, is dominated by the city of York. The first settlement of any note here was created by the Romans, who named their garrison town 'Eboracum', and, from then on, York has been an important and influential force not only in Yorkshire but also in the rest of the country. Known to the Saxons as 'Eoferwic' and the Vikings as 'Jorvik', it was the creation of the magnificent Minster, started in the

York Minster in Winter

early 13th century that saw the city truly begin to develop. A major trading centre and, at one time, the second largest city in the country, York is also remembered as the heart of the railway network in the north of England. Not surprisingly, there is plenty to see here and, along with the numerous imaginative museums and galleries, visitors will want to walk around its medieval streets and soak up the atmosphere that encompasses architectural styles from at least the last 700 years.

Nun Monkton, nr York

109

104 JORVIK VIKING
CENTRE

York

The world famous **JORVIK** centre in York transports visitors back in time to experience the sights, sounds and - perhaps most famously - the smells of 10th century York

🏛 *see page 276*

YORK

'The history of York is the history of England,' said the Duke of York, later to become George VI. A bold claim but well justified. For almost 2,000 years the city has been at the centre of great events and, better than any other city in England, it has preserved the evidence of each era of its glorious past.

One of the grandest cityscapes in the country opens up as you walk along the old city walls towards **York Minster,** a sublime expression of medieval faith. The Minster stands on the site of an even older building, the headquarters of the Roman legions. The Imperial troops arrived here in AD 71 when the governor, Quintus Petilius Cerealis, chose this strategic position astride the Rivers Ouse and Foss as his base for a campaign against the pesky tribe of the Brigantes. The settlement was named Eboracum. From this garrison, Hadrian directed the

construction of his great wall and a later general, Constantine, was proclaimed Emperor here. The legions finally left the city around AD 410, but the evidence of their three-and-a-half centuries of occupation is manifest all around York in buildings like the **Multangular Tower,** in rich artefacts treasured in the city's museums and even in a pub: at the **Roman Bath Inn** you can see the remains of steam baths used by the garrison residents.

Little is known of York during the Dark Ages but by the 8th century the city had been colonised by the Anglo-Saxons, who named it Eoferwic, and it was already an important Christian and academic centre. The Vikings put an end to that when they invaded in the 9th century and changed the name once again, this time to Jorvik. The story of York during those years of Danish rule is imaginatively told in the many displays at the **Jorvik Viking Centre** (see panel) in Coppergate, celebrating a 1000-year-old story. This world-famous centre transports visitors back in time to experience the sights, sounds and – perhaps most famously – the smells of 10th-century York. Visitors are shown that, in AD 975, York was a bustling commercial centre where 10,000 people lived and worked. Travelling in state-of-the-art 'time capsules', visitors are carried past and through two-storey dwellings, enjoying views over back gardens and rooftops, and even glimpsing the Viking Age equivalent of

Multangular Tower, York

today's Minster. Journeying through representations of real-life Viking Age Britain, you pass through a bustling market thronged with Danes bartering for chickens, corn and other provisions and wares, penetrate dark smoky houses, cross a busy wharf where goods, transported along the rivers Ouse and Foss, are being off-loaded. Both fun and educational, 20 years after it first opened, Jorvik still retains its status as one of the world's iconic attractions, and its many superb features make it an enduring favourite with children and adults alike.

After the Norman Conquest, the city suffered badly during the Harrowing of the North when William the Conqueror mounted a brutal campaign against his rebellious northern subjects. Vast tracts of Yorkshire and Northumberland were laid waste and some historians reckon that it took more than 100 years for the area to recover from this wholesale devastation.

In later Norman times, however, York entered one of its most glorious periods. It was at this time that **Clifford's Tower** (see panel) was built, a mightily impressive structure set atop a huge mound. It was built in the shape of a quatrefoil, the only castle in England of this kind. It was originally part of York Castle but was re-named after a man called Clifford was hanged here in 1332.

The Minster, the largest Gothic cathedral in Northern Europe, was begun around 1230 and the work

was on such a scale that it would not be completed until two-and-a-half centuries later. Its stained glass windows – there are more than 100 of them – cast a celestial light over the many treasures within. A guided tour of the Great Tower gives dizzying views across the city; a visit to the crypt reveals some of the relics from the Roman fortress that stood here nearly 2,000 years ago.

This superb building has survived three major fires. The first occurred in 1829 and was started

105 CLIFFORD'S TOWER

York

The sweeping views of the city from the tower still show why it played such an important part in controlling northern England.

🏛 see page 276

York Minster

by a madman, Jonathan Martin. Believing that God wanted him to destroy the church, he started a fire using prayer and hymn books. The fire was not discovered until the following morning by which time the east end of the Minster had been severely damaged. A second blaze, in 1840, was caused by a workman leaving a candle burning. As a result of his carelessness, the central part of the nave was destroyed. The most recent conflagration was in July 1984, shortly after a controversial Bishop of Durham had been installed. Some attributed the fire to God's wrath at the Bishop's appointment; the more prosaic view was that it had been caused by lightning. The subsequent restoration has allowed modern masons and craftsmen to demonstrate that they possess skills just as impressive as those of their medieval forebears.

The network of medieval streets around the Minster is one of the city's major delights. Narrow lanes are criss-crossed by even narrower footpaths – ginnels, snickets or 'snickelways', which have survived as public rights of way despite being built over, above and around. Narrowest of all the snickelways is Pope's Head Alley, more than 100 feet long but only 31 inches wide. The alley became known as Introduction Lane – if you wanted to know someone better, you simply timed your walk along the lane so as to meet the other party half-way. Whip-ma-Whop-ma-Gate, allegedly, is where felons used to be 'whipped and whopped'. Probably most famous of these ancient streets is **The Shambles**. Its name comes from 'Fleshammels', the street of butchers and slaughter houses. The houses here were deliberately built to keep the street out of direct sunlight, thus protecting the carcasses which were hung outside the houses on hooks. Many of the hooks are still in place.

During these years, York was the second largest city in England and it was then that the town walls and their 'bars', or gates, were built. The trade guilds were also at their most powerful and in Fossgate one of them built the lovely black and white timbered **Merchant Adventurers Hall**. The Merchant Adventurers controlled the lucrative trade in 'all goods bought and sold foreign' and they spared no expense in building the Great Hall where they conducted their affairs beneath a complex timbered roof displaying many colourful banners of York's medieval guilds. To this period, too, belong the **York Mystery Plays**, first performed in 1397 and subsequently every four years.

During Tudor times, York's importance steadily declined but re-emerged in the 18th century as a fashionable social centre. Many

Merchant Adventurers Hall, York

elegant Georgian houses, of which **Fairfax House** in Castlegate is perhaps the most splendid, were built at this time and they add another attractive architectural dimension to the city. Fairfax House was built in the early 1700s and elegantly remodelled by John Carr half a century later. The gracious old house has had an unfortunate history. It passed through a succession of private owners and by 1909 was divided between three building societies and the York City Club. The final indignity came in 1919 when the city council permitted a cinema to be built alongside and its superb first floor rooms to be converted into a dance hall. The York Civic Trust was able to purchase the house in 1981 and has restored this splendid old mansion to its former state of grace. The original furnishings have long since been dispersed but in their place are the marvellous pieces from the Noel Terry collection of fine furniture and clocks which includes many rare and unusual pieces.

The 19th century saw York take on a completely different role as the hub of the railway system in the north. At the heart of this transformation was the charismatic entrepreneur George Hudson, founder of what became the Great Northern Railway. Part visionary, part crook, Hudson's wheeler-dealing eventually led to his disgrace but even then the citizens of York twice elected him as Lord Mayor and he has a street named after him. It was thanks to Hudson that York's magnificent railway station, with its great curving roof of glass, was built, a tourist attraction in its own right.

Fairfax House, York

Another aspect of railway history is on view at the **York Model Railway**, next door to the station, which has almost one third of a mile of track and up to 14 trains running at any one time.

For real trains, however, a visit to the **National Railway Museum** (free) is a must. The world's largest railway museum, it has 3 enormous halls where you'll find iconic locomotives such as *Mallard,* the world's fastest steam engine, a Japanese Bullet Train, and the Chinese Locomotive, one of the largest steam locomotives ever built in Britain. There's also a wealth of interactive exhibits and daily demonstrations.

Within the same site is the **Yorkshire Wheel,** York's answer to the London Eye. Rising to some 80 metres, the Wheel provides spectacular views of the city and surrounding countryside.

A city with such a long and colourful history naturally boasts some fine museums. Set in botanical gardens close to the Minster and beside the River Ouse,

113

106 THE DUKE OF YORK

Gate Helmsley

Charming traditional country pub serving excellent food and real ales; beer garden and children's play area.

🍴 *see page 277*

107 THE FOX INN

Stockton-on-the-Forest

Outstanding village inn serving appetising food and real ales; patio and function room.

🍴 *see page 278*

the **Yorkshire Museum & Gardens** has an outstanding collection of Roman, Viking and medieval artefacts, including the exquisite Middleham Jewel which was uncovered close to Middleham Castle. Made of finely engraved gold and adorned with a brilliant sapphire it is one of the most dazzling pieces to have been discovered from that period.

At the **York Castle Museum** visitors can venture into the prison cell of notorious highwayman Dick Turpin; stroll along Victorian and Edwardian streets complete with fully equipped shops, hostelries and houses; or browse among the more than 100,000 items on display. One of the country's most popular museums of everyday life, its exhibits range from crafts and costumes to automobiles and machine guns, from mod cons and medicines to toys and technology.

Insights into medieval daily life are provided at **Barley Hall,** a superbly restored late medieval townhouse which in Tudor times was the home of William Snawsell, a goldsmith who became Lord Mayor of York. Visitors can try out the furniture, handle all the pottery, glass and metal wares, and even try on some medieval costumes.

In a beautifully restored church close to the Shambles is the **Archaeological Research Centre,** an award-winning hands-on exploration of archaeology for visitors of all ages. Here you can meet practising archaeologists who will demonstrate how to sort and identify genuine finds or to try out

ancient crafts. For the more technically minded, there's a series of interactive computer displays which illustrate how modern technology helps to discover and interpret the past.

The latest addition to the city's attractions is the **Quilt Museum and Gallery**, opened in June 2008. Housed in a 15th century guidhall, it is Europe's first museum dedicated to quilt making and textile arts and is home to the Quilters' Guild of the British Isles and its world-famous Heritage Quilt Collection.

It's impossible here to list all York's museums, galleries and fine buildings, but you will find a wealth of additional information at the Tourist Information Centre close to one of the historic old gateways to the city, **Bootham Bar.**

NORTH OF YORK

MURTON

3 miles E of York off the A64

Although a small village, Murton is an important, modern livestock centre and it is also home to the **Yorkshire Museum of Farming**, found at Murton Park. As well as wandering around the fields and pens, visitors can also see reconstructions of a Roman fort, a Danelaw village from the Dark Ages and Celtic Roundhouses along with bumping into Romans, Viking and Saxons. Other attractions at the park include the Derwent Valley Light Railway, a children's play area and a café fashioned on a farmhouse kitchen.

Murton also hosts a large farmers' market on the 3rd Saturday of each month.

BISHOP WILTON

8½ miles E of York off the A166

A small and unspoilt village between Stamford Bridge to the west and Pocklington to the south, in Saxon times Bishop Wilton was a country retreat for the bishops of York. The Saxons – whose bishops gave the village its name – began the lovely village church, which has a fine Norman chancel arch and doorway. The remarkable black-and-white marble flooring is copied from the Vatican.

STAMFORD BRIDGE

7 miles NE of York on the A166

Everyone knows that 1066 was the year of the Battle of Hastings but, just a few days before that battle, King Harold had clashed at Stamford Bridge with his half-brother Tostig and Hardrada, King of Norway who between them had mustered some 60,000 men. On a rise near the corn mill is a stone commemorating the event with an inscription in English and Danish. Up until 1878, a Sunday in September was designated 'Spear Day Feast' in commemoration of the battle. On this day, boat-shaped pies were made bearing the impression of a spear, in memory of the Saxon soldier in his boat who slew the single Norseman defending the wooden bridge over the River Derwent. Harold's troops were triumphant but immediately after this victory they marched

Beningbrough Hall, nr Newton-on-Ouse

southwards to Hastings and a much more famous defeat.

NEWTON-ON-OUSE

7 miles NW of York off the A19

About a mile to the south of Newton-on-Ouse is **Beningbrough Hall** (National Trust), a baroque masterpiece from the early 18th century with seven acres of gardens, wilderness play area, pike ponds and scenic walks. There's also a fully-operational Victorian laundry which demonstrates the painstaking drudgery of a 19th-century washing day. A major attraction here is the permanent exhibition of more than 100 portraits on loan from the National Portrait Gallery. Other exhibitions are often held at the Hall – for these there is usually an additional charge.

EASINGWOLD

This agreeable market town was once surrounded by the Forest of Galtres, a vast hunting preserve of Norman kings. It lies at the foot of the Howardian Hills, an Area of

108 THE BLACK HORSE

Tollerton

This traditional pub caters for every age group, with a 'Tap Room' and regular real ales, recently opened beer garden and children's playground.

see page 279

109 SUTTON PARK

Sutton-on-the-Forest

Sutton Park is a charming lived-in house, built of mellow brick in 1730 by Thomas Atkinson.

 see page 278

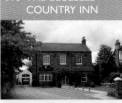

110 THE BLUEBELL COUNTRY INN

Alne

Superb village inn, formerly a farmhouse, noted for its outstanding cuisine, real ales and quality en suite rooms.

see page 280

Outstanding Natural Beauty covering 77 acres of woods, farmland and historic parkland. Easingwold's prosperity dates back to the 18th century when it flourished as a major stage coach post – at that period the town could offer a choice of some 26 public houses and inns. Until the recent construction of a bypass the old town was clogged with traffic but it is now a pleasure again to wander around the marketplace with its impressive **Market Cross** and, nearby, the outline of the old bull-baiting ring set in the cobbles. Easingwold used to enjoy the distinction of having its own private railway, a two-and-a-half mile stretch of track along which it took all of 10 minutes to reach the main east coast line at Alne. Older residents fondly remember the ancient, tall-chimneyed steam locomotive that plied this route until its deeply regretted closure to passenger traffic in 1948.

A little to the south of Easingwold, on the B1363, is **Sutton Park** (see panel), a noble early 18th-century mansion, built in 1730 by Thomas Atkinson and containing some fine examples of Sheraton and Chippendale furniture, and much admired decorative plasterwork by the Italian maestro in this craft, Cortese. The ubiquitous Capability Brown designed the lovely gardens and parkland in which you'll find a Georgian ice-house, well-signposted woodland walks and a nature trail. There's also a gift shop and a café.

AROUND EASINGWOLD

STILLINGTON

4 miles E of Easingwold on the B1363

In 1758, one of the great works of English literature almost perished in the fireplace of Stillington Hall. The parson of Coxwold had been invited to dinner and when the meal ended was asked to read from a book he had just completed. The guests had all wined and dined well and were soon dozing off. Incensed by their inattention the parson threw the pages of his manuscript onto the fire. Fortunately his host, the Squire of Stillington, rescued them from the flames and Laurence Sterne's immortal *Tristram Shandy* was saved for posterity.

HUSTHWAITE

4 miles N of Easingwold off the A19

Old stone houses mingle with mellow Victorian and Edwardian brick and overlooking the village green, where three lanes meet, the Church of St Nicholas still retains its original Norman doorway. Just outside the village, on the road to Coxwold, there's a stunning view across to the Hambleton Hills and the White Horse of Kilburn.

COXWOLD

5 miles N of Easingwold off the A19 or A170

Coxwold enjoys a particularly lovely setting in the narrow valley that runs between the Hambleton and Howardian Hills. At the western end of the village stands the 500-year-old **Shandy Hall**, home of

Shandy Hall Garden

Laurence Sterne, vicar of Coxwold in the 1760s. Sterne was the author of *Tristram Shandy*, that wonderfully bizarre novel which opened a vein of English surreal comedy leading directly to The Goons and the Monty Python team. The architecture of the Hall, Tudor in origin, includes some appropriately eccentric features – strangely-shaped balustrades on the wooden staircases, a Heath Robinson kind of contraption in the bedroom powder-closet by which Sterne could draw up pails of water for his ablutions, and a tiny, eye-shaped window in the huge chimney stack opening from the study to the right of the entrance. A more conventional attraction is the priceless collection of Sterne's books and manuscripts.

The Revd Sterne much preferred the cosmopolitan diversions of London to the rustic pleasures of his Yorkshire parish and rarely officiated at the imposing **Church of St Michael** nearby with its striking octagonal tower, three-decker pulpit and Fauconberg family tombs. A curiosity here is a floor brass in the nave recording the death of Sir John Manston in 1464. A space was left for his wife Elizabeth's name to be added at a later date. The space is still blank. Outside, against the wall of the nave, is Sterne's original tombstone, moved here from London's Bayswater when the churchyard there was deconsecrated in 1969.

Just to the south of Coxwold is **Newburgh Priory,** founded in 1145 as an Augustinian monastery and now a mostly Georgian country house with fine interiors and a beautiful water garden. Since 1538, the Priory has been the home of the Fauconberg family. An old tradition asserts that Oliver Cromwell's body is interred here. Cromwell's daughter, Mary, was married to

Newburgh Priory, nr Coxwold

111 MOUSEMAN VISITOR CENTRE

Kilburn

The new Mouseman Visitor Centre will take you on an amazing journey through the life and times of the Mouseman from humble beginnings to furniture legend.

see page 281

Lord Fauconberg and when Charles II had her father's corpse hanged at Tyburn and his head struck off, Lady Fauconberg claimed the decapitated body, brought it to Newburgh and, it is said, buried the remains under the floorboards of an attic room. The supposed tomb has never been opened, the Fauconbergs even resisting a royal appeal from Edward VII when, as Prince of Wales, he was a guest at the Priory. The house, which is still the home of the Earls of Fauconberg, and its extensive grounds are open to the public during the spring and summer months.

From Coxwold, follow the minor road northeastwards towards Ampleforth. After about two miles, you will see the lovely, cream-coloured ruins of **Byland Abbey** (English Heritage). The Cistercians began building their vast compound in 1177 and it grew to become the largest Cistercian church in Britain. Much of the damage to its fabric was caused by Scottish soldiers after the Battle of Byland in 1322. The English king, Edward II had been staying at the Abbey but fled after his defeat, abandoning vital stores and priceless treasures. In a frenzy of looting, the Scots made off with everything the king had left and ransacked the Abbey for good

Byland Abbey, nr Coxwold

measure. The ruined west front of the Abbey, although only the lower arc of its great rose window is still in place, gives a vivid impression of how glorious this building once was.

AMPLEFORTH
6 miles N of Easingwold off the A170

Set on the southern slopes of the Hambleton Hills, Ampleforth is perhaps best known for its Roman Catholic public school, Ampleforth College, established by the Benedictine community that came here in 1809, fleeing from persecution in post-revolutionary France. The monks built an austere-looking Abbey in the Romanesque style among whose treasures are an altar stone rescued from Byland Abbey and finely crafted woodwork by the 'Mouseman of Kilburn', Robert Thompson.

KILBURN
6 miles N of Easingwold off the A170

Kilburn was the home of one of the most famous of modern Yorkshire craftsmen, Robert Thompson – the '**Mouseman of Kilburn**'. Robert's father was a carpenter but he apprenticed his son to an engineer. At the age of 20 however, inspired by seeing the medieval wood carvings in Ripon Cathedral, Robert returned to Kilburn and begged his father to train him as a carpenter. An early commission from Ampleforth Abbey to carve a cross settled his destiny: from then until his death in 1955 Robert's beautifully crafted ecclesiastical and domestic furniture was in constant demand. His work can be seen in more than 700 churches, including Westminster Abbey and York Minster. Each piece bears his 'signature' – a tiny carved mouse placed in some inconspicuous corner of the work. According to a family story, Robert adopted this symbol when one of his assistants happened to use the phrase 'as poor as a church mouse'. (Signing one's work wasn't an entirely new tradition: the 17th-century woodcarver Grinling Gibbons' personal stamp was a pod of peas). Robert Thompson's two grandsons have continued his work and their grandfather's former home (see panel) is now both a memorial to his genius and a showroom for their own creations.

You can see several of the Mouseman's creations in Kilburn village church – there's one perched on the traceried pulpit, another clinging to a desk in the sanctuary, and a third sitting cheekily on the lectern.

From the northern end of the village a winding lane leads to the famous **White Horse,** inspired by the prehistoric White Horse hill-carving at Uffingham in Berkshire. John Hodgson, Kilburn's village schoolmaster, enthused his pupils and villagers into creating this splendid folly in 1857. It is 314 feet long and 228 feet high and visible from as far away as Harrogate and Otley. Unlike its prehistoric predecessor in Berkshire, where the chalk hillside keeps it naturally white, Kilburn's 'White' horse is scraped from grey limestone which needs to be regularly groomed with lime-washing and a liberal spreading of chalk chippings.

SOUTH OF YORK

ELVINGTON

7 miles SE of York off the B1228

During the Second World War RAF Elvington was the base for British, Canadian and French bomber crews flying missions to occupied Europe. With virtually all its original buildings still intact, the base now provides an authentic setting for the **Yorkshire Air Museum** and is the largest Second World War Bomber Command Station open to the public in the UK. In addition to examining the many exhibits tracing the history of aviation, including a unique Halifax bomber, visitors can visit the control tower, browse among the historic military vehicle collection, watch engineers restoring vintage planes – and enjoy home-cooked food in the NAAFI restaurant. The

112 THE YORKSHIRE AIR MUSEUM

Elvington
Over the past few years the Yorkshire Air Museum has become one of the most fascinating and dynamic Museums of its type in the country.

🏛 *see page 281*

113 THE BLACK BULL INN

Escrick
Former coaching inn in idyllic village offering excellent cuisine, real ales and quality en suite rooms.

🍴 🛏 *see page 282*

White Horse of Kilburn

Marston Moor Memorial

museum hosts many special events throughout the year and offers conference and corporate event facilities.

LONG MARSTON

7 miles W of York off the B1224

Lying on the edge of the Vale of York and sheltered by a hill, this village is an ancient agricultural community. However, in July 1644, its tranquillity was shattered by the battle of Marston Moor, one of the most important encounters of the Civil War and one which the Royalists lost. The night before the battle, Oliver Cromwell and his chief officers stayed at Long Marston Hall and the bedroom they used is still called The Cromwell Room.

Each year the anniversary of the battle is commemorated by the members of the Sealed Knot and, it is said, that the ghosts of those who fell in battle haunt the site. Certainly, local farmers still occasionally unearth cannonballs used in the battle when they are out ploughing the fields.

TADCASTER

9 miles SW of York off the A64

The lovely magnesian limestone used in so many fine Yorkshire churches came from the quarries established here in Roman times. Their name for Tadcaster was simply 'Calcaria' – limestone. By 1341 however, brewing had become the town's major industry, using water from River Wharfe. Three major breweries are still based in Tadcaster: Samuel Smiths, established in 1758 and the oldest in Yorkshire; John Smith's, whose bitter is the best-selling ale in Britain; and Coors Tower Brewery. The distinctive brewery buildings dominate the town's skyline and provide the basis of its prosperity. Guided tours of the breweries are available by prior booking.

Also worth visiting is **The Ark**, the oldest building in Tadcaster dating back to the 1490s. During its long history, The Ark has served as a meeting place, a post office, an inn, a butcher's shop, and a museum. It now houses the Town Council offices and is open to the public in office hours. This appealing half-timbered building takes its name from the two carved heads on the first floor beams. They are thought to represent Noah and his wife, hence the name. Tadcaster also offers some attractive riverside walks, one of which takes you across the 'Virgin Viaduct' over the River Wharfe. Built in 1849 by the great railway entrepreneur George Hudson, the viaduct was intended to be part of a direct line from Leeds to York. Before the tracks were laid however Hudson was convicted of fraud on a stupendous scale and this route was never completed.

About four miles southwest of Tadcaster is Hazelwood Castle, now a superb hotel and conference centre; but for more than eight centuries it was the home of the Vavasour family who built it with the lovely white limestone from their quarry at Thevesdale – the same quarry that provided the stone for York Minster and King's College Chapel, Cambridge. The well-maintained gardens and nature trail are open every afternoon (tea room and shop open on Sundays only), and guided tours of the Castle with its superb Great Hall and 13th-century Chapel are available by arrangement.

BOSTON SPA
11 miles SW of York on the A659

Set beside the broad-flowing River Wharfe, this attractive little town enjoyed many years of prosperity after a Mr John Shires discovered a mineral spring here in 1744. The spa activities have long since ceased. There's a pleasant riverside walk which can be continued along the track of a dismantled railway as far as Tadcaster in one direction, Wetherby in the other. The town's impressive 19th-century church is notable for its stately tower and the 36 stone angels supporting the nave and aisles.

WETHERBY
11 miles SW of York on the A661

Situated on the Great North Road, at a point midway between Edinburgh and London, Wetherby was renowned for its coaching inns, of which the two most famous were The Angel and The Swan &

Talbot. It is rumoured that serving positions at these inns were considered so lucrative that employees had to pay for the privilege of employment in them!

The town has remained unspoilt and has a quaint appearance with a central marketplace that was first granted to the Knights Templar. Many of the houses in the town are Georgian, Regency, or early Victorian. Apart from its shops, galleries, old pubs, and cafés, there is also a popular racecourse nearby. Another feature is the renowned 18th-century bridge with a long weir which once provided power for Wetherby's corn mill and possibly dates from medieval times. The bridge once carried traffic along the Great North Road; the A1 now by-passes the town.

About five miles south of Wetherby, **Bramham Park** is noted for its magnificent gardens, 66 acres of them, and its pleasure grounds which cover a further 100 acres. They are the only example of a formal, early 18th-century landscape in Britain. Temples, ornamental ponds, cascades, a two-mile long avenue of beech trees and one of the best wildflower gardens in the country are just some of the attractions. In early June, the park hosts the Bramham Horse Trials. The house itself, an attractive Queen Anne building, is open to groups of six or more by appointment only.

114 THE CHEQUERS INN

Bilton-in-Ainsty

Family-run country inn with quality food, real ales, lovely beer garden and excellent en suite rooms.

see page 283

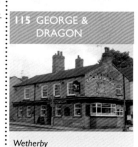

115 GEORGE & DRAGON

Wetherby

Former coaching inn adjacent to the River Wharfe serving good, hearty food and real ale.

see page 284

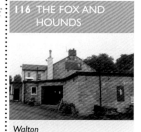

116 THE FOX AND HOUNDS

Walton

A food-led pub with a friendly atmosphere using the best ingredients, prepared and presented well. Also host three real ales.

see page 285

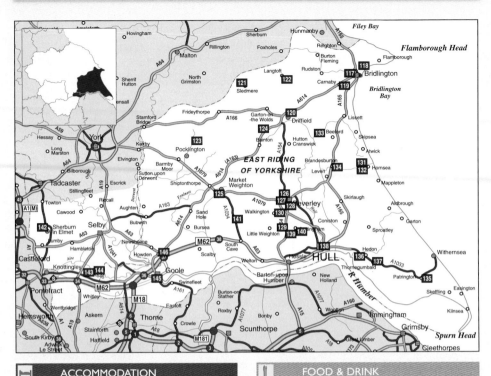

East Yorkshire

Fold upon fold of encircling hills, piled rich and golden – such was the author Winifred Holtby's fond memory of the Wolds landscape. She was born in 1898 in Rudston on the northern edge of the Wolds, a village dominated by the prehistoric Rudston Monolith. This colossal block of stone, a daunting symbol of some misty pagan belief, stands challengingly close to Rudston's Christian parish church. At 25 feet (7.6 metres) high, it is the tallest standing stone in Britain. Winifred Holtby left the village and became a leading figure in London literary circles, editor of the influential magazine *Time and Tide*, but in her own books it was those 'rich and golden hills' that still enthralled her. In her most successful novel, *South Riding*, the fictional Riding is unmistakably recognisable as the Wolds among whose gently rolling acres she had spent her childhood.

The Wolds are a great crescent of chalk hills that sweep round from the coast near Flamborough Head to the outskirts of Hull. There were settlers here some 10,000 years ago – but never very many. In the early 1700s, Daniel Defoe described the area as 'very thin of towns and people' and also noted the 'great number of sheep'. Little has changed: the Wolds remain an unspoilt tract of scattered farmsteads and somnolent villages with one of the lowest population densities in the country. Artists remark on the striking quality of the light and air, and on the long views that open up, perhaps across undulating hills to the twin towers of Beverley Minster or to the great towers of the Minster at York. The Wolds never rise above 800 feet but the open landscape makes them particularly vulnerable to winter snowstorms: children have been marooned in their schools, the dipping and twisting country roads, even in recent years, have been blocked for weeks at a time.

The south-eastern corner of Yorkshire tends to be overlooked by many visitors. If only they knew what they were missing. Beverley is one of the most beguiling of Yorkshire towns and its Minster one of the greatest glories of Gothic architecture. Its parish church, built by a medieval guild, rivals the Minster in its grandeur and in its colourful interior. The whole town has the indefinable dignity you might expect from a community that was a capital of the East Riding in former days when Hull, just six miles to the south, was still a rather scruffy little port.

To the east and south of Beverley lies the old Land of Holderness, its character quite different from anywhere else in Yorkshire. A wide plain, it stretches to the coast where for aeons the land has been fighting an incessant, and losing, battle against the onslaught of North Sea billows. The whole length of the Holderness coast is being eroded at an average rate of three inches a year, but in some locations up to three feet or more gets gnawed away. At its southernmost tip, Spurn Point curls around the mouth of the Humber estuary, a cruelly exposed tip of land whose contours get re-arranged after every winter storm. The coastal towns and villages have a bleached and scoured look to them, perhaps a little forbidding at first. It doesn't take long however for visitors to succumb to the appeal of this region of wide vistas, secluded villages and lonely shores.

Selby is the most southerly of the eight districts that make up the vast, sprawling county of North Yorkshire. Here, the level plains of the Vale of York stretch for miles – rich, agricultural land watered by the four great Yorkshire rivers, Ouse, Wharfe, Derwent and Aire, and by the Selby Canal. It is ideal country for walking and cycling, or for exploring the waterways on which a wide variety of rivercraft is available for hire.

123

117 THE PACK HORSE INN

Old Bridlington

Outstanding inn offering appetising, home-cooked food and real ales; delightful garden and patio.

🍴 see page 285

BRIDLINGTON

Bridlington lies at the northern tip of the crescent of hills that form the Wolds. This bustling seaside resort with its manifold visitor amusements and attractions has been understandably popular since early Victorian times. The attractions of a vast, 10-mile stretch of sandy beach distract most visitors from the Old Town which lies half a mile inland from the beach. Narrow, medieval streets are lined with unspoilt buildings many of which are now tea rooms, speciality and antiques shops. Also within the Old Town is **Bridlington Priory** which was one of the wealthiest in England until it was ruthlessly pillaged during the Reformation. Externally it is somewhat unprepossessing, but step inside and the majestic 13th-century nave is unforgettably impressive.

A corner of the Priory churchyard recalls one of the most tragic days in the town's history. During a fearsome gale in January 1871, a whole fleet of ships foundered along the coast. Bridlington's lifeboat was launched but within minutes it was "smashed to matchwood"; most of its crew perished. Twenty bodies were washed ashore and later buried in the churchyard here.; it was estimated that 20 times as many souls found a watery grave. This awesome tragedy is still recalled each year with a solemn service of remembrance and the lifeboat is drawn through the town.

Another dangerous event, though fortunately not fatal, occurred during Queen Henrietta Maria's visit to Bridlington in February 1643. She landed here on a Dutch ship laden with arms and aid for her beleaguered husband, Charles I. Parliamentary naval vessels were in hot pursuit and having failed to capture their quarry, bombarded the town. Their cannon balls actually hit the Queen's lodging. Henrietta was forced to take cover in a ditch where, as she reported in a letter to her husband, 'the balls sang merrily over our heads, and a sergeant was killed not 20 paces from me.' At this point Her Majesty deemed it prudent to retreat to the safety of Boynton Hall, three miles inland and well beyond the range of the Parliamentary cannons.

North Beach, Bridlington

These stirring events, and many others in the long history of Bridlington and its people, are vividly brought to life with the help of evocative old paintings, photographs and artefacts in the **Bayle Museum**. Quite apart from its fascinating exhibits the museum is well worth visiting for its setting inside the old gatehouse to the town, much of it built in the late 12th century. The museum is owned and run by a body called the Lords Feoffees, a charitable trust established in 1636.

Bridlington Gatehouse

The Lords Feoffees also own and manage **Beside the Seaside**, an all-weather venue where visitors can take a promenade through Bridlington's heyday as a resort, sampling the sights, sounds and characters of a seaside town. Film shows and period amusements such as antique coin-in-the-slot games and a Punch & Judy Show, displays reconstructing a 1950s boarding house as well as the town's maritime history – the museum provides a satisfying experience for both the nostalgic and those with a general curiosity about the town's past.

Penny arcades were once an indispensable feature of seaside resorts. At the **Old Penny Memories Museum** (free) you can see 'What the Butler Saw', have your fortune told, test your strength on the Minigrip, discover your matrimonial prospects, pit your skills against a pinball machine, and enjoy a host of other entertainments on the extensive collection of antique slot machines

– and all for just one old penny each. There's also a sixties café with lots of colourful memorabilia of the period.

Lovers of the Art Deco style should find a reason to visit the Royal Hall at **The Spa Bridlington**. The Hall is exquisitely adorned in the short-lived 1930s fashionable vogue. The Spa has recently had a multi-million-pound redevelopment and was re-launched as the East Coast's premier entertainment venue in the spring of 2008. It hosts concerts by top bands, quality drama, dancing, exhibitions, music and more.

On the north-eastern outskirts of Bridlington is **Sewerby Hall** (see panel), a monumental mansion built on the cusp of the Queen Anne and early Georgian years, between 1714 and 1720. Set in 50 acres of garden and parkland (where there's also a small zoo), the house was purchased by Bridlington Borough Council in 1934 and opened to the public two years later by Amy Johnson, the

An excellent way to get an overview of the town and the coast is to take a ride on the Eye on the Bay, a 130 feet high observation wheel with 24 pods, each seating up to 6 people.

118 SEWERBY HALL AND GARDENS

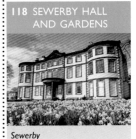

Sewerby

Sewerby Hall is situated 2 miles north of the seaside resort of Bridlington, on the East Yorkshire coast.

🏛 see page 286

125

Close by Sewerby Hall is Bondville Miniature Village, one of the finest model villages in the country. The display includes more than 1000 hand-made and painted characters, over 200 individual and unique villages, and carefully crafted scenes of everyday life, all set in a beautifully landscaped one acre site. The Village is naturally popular with children who are fascinated by features such as the steam train crossing the tiny river and passing the harbour with its fishing boats and cruisers.

dashing, Yorkshire-born pilot who had captured the public imagination by her daring solo flights to South Africa and Australia. The Museum of East Yorkshire here houses some fascinating memorabilia of Amy's pioneering feats along with displays of motor vehicles, archaeological finds and some remarkable paintings among which is perhaps the most famous portrait of Queen Henrietta Maria, wife of Charles I. Queen Henrietta loved this romantic image of herself as a young, carefree woman, but during the dark days of the Civil War she felt compelled to sell it to raise funds for the doomed Royalist cause which ended with her husband's execution. After passing through several hands, this haunting portrait of a queen touched by tragedy found its last resting place at Sewerby Hall.

Other amenities at Sewerby Hall include a pitch and putt course, putting green, children's play area, tearooms, craft units and a souvenir and gift shop.

AROUND BRIDLINGTON

FLAMBOROUGH

4 miles NE of Bridlington on the B1255.

At **Flamborough Head,** sea and land are locked in an unremitting battle. At the North Landing, huge, foam-spumed waves roll in between gigantic cliffs, slowly but remorselessly washing away the shoreline. Paradoxically, the outcome of this elemental conflict is to produce one of the most picturesque locations on the Yorkshire coast, much visited and much photographed.

Flamborough has a long and lively maritime history, not least for being the site of one of the most stubborn naval battles in British history, which took place off Flamborough Head between the American squadron led by John Paul Jones and two British ships of war. Taking place during the War of Independence in 1779, watchers on the coast were transfixed by this intense battle that eventually led to the defeat of the British, when British Captain Pearson surrendered his sword to John Paul Jones. Shortly afterwards, the American's ship began to sink and he was lucky to escape with his life.

Victorian travel writers, in their time, also came to appreciate and honour Flamborough, not just for its dramatic setting but also for its people. They were so clannish and

Flamborough

believed in such strange superstitions. No boat would ever set sail on a Sunday; wool could not be wound in lamplight; anyone who mentioned a hare or pig while baiting the fishing lines was inviting doom. No fisherman would leave harbour unless he was wearing a navy-blue jersey, knitted by his wife in a cable, diamond mesh peculiar to the village and still worn today. Every year the villagers would slash their way through Flamborough in a sword-dancing frenzy introduced here in the 8th century by the Vikings. Eventually, local fishermen grew weary of this primitive role so although the sword dance still takes place it is now performed by boys from the primary school, wearing white trousers, red caps and the traditional navy-blue jerseys.

Flamborough's parish church contains two particularly interesting monuments. One is the **Tomb of Sir Marmaduke Constable** which shows him with his chest cut open to reveal his heart being devoured by a toad. The knight's death in 1518 had been caused, the story goes, by his swallowing the toad which had been drowsing in Sir Marmaduke's lunchtime pint of ale. The creature then devoured his heart. The other notable monument is a statue of St Oswald, patron saint of fishermen. This fishing connection is renewed every year, on the second Sunday in October, by a service dedicated to the **Harvest of the Sea,** when the area's seafarers gather together in a church decorated with crab pots and fishing nets.

Flamborough Head's first, and England's oldest surviving **lighthouse,** is the octagonal chalk tower on the landward side of the present lighthouse. Built in 1674, its beacon was a basket of burning coal. The lighthouse that is still in use was built in 1806. Originally signalling four white flashes, developments over the years have included a fog horn in 1859 and, in more recent years, a signal of radio bleeps. Until it was automated in 1995, it was the last manned lighthouse on the east coast. Boat trips around the lighthouses are available during the season.

Just to the north of Flamborough is **Danes Dyke,** a huge rampart 4 miles long designed to cut off the headland from hostile invaders. The Danes had nothing to do with it, the dyke was in place long before they arrived. Sometime during the Bronze or Stone Age, early Britons constructed this extraordinary defensive ditch. A mile and a quarter of its southern length is open to the public as a Nature Trail.

The South Landing area of Flamborough Head is designated as a Local Nature Reserve and an attractive feature here is the Sculpture Trail. There are currently 16 sculptures made from various materials and the subjects include two donkeys hand crafted with cement, a Totem Pole intricately carved with objects associated with the sea, and various living willow sculptures.

Danes Dyke, nr Flamborough

Gannets at RSPB Reserve, Bempton Cliffs

119 MANOR COURT HOTEL & AZZURRO RESTAURANT

Carnaby

Surrounded by countryside, this high quality gem has a huge choice of menus, including Azzurro, a contemporary Italian restaurant, and a selection of stylish en-suite rooms.

see page 287

BEMPTON

3 miles N of Bridlington on the B1229

Bempton Cliffs, 400 feet high, mark the northernmost tip of the great belt of chalk that runs diagonally across England from the Isle of Wight to Flamborough Head. The sheer cliffs at Bempton provide an ideal nesting place for huge colonies of fulmars, guillemots, puffins and Britain's largest seabird, the gannet, with a wingspan six feet wide. In Victorian times, a popular holiday sport was to shoot the birds from boats. Above them, crowds gathered to watch gangs of 'climmers' make a hair-raising descent by rope down the cliffs to gather the birds' eggs. Most were sold for food, but many went to egg collectors. The climmers also massacred kittiwakes in their thousands: kittiwake feathers were highly prized as accessories for hats and for stuffing mattresses. The first Bird Protection Act of 1869 was specifically designed to protect the kittiwakes at Bempton. A ban on collecting eggs here didn't come into force until 1954. Bempton Cliffs are now an RSPB bird sanctuary, a refuge during the April to August breeding season for more than 200,000 seabirds making this the largest colony in England. The RSPB provides safe viewpoints allowing close-up watching and there's also a visitor centre, shop and refreshments.

BARMSTON

5 miles S of Bridlington off the A165

The road leading from Barmston village to the sands is just over half a mile long: in Viking times it stretched twice as far. The whole of this coast is being eroded at an average rate of three inches every year, and as much as three feet a year in the most vulnerable locations. Fortunately, that still leaves plenty of time to visit Barmston's village pub before it tumbles into the sea!

CARNABY

2 miles SW of Bridlington on the A614

Leaving Bridlington on the A166 will shortly bring you to **John Bull – World of Rock** which has become a premier tourist attraction in this part of East Yorkshire and really is a great day out. Whether you are young or old, you will be fascinated as you discover the history and delights of rock making. The older generation will particularly revel in the smell of the old-fashioned way of making toffee and the interesting bygone displays.

Animation and taped conversation accompany you as you explore the establishment which is described as a total sensory experience. You can even try your hand at making a personalised stick of rock.

Also in Carnaby, set in 3½ acres of natural woodland, is the **Park Rose Owl & Bird of Prey Centre**, home to a variety of eagle owls, hawks, buzzards, vultures and owls. There are daily flying displays, weather permitting, and the centre runs courses on falconry.

BURTON AGNES

5 miles SW of Bridlington on the A166

The overwhelming attraction in this unspoilt village is the sublime Elizabethan mansion, Burton Agnes Hall, but visitors should not ignore **Burton Agnes Manor House** (English Heritage), a rare example of a Norman house: a building of great historical importance but burdened with a grimly functional architecture, almost 800 years old, that chills one's soul. As Lloyd Grossman might say, 'How could anyone live in a house like this?'

Burton Agnes Hall is much more appealing. An outstanding Elizabethan house, built between 1598 and 1610 and little altered, Burton Agnes is particularly famous for its splendid Jacobean gatehouse, wondrously decorated ceilings and overmantels carved in oak, plaster and alabaster. It also has a valuable collection of paintings and furniture from between the 17th and 19th centuries – including a portrait of Oliver Cromwell 'warts and all' – and a large collection of

Impressionist paintings. The gardens are extensive with more than 2000 plants, a maze and giant board games in the Coloured Gardens. Other visitor facilities include an ice cream parlour, a dried-flower and herb shop, a children's animal corner, and an artists' studio. A very popular addition is the plant sales where numerous uncommon varieties can be obtained. The Impressionist Café, open throughout the Hall's season, seats 64 inside and, in good weather, 56 outside. Licensed and offering only the very best in home cooking, the café serves some particularly delicious scones.

HARPHAM

6 miles SW of Bridlington off the A614

To the south of this village, where the manor once stood, stands **Drummers Well** which gained its interesting name during the 14th century. Then, the Lord of the Manor, in the midst of holding an archery day, accidentally pushed his

Burton Agnes Hall

120 THE BUCK HOTEL

Driffield

Fine old traditional hostelry serving a good selection of home-made food and a real ale; patio area outside and regular weekly karaoke.

¶ see page 286

Great Driffield was once the capital of the Saxon Kingdom of Dear, a vast domain extending over the whole of Northumbria and Yorkshire. It was a King of Dear who, for administrative convenience, divided the southern part of his realm into three parts, 'thriddings', a word which gradually evolved into the famous 'Ridings' of Yorkshire.

drummer boy into the well, where he subsequently drowned. The boy's mother, who was also the local wise woman, on hearing the news proclaimed that from then on the sound of drumming from the well would precede the death of any member of the lord's family.

RUDSTON

4 miles W of Bridlington on the B1253

This village takes its name from the giant **Monolith** or 'rood stone' which stands in the village churchyard. At some 26 feet high, it is reputed to be the tallest in Britain, and local legends say that the monolith was a hugh gritstone spear thrown by the Devil who was angered when a church was built on what had been a sacred pagan site. However, it is far more likely that the giant stone was dragged here from Cayton Bay, some 10 miles away, or that it may be a relic from the Ice Age.

FOSTON ON THE WOLDS

7 miles SW of Bridlington off the B1249 or A165

If you can't tell a Gloucester Old Spot from a Saddleback, or a Belted Galloway from a Belgian Blue, then take a trip to **Cruckley Animal Farm** where all will become clear. This working farm supports many different varieties of cattle, sheep, pigs, poultry and horses. Some of the animals are endangered – Greyfaced Dartmoor and Whitefaced Woodland Sheep, for example, and the farm also safeguards all seven breeds of rare British pigs.

The farm has been approved by the Rare Breeds Survival Trust since 1994 and is the only farm in East Yorkshire to achieve this accolade. Enormously popular with children, the 60-acre farm is home to more than 50 varieties of farm animals. There are daily milking demonstrations, seasonal events such as sheep-clipping and harvesting, and a children's paddock with hand-reared small animals where the undoubted star is Cecil the Vietnamese pot-bellied pig.

GREAT DRIFFIELD

Located on the edge of the Wolds, Great Driffield is a busy little market town at the heart of an important corn growing area. A cattle market is held here every Thursday; a general market on both Thursday and Saturday, and the annual agricultural show has been going strong since 1854. All Saints Parish Church, dating back to the 12th century, has one of the highest towers in the county and some lovely stained glass windows portraying local nobility.

Driffield has expanded westwards to meet up with its smaller neighbour, Little Driffield. A tablet in the church here claims that, in the Saxon monastery that stood on this site, Aldred, King of Northumbria was buried in AD 705 after being wounded in a battle against the Danes.

AROUND GREAT DRIFFIELD

SLEDMERE

7 miles NW of Driffield on the B1252/B1253

Sledmere House (see panel) is a noble Georgian mansion built by the Sykes family in the 1750s when this area was still a wilderness infested with packs of marauding wolves. Inside, there is fine furniture by Chippendale and Sheraton, and decorated plasterwork by Joseph Rose. The copy of a naked, and well-endowed, Apollo Belvedere in the landing alcove must have caused many a maidenly blush in Victorian times, and the Turkish Room – inspired by the Sultan's salon in Istanbul's Valideh Mosque – is a dazzling example of oriental opulence. Outside, the gardens and the 220 acres of parkland were landscaped by Capability Brown.

The Sykes family set a shining example to other landowners in the Wolds by agricultural improvements that transformed a 'blank and barren tract of land' into one of the most productive and best cultivated districts in the county. They founded the famous Sledmere Stud, and the second Sir Tatton Sykes spent nearly two million pounds on building and restoring churches in the area. Sledmere House itself was ravaged by fire in 1911. Sir Tatton was enjoying his favourite lunchtime dessert of rice pudding when a servant rushed in with news of the fire and urged him to leave the house. 'First, I must finish my pudding, finish my pudding,' he declared, and did so. An armchair was set up for him on the lawn and Sir Tatton, then 85 years old, 'followed the progress of the conflagration' as the household staff laboured to rescue the house's many treasures. After the fire, Sledmere was quickly restored and the Sykes family is still in residence. The house is open to the public and music lovers should make sure they visit between 2 and 4pm on Wednesday or Sunday when the enormous pipe organ is being played.

Across the road from Sledmere House are two remarkable, elaborately detailed, monuments. The **Eleanor Cross** – modelled on those set up by Edward I in memory of his Queen, was erected by Sir Tatton Sykes in 1900; the **Wagoners Memorial** designed by Sir Mark Sykes, commemorates the 1000-strong company of men he raised from the Wolds during the First World War. Their knowledge of horses was invaluable in their role as members of the Army Service Corps. The finely-carved monument is like a 'storyboard', its panels depicting the Wagoners' varied duties during the war. In the main house itself, a recently re-designed exhibit tells the story of the Wagoners Special Reserve through old photographs, memorabilia and some of the medals they were awarded.

HUGGATE

10 miles W of Great Driffield off the B1246 or B1248

Huggate is tucked away deep in the heart of the Wolds with two long-

121 SLEDMERE HOUSE

Sledmere

There has been a **manor house** at Sledmere since medieval times. The present house was built in 1751 by Sir Christopher Sykes 2nd Baronet.

🏛 see page 288

122 THE OLD MILL HOTEL & RESTAURANT

Langtoft

This family-run hotel and restaurant extends a warm welcome, excellent homemade food and a peaceful and tranquil setting.

🛏 ¶ see page 288

131

Millington

Traditional village inn serving appetising food and real ales; superb beer garden.

see page 289

124 QUEENS HEAD

Kickburn

Set in the beautiful and peaceful Yorkshire Wolds, the Queens Head offers some of the best home-cooked food around.

see page 290

Saxon Cross, Nunburnholme

132

distance walks, the Minster Way and the Wolds Way, skirting it to the north and south. The village clusters around a large green with a well which is claimed to be the deepest in England.

About 4 miles south of Huggate, in the pretty village of Warter, is where the 'oldest horse race in England' has its winning post. The post is inscribed with the date 1519, the year in which the **Kipling Cotes Derby** was first run. This demanding steeple chase passes through several parishes and is still held annually on the third Thursday in March.

KIRKBURN

3 miles SW of Driffield on the A614

The architectural guru Nikolaus Pevsner considered **St Mary's Church** in Kirkburn to be one of the two best Norman parish churches in the East Riding. Dating from 1119, the church has an unusual tower staircase, a richly carved and decorated Victorian screen, and a spectacular early Norman font covered with carved symbolic figures.

NUNBURNHOLME

13 miles SW of Great Driffield off the A1079

This small village close to the Yorkshire Wolds Way was named after the Benedictine nuns who first settled here. The village church is well worth a visit as just inside is a 1000-year-old **Saxon Cross** elaborately carved with arches, animals and representations of the Madonna. It was also here that the famous ornithologist the Reverend Francis Orpen Morris was born. Heavily influenced by the 18th-century naturalist Gilbert White, Morris penned the multi-volumed *History of British Birds*.

POCKLINGTON

14 miles SW of Great Driffield off the A1079

Set amidst rich agricultural land with the Wolds rising to the east, Pocklington is a lively market town with an unusual layout of twisting alleys running off the marketplace. Its splendid church, mostly 15th century but with fragments of an earlier Norman building, certainly justifies its title as the Cathedral of the Wolds (although strictly speaking Pocklington is just outside the Wolds). William Wilberforce went to the old grammar school here and, a more dubious claim to fame, the last burning of a witch in England took place in Pocklington in 1630.

Founded in Anglo-Saxon times by 'Pocela's people', by the time the *Domesday Book* was compiled Pocklington was recorded as one of the only two boroughs in the East Riding. A market followed in the 13th century, but it was the building in 1815 of a canal linking the town to the River Ouse, and the later arrival of the railway, that set the seal on the town's prosperity.

The people of Pocklington have good reason to be grateful to Major P. M. Stewart who, on his death in 1962, bequeathed **Burnby Hall and Gardens** to the town.

The eight acres of gardens are world-famous for the rare collection of water-lilies planted in the two large lakes. There are some 80 varieties and in the main flowering season from July to early September they present a dazzling spectacle. The Major and his wife had travelled extensively before settling down at Burnby and there's a small museum in the Hall displaying his collection of sporting trophies. On Sunday afternoons, the Gardens are the venue for concerts given by some of Yorkshire's most popular bands.

A mile outside the town is **Kilnwick Percy Hall**, a magnificent Georgian mansion of 1784 built for the Lord of the Manor of Pocklington. It now houses the Madhyamaka Centre, the largest Buddhist settlement in the western world. Visitors can stay in converted stables at the Hall, either to take part in one of the residential courses or to use as a base for exploring the area. There's a modest charge for full board; smoking and drinking alcohol are not allowed.

A few miles to the south of Pocklington is **Londesborough Park,** a 400-acre estate which was once owned by the legendary railway entrepreneur, George Hudson. He had the York to Market Weighton railway diverted here so that he could build himself a comfortable private station. The railway has now disappeared but part of its route is included in the popular long-distance footpath, the Wolds Way.

GOODMANHAM

14 miles SW of Driffield off the A1079

Goodmanham is always mentioned in accounts of early Christianity in northern England. During Saxon times, according to the Venerable Bede, there was a pagan temple at Goodmanham. In AD 627 its priest, Coifu, was converted to the Christian faith and with his own hands destroyed the heathen shrine. Coifu's conversion so impressed Edwin, King of Northumbria, that he also was baptised and made Christianity the official religion of his kingdom. Other versions of the story attribute King Edwin's conversion to a different cause. They say he was hopelessly enamoured of the beautiful Princess Aethelburh, daughter of the King of Kent. Aethelburh, however, was a Christian and she refused to marry Edwin until he had adopted her faith.

MARKET WEIGHTON

16 miles SW of Driffield on the A614/A1069

Recorded in the *Domesday Book* as 'Wicstun', Market Weighton is a busy little town where mellow 18th-century houses cluster around an early Norman church. Buried somewhere in the churchyard is William Bradley who was born at Market Weighton in 1787 and grew up to become the tallest man in England. He stood 7 feet 8 inches high and weighed 27 stones. William made a fortune by travelling the country and placing himself on display. He was even received at Court by George III

125 THE WICSTUN CAFÉ

Market Weighton

Popular town centre eating place serving delicious home-baked cakes, pies and puddings, as well as cooked meals.

see page 291

who, taking a fancy to the giant, gave him a huge gold watch to wear across his chest.

SOUTH DALTON

13 miles SW of Driffield off the B1248

The most prominent church in East Yorkshire, **St Mary's Church**, has a soaring spire more than 200 feet high, an unmistakable landmark that has been described as 'an arrow in the breast of the Wold'. Built in 1861 for Lord Beaumont Hotham, the church was designed by the famous Victorian architect JL Pearson and is regarded as one of his best works.

North Bar, Beverley

BEVERLEY

'For those who do not know this town, there is a great surprise in store ... Beverley is made for walking and living in.' Such was the considered opinion of the late Poet Laureate, John Betjeman. In medieval times, Beverley was one of England's most prosperous towns and it remains one of the most gracious. Its greatest glory is the **Minster** whose twin towers, built in glowing magnesian limestone, soar above this, the oldest town in East Yorkshire. More than two centuries in the making, from around 1220 to 1450, the Minster provides a textbook demonstration of the evolving architectural styles of those years. Among its many treasures are superb, fine wood carvings from the Ripon school, and a 1,000-year-old *fridstol*, or sanctuary seat. Carved from a single block of stone, the fridstol is a relic from the earlier Saxon church on this site. Under Saxon law, the fridstol provided refuge for any offender who managed to reach it. The canons would then try to resolve the dispute between the fugitive and his pursuer. If after 30 days no solution had been found, the seeker of sanctuary was given safe escort to the county boundary or the nearest port. The custom survived right up until Henry VIII's closure of the monasteries.

Unlike the plain-cut fridstol, the canopy of the 14th-century Percy Shrine is prodigal in its ornamentation – 'the finest piece of work of the finest craftsmen of the finest period in British building.' The behaviour of some visitors to this glorious Shrine was not, it seems, always as reverent as it might have been. When Celia Fiennes toured the Minster in 1697 she recorded that the tomb of 'Great Percy, Earle of Northumberland was a little fallen in and a hole so bigg as many put their hands in and touch'd the body which was much of it entire.' Great Percy's remains are now decently concealed once again.

As well as the incomparable stone carvings on the shrine, the Minster also has a wealth of wonderful carvings in wood. Seek out those representing Stomach Ache, Toothache, Sciatica and Lumbago – four afflictions probably almost as fearsome to medieval people as the Four Riders of the Apocalypse.

Close by is the **North Bar,** the only one of the town's five medieval gatehouses to have survived. Unlike many towns in the Middle Ages, Beverley did not have an encircling wall. Instead, the town fathers had a deep ditch excavated around it so that all goods had to pass through one of the gates and pay a toll. North Bar was built in 1409 and, with headroom of little more than 10 feet, is something of a traffic hazard, albeit a very attractive one. Next door is Bar House, in which Charles I and his sons stayed in the 1630s. Another visitor to the town, famous for very different reasons, was the highwayman Dick Turpin who, in

1739, was brought before a magistrates' hearing conducted at one of the town's inns. That inn has long since gone and its site is now occupied by the Beverley Arms.

St Mary's Church, just across the road from the Beverley Arms, tends to be overshadowed by the glories of Beverley Minster. But this is another superb medieval building, richly endowed with fine carvings, many brightly coloured, and striking sculptures. A series of ceiling panels depicts all the Kings of England from Sigebert (AD 623-37) to Henry VI. Originally, four legendary kings were also included, but one of them was replaced in recent times by a portrait of George VI. Lewis Carroll visited St Mary's when he stayed with friends in the town and was very taken with a stone carving of a rabbit – the inspiration, it is believed, for the March Hare in *Alice in Wonderland.* Certainly the carving bears an uncanny resemblance to Tenniel's famous drawing of the Mad Hatter.

The wide market square in the heart of the town is graced by an elegant **Market Cross,** a circular pillared building rather like a small Greek temple. It bears the arms of Queen Anne in whose reign it was built at the expense of the town's two Members of Parliament. At that time of course parliamentary elections were flagrantly corrupt but at Beverley the tradition continued longer than in most places – in 1868 the author Anthony Trollope stood as a

126 THE WOOLPACK INN

Beverley

Fine old traditional inn with appetising home-cooked food and half a dozen real ales; regular entertainment.

see page 291

127 GINGERS

Beverley

Gingers offers a truly enticing array of superb home baking with scones as the speciality of the house.

see page 292

128 THE POPPY SEED

Beverley

Outstanding delicatessen and coffee shop serving quality home-cooked food prepared to the highest standards.

see page 292

Bishop Burton, nr Beverley

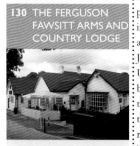

129 HALF MOON INN

Skidby

Delightful former coaching inn serving appetising cuisine and real ales.

❚❚ see page 292

130 THE FERGUSON FAWSITT ARMS AND COUNTRY LODGE

Walkington

Offers first class food, warm friendly service and excellent facilities, as well new luxury en-suite bedrooms, including a honeymoon suite.

❚❚ ⊨ see page 293

candidate here but was defeated in what was acknowledged as a breathtakingly fraudulent election.

The Guildhall nearby was built in 1762 and is still used as a courtroom. The impressive courtroom has an ornate plasterwork ceiling on which there is an imposing Royal Coat of Arms and also the familiar figure of Justice holding a pair of scales. Unusually, she is not wearing a blindfold. When an 18th-century town clerk was asked the reason for this departure from tradition, he replied, 'In Beverley, Justice is not blind.'

Beverley boasts two separate museums and galleries. The **Beverley Art Gallery** contains an impressive collection of local works including those by Frederick Elwell

RA and the **East Yorkshire Regimental Museum** has six rooms of exhibits chronicling the area's long association with the regiment.

Walkington village, just a mile or so southwest of the town, hosts the **Walkington Victorian Hayride** on the 3rd Sunday of June each year. A colourful parade of heavy and light horses with wagons and carts processes through the village accompanied by villagers in Victorian costume. The event reflects past times when the community would travel in wagons to the coast for a day out at the end of hay-making.

From Beverley, serious walkers might care to follow some or all of the 15-mile **Hudson Way**, a level route that follows the track of the old railway from Beverley to Market Weighton. The route wanders through the Wolds, sometimes deep in a cutting, sometimes high on an embankment, past an old windmill at Etton and through eerily abandoned stations.

AROUND BEVERLEY

SKIDBY

4 miles S of Beverley off the A164

In the 1800s more than 200 windmills were scattered across the Wolds. Today, **Skidby Mill** is the only one still grinding grain and producing its own wholemeal flour. Built in 1821, it has three pairs of millstones powered by four 12-metre sails, each weighing more than 1.25 tonnes.

136

The mill is run, weather permitting, by the miller and mill volunteers between Wednesdays and Sundays, and produces various grades of wholemeal flour from East Riding-grown 'Hereward' variety grain, which is available for purchase in the mill shop, along with a wide range of souvenir and other items, and books. The Mill's courtyard contains various exhibits including a blacksmith's forge, and a café. At the side of the mill is a sheltered garden picnic area, Wildlife Garden and pond.

At the same location is the **Museum of East Riding Rural Life** where the farming year is chronicled using historic implements and fascinating photographs. The displays feature the Thompson family, who owned Skidby Mill for more than a century, and other local characters.

Skidby Mill, Skidby

HOLDERNESS

*Lordings, there is in Yorkshire, as I guess
A marshy country called Holdernesse.*
With these words Chaucer begins the Summoner's story in the *Canterbury Tales*. It's not surprising that this area was then largely marshland since most of the land lies at less than 10 metres above sea level. The name Holderness comes from Viking times: a 'hold' was a man of high rank in the Danelaw, 'ness' has stayed in the language with its meaning of promontory. The precise boundaries of the Land of Holderness are clear enough to the east where it runs to the coast, and to the south where Holderness ends with Yorkshire itself at Spurn Point. They are less well-defined to the north and west where they run somewhere close to the great crescent of the Wolds. For the purposes of this book, we have taken as the northern limit of Holderness the village of Skipsea, where, as you'll discover in the next entry, some early Norman Lords of Holderness showed a remarkable lack of loyalty to their King.

HORNSEA

This small coastal town with its Blue Flag beach can boast not only one of the most popular visitor attractions in Humberside, **Freeport**

131 THE ROSE & CROWN

Hornsea

Striking, medieval-looking town centre inn serving wholesome and appetising food and real ales; outdoor patio and regular entertainment.

see page 294

132 HORNSEA FOLK MUSEUM

Hornsea

Established in 1978, the excellent **Hornsea Folk Museum** occupies a Grade II listed former farmhouse where successive generations of the Burn family lived for 300 years up until 1952.

see page 295

Hornsea, but also Yorkshire's largest freshwater lake, **Hornsea Mere**. The mere, two miles long and one mile wide, provides a refuge for more than 170 species of birds and a peaceful setting for many varieties of rare flowers. Human visitors are well provided for, too, with facilities for fishing, boating and sailing.

Hornsea also has an award-winning promenade, a church built with cobbles gathered from the shore, well-tended public gardens and a breezy, mile-long promenade all adding to the town's popularity.

The excellent **Hornsea Museum** (see panel), established in 1978, is a folk museum that has won numerous national awards over the years as well as being featured several times on television. The museum occupies a Grade II listed building, a former farmhouse where successive generations of the Burn family lived for 300 years up until 1952. Their way of life, the personalities and characters who influenced the development of the town or found fame in other ways, are explored in meticulously restored rooms brimming with furniture, decorations, utensils and tools of the Victorian period. The kitchen, parlour and bedroom have fascinating displays of authentic contemporary artefacts, and the museum complex also includes a laundry, workshop, blacksmith's shop and a barn stocked with vintage agricultural implements.

In Swallow Cottage next door, children can undergo the Victorian school experience under the tutelage of 'Miss Grim' – writing on slates,

having good deportment instilled and, above all, observing the maxim 'Silence is Golden.' The cottage also houses a comprehensive and varied display of early Hornsea pottery, various temporary exhibitions, and, in summer, a refreshment room for visitors. Remarkably, this outstanding museum is staffed entirely by volunteers.

For a satisfying shop-till-you-drop experience, **Hornsea Freeport** – the 'Independent State of Low Prices' – is hard to beat. There are discounts of up to 50 per cent or more on everything from designer wear, children's wear and sportswear to chinaware, kitchenware and glassware. There are themed leisure attractions and bright, fun-filled play areas to keep the children amused. One of these, **Butterfly World,** is home to more than 200 species of colourful butterflies.

Just to the north of the town, **Honeysuckle Farm** promises a great day out for all the family. There are shire horses giving cart rides, other farm animals, indoor and outdoor play areas, woodland walks, picnic areas and a souvenir shop. There's also a tea room and an ice cream parlour selling ice creams made with milk from the farm's own Jersey cows.

AROUND HORNSEA

ATWICK

2 miles NW of Hornsea on the B1242

Like Hornsea, Atwick once had its own mere. Some years ago, excavations in its dried-up bed revealed fossilised remains of a huge Irish elk and the tusk of an ancient elephant, clear proof of the tropical climate East Yorkshire enjoyed in those far-off days. Atwick is a picturesque village on the coast, just two miles north of Hornsea. It has been a regular winner of local – and, in 1997, county – awards in the "Britain in Bloom" competition.

SKIPSEA

5 miles NW of Hornsea on the B1242

When William the Conqueror granted Drogo de Bevrere the Lordship of Holderness, Drogo decided to raise his **Castle** on an island in the shallow lake known as Skipsea Mere. Built mostly of timber, the castle had not long been completed when Drogo made the foolish mistake of murdering his wife. In the normal course of events, a Norman lord could murder whomever he wished, but Drogo's action was foolish because his wife was a kinswoman of the Conqueror himself. Drogo was banished and his lands granted to a succession of other royal relatives, most of whom also came to a sticky end after becoming involved in rebellions and treasonable acts. The castle was finally abandoned in the mid-13th century and all that remains now is the great motte, or mound, on which it was built and the earth ramparts surrounding it.

WEST NEWTON

5 miles S of Hornsea off the B1238

To the south of the village of West Newton is **Burton Constable**

Hall, named after Sir John Constable who, in 1570, built a stately mansion here which incorporated parts of an even older house, dating back to the reign of King Stephen in the 1100s. The Hall was again remodelled, on Jacobean lines, in the 18th century and contains some fine work by Chippendale, Adam and James Wyatt. In the famous Long Gallery with its 15th-century Flemish stained glass, hangs a remarkable collection of paintings, among them Holbein's portraits of Sir Thomas Cranmer and Sir Thomas More, and Zucchero's Mary, Queen of Scots. Dragons abound in the dazzling Chinese Room, an exercise in oriental exotica that long pre-dates the Prince Regent's similar extravaganza at the Brighton Pavilion. Thomas Chippendale himself designed the fantastical Dragon Chair, fit for a Ming Emperor. Outside, there are extensive parklands designed by Capability Brown, and apparently

133 THE BLUE POST

North Frodingham

Welcoming village hostelry serving excellent food and real ales; regular entertainment.

see page 295

Burton Constable Hall, West Newton

134 THE DACRE ARMS

Brandesburton

Captivating village hostelry rich in history and noted for its excellent cuisine and real ales.

see page 296

inspired by the gardens at Versailles. Perhaps it was this connection that motivated the Constable family to suggest loaning the Hall to Louis XVIII of France during his years of exile after the Revolution. (Louis politely declined the offer, preferring to settle rather closer to London, at Hartwell in Buckinghamshire.) Also in the grounds of the Hall are collections of agricultural machinery, horse-drawn carriages and 18th-century scientific apparatus.

The descendants of the Constable family still bear the title 'Lords of Holderness' and along with it the rights to any flotsam and jetsam washed ashore on the Holderness peninsula. Many years ago, when the late Brigadier Chichester Constable was congratulated on enjoying such a privilege, he retorted, 'I also have to pay for burying, or otherwise disposing of, any whale grounded on the Holderness shore – and it costs me about £20 a time!' The huge bones of one such whale are still on show in the grounds of the Hall.

WITHERNSEA

The next place of interest down the Holderness coast is Withernsea. Long, golden sandy beaches stretch for miles both north and south, albeit a mile further inland than they were in the days of William the Conqueror. Over the years, 22 towns and villages have been lost to the encroaching sea.

Withernsea hosts an outdoor market every Thursday, Saturday, Sunday and Bank Holidays, has a promenade nearly a mile long, and a beautifully landscaped open space, Valley Gardens, that has recently been refurbished.

The old **Lighthouse** is a striking feature of the town and those energetic enough to climb the 144 steps of the 127 feet tower are rewarded by some marvellous views from the lamp room. The lighthouse was decommissioned in 1976 and now houses two small museums. One is dedicated to the history of the Royal National Lifeboat Institution; the other to the actress Kay Kendall. Her grandfather helped build the lighthouse in 1892 and was the last coxswain of the deep sea lifeboat. Kay was born in Withernsea and later achieved great success in the London theatre as a sophisticated comedienne but she is probably best remembered for the rousing

Withernsea Lighthouse

trumpet solo she delivered in the Ealing Studios hit film *Genevieve*. The museum shows video excerpts from some of her most popular films.

South of Withernsea stretches a desolate spit of flat windswept dunes. This is **Spurn Point** which leads to Spurn Head, the narrow hook of ever-shifting sands that curls around the mouth of the Humber estuary. This bleak but curiously invigorating tag end of Yorkshire is nevertheless heavily populated – by hundreds of species of rare and solitary wild fowl, by playful seals, and also by the small contingent of lifeboatmen who operate the only permanently manned lifeboat station in Britain. Please note that this is a National Nature Reserve and a toll is payable beyond the village of Kilnsea. Access to Spurn Head itself is only on foot.

AROUND WITHERNSEA

HOLMPTON
3 miles S of Withernsea off the A1033

RAF Holmpton was built between 1951 and 1952 and started its operational life in 1953 as an Early Warning Radar Station. It was equipped with a massive Nuclear Bunker almost 100 feet below ground and covering nearly 35,000 square feet. This **Underground Bunker** is now open to the public with fully guided tours lasting about an hour and a half. The tours visit all the working and living areas as well as the Weapons of Mass

Destruction Gallery, all brought to life with films, shows and demonstrations.

PATRINGTON
4 miles SW of Withernsea on the A1033

Shortly after it was built, **St Patrick's Church** at Patrington was dubbed 'Queen of Holderness', and Queen it remains. "It sails like a galleon of stone over the wide, flat expanse of Holderness" wrote John Betjeman. This sublime church took more than 100 years to build, from around 1310 to 1420, and it is one of the most glorious examples of

135 THE RAILWAY

Patrington
Fine old hostelry in delightful village serving appetising food and real ales; patio and regular live entertainment.

🍴 *see page 297*

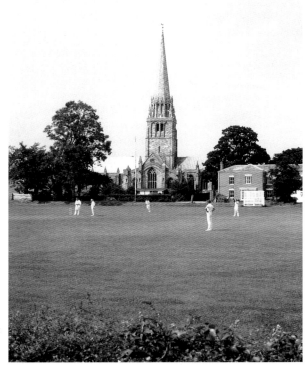

St Patrick's Church, Patrington

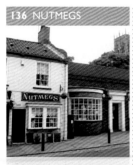

136 NUTMEGS

Hedon

Irresistible home cooking and baking in delightful town centre eating place.

see page 297

137 THE BARN FARM

Hull

Stunning converted farmhouse, with a popular Sunday Carvey and massive range of meals throughout the week

see page 298

the eye-pleasing style known as English Decorated. Its spire soars almost 180 feet into the sky making it the most distinctive feature in the level plains of Holderness. St Patrick's has the presence and proportions of a cathedral although only enjoying the status of a parish church. A parish church, nevertheless, which experts consider among the finest dozen churches in Britain for architectural beauty. Patrington's parish council go further: a notice displayed inside St Patrick's states unequivocally, 'This is England's finest village Church.' Clustering around it, picturesque Dutch-style cottages complete an entrancing picture and just to the east of the village the Dutch theme continues in a fine old windmill.

HALSHAM

4 miles W of Withernsea off the B1362

Halsham was once the seat of the Constable family, Lords of Holderness, before they moved to their new mansion at Burton Constable. On the edge of Halsham village, they left behind their imposing, domed mausoleum built in the late 1700s to house ancestors going back to the 12th century. The mausoleum is not open to the public but is clearly visible from the B1362 Hull to Withernsea road.

HEDON

10 miles W of Withernsea off the A1033

Founded around AD 1130 by William le Gros, Lord of Holderness, Hedon quickly became

a port and market town of great importance. Its market still takes place every Wednesday in the square with its row of Georgian shops and early 19th-century dwellings. Nearby, in St Augustine's Gate, is the handsome Town Hall, built in 1692. From time to time, the town's Civic Silver Collection is on display here. It includes the oldest civic mace in the country, dating back to 1415. The volunteer-run **Hedon Museum** (free) has displays of maps, photographs and artefacts relating to the history of Hedon and Holderness; these are changed regularly. Limited opening times.

PAULL

12 miles W of Withernsea off the A1033

Fort Paull's role as a frontier landing and watch point goes back to at least Viking times. Henry VIII built a fortress here in the mid-1500s; a second fort was added at the time of the Napoleonic wars. Charles I based himself at Fort Paull for some time during the Civil War; Winston Churchill visited its anti-aircraft installations during the Second World War.

Today, the spacious 10-acre site on the bank of the Humber Estuary offers a wide variety of attractions for all the family. In addition to the historical displays, including rare period and contemporary artillery, there are classic military vehicles, an array of waxwork creations, a parade ground where re-enactments take place, an assault course for youngsters, a Bird of Prey Centre, museum, gift shop, bar and restaurant. The fort is open seven days a week, all year.

HULL

During the Second World War Hull was mercilessly battered by the Luftwaffe: 7000 of its people were killed and 92 per cent of its houses suffered bomb damage. Then in the post-war years its once huge fishing fleet steadily dwindled. But Hull has risen phoenix-like from those ashes and is today the fastest-growing port in England. The port area extends for seven miles along the Humber with 10 miles of quays servicing a constant flow of commercial traffic arriving from, or departing for, every quarter of the globe. Every day, a succession of vehicle ferries link the city to the European gateways of Zeebrugge and Rotterdam. Hull is unmistakably part of Yorkshire but it also has the freewheeling, open-minded character of a cosmopolitan port.

Hull's history as an important port goes back to 1293 when Edward I, travelling north on his way to fight the Scots, stopped off here and immediately recognised the potential of the muddy junction where the River Hull flows into the Humber. The king bought the land from the monks of Meaux Abbey (at the usual royal discount) and the settlement thenceforth was known as 'Kinges town upon Hull'.

The port grew steadily through the centuries and at one time had the largest fishing fleet of any port in the country with more than 300

The Marina, Hull

trawlers on its register. The port's rather primitive facilities were greatly improved by the construction of a state-of-the-art dock in 1778. Now superseded, that dock has been converted into the handsome Queen's Gardens, one of the many attractive open spaces created by this flower-conscious city which also loves lining its streets with trees, setting up fountains here and there, and planting flower beds in any available space. And waymarked walks such as the **Maritime Heritage Trail** and the **Seven Seas Fish Trail** make the most of the city's dramatic waterfront. The tourist information centre also publishes a leaflet detailing the Hull Ale Trail, a guide to almost 30 of the city's hostelries. Remarkably, despite the battering Hull received in World War II, many splendid Victorian pubs have survived with their opulent furnishings and decoration intact.

138 THE DEEP

Hull

This award-winning Yorkshire family attraction is home to 40 sharks and over 3,500 fish.

🏛 see page 298

143

A visit to Hull is an exhilarating experience at any time of the year but especially so in October. Back in the late 1200s the city was granted a charter to hold an autumn fair. This began as a fairly modest cattle and sheep mart but over the centuries it burgeoned into the largest gathering of its kind in Europe. Hull Fair is now a nine day extravaganza occupying a 14-acre site and offering every imaginable variety of entertainment. That takes care of October, but Hull also hosts an Easter Festival, an International Festival (some 300 events from mid-June to late July), a Jazz on the Waterfront celebration (August), an International Sea Shanty Festival (September) and a Literature Festival in November.

Throughout the year, Hull's tourism office modestly suggests you explore its 'Marvellous Museums – Fabulous and Free' – a quite remarkable collection of eight historic houses, art galleries and museums, all with free entry. Perhaps the most evocative is the **Wilberforce House Museum** in the old High Street. William Wilberforce was born here in 1759 and, later, it was from here that he and his father lavished thousands of pounds in bribes to get William elected as Hull's Member of Parliament. Nothing unusual about that kind of corruption at the time, but William then redeemed himself by his resolute opposition to slavery. His campaign took more than 30 years and William was already on his deathbed before a reluctant Parliament finally outlawed the despicable trade. Re-opened in 2007 after a £1.6 million refit, the museum presents a shaming history of the slave trade along with a more uplifting story of Wilberforce's efforts to eliminate it for ever.

Other stars of the 'Magnificent Eight' are **The Ferens Art Gallery** which houses a sumptuous collection of paintings and sculpture that ranges from European Old Masters (including some Canalettos and works by Franz Hals) to challenging contemporary art; and the **Hull Maritime Museum** which celebrates seven centuries of Hull's maritime heritage and includes a fine collection of scrimshaw. A more unusual museum is the **Spurn Lightship.** Once stationed on active duty 4.5 miles east of Spurn Point, the 200-ton, 33-metre long craft is now moored in Hull's vibrant Marina. Visitors can explore the 75-year-old vessel with the help of its knowledgeable crew. Another aspect of the city's maritime heritage can be investigated in the **Arctic Corsair,** the city's last sidewinder trawler. Experienced guides recount the hazardous conditions endured by deep sea trawler men in the 1960s.

The city's noisiest museum is the **Streetlife Transport Museum** which traces 200 years of transport history. Visitors are transported back to the days of horse-drawn carriages, steam trains, trams and penny-farthing cycles. There are curiosities such as the 'Velocipede', the Automobile à Vapeur (an early steam-driven car), and Lady Chesterfield's ornamental sleigh, caparisoned with a swan, rearing unicorn and a panoply of bells to herald her approach.

One of Hull's largest and most impressive buildings is the Victorian **Guildhall** which houses a wonderful collection of paintings, sculptures, antiques, silver and the unique Hull Tapestry. And then there's the **Hull & East Riding Museum** where you can stroll through an Iron Age Village, visit a Roman bath-house, encounter mysterious Bronze Age warriors and inspect dinosaur bones. There are more relics of these ever-fascinating creatures at **Dinostar - The Dinosaur Experience.** The exhibition of fossils and dinosaurs includes a full size T-Rex skull and Triceratops leg bones you can touch.

At **The Deep** (see panel on page 143), the world's only submarium, visitors can have a close encounter with the ocean's greatest predator. There are some 40 sharks here and more than 3500 fish. In the Slime! Exhibit you can discover animals that ooze, stick and slide to survive. A recent addition to the displays is the ultimate shark film in 4D, a 20-minute spectacular with theatrical effects.

AROUND HULL

HESSLE

5 miles W of Hull off the A63

At Hessle the River Humber narrows and it was here that the Romans maintained a ferry, the *Transitus Maximus*, a vital link in the route between Lincoln and York. The ferry remained in operation for almost 2000 years until it was replaced in 1981 by the **Humber Bridge** whose mighty pylons soar more than 500 feet above the village.

It is undoubtedly one of the most impressive bridges on earth, and also one of the least used – someone described it as the least likely place in Britain to find a traffic jam. With an overall length of 2,428 yards (2,220 metres), it is one of the world's longest single-span bridges. For more than a third of a mile only four concrete pillars, two at each end, are saving you from a watery death. From these

huge pylons, 510 feet (155 metres) high, gossamer cables of thin-wired steel support a gently curving roadway. Both sets of pylons rise vertically, but because of the curvature of the earth they actually lean away from each other by several inches. The bridge is particularly striking at night when the vast structure is floodlit.

The great bridge dwarfs Cliff Mill, built in 1810 to mill the local chalk. It remained wind-driven until 1925 when a gas engine was installed. Although it is no longer working, the mill provides a scenic feature within the **Humber Bridge Country Park**. This well laid out park gives visitors a true back-to-nature tour a short distance from one of modern man's greatest feats of engineering. The former chalk quarry has been attractively landscaped, providing a nature trail, extensive walks through woodlands and meadows, picnic and play areas, and picturesque water features.

WELTON

10 miles W of Hull off the A63

A little further south is the pretty village of Welton where a stream flows past the green, under bridges and into a tree-encircled duck pond. It has a church dating from Norman times which boasts a striking 13th-century doorway and Pre-Raphaelite windows made by William Morris' company of craftsmen. In the graveyard stands a memorial to Jeremiah Found, a resilient local reputed to have outlived eight wives.

139 THE BLUE BELL

Cottingham
Attractive location, excellent menu and Specials Board, and Open Mic Night-everyone will love this!

see page 299

140 THE TIGER INN

Cottingham
Quality hospitality and regular entertainment, as well as freshly cooked meals (fish being a speciality), and delicious Sunday Lunches.

see page 300

The notorious highwayman Dick Turpin was not a local but his villainous, if romantic, career came to an end at Welton village when he was apprehended inside the Green Dragon Inn. Local legend has it that this establishment gave him hospitality before he was taken off to the magistrates at Beverley who committed him to the Assizes at York where he was found guilty and hanged in 1739.

145

141 THE TIGER INN

North Newbald

Delightful family-run village Pub serving excellent home-cooked food and real ales.

🍴 see page 300

BRANTINGHAM

11 miles W of Hull off the A63

The village of Brantingham, just off the A63, is worth a short diversion to see its remarkable **War Memorial,** once described as 'lovingly awful'. Conceived on a monumental scale, the memorial was built using masonry recycled from Hull's old Guildhall when that was being reconstructed in 1914. Various stone urns placed around the village came from the same source.

NORTH FERRIBY

18 miles SE of Pocklington on the B1231

It was here, in 1946, that some late Bronze Age boats dating from 890 BC to about 590 BC were found on the shore. Made from planks held together with strips of yew, they indicate that travel on the River Humber began much earlier than had been previously thought. A model of the boats can be seen in Hull's Transport and Archaeology Museum.

SOUTH CAVE

14 miles W of Hull off the A63

The village of South Cave is, officially, a town with its very own Town Hall in the marketplace. The name is said to be a corruption of South Cove since the southern part of the parish is set around a backwater of the Humber. The village is separated into two distinct areas by the grounds of the Cave Castle Golf Hotel. This building dates back to Elizabethan times and was once the home of George Washington's great grandfather.

SELBY

In 1069 a young monk named Benedict, from Auxerre in France, had a vision. It's not known exactly what the vision was but it inspired him to set sail for York. As his ship was sailing up the Ouse near Selby, three swans flew in formation across its bows. (Three swans, incidentally, still form part of the town's coat of arms). Interpreting

Selby Abbey

this as a sign of the Holy Trinity, Benedict promptly went ashore and set up a preaching cross under a great oak called the Stirhac. The small religious community he established went from strength to strength, acquiring many grants of land and, in 1100, permission to build a monastery. Over the course of the next 120 years, the great **Selby Abbey** slowly took shape, the massively heavy Norman style of the earlier building gradually modulating into the much more delicate early English style. All of the abbey was built using a lovely cream-coloured stone.

Over the centuries this sublime church has suffered more than most. During the Civil War it was severely damaged by Cromwell's troops who destroyed many of its statues and smashed much of its stained glass. Then in 1690 the central tower collapsed. For years after that the Abbey was neglected and by the middle of the 18th century a wall had been built across the chancel so that the nave could be used as a warehouse. That wall was removed during a major restoration during the 19th century but in 1906 there was another calamity when a disastrous fire swept through the Abbey. Visiting this serene and peaceful church today it's difficult to believe that it has endured so many misfortunes and yet remains so beautiful. Throughout all the Abbey's misfortunes one particular feature survived intact – the famous Washington Window which depicts

the coat of arms of John de Washington, Prior of the Abbey around 1415 and a direct ancestor of George Washington. Prominently displayed in this heraldic device is the stars and stripes motif later adapted for the national flag of the United States. Guided tours of the cathedral are available.

ROUND SELBY

RICCALL

4 miles N of Selby on the A19

The ancient village of Riccall was mentioned in the *Domesday Book* and has a church that was built not long after. The south doorway of the church dates back to about 1160 and its fine details have been well-preserved by a porch added in the 15th century. The village's great moment in history came in 1066 when the gigantic King Harold Hardrada of Norway and Earl Tostig sailed this far up the Ouse with some 300 ships. They had come to claim Northumbria from Tostig's half-brother King Harold of England but they were comprehensively defeated at the Battle of Stamford Bridge.

Riccall is popular with walkers: from the village you can either go southwards alongside the River Ouse to Selby, or strike northwards towards Bishopthorpe on the outskirts of York following the track of the dismantled York to Selby railway. This latter path is part of the 150-mile-long Trans Pennine Trail linking Liverpool and Hull.

Devotees of railway history will want to pay their respects to Selby's old railway station. Built at the incredibly early date of 1834 it is the oldest surviving station in Britain. From Selby the railway track runs straight as a ruler for 18 miles to Hull – the longest such stretch in Britain.

142 THE WHEATSHEAF

Sherburn-in-Elmet

Outstanding hostelry serving wholesome home-made food; lounge with SKY Sports and attractive beer garden.

🍴 see page 301

143 LA ANCHOR BAR & PIZZERIA

Hensall

This classy premises has an Italian style restaurant, where you can watch your meal being prepared from the open kitchen.

🍴 see page 302

144 THE ROYAL OAK INN

Hirst Courtney

Quality accommodation, well kept ales and super food, as well as a patio and pool table.

🍴 🛏 see page 301

SKIPWITH

5 miles NE of Selby off the A163

Just to the south of Skipwith, the Yorkshire Wildlife Trust maintains the **Skipwith Common Nature Reserve.** This 500 acres of lowland heath is one of the last such areas remaining in the north of England and is of national importance. The principal interest is the variety of insect and birdlife, but the reserve also contains a number of ancient burial sites.

SOUTH MILFORD

9 miles W of Selby off the A162

About nine miles west of Selby, near the village of South Milford, is the imposing 14th-century **Steeton Hall Gatehouse**, all that remains of a medieval castle once owned by the Fairfax family. A forebear of the famous Cromwellian general is said to have ridden out from here on his way to carry off one of the nuns at Nun Appleton Priory to make her his bride. He was Sir William Fairfax; she was Isabel Thwaites, a wealthy heiress.

SHERBURN-IN-ELMET

10 miles W of Selby on the A162

This attractive village was once the capital of the Celtic Kingdom of Elmete. Well worth visiting is **All Saints' Church** which stands on a hill to the west and dates from about 1120. Its great glory is the nave with its mighty Norman pillars and arcades. A curiosity here is a 15th-century Janus cross which was discovered in the churchyard during the 1770s. The vicar and churchwarden of the time both claimed it as their own. Unable to resolve their dispute, they had the cross sawn in half: the two beautifully carved segments are displayed on opposite sides of the south aisle.

WEST HADDLESEY

5 miles SW of Selby on the A19

At **Yorkshire Garden World** gardeners will find endless inspiration in its six acres of beautiful display and nursery gardens. Organically grown herbs, heathers, ornamental perennials, wild flowers and climbers are all on sale; the gift shop has a huge variety of home made crafts, herbal products, Leeds pottery and garden products; and the many different gardens include a Heather and Conifer Garden, an Aromatherapy Garden, an Open Air Herb Museum, a Lovers' Garden, and the Hall Owl Maze for children.

CARLTON

6 miles S of Selby on the A1041

A mile or so south of Camblesforth, off the A1041, is **Carlton Towers**, a stately home that should on no account be missed. This extraordinary building, 'something between the Houses of Parliament and St Pancras Station', was created in the 1870s by two young English eccentrics, Henry, 9th Lord Beaumont, and Edward Welby Pugin, son of the eminent Victorian architect, A.G. Pugin. Together, they transformed a traditional Jacobean house into an exuberant mock medieval fantasy in stone, abounding with turrets, towers, gargoyles and heraldic shields. The richly-decorated High Victorian interior, designed in the manner of medieval banqueting halls, contains a minstrels' gallery and a vast Venetian-style drawing room. Both Beaumont and Pugin died in their forties, both bankrupt. Carlton Towers is now the Yorkshire home of the Duke of Norfolk and is open to the public during the summer months.

In Carlton village the Comus Inn is the only licensed premises in the country to bear that name. It is believed to have been named after the Greek god of sensual pleasure, Comus, the son of Bacchus.

About 3 miles southeast of Carlton is the village of Drax which, as well as supplying Ian Fleming with a sinister-sounding name for one of the villains in his James Bond thrillers, also provides the National Grid with 10% of all the electricity used in England and Wales. The largest coal-powered power station in Europe, Drax's vast cooling towers dominate the low-lying terrain between the rivers Ouse and Aire. Drax power station has found an unusual way of harnessing its waste heat by channelling some of it to a huge complex of greenhouses covering 20 acres. Part of the heat goes to specially constructed ponds in which young eels are bred for the export market. Guided tours of the power station are available by prior arrangement.

GOOLE

10 miles SE of Selby on the A614

Britain's most inland port, some 50 miles from the sea, Goole lies at the hub of a waterways network that includes the River Ouse, the River Don (known here as the Dutch

145 BIZZY LIZZIE LICENSED CAFÉ

Goole

Popular eating place with extensive menu of wholesome home-cooked food.

🍴 see page 304

Goole Waterways Museum

149

River), the River Aire and the Aire & Calder Navigation. The **Waterways Museum** (free), located on the dockside, tells the story of Goole's development as a canal terminus and also as a port connecting to the North Sea. The museum displays model ships and many photographs dating from 1905 to the present day, and visitors can explore an original Humber Keel, *Sobriety*, and watch crafts people at work. There are also occasional short boat trips available.

More of the town's history is in evidence at **Goole Museum & Art Gallery** (free) which displays ship models, marine paintings and a changing programme of exhibitions. Other attractions in the town include its refurbished Victorian Market Hall, open all year Wednesday to Saturday, and a well-equipped Leisure Centre which provides a wide range of facilities for all ages.

HEMINGBROUGH

4 miles E of Selby off the A63

Anyone interested in remarkable churches should seek out **St Mary's Church** at Hemingbrough. Built in a pale rose-coloured brick, it has an extraordinarily lofty and elegant spire soaring 190 feet high and, inside, what is believed to be Britain's oldest misericord. Misericords are hinged wooden seats for the choir which could be folded back when they stood to sing. Medieval woodcarvers delighted in adorning the underside of the seat with intricate carvings. The misericord at Hemingbrough dates back to around 1200.

HOWDEN

9 miles E of Selby on the A63

Despite the fact that its chancel collapsed in 1696 and has not been used for worship ever since, **Howden Minster** is still one of the largest parish churches in East Yorkshire and also one of its most impressive, cathedral-like in size. From the top of its soaring tower, 135 feet high, there are wonderful views of the surrounding

Howden Minster, Howden

150

countryside – but it's not for the faint-hearted. The ruined chapter house, lavishly decorated with a wealth of carved mouldings, has been described as one of the most exquisite small buildings in England.

When the medieval Prince-Bishops of Durham held sway over most of northern England, they built a palace at Howden which they used as a pied-à-terre during their semi-royal progresses and as a summer residence. The Hall of that 14th-century palace still stands, although much altered now.

Howden town is a pleasing jumble of narrow, flagged and setted streets with a picturesque stone and brick Market Hall in the marketplace. The celebrated aircraft designer Barnes Wallis knew Howden well: he lived here while working on the R100 airship which was built at Hedon airfield nearby. It made its maiden flight in 1929

and successfully crossed the Atlantic. At the nearby Breighton Aerodrome is the **Real Aeroplane Museum**, which illustrates the history of flight through the work of Yorkshire aviation pioneers.

About four miles northwest of Howden are the striking remains of **Wressle Castle**, built in 1380 for Sir Henry Percy and the only surviving example in East Yorkshire of a medieval fortified house. At the end of the Civil War, three of the castle's sides were pulled down and much of the rest was destroyed by fire in 1796. But two massive towers with walls six feet thick, the hall and kitchens remain. The castle is not open to the public but there are excellent views from the village road and from a footpath that runs alongside the River Derwent. A fine old windmill nearby provides an extra visual bonus.

146 THE WHEATSHEAF

Howden

Exceptional choice of food and outstanding hospitality; both young and old are at home here.

see page 303

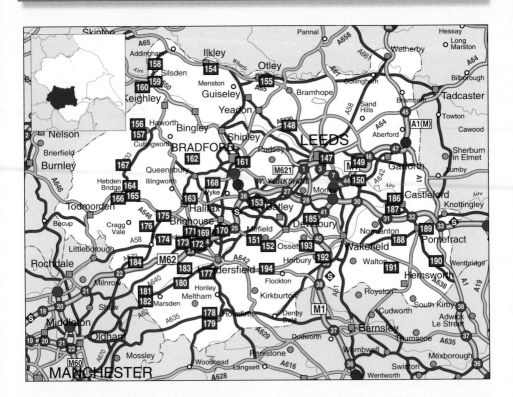

152

West Yorkshire

Smoking mill chimneys and bleak Wuthering Heights-style moors - the old perception of West Yorkshire is surprisingly durable even though most of the chimneys have gone and many of the mills have been converted into upmarket apartments. But although the Yorkshire woollen textile industry is now almost a thing of the past, the heritage of those prosperous days can be seen in almost any town or village of the region. The wealthy mill owners built grand villas for themselves and also contributed to the construction of the marvellous array of opulent civic buildings that are such a feature of West Yorkshire towns. Today, many of the mills which have remained redundant for decades are being put to other uses while places such as Bradford, Leeds, Huddersfield and Wakefield are finding new industries to take the place of the old. There is a wealth of interesting museums here that concentrate on the wool industry but there are also others such as the National Media

Centre in Bradford, that look towards the future. Coal mining, too, was a feature of West Yorkshire and the National Coal Mining Museum, near Wakefield, provides visitors with the opportunity to go down a real mine shaft.

West Yorkshire boasts several grand stately homes in the area, such as Temple Newsam near Leeds, East Riddlesden Hall near Bradford and the magnificent Harewood House, but the foremost residence that most people make a pilgrimage to in West Yorkshire is The Parsonage at Howarth. It was here that the Brontë family moved to in 1820 and, surrounded by the wild Pennine landscape, the three sisters, Charlotte, Anne and Emily, became inspired by their surroundings and wrote some of the most famous novels in the English language. Now a museum dedicated to the tragic sisters, this fine Georgian house is a starting point for a 40-mile footpath that takes in many of the places that feature in the Brontë novels.

147 HENRY MOORE
INSTITUTE

Leeds

The Henry Moore Institute in Leeds is a unique resource devoted exclusively to sculpture, with a programme comprising exhibitions, collections and research.

see page 304

LEEDS

In recent years, the city of Leeds has seen something of a renaissance. Its waterfront, neglected and derelict for so long, is now buzzing with new developments. Abandoned warehouses have been imaginatively transformed into fashionable bars, restaurants and tourist attractions, all less than 15 minutes walk from the shopping centre. Debenhams has recently opened a new flagship store in the heart of the city and other high profile stores are also flocking to the city. Perhaps the most talked about store is Harvey Nichols whose Knightsbridge emporium enjoyed a heightened reputation in the 1990s thanks to the BBC series *Absolutely Fabulous*. In parallel with these developments the Aire and Calder Navigation, which commenced construction in 1704, is being transformed to enable leisure traffic to use the waterway as well as freight.

The city is also a major European cultural centre with its own opera and ballet companies, Northern Ballet Theatre and Opera North, while the West Yorkshire Playhouse, regarded as the 'National Theatre of North', provides a showcase for classic British and European drama as well as work by new Yorkshire writers. The Leeds International Film Festival, held every October since 1986, has hosted major world premieres for films such as *Brassed Off*.

Leeds boasts some outstanding galleries and museums. Located right next to the monumental Town Hall, the **Leeds City Art Gallery** showcases an exceptional collection of Victorian and French Post-Impressionist paintings, along with major works by Courbet, Lowry, Sickert, Stanley Spencer and Bridget Riley. Linked to the gallery is the **Henry Moore Institute** (see panel), the first centre in Europe devoted to the display and study of sculpture of all periods. There's also a Craft and Design shop selling cards, jewellery and pottery; and an art library.

The **Thackray Medical Museum**, one of the largest museums of its kind in Europe, possesses more than 25,000 extraordinary objects in its collection. They range from a surgical chain saw and Prince Albert's Medical Chest through to a 17th-century correction frame. Visitors can listen in to the thoughts and feelings of a surgeon, his assistants and Hannah Dyson, an 11-year-old girl whose leg has been crushed in a factory accident, as they prepare for the amputation of Hannah's leg. Or you might prefer to walk through a giant gut in Bodyworks and find out exactly why your tummy rumbles.

Opened by Queen Elizabeth II in 1998, the **Royal Armouries** trace the development of arms and armour from the 5th century BC to modern times. The museum utilises interactive computer displays, videos, films, music and poetry to tell the story of arms and armour in battle, self-defence, sport and fashion. Outside, the Tiltyard features jousting and hunting tournaments daily from April to September, while a bustling Menagerie Court includes displays of falcons, hunting dogs and horses.

Leeds in the 1880s is the theme of **Abbey House Museum** where visitors can experience the signs and sounds of everyday life in Victorian Leeds, learn about a city steeped in history and walk through the carefully reconstructed streets of a once small market town. **Armley Mills,** once the world's largest woollen mill, is now an award-winning industrial museum. It contains exhibits dating from the 18th and 19th centuries showing the history of textiles, clothing, engines and locomotive manufacture in the area. The museum also illustrates the history of cinema projections, including the first moving pictures taken in Leeds, as well as 1920s silent movies. During the regular 'working weekends' several exhibits are operated including water wheels and a steam engine.

To the northwest of the city, **Kirkstall Abbey** is one of the most complete ruins in this part of Yorkshire. Building started in 1152 by the Cistercians and was completed within a generation, so Kirkstall is regarded by many as representing Cistercian architecture at its most monumental. It was executed with typical early Cistercian austerity as can be seen in the simplicity of the outer domestic buildings. The bell tower, a 16th century addition, was in contravention of the rule of the Order that there were to be no stone bell towers as they were considered an unnecessary vanity.

A few miles north of Leeds city centre, in Roundhay Park, is one of the UK's most popular garden tourist attractions and home to the largest collection of tropical plants outside Kew Gardens – **Tropical World**. Visitors can follow the 'Tropical Trail' into an Amazon rain forest where waterfalls tumble into jungle pools and birds of every hue fly through the trees. There's also a 'Desert World' and a 'Nocturnal House' where fruit bats, monkeys, bush babies and rock cavies reside – animals that can normally only be seen during twilight hours.

148 THE BRIDGE LOW LANE

Horsforth

Popular village inn serving quality food and a selection of real ales.

see page 304

Kirkstall Abbey, nr Leeds

149 TEMPLE NEWSAM

Leeds

Set in over 1,500 acres of land, this magnificent Tudor-Jacobean house is home to rich collections of works of art, and the superb gardens are a delight.

🏛 see page 305

150 HAPPY BUNNY CAFÉ

Rothwell

Family-friendly town centre café offering wide selection of hot and cold meals and snacks.

🍴 see page 305

A couple of miles southwest of the city is **Temple Newsam House** (see panel), often referred to as the 'Hampton Court of the North'. Set in 1200 acres of parkland (entry to which is free), this Tudor-Jacobean gem boasts extensive collections of decorative arts displayed in their original room settings. Among them is one of the largest collections of Chippendale furniture in the country. Adjacent to Temple Newsam House is the country's largest approved Rare Breeds Centre – **Home Farm**. Visitors to this working farm will see pigs, goats, horses and poultry alongside interesting displays of vintage farm machinery and past farming methods.

AROUND LEEDS

HAREWOOD

8 miles N of Leeds on the A61

One of the grandest stately homes in the country, **Harewood House**

was built at a time when many of the most illustrious names in the history of English architecture, interior decoration, furniture making and landscape gardening were at the peak of their powers.

For the creation of Harewood in the mid-1700s, Edwin Lascelles was able to employ the dazzling talents of Robert Adam, John Carr, Thomas Chippendale and Capability Brown. Edwin's son, Edward, was one of the first to patronise a young artist named JMW Turner and many of Turner's paintings are still here along with hundreds by other distinguished painters collected by later generations of the family.

Many of the finest of them are displayed in a superb gallery that extends along the whole west end of the house. Among the masterpieces on show are works by Bellini, Titian, Veronese, El Greco and Tintoretto, while family portraits by Reynolds, Hoppner and Gainsborough look down from the silk-covered walls of the opulent drawing rooms. Along with superb gardens, charming walks, a bird garden which is home to some 120 exotic species, an adventure playground, boat trips on the lake, and an extensive events and exhibitions programme, Harewood House is indisputably one of Yorkshire's must-see attractions.

BRAMHAM

8 miles NE of Leeds off the A1

Bramham Park is one of Yorkshire's most exquisite country houses and is special for a number

Harewood House, Harewood

of reasons. The house itself dates from the Queen Anne era. It was built for Robert Benson, Lord Bingley, between 1698 and 1710, and is superbly proportioned in an elegant and restrained classical style. The final effect is more French than English and indeed the gardens were modelled on Louis XIV's Versailles, with ornamental canals and ponds, beech groves, statues, long avenues and an arboretum with an impressive collection of rare and unusual trees. The interior contains elegant furniture and paintings by major artists such as Kneller and Sir Joshua Reynolds.

Lotherton Hall Estate, Aberford

ABERFORD

13 miles E of Leeds on the B1217

To the southeast of this village lies an elegant Edwardian mansion, **Lotherton Estate and Gardens**, providing a fascinating insight into life in those serene days before the First World War. It was once the home of the Gascoigne family who were local land and coal mine owners. They were also enthusiastic travellers and collectors with a discriminating taste that is evident in the family paintings, furnishings and works of art on display.

The house, gardens and estate were given to the citizens of Leeds in 1968 by Sir Alvary and Lady Gascoigne. Since then their collections have been added to and now include superb 19th- and 20th-century decorative art as well as costume and Oriental art. Other attractions include the Edwardian formal gardens, a walled garden with some quirky spiral topiary, a bird garden with more than 200 species of rare and endangered birds, a 12th-century Chapel of Ease, deer park and café.

BATLEY

6 miles S of Leeds on the A653

This typical industrial town is home to the **Bagshaw Museum** (free), housed inside a strangely Gothic residence in Wilton Park. The museum was founded by the Bagshaw family and many of the collections here were gathered by them on their travels, including items brought back from Alaska by Violet Bagshaw in her 100th year! There are all manner of exhibits, ranging from ancient Egypt to Asia and the Americas, displayed in the exotic interior of this Victorian house. The museum is currently closed as two new galleries are being built. It is scheduled to re-open in the autumn of 2008. In the park itself there are nature trails

151 CAFÉ BOO

Mirfield

Stylish eating place offering excellent range of appetising food; fully licensed and with regular Tapas evenings.

¶ see page 306

152 NOSH CAFÉ BAR

Mirfield

Popular town centre café and take out noted for its superb roasts and home-made pies.

¶ see page 305

and also the **Butterfly Conservation Centre** (free) which houses a rich assortment of butterflies, many of which are close to extinction in the wild.

Elsewhere in the town there is the **Batley Art Gallery,** which plays host to a changing programme of exhibitions that, in particular, feature local artists. In the historic Alexandra Mill there is the **Yorkshire Motor Museum** (free). The collection of cars on display here ranges from a Benz Motor Wagon of 1885 to the latest Ferrari F40. The museum also boasts the only surviving Bramham – chassis number 128.

BIRSTALL

6 miles SW of Leeds on the A653

This town is home to **Oakwell Hall**, an Elizabethan manor house that dates from 1583 and is one of England's most charming historic houses. Now set out as a 17th-century home, the panelled rooms

contain a fine collection of oak furniture, reproduction soft furnishings and items of domestic life. The gardens contain period plants, including culinary and medicinal herbs, while the grounds are now **Oakwell Hall Country Park**. Charlotte Brontë visited the Hall in the 19th century and it appears as 'Fieldhead' in her novel *Shirley*.

DEWSBURY

8 miles SW of Leeds on the A653

Dewsbury is an extremely old town which once had considerable influence. It has one of the region's oldest town centres with an imposing Town Hall designed by Henry Ashton and George Fox. It also has a number of other notable public and commercial buildings, a substantial shopping area (with some 443,500 square feet of retail floorspace) and a famous open market.

According to legend, **Dewsbury Minster** is situated at the very spot where, in AD 627, St Paulinus baptised converts to Christianity in the River Calder. The church dates from the 12th century although the tower was erected in 1767 to a design by the eminent York architect, John Carr. The interior has some interesting features, among them fragments of an Anglo-Saxon cross and coffin lids. The Minster is perhaps best known for its custom of tolling the 'Devil's Knell' on Christmas Eve to ward off evil spirits with a bell known as Black Tom. There are Brontë connections here. Patrick

Oakwell Hall Country Park, Birstall

Brontë was curate of Dewsbury between 1809-11, and Charlotte taught at Wealds House School nearby. The school was run by a Miss Wooler who later gave her away when she was married.

The **Dewsbury Museum** (free) is dedicated to childhood and takes visitors on a fascinating journey right back to the first decades of the 20th century, as seen through the eyes of a child.

GOMERSAL
8 miles SW of Leeds on the A643

This ancient village, which featured in the *Domesday Book*, is home to another house that featured in Charlotte Brontë's famous novel, *Shirley*. The **Red House Museum and Brontë Gallery** (see panel), which dates back to 1660, was the home of woollen cloth merchants the Taylor family, and the author often came here to see her close friend Mary Taylor in the 1830s. The house features as 'Briarmains' in the novel. Today the house is just as the two young Victorian ladies would have remembered it, and it portrays, faithfully, middle-class domestic life of the time. There is an elegant parlour and a stone-floored kitchen while, outside in the restored barn, the Secret's Out Gallery explores the author's connections with the Spen Valley.

ILKLEY

Originally an Iron Age settlement, Ilkley was eventually occupied by the Romans who built a camp here to protect their crossing of the River Wharfe. They named their town *Olicana*, so giving rise to the present name with the addition of the familiar *ley* (Anglo-Saxon for 'pasture'). Behind the medieval church is a grassy mound where a little fort was built and in the town's museum are altars carved in gritstone, dedicated to the Roman gods.

The spring at **White Wells** (free) brought more visitors to the town in the 18th century. A small bath house was built where genteel and elderly patients were encouraged to take a dip in the healing waters of the heather spa. Two baths were built here, one of which can still be used. Early Victorian times saw the development of the Hydros – hydropathic treatment hotels – providing hot and cold treatments based on the idea of Dr Preissnitz of Austria who, in 1843, became the director of Britain's first Hydro at nearby Ben Rhydding.

The coming of the railways from Leeds and Bradford in the 1860s and '70s, during a period of

153 RED HOUSE

Gomersal

This delightful house now looks very much as it would have done in Charlotte Bronte's time when she used it as a model for the Briarmains of her novel *Shirley*.

🏛 see page 306

154 THE DALESWAY HOTEL

Ilkley

Welcoming traditional town centre hostelry noted for its excellent food, real ales and quality en suite rooms.

🍴 🛏 see page 307

River Wharfe, Ilkley

159

Ilkley's patrons and well-to-do citizens gave the town a splendid Town Hall, Library, Winter Gardens and King's Hall and a sense of elegance is still present along The Grove. It is still a delight to have morning coffee in the famous Betty's coffee house and discerning shoppers will find a wealth of choice, some in a perfectly preserved Victorian arcade complete with potted palms and balconies.

growth in the Yorkshire woollen industry, saw the town take on a new role as a fashionable commuter town. Wool manufacturers and their better-paid employees came, not only to enjoy the superb amenities, but to build handsome villas. If Bradford and Leeds were where people made their brass, so it was said at the time, then it was usually at Ilkley that it was spent. Even today, Ilkley sports some remarkable and opulent Victorian architecture.

Between the remains of the Roman fort and the River Wharfe lie the **Riverside Gardens**, a favourite place for a stroll that might lead over a 17th-century packhorse bridge across the river. On the side of this bridge, beside the stone steps, the flood levels of the river have been marked, along with the dates. On the opposite side of the river is The Lido, one of the few surviving outdoor swimming pools in Yorkshire. Its idyllic surroundings and extensive terraces make it a popular place in summer. Next to the Lido is an indoor pool open all year round. From the Lido a footpath leads up to Middleton Woods, in May a sea of bluebells.

Housed in a building that dates from the 15th, 16th and 17th centuries, complete with mullioned windows, carved beams and an interesting wall privy, **Manor House** (free) tells the history of Ilkley from its prehistoric roots through to its development as a Victorian spa town. Upstairs is an art gallery hosting a programme of temporary exhibitions throughout the year.

A very different kind of museum, the **Ilkley Toy Museum** displays one of the finest private collections of toys in the north of England. Amongst the many exhibits are dolls, dolls houses, teddies, tin plate toys, lead figures and games.

One of the most famous West Yorkshire attractions has to be **Ilkley Moor**, immortalised in the well-known song. Like any of the Yorkshire moors, Ilkley Moor can look inviting and attractive on a sunny day but ominous and forbidding when the weather takes a turn for the worse. The River Wharfe runs along the edge of the moor and through the town of Ilkley which is clustered within a narrow section of the valley in the

Toy Museum, Ilkley

160

midst of heather moorland, craggy gritstone and wooded hillside. Few places in the north can equal Ilkley Moor or, more correctly, Rombalds Moor. The moorland, much of it still covered in heather, is also an area of national importance for its archaeology. There is a series of mysteriously marked **Cup and Ring Stones** dating from the Bronze Age. Almost in the centre of the moor is an ancient stone circle, no doubt a site of some religious importance. Only the keen walker is likely to find these, located high up on the moor, but there is a fine example of a cup and ring stone in the lower part of St Margaret's churchyard in Queen's Road.

Cup and Ring Stone, Ilkley Moor

AROUND ILKLEY

BEN RHYDDING

1 mile E of Ilkley off the A65

'A few weeks spent at Ben Rhydding seem to effect a complete change in the system', wrote one Victorian visitor to the spa. 'I have seen delicate women, scarcely able to walk feebly round the garden on their first arrival, become strong enough to walk to the Hunting-tower, a lovely point in the heart of the moor at some distance from the house.'

The original Ben Rhydding Hydropathic Hotel, opened in 1844 by a consortium of Leeds businessmen, was built in the Scottish baronial style so popular at the time. By 1908, interest in hydropathy had declined and the exuberant building became the Ben Rhydding Golf Hotel. Later it was turned into flats but finally demolished in 1955.

Athough the name suggests some Scottish connection – and the surrounding scenery certainly has a Caledonian grandeur – 'Ben Rhydding' is actually derived from nearby Bean Rhydding, or bean clearing.

BURLEY IN WHARFEDALE

3 miles SE of Ilkley on the A65

Mentioned in the Anglo-Saxon Chronicle in AD 972 as Burhleg and in the *Domesday Book* as Burghelai, Burley remained a small riverside settlement until the 1790s when the Industrial Revolution reached the village. Many of the terraces of stone-built cottages, designed for the mill workers, have survived and are now highly desirable residences. Burley's population has doubled since the 1920s but the Main Street is still lined with Yorkshire stone cottages and houses, and the surrounding hills frame every view.

Looking at a map of the area around Ilkley, many people's attention is drawn to the curiously named Cow and Calf Rocks which form a striking moor-edge landmark above Ben Rhydding. The Cow is a great gritstone outcrop concealing an old quarry, popular with climbers, while the free-standing Calf is a giant boulder.

155 THE RED LION

Otley

Popular town centre hostelry serving excellent home-cooked food at honest-to-goodness prices; regular live entertainment.

🍴 see page 307

•

An attractive feature of the town is The Chevin Forest Park, a forested ridge above the town which can be reached by a delightful walk that starts in the town. There is also a pleasant walk along the River Wharfe.

•

OTLEY

6 miles SE of Ilkley on the A660

Although it now forms part of the Leeds Metropolitan District, Otley has retained its distinctive character, still boasting a busy cobbled marketplace and many little alleyways and courtyards. Each May the Wharfedale Agricultural Show, founded in 1799 and the oldest show of its kind in England, is held in a nearby field.

Even older is Prince Henry's Grammar School, founded in 1602 by James I and named after his eldest son. In front of the building in Manor Square is a statue of Thomas Chippendale, the great furniture maker who was born in Otley in 1718. In 1754 Chippendale published *The Gentleman and Cabinet-Maker's Directory,* which was immensely influential in both Britain and the USA. His own workshop produced a comparatively small number of pieces but he gave his name to a style that dominated a generation and is still highly prized.

In addition to the statue on the front of the Grammar School, Otley's most famous son is commemorated by a plaque on the wall of Browns Gallery which records that Thomas Chippendale was born in 1718 in a cottage that stood on this spot.

Otley's parish church dates from Saxon times although the main body was constructed in the 11th century. An unusual memorial, close by, is a stone model of Bramhope Railway Tunnel with its impressive crenellated entrance

portals. It was built in the 1830s on the Leeds-Thirsk railway line and more than 30 labourers died during its construction – a tragic loss of life which the model commemorates.

GUISELEY

7 miles SE of Ilkley on the A65

Guiseley boasts the most famous fish and chip shop in the world, Harry Ramsden's. Harry's career as the world's most successful fish frier began in Bradford where he was the first to offer a sit-down fish and chip meal. He moved to Guiseley in 1928 and the original white-painted wooden hut, 10 feet by 6 feet, in which he started business is still on the site today. The present building holds its place in the *Guinness Book of Records* as the world's busiest fish and chip restaurant, serving nearly one million customers each year.

ADDINGHAM

3 miles W of Ilkley off the A65

Although Addingham dates back to Saxon times (it was named after a Saxon chieftain, Adda), the village enjoyed its greatest prosperity in the 18th century when no fewer than five water mills lined the banks of the Wharfe. Four of them were textile mills and no longer operate, but the fifth, a timber mill, is still working.

HAWORTH

Once a bleak moorland town in a dramatic setting that fired the romantic imaginations of the

162

Brontë sisters, Haworth has been transformed into a lively, attractive place, with wonderful tea houses, street theatre, and antique and craft shops, very different to how it must have been in the Brontë's days. It was then a thriving industrial town, squalid amidst the smoke from its chimneys, filled with the noise of the clattering looms, which were rarely still. It is worth exploring the ginnels and back roads off the steeply rising high street, to get a feeling of what the place was like in the days of the Brontës.

The Parsonage, built in 1777, is the focus of most Brontë pilgrimages and is now given over to the **Brontë Parsonage Museum**. The Brontë Society has restored the interior to resemble as closely as possible the house in which the sisters lived with their father and brother. There are exhibitions and displays of contemporary material, personal belongings, letters, and portraits, as well as a priceless collection of manuscripts, first editions, and memorabilia in the newer extension.

The Brontë family moved to Haworth in 1820 when their father, Patrick, took up the position of rector. Within five years, both Maria Brontë (the mother) and two of the five girls died; the unhealthy climate having begun to take its toll. Though all the remaining children did receive an education, it was in a somewhat haphazard way and they spent much of their time with each other isolated at the parsonage. After various attempts at working,

Brontë Parsonage Museum, Haworth

generally as teachers, the girls, and their brother Branwell, all returned to the parsonage in the mid-1840s and this is when their writing began in earnest.

Taking their inspiration from the surrounding bleak and lonely Haworth Moor and from the stories they made up as children, the three sisters, Anne, Charlotte, and Emily, under male *noms de plume*, all became published authors while Branwell, though by all accounts a scholar, sought refuge in the beer at the local inn. Then the tuberculosis that had attacked the family earlier returned and, one by one, Patrick Brontë's children succumbed to the terrible disease. The story of the Brontë family is

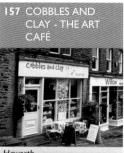

Haworth

Licensed town centre café offering appetising food and the opportunity to create your own pottery.

🍴 🏛 see page 308

•

The countryside around Haworth inspires the modern visitor as much as it did the Brontës. This is excellent walking country and it is worth taking a trip through the Penistone Hill Country Park, following the rough track by old moorland farms to the Brontë Falls and stone footbridge. For the energetic, the path eventually leads to the deserted ruins of Top Withins Farm, said to have been the inspiration for the setting of Wuthering Heights.

•

one of tragedy but the circumstances of their deaths were all too common in the 19th century.

Many visitors are drawn to the area by the story of the family and the **Brontë Way,** a 40-mile linear footpath with a series of four guided walks, links the places that provided inspiration to the sisters. The most exhilarating and popular excursion is that to **Top Withins**, a favourite place of Emily's and the inspiration for the 'Wuthering Heights' of the novel. The route also takes into account a great variety of scenery, from wild moorlands to pastoral countryside.

Brontë enthusiasts can also sit in the Black Bull, where Branwell sent himself to an early grave on a mixture of strong Yorkshire ale, opium, and despair. The Post Office, from where the sisters sent their manuscripts to London publishers, is still as it was, as is the Sunday School at which they all taught. Sadly, the church which they all attended no longer exists, although Charlotte, Emily, and Branwell (Anne is buried in Scarborough) all lie in a vault in the new church which dates from 1879.

As well as attracting devotees of the Brontë legend, Haworth is also popular with steam railway fans. The town is the headquarters of the **Keighley & Worth Valley Railway,** a thriving volunteer-run enterprise which serves 6 stations, most of them still gas-lit, in the course of its 4¼ mile route. The railway owns a large and varied collection of steam and heritage diesel locomotives and everything

combines to re-create the atmosphere of the days of steam. There are daily services during July and August, and intermittent services throughout the rest of the year. Many scenes for the classic film *The Railway Children* (1970) were filmed on the railway, mostly on the stretch between Keighley and Oxenhope. Oakworth Station in the film is indeed the actual Oakworth station, and the house of stationmaster Perks, played by Bernard Cribbins, is just over the level crossing.

AROUND HAWORTH

OAKWORTH

1 mile N of Haworth on the B6143

Those visiting Oakworth may find its Edwardian station, on the Keighley and Worth Valley Railway line somewhat familiar. In fact, not only did it feature in the classic film *The Railway Children*, but also in episodes of the TV series *Sherlock Holmes*.

HAINWORTH

1 mile N of Haworth off the A650

The **Worth Way** is an interesting five mile walk from the heart of industrial Keighley to the eastern edge of the Worth Valley at Oxenhope. This landscape has changed little since the time when Mrs Gaskell wrote about the area while visiting Charlotte Brontë in 1856. En route, the Worth Way passes close to the village of Hainworth which stands high on the hillside and commands some grand views of Harden Moor.

KEIGHLEY

3 miles N of Haworth on the A650

Lying at the junction of the Rivers Worth and Aire, this bustling textile and engineering town, despite its modern redevelopment, still retains a strangely nostalgic air of the Victorian Industrial Revolution. It was that era of rapid growth that created the town seen today, beginning at Low Mill in 1780, when cotton spinning on a factory scale was first introduced. Reminders of hardship endured by the many factory workers of that time can be seen in the labyrinth of ginnels and terraces which lie amid the many elaborately decorated mills. There are delightful carvings and on one early mill chimney are three heads, one wearing a top hat; in contrast is the classical French-styled **Dalton Mill** in Dalton Lane with its ornate viewing gallery.

Close to the town centre is **Cliffe Castle** which, despite its name, is actually a grand late-19th century mansion complete with a tower, battlements and parkland. It was built for local mill owners, the Butterfields, but now house the Keighley Museum which concentrates on the fascinating local topography and geology of Airedale as well as the history of the town. Also on display is the hand loom, complete with unfinished cloth, used by Timmy Feather, the last hand loom weaver in England. Part of the building is still furnished and decorated in the lavish style of the 1880s.

Keighley is the northern terminus of the **Keighley and Worth Valley Railway** which runs to Haworth and Oxenhope. This restored steam railway line passes through some attractive small villages and some notable stations complete with vintage advertising signs, gas lighting and coal fires in the waiting rooms. At Ingrow Station, **The Museum of Rail Travel** contains some fascinating items connected with Victorian travel, among them three small locomotives, coaches in various liveries, the clock from Manchester's Mayfield Station, an

The centre of Keighley is dominated by impressive Victorian civic buildings and a beautifully set out covered shopping precinct, where the statue of legendary local giant, Rombald, stands. The parish church, also in the centre, is famous as the site where Patrick Brontë often officiated at marriages. The graveyard contains 15th-century headstones, as well as a crude cross made from four carved heads which is believed to be Saxon in origin.

Cliffe Castle Museum, Keighley

interesting collection of posters and other memorabilia from the golden age of steam.

Celebrating another form of transport, the **Keighley Bus Museum** has a collection of more than 50 buses, coaches, trolleybuses and ancillary vehicles, mainly with West Yorkshire connections and dating from 1924 to 1982.

Above the town, by way of escaping the industrial past, one might enjoy a walk in Park Woods, taking the cobbled path to Thwaites Brow, which affords magnificent views of the town below.

SILSDEN

7 miles N of Haworth on the A6034

This well-contained stone built industrial town, which spreads uphill from the Leeds and Liverpool Canal, owes its development to the textile industry. Rows of terraced cottages and houses line the steep hillsides and there is newer housing on the outskirts of the town. It was the birthplace of Augustus Spencer, Principal of the Royal College of Art (1900-20), whose memorial can be seen in the 18th-century parish church.

Outside The King's Arms, in the centre of the village, stands an old mounting block, a survival from the days when this was a coaching and post house inn.

RIDDLESDEN

4 miles NE of Haworth off the A629

Parts of **East Riddlesden Hall** (National Trust) date back to Saxon times. The main building, however, was constructed in the 1630s by James Murgatroyd, a wealthy Halifax clothier and merchant. A fine example of a 17th-century manor house, the gabled hall is built of dark stone with mullioned windows, and it retains its original centre hall, superb period fireplaces, oak panelling, and plaster ceilings. The house is furnished in Jacobean style, which is complemented by carved likenesses of Charles Stuart and Henrietta Maria. East Riddlesden Hall also has one of the largest and most impressive timber framed barns in the North of England which now houses a collection of farm wagons and agricultural equipment. The hall is said to be haunted by the ghost of a lady dressed in blue who wanders along the building's passageways and sets the child's cradle rocking.

OXENHOPE

2 miles S of Haworth on the A6033

This village contains more than 70 listed buildings, including a Donkey Bridge, two milestones, a mounting block, a cowshed, and a pigsty. The early farmhouses had narrow mullioned windows which gave maximum light for weaving and some had a door at first-storey level so that the pieces could be taken out. The first mill here was built in 1792 and, during the 19th century, there were up to 20 mills producing worsted.

Many scenes for *The Railway Children* were set here in 1970 using local views and local people. A station on the Keighley and

Worth Valley Railway also serves the village.

STANBURY

2 miles W of Haworth off the B6143

Close to the village stands **Ponden Mill** which was, in the heyday of Yorkshire's textile industry, one of the largest working mills in the country. At the height of production, cloth from Ponden Mill was exported around the world. Though the vast majority of the mills have now closed and the Yorkshire textile industry is virtually a thing of the past, Ponden Mill is still open, this time as a retail centre selling all manner of textiles from home furnishings and linens to country clothing. To round off your visit, have a look in the clog shop where traditional methods of manufacture are still on show.

BRADFORD

Bradford is a city with much to offer the visitor. In terms of numbers, the most popular attraction is undoubtedly the re-named **National Media Museum**, which houses IMAX, one of the largest cinema screens in the world. If you suffer from vertigo you'll need to close your eyes as the huge, wrap-around screen shows such heart-stopping scenes as roller-coaster rides and Alpine mountaineering. There's plenty to keep you occupied here for hours – virtual reality exhibits, the Kodak Gallery which leads you on a journey through the history of

popular photography, an extensive TV display which ranges from the world's first TV pictures to the very latest, and much, much more. A recent addition is a vast new space presenting world-class exhibitions on photography, film, TV and new media.

A short walk from the museum brings you to Bradford's latest two cultural offerings, the **Impressions Gallery** and **Bradford 1 Gallery** which have changing programmes of photography and art exhibitions respectively.

Of related interest is Britain's only **Museum of Colour**. 'The World of Colour' gallery looks at the concept of colour, how it is perceived and its importance. Visitors can see how the world looks to other animals, mix coloured lights and experience strange colour illusions. In the 'Colour and Textiles' gallery you can discover the fascinating story of dyeing and textile printing from Ancient Egypt to the present day. Computerised technology allows

National Media Museum, Bradford

161 BOLLING HALL MUSEUM

Bradford

Bolling Hall offers visitors a fascinating journey through the lives and times of the Bradford families for whom it provided a home over five hundred years.

🏛 see page 310

you to take charge of a dye-making factory and decorate a room. Visits to the museum are by appointment only.

Occupying a spectacularly exuberant Victorian pile in Lister Park, the collections at the **Cartwright Hall Art Gallery** (free) reflect the diverse cultural mix that helps to make Bradford the vibrant and unique city it has become in the 21st century. From Victorian paintings and sumptuous Indian silks to works by David Hockney, this gallery is as interesting and far-reaching as the city itself.

Also in Lister Park is the most striking building in this city of impressive buildings, **Lister's Mill**. Its huge ornate chimney dominates the city's northern skyline and its claimed that it is wide enough at the top to drive a horse and cart around. The mill fell silent some years ago though its exterior has been cleaned up and it is currently being converted into up-market apartments.

The **Bradford Industrial Museum** (free) celebrates the city's industrial heritage. It is housed in an original worsted spinning mill complex built in 1875 and re-creates life in Bradford in late Victorian times. Open all year, the museum also offers horse-bus and tram rides, a shire horse centre, a reconstructed mill owner's house and the working men's back to back cottages. The complex also includes a café, shop and picnic area.

Bolling Hall Museum (see panel - free) is a primarily 17th century mansion house containing period furnished rooms as well as temporary exhibitions. The furnishings come from the collections of Bradford Museums, Galleries and Heritage.Unique in the UK, the **Peace Museum** (free) covers the history of non-violence movements and conflict resolution.

A rather quirkier sign of the city's former riches is **Undercliffe Cemetery**. Here the wool barons were buried, each in a more opulent Gothic mausoleum than the last. It is easy to spend an hour here admiring the Victorian funereal art on show with the cityscape laid out before you.

The fact that the city has a **Cathedral** is an indication of its importance. The first evidence of worship on the site is provided by the remains of a Saxon preaching cross. Today the cathedral contains many items of interest, including beautiful stained glass windows, some of which were designed by William Morris, carvings and statuary.

AROUND BRADFORD

SHIPLEY

4 miles N of Bradford on the A6037

Although Shipley town is mainly industrial, **Shipley Glen** is a very popular area for tourists. Within the grounds is a narrow gauge, cable hauled tramway, built in 1895, that carries passengers a quarter of a mile up the side of a steep hill, passing en route through Walker Wood, famous for its bluebells.

In Shipley itself, the **Saltaire Brewery** is a state of the art micro-brewery. It features a Visitor Centre with a mezzanine bar and an exhibition about the science of brewing.

THORNTON

4 miles W of Bradford on the B6145

Thornton is an essential stopping place on the Brontë trail for it was here that the three sisters were born, at No. 74 Market Street, now open to the public as the **Brontë Birthplace**. Their father was the vicar of Thornton and one of the treasures of his parish church is a font, inscribed with the date 1687, in which Charlotte, Emily and Anne were all baptised. Charlotte was only four years old, her two sisters still toddlers, when the family moved a few miles northwest to Haworth where their father had been appointed rector.

SALTAIRE

4 miles NW of Bradford off the A657

A UNESCO World Heritage Site, **Saltaire** is the model village created by Titus Salt for the workers at his mill. Salt was a very benevolent employer and determined to provide his workers with everything essential for a decent standard of living. Built between 1851 and 1876, the facilities in the village were designed to cater for all their needs – health, leisure and education, but there were no public houses. The spiritual needs of the work force were attended to by the elegant Congregational church which has been described as the

Shipley Glen Cable Tramway

most beautiful Free Church in the north of England.

A statue of Titus Salt stands in nearby Robert's Park (where swearing and gambling were banned) above the figures of a llama and an alpaca whose wool he imported for spinning in his mills.

Titus Salt's ban on the sale of alcohol in Saltaire has finally been overturned. The Victoria Boat House on the banks of the River Aire was built in 1871 but has recently been converted into a stylish bar and restaurant.

Also in Saltaire is the **Museum of Reed Organs and Harmoniums** which has a collection of around 100 instruments, including harmonicas and an American organ, which are demonstrated from time to time, and some of which are available for visitors to try. Original catalogues, posters, trade cards and glass plate negatives create a lively impression of the industry in its heyday.

Saltaire isn't completely locked in the past. The former Salt's Mill

162 GILLY'S FRIENDLY CAFÉ

Thornton

Warm and inviting long-established café with extensive menu of light meals.

see page 310

169

has been converted into the **1853 David Hockney Gallery** which displays one of the largest collections in the world of paintings by the internationally acclaimed artist who was born in Bradford in 1937.

HALIFAX

Halifax has been dubbed "the most complete Victorian town in Britain". Amongst its numerous impressive examples of municipal architecture from that period is one glorious building from the previous century, **Piece Hall**. It was originally built as a Cloth Hall housing some 300 merchants selling 'pieces' of woven woollen cloth. Today the Hall houses forty bespoke shops ranging from designer glassware to traditional and old-fashioned sweets. It

Gibbet Street, Halifax

possesses a large quadrangle where regular markets are held on Fridays and Saturdays, surrounded by colonnades and balconies behind which are some 40 specialist shops. On Thursdays a flea market is held here and there's a lively and varied programme of events for all the family throughout the season. There's also an art gallery with a varied

programme of contemporary exhibitions and workshops, a visitor centre, museum and tea room.

The **Town Hall** is another notable building, designed by Sir Charles Barry, architect of the Houses of Parliament, and there's an attractive Borough Market, constructed in cast iron and glass with an ornate central clock.

Halifax also boasts the largest parish church in England. Of almost cathedral sized proportions, the **Church of St John** dates from the 12th and 13th centuries although most of the present building is from the 1400s. It has a lovely wooden ceiling, constructed in 1635, and visitors should look out for 'Old Tristram', a life-sized wooden effigy of a beggar, reputedly based on a local character. It was designed to serve as the church poor box – and still does.

There are many hidden places in old Halifax to explore. From Shear's Inn, an old weavers' inn near the town centre, one can walk up the cobbled Boy's Lane, very little changed from Victorian times, or trace out the ancient *Magna Via*, a medieval path to the summit of Beacon Hill. In **Gibbet Street** stands a grisly reminder of the past – a replica of the Halifax guillotine, the original blade being kept in the Piece Hall Museum. Halifax appears to have been unique in using the guillotine to execute condemned criminals. It is reported that if the offender was to be executed for stealing an animal, the end of a rope was fastened to the pin holding the blade in place and tied to the animal, which was then driven off, causing the pin to pull out and the blade to drop. The use of the guillotine was first recorded in 1286; the last two offenders to die by this method perished in 1650.

Situated next to Halifax railway station, **Eureka!** is Britain's first and only interactive museum designed especially for children between three and 12 years old. With more than 400 larger than life exhibits and exciting activities available, Eureka! opens up a fascinating world of hands-on exploration. A team of 'Enablers' helps children make the most of their visit; there are regular temporary exhibitions, and the complex includes a café and gift shop.

Now a vibrant complex of businesses, galleries, theatre, and design and book shops, **Dean Clough** is housed in a magnificent Victorian carpet mill. Built between 1840 and 1870 by the Crossley family, this mill was once home to one of the world's leading carpet factories. It ceased production in 1982. The complex also includes artists studios and workshops, a café/bar and a licensed restaurant.

Shibden Hall and Park, about a mile out of town, is somewhere very special that should not be missed. The Old Hall lies in a valley on the outskirts of the town and is surrounded by 90 acres of parkland. This distinctive timber framed house dates from 1420 and has been carefully furnished to

reflect the various periods of its history. The 17th-century barn behind the Hall houses a fine collection of horse-drawn vehicles and the original buildings have been transformed into a 19th-century village centre with a pub, estate worker's cottage, saddler's, blacksmith's, wheelwright's and potter's workshop. The grounds of the Hall are now a public park with a boating lake, pitch and putt, children's playground and a miniature railway.

On the northern outskirts of the town is the **Bankfield Museum** (see panel), the home between 1837 and 1886 of Edward Akroyd, the largest wool manufacturer in Britain. He lavished money and attention on the building, transforming it from a modest town house into a magnificent Italianate mansion with elaborate ceilings, staircases and plasterwork. After his death, his sumptuous home became a museum and now houses an

163 BANKFIELD MUSEUM

Halifax

Set in a Victorian mill owner's house, there is an important collection of textiles, various objects from around the world plus a programme of exhibitions and activities.

🏛 see page 311

Eureka!, Halifax

First Bridge, Hebden Bridge

164 WHITE LION HOTEL

Hebden Bridge

17th century coaching inn with riverside location offering quality food, real ales and en suite rooms.

see page 311

165 COPA HOUSE

Hebden Bridge

Stylish town centre licensed restaurant/coffee shop offering imaginative cuisine.

see page 311

internationally important collection of textiles and costumes from around the world. Contemporary crafts are also featured and the museum hosts an interesting programme of temporary exhibitions, workshops, seminars, master classes and gallery demonstrations. Here, too, is a Toy Gallery, the Duke of Wellington's Regimental Museum and the Marble Gallery that sells contemporary crafts. Surrounding his house, Akroyd built a model village called Akroydon that, with its terraced houses, allotments, park and church was the first 'urban' village.

AROUND HALIFAX

HEBDEN BRIDGE

6 miles NW of Halifax on the A646

This mill town is characterised by the stepped formation of its houses which were stacked one above the other up the steep sides of the Calder valley. There has been a

village here for many years, centred around the crossing-point of the River Calder. When the first bridge was built is not known but as early as the beginning of the 16th century its state of repair was causing concern and, in a style typical of this area of Yorkshire, a stone bridge was erected close by. In the heart of the town, the historic **Hebden Bridge Mill** has, for almost 700 years now, been powered by the fast-flowing waters of the River Hebden. For more than four centuries this was a manorial corn mill before it was converted into a textile mill that was finally abandoned in the 1950s. Now lovingly restored, the mill is home to various stylish shops, restaurants and craft workshops.

The **Rochdale Canal**, which slices through the town, was completed in 1798. It was constructed to link the Calder and Hebble Navigation with the Bridgewater and Ashton canals from Lancashire. Used by commercial traffic since 1939, the canal has been repaired and sections of it, including that between Hebden Bridge and Todmorden, are now open to traffic. Motor boat cruises are available from the marina.

To the northwest of Hebden Bridge is the **Land Farm Sculpture Garden and Gallery**, a delightful woodland garden created over some 30 years from a barren Pennine hillside that faces north and is 1000 feet above sea level.

From Hebden Bridge a riverside walk leads to **Hardcastle**

Crags (National Trust, free), 400 acres of unspoilt woodlands encompassing deep rocky ravines, tumbling streams, oak, beech and pine woods and some of the best examples of upland meadows in the country. At the heart of the site is **Gibson Mill,** a 19th century former cotton mill. It went out of business in the early 1900s because it could not compete against the Lancashire mills with their better transport links. Its owners re-invented the mill area by introducing funfairs, a skating rink and restaurants. It has recently been redeveloped as an example of sustainable tourism. So the mill has no mains electricity, gas, water or sewers - the only outside service is the telephone. There are many hands-on family-orientated exhibits allowing visitors to learn more about the industrial and social heritage of the mill and the natural surroundings of Hardcastle Crags.

HEPTONSTALL

7 miles NW of Halifax off the A646

This picturesque hilltop village, one of the main tourist centres in Calderdale, overlooks Hebden Bridge and **Hardcastle Crags** (National Trust). Within this beautiful wooded valley there are several interesting walks along purpose built footpaths.

Occupying what was the village grammar school, **Heptonstall Museum** has a range of displays reflecting life in the area over the last four centuries. Two of the school's long black oak desks have survived, complete with graffiti, as well as the Headmaster's desk and a fine collection of Victorian school books. The story of the Cragg Vale Coiners is told, a tale of a small band of local men who produced counterfeit coins and committed murder to escape capture. Also on display are photographs from the Alice Longstaff Collection which gives unique insights into local life between the 1960s and 1990s.

Heptonstall is one of only three places in Britain where two churches occupy the same churchyard. In this case, the original church, which dates from 1256, was struck by lightning in the 1830s and a new church was built next to the ruin. Within the churchyard is the grave of David Hartley, the leader of the Cragg Vale Coiners, who was hung in 1770 in York.

Every year, on Good Friday, the **Paceggers Play** takes place in Weavers Square. It's an ancient method of story-telling with actors dressed in elaborate costumes recounting the legend of St George.

SHELF

4 miles NE of Halifax on the A6036

At Pepper Hill in Shelf a congregation was established in 1858 as a mission from Halifax. The building was built in 1861 and extensively rebuilt in 1936 after the roof collapsed. It is a simple building befitting its rural setting and has some attractive Art Deco 'Rising Sun' pattern windows dating from the 1930s.

166 WHITE LION

Heptonstall

Impressive stone-built hostelry serving quality food and real ales; regular live entertainment, and en suite accommodation.

see page 312

167 GRAIN FARM

Pecket Well

Quality bed & breakfast accommodation in Pennine farmhouse set amidst breathtaking scenery.

see page 313

168 THE WINDMILL INN

Shelf

Welcoming village inn with glowing reputation for superb home cooked-food and real ales; beer garden and children's play area.

see page 313

169 CAFÉ ETC

Elland

Popular town centre eating place serving great home-made food in comfortable and pleasant atmosphere.

see page 314

170 THE CLOUGH HOUSE INN

Rastrick

Popular village inn with pool room and beer garden serving quality food and real ales.

see page 315

171 CORNER CAFÉ

Greetland

Gem of a café and take-out with extensive choice of delicious home-made food.

see page 316

172 THE GOLDEN FLEECE

Blackley

Full of charm and character and enjoying breathtaking views, the inn serves a good choice of wholesome food and real ales.

see page 317

BRIGHOUSE

4 miles SE of Halifax on the A643/A644

Brighouse lies in the so called "golden triangle" commuter belt between Halifax, Ripponden and Brighouse with convenient access to the M62. Currently, there is an extensive programme of renovation of Brighouse mills which are being converted into loft style apartments.

The **Smith Art Gallery** is named after its founder, William Smith, Mayor of Brighouse in 1893. He was passionate about art and amassed a large collection of works that reflect the tastes of the late Victorian period, pieces like Atkinson Grimshaw's Mossy Glen and Marcus Stone's Silent Pleading. One of the two galleries displays his collection as a permanent exhibition; the other has a programme of temporary exhibitions, including work by local artists, as well as touring exhibitions by national and internationally renowned artists.

SOWERBY BRIDGE

2 miles SW of Halifax on the A58

Sowerby Bridge has a flower-bedecked canal wharf, a reputation as a gourmet destination, many specialist shops, an award-winning sculpture trail and, in the spirit of the times, a solar-powered market.

The town has a rather odd connection with the Brontës. For a while, Branwell Brontë worked as a booking clerk at the railway station here. He was dismissed in March 1842 when discrepancies were found in his accounts. Branwell also worked in the same role at nearby Luddenden Foot where he was a member of the library at the White Swan inn. (At that time, several hostelries provided this amenity for their patrons.) A condition of membership of the library stipulated 'sobriety and decorous conduct' on pain of a fine of 2d (0.8p) for each offence. This requirement must have caused Branwell some difficulty as he was a scandalously heavy drinker.

An important crossing of both the Rivers Ryburn and Calder in medieval times, and possibly as far back as the Roman occupation, Sowerby Bridge first had water-powered mills as early as the 14th century. The mills, first used for grinding corn, moved into textile production and by the 1850s were all steam-driven. Greenups Mill, built in 1792, was the first integrated woollen mill in Yorkshire with all the textile processes brought under one roof. Sowerby Bridge also boasted one of the first turnpike roads in Britain, constructed in 1735. Just a short time later the Calder and Hebble Navigation, surveyed by John Smeaton, the designer of the Eddystone Lighthouse, was opened in 1770, followed by the Rochdale Canal in 1804. A reminder of the busy days of the canal is **Tuel Lane Lock and Tunnel** which joined the two man-made waterways. It re-opened in 1996 and it is a grand sight to watch the narrowboats negotiating what is the deepest lock in the country.

RIPPONDEN

6 miles SW of Halifax on the A58

Ripponden lies in the valley of the Ryburn, a tributary of the Calder. An ancient packhorse bridge crosses the river and, right beside it, the Old Bridge Inn which is one of the oldest inns in Yorkshire. It was already in existence in 1313 and its interior, with its sloping floors and different levels, has been compared to a funfair crazy house. The inn hosts an annual Pork Pie Festival.

MYTHOLMROYD

5 miles W of Halifax on the A646

Prior to the 1600s, the valley bottom in what is now Mytholmroyd, was marshy and of little use as foundations for a village, though some of the outlying farms in the area date from the late 14th century. However, with the need to build more mills close to a supply of water, the land was improved and Mytholmroyd joined the age of the Industrial Revolution.

Each spring the town is host to the **World Dock Pudding Championships**. Dock Pudding is unique to this corner of the county and is made from the weed *Polygonum Bistorta* or sweet dock (which should never be confused with the larger docks that are commonly used for easing nettle stings). In spring the plant grows profusely and local people pick it by the bagful. The docks are then mixed with young nettles and other essential ingredients and cooked to produce a green and slimy delicacy the appearance of which is found by many to be rather off-putting. It is usually served with bacon after having been fried in bacon fat and is believed to cure acne and cleanse the blood.

Mytholmroyd is also home to **Walkley Clogs,** one of the last UK producers to make and sell the genuine article.

TODMORDEN

12 miles W of Halifax on the A646

This is another typical mill town that grew with the expansion of the textile industry. Before the 19th century, Todmorden had been a spartan place with many of the villagers eking out frugal lives by hand loom weaving. Following the building of the first mill here, Todmorden began to grow and the highly ornate and flamboyant public buildings were, in the main, built by the mill owners. Though many towns which owe their existence to industry also bear the scars, Todmorden has retained all its charm and character and is an excellent place to visit for those interested in architecture. It boasts a magnificent **Town Hall** designed by John Gibson and opened in 1875. One of the finest municipal buildings of its size in the country, the grand old building stands half in Yorkshire and half in Lancashire. So the ornate carving in the pediment represents the farming and iron trades of Yorkshire in the right panel; the cotton trade of Lancashire in the left.

173 THE DUKE OF YORK

Stainland

Spacious and impressive hostelry serving superb home-cooked food and up to 4 real ales.

see page 317

174 GRIFFIN INN

Barkisland

Family-run village hostelry serving outstanding home-made food and real ales.

see page 318

175 THE WHARF

Sowerby Bridge

Popular town centre pub with wholesome food, real ales, and regular entertainment sessions.

see page 318

176 THE ALMA INN

Sowerby Bridge

Outstanding traditional country hostelry offering fine cuisine, real ales and luxurious en suite accommodation.

see page 319

175

HUDDERSFIELD

Huddersfield is home to two canals that helped to link Huddersfield not only with the national canal network but also with other industrial towns. Completed in 1780 and paid for by the Ramsden family, the Huddersfield Broad Canal was constructed to link the town with the Calder and Hebble Navigation. The canal's Aspley Basin is today home to a marina. In 1794, work began on the Huddersfield Narrow Canal, linking the town with Ashton-under-Lyne. Its centrepiece, the Standedge Tunnel, took 17 years to complete and is the longest, highest and deepest canal tunnel in the country. The Standedge Experience at Marsden houses an exciting and interactive exhibition telling the story of the canal and the tunnel. The surrounding countryside offers a wide range of activities including walking, cycling and fishing, and this area of outstanding natural beauty is also a haven for wildlife.

Huddersfield's earliest roots can be found on the 1000-feet high Castle Hill which has been occupied as a defence since the Stone Age. Simple tools, flints, bone needles, combs and pottery dating back to 2000 BC have been unearthed here. The much later ramparts of an Iron Age fort, built here around 600 BC can still be seen. In 1147 the Normans repaired the earthworks and built a motte and bailey castle which was apparently used as a base for hunting. The hill was also used as a beacon when England was threatened by the Spanish Armada, and again during the Napoleonic wars. The lofty Jubilee Tower, built in 1897 to celebrate Queen Victoria's Diamond Jubilee, is the most recent structure on the summit and was funded by public subscription. Inside the tower there's a museum which traces the hill's 4000 years of history.

With its steep, often cobbled streets, millstone grit cottages and larger Victorian dwellings, Huddersfield has a very distinctive character all of its own. The town flourished in Victorian times and its most impressive buildings date from that era. The stately railway station was designed by James Pigott of York and built between 1846-50, to be followed by the Italianate Town Hall.

Back in the town, the **Tolson Memorial Museum** (free) has displays that range from the tools of the earliest settlers in the area to modern day collections contributed by local people. One of the most popular exhibits is the collection of vintage vehicles and motoring memorabilia in the 'Going Places' collection. Other displays trace the story of the Industrial Revolution, so important to the growth of the town, and the political protests it engendered.

Huddersfield Art Gallery holds the Kirklees Collection of British Art covering the last 150 years, with a lively programme of exhibitions that feature contemporary works from regional, national and international artists.

AROUND HUDDERSFIELD

FARNLEY TYAS

3 miles SE of Huddersfield off the A626 or A629

Farnley Tyas is another attractive Pennine village with scattered stone farmhouses and barns, and 18th- and 19th-century workers' cottages grouped around the crossroads. It is mentioned in the *Domesday Book* as 'Fereleia': the Tyas part of its name comes from the Le Teyeis family which owned much of the land hereabouts from the 13th century.

DENBY DALE

8 miles SE of Huddersfield on the A635/A636

Denby Dale is, of course, famous for its production of gigantic meat pies. The first of these Desperate Dan-sized dishes was baked in 1788 to celebrate George III's return to sanity; later ones marked the victory of Waterloo and Queen Victoria's Jubilee. The 1928 monster meal was organised to raise funds for the Huddersfield Royal Infirmary but the festivities were almost cancelled when the organisers discovered that a large part of the pie had gone bad. Four barrowloads of stinking meat were secretly spirited away.

Perhaps because of that mishap, no more great pies were attempted until 1964 when it was decided to commemorate the four royal births of that year. On this occasion two walls of Mr Hector Buckley's barn, in which the pie had been baked, had to be demolished to get it out. The most recent pie was made in 2000 as part of the town's Millennium celebrations. It weighed a hearty 12 tonnes and contained 100kg of John Smith's Best Bitter.

CLAYTON WEST

8 miles SE of Huddersfield on the A636

A popular attraction at Clayton West is the **Kirklees Light Railway**, a 15" gauge steam railway which runs along the old Lancashire & Yorkshire Clayton West branch line. The track runs through gently rolling farmland for about four miles with a quarter-mile long tunnel adding to the thrill. The large station/visitor centre at Clayton West provides passengers with comfortable, spacious surroundings to await their train or take advantage of the light refreshment café and the souvenir shop. The railway operates daily during the season and every

weekend throughout the year

ARMITAGE BRIDGE

2½ miles S of Huddersfield on the A616

This village is home to the North Light Gallery which concentrates on hosting major exhibitions of the very best in 20th-century and contemporary art while, throughout the year, the North Light Studio holds classes and a programme of weekend workshops.

HONLEY

3 miles S of Huddersfield off the A616

The centre of this delightful little Pennine village has been designated as a site of historic interest. There are charming terraces of weavers' cottages and lots of interesting alleyways, and the old village stocks still stand in the churchyard of St Mary's. The Coach and Horses Inn has strong connections with the Luddite movement of the early 1800s. It was here, in 1812, that two Luddites, Benjamin Walker and Thomas Smith, spent the night drinking after murdering a mill owner at nearby Marsden. They were later arrested, convicted and executed at York. Not far from the inn is another interesting feature – an old well dated 1796 whose date stone warns passers-by they will be fined 10 shillings (50p) for 'defouling' the water.

MELTHAM

5 miles S of Huddersfield on the B6107/B6108

A typical Pennine mill town, Meltham is mostly Victorian but with a handsome Georgian parish

177 THE SANDS HOUSE

Crosland Hill

Excellent traditional country inn serving outstanding food and real ales; beer garden and regular entertainment.

see page 320

178 LAST OF THE SUMMER WINE EXHIBITION

Holmfirth

Back in the early 1970s, the sleepy Pennine town of Holmfirth was turned head over heels by the introduction of three rascally men.

🏛 *see page 319*

179 HERVEY'S WINE BAR

Holmfirth

Quality wine bar also serving real ales and delicious home-cooked food; outdoor patio and host to annual folk festival.

🍴 *see page 321*

church dating from 1786 which is challenged in size by the spacious Baptist Chapel, rebuilt in 1864. Only two mills have survived but the Meltham Mills Band, founded in 1845, is still thriving and has won many competitions throughout the country, including the British Championship.

Meltham used to have an assembly plant for building tractors. The **David Brown Tractor Museum** showcases memorabilia and archives from the history of that once well-known company. The displays includes one of the first tractors built here in 1943 and also the last tractor built here. Limited opening times.

THONGSBRIDGE

5 miles S of Huddersfield on the A616

Upperthong, Netherthong and Thongsbridge derive the common element of their names from the Danish word 'thing' meaning an assembly or council. Thongsbridge is set beside a tributary of the River Holme and is very much a part of the *Last of the Summer Wine* country.

HOLMFIRTH

6 miles S of Huddersfield on the A6024/A635

BBC-TV's longest running situation comedy, *Last of the Summer Wine*, has made the little Pennine town of Holmfirth familiar to viewers around the world. Visitors can enjoy an authentic bacon buttie in the Wrinkled Stocking Tea Room, gaze at Nora Batty's cottage and sit in the famous pub. The rest of the town offers a network of side lanes, courts and alleyways while

the terraces of weavers' cottages are typical of a town famous for its production of wool textiles. In recent years, the influx of *Last of the Summer Wine* (see panel) tourists has generated the growth of a number of speciality shops and galleries, including the Ashley Jackson Gallery featuring the distinctive watercolour paintings of brooding moorland by the popular artist.

Holmfirth has a lovely Georgian church, built in 1777-8 in neo-classical style to the designs of Joseph Jagger. The gable faces the street and the tower is constructed at the eastern end against a steep hillside.

During the first half of the 20th century a comprehensive range of traditional saucy seaside postcards was produced by Bamforths of Holmfirth. The company also printed hymn sheets and, rather surprisingly, made many early silent movies. Bamforths also owned a cinema in the town which has recently been restored as **Picturedrome**. The re-instated building now hosts a wide range of film events and other entertainment, and also displays a selection of the vintage postcards.

As with so many of these moorland villages, there is a lot of surrounding water and in its time Holmfirth has suffered three major floods. The worse occurred in 1852 when the nearby Bilberry Reservoir burst its banks, destroying mills, cottages and farms, and killing 81 people. A pillar near the church records the height the waters reached.

HOLMBRIDGE

7 miles S of Huddersfield on the A6024

This charming village stands at the head of a steep-sided valley and enjoys picture postcard views of the Pennines and the Holme valley. There are cottages here dating from the 1700s and the area is known for its unusual style of architecture, four-decker cottages dug into the hillside. The lower cottage is approached from the front, the upper cottage is reached by a steep flight of stone steps leading round the back.

HEPWORTH

7 miles S of Huddersfield on the A616

What is one to make of a village that lies on the River Jordan, has a house that has always been known as Solomon's Temple (although no one knows why), and a parcel of land called Paradise, the only place it is said where fruit trees will grow? There are some other curious names here, including Meal Hill, where the Romans brought their hand-mill stones to grind corn, and **Barracks Fold** where, during the plague, the healthy barricaded themselves against the infected. There are still some triangular patches of land in the village that are believed to contain the common graves of the plague victims.

MARSDEN

7 miles SW of Huddersfield on the A62

Situated at the head of the Colne Valley, this village is an historic Trans-Pennine crossing point with the Standedge rail, canal tunnels and a packhorse route that leads out of the valley.

Situated above the village is the **Marsden Moor Estate** (National Trust), a tract of nearly 6000 acres of Pennine moorland that is full of industrial architecture. Public footpaths criss-cross this land which, as well as providing grazing for sheep, is home to numerous moorland birds including golden plover, grouse, curlew, snipe and twite. Meanwhile, the moorland's deep peat provides a habitat for acid-loving plants and for animals that can survive in this bleak and exposed environment.

SCAPEGOAT HILL

3 miles W of Huddersfield off the A62 or A640

About a mile south of the oddly-named Scapegoat Hill the **Colne Valley Museum** (see panel) is housed in three 19th-century weavers' cottages near the parish church. Visitors can see a loom chamber with working hand looms and a Spinning Jenny; a weavers' living room of 1850 and a gas-lit clogger's shop of 1910. On two weekends a year, a craft weekend is held when many different skills are demonstrated. Light refreshments are available and there's also a museum shop. Run entirely by its members, the museum has featured many times on TV and is open weekends and Bank Holidays throughout the year but party visits can be arranged at other times.

180 WHARFESIDE INN

Slaithwaite

Located in the picturesque Colne Valley, this cosy inn serves fresh food daily, real ales and has 4 en-suite guest rooms available all year round

🍽 🛏 see page 322

181 COOKHOUSE CAFÉ

Slaithwaite

Popular town centre café serving magnificent breakfasts and delicious home-made pies.

🍽 see page 321

182 THE GREAT WESTERN INN

Marsden

Former coaching inn in stunning location serving top quality food and real ales.

🍽 see page 323

183 COLNE VALLEY MUSEUM

Golcar

Set in three 19th century weavers cottages, the museum offers an insight into the life and work of the time.

🏛 see page 323

Chantry Chapel on Chantry Bridge, Wakefield

Many students of the Robin Hood legends claim that the famous outlaw had his origins in Wakefield. As evidence they cite the Court Rolls in which one Robin Hode is noted as living here in the 14th century with his wife Matilda. Also medieval in origin are the Wakefield Mystery Plays which explore Old and New Testament stories in vivid language.

WAKEFIELD

One of the oldest towns in Yorkshire, Wakefield stands on a hill guarding an important crossing of the River Calder. Its defensive position has always been important and it was the Battle of Wakefield in 1460, when the Duke of York was defeated, that gave rise to the mocking song *The Grand Old Duke of York*.

There are four main streets in the city, Westgate, Northgate, Warrengate and Kirkgate, which still preserve the medieval city plan. One of the most striking surviving buildings of that time is the tiny **Chantry Chapel on Chantry Bridge** which dates from the mid-1300s and is the best of only four such examples of bridge chapels in England. It is believed to have been built by Edward IV to commemorate the brutal murder of his brother Edmund. Grandest of all though is **Wakefield Cathedral** which was begun in Norman times, rebuilt in 1329 and refashioned in 1470 when its magnificent 247-feet high spire – the highest in Yorkshire – was added. The eastern extension was added in 1905 and was considered necessary after the church became a Cathedral in 1888. Other interesting buildings in the town include the stately Town Hall, the huge County Hall, the recently restored Victorian Theatre Royal and many fine Georgian and Regency terraces and squares.

Wakefield's cultural attractions include **Wakefield Art Gallery**, housed in an attractive former Victorian vicarage just a short stroll from the town centre. Collections include many early works by locally born sculptors Henry Moore and Barbara Hepworth along with important work by many other major British modern artists. Currently, work is well underway for the construction of a £26m art gallery and creative centre, The Hepworth Wakefield, which is scheduled to open in 2010. It will showcase the present gallery's treasures as well as the Gott Collection of more than 1200 images of Yorkshire.

Wakefield Museum, located in an 1820s building next to the Town Hall, was originally a music saloon and then a Mechanics' Institute. It now houses collections illustrating the history and archaeology of Wakefield and its people from prehistoric times to the present day. There is also a permanent display of exotic birds and animals garnered by the noted

19th-century traveller, naturalist and eccentric Charles Waterton, who lived at nearby Walton Hall where he created the world's first nature reserve. Also of interest is the **Stephen G Beaumont Museum** (free) which houses an unusual exhibition of medical memorabilia and exhibits telling the story of the West Riding Pauper Lunatic Asylum that was founded in 1818 and only closed in 1995. The exhibition includes restraining equipment, a padded cell, photographs dating from 1862 plus medical and surgical equipment and documents. The museum, which has a scale model of the early 19th-century building, is only open on Wednesdays.

Just south of the city centre stands **Sandal Castle**, a 12th-century motte-and-bailey fortress that was later replaced by a stone structure. It overlooks the site of the Battle of Wakefield in 1460. Such was this castle's importance that Richard III was planning to make Sandal his permanent northern stronghold when he was killed at Bosworth Field. Today all that remains are ruins as the castle was destroyed by Cromwell's troops after a siege in 1645. From the castle there are magnificent views across the Calder Valley. Discoveries made during recent excavations of the site can be found in Wakefield's new Interpretive Centre.

To the north of the city centre, **Clarke Hall** is a late-17th century brick-built gentleman farmer's residence with contemporary and replica furnishings and now used as a living history museum. Because of its size the Hall is reserved for use by school groups during term time. The gardens have also been restored in 17th century style and there's a modern visitor centre with exhibits and displays relating to the history of the Hall and its owners.

About 5 miles southeast of Wakefield, **Nostell Priory** is one of the most popular tourist venues in this area. The word 'priory' is misleading since it evokes the picture of an ecclesiastical structure. But Nostell is in fact a large Palladian building erected on the site of an old Augustinian priory. It was in 1733 that the owner, Sir Rowland Winn,

184 THE TURNPIKE INN

Rishworth

Recently refurbished country inn offering quality food, real ales and excellent en suite accommodation.

🍽 🛏 see page 324

185 THE STAR INN

Kirkhamgate

19th century inn with real charm offering first class cuisine and real ale; beer garden and children's play area.

🍽 see page 325

Nostell Priory

181

186 THE BOAT PUB & RESTAURANT

Allerton Bywater

Traditional country hostelry in lovely riverside setting serving quality food and real ales.

see page 326

187 THE NEW QUEEN

Lower Mickletown

Welcoming country hostelry in picturesque village offering quality food, real ales and regular entertainment.

see page 327

commissioned James Paine to build a grand mansion here. Paine was only 19 at the time and this was his first major project. Thirty years later, only half the state rooms were constructed and Sir Rowland's son, also named Rowland, engaged an up and coming young designer to complete the decoration. The young man's name was Robert Adam and between 1766 and 1776 his dazzling designs produced an incomparable sequence of interiors.

There was a third man of genius involved in the story of Nostell Priory – the cabinet maker Thomas Chippendale. What is believed to be his 'apprentice piece', made around 1735, is on display here – an extraordinary doll's house six feet high and replete with the most elaborate detail, every minuscule door, window or desk drawer functioning perfectly. Today, Nostell Priory can boast the most comprehensive collection in the world of Chippendale's work.

Another interesting piece of furniture is John Harrison's Clock. John was the son of Nostell Estate's carpenter and went on to solve the Longitude problem. The movement of the clock on display here is made entirely of wood.

AROUND WAKEFIELD

CASTLEFORD

9 miles NE of Wakefield on the A656

It was here at Castleford that the Romans crossed the River Aire and then built a fort to protect this important crossing. Sadly little remains of the settlement that the Romans called 'Legioleum', although archaeological finds from that period can be seen in the town's excellent Castleford Museum Room at the town library. Here, not only are these remains exhibited but there are also displays on the lives of ordinary people in Victorian Castleford.

The home of Allison's flour, which is still stone-ground on the banks of the river, Castleford was also, in 1898, the birthplace of the internationally-renowned sculptor Henry Moore. One of the most influential artists of the 20th century, the town has honoured its famous son with Moore Square, a fine area of York stone paving with a series of large stone archways that stands close to the place where the family's home once stood – the house itself was demolished in the 1970s.

NORMANTON

4 miles E of Wakefield off the A655

A former mining town, Normanton has a spacious park, a moat round a hill where the Romans built a camp, and a large, mostly 15th-century church with a fine 500-year-old font. The stained glass windows here are something of an oddity since none of them originally belonged to the church. They were part of a collection amassed by a 19th-century resident of the town who was himself a glass painter and bequeathed the unrelated pieces to the church. The most striking is a 15th-century *Pietà* in the east

Aerial View, Pontefract Castle

window which has been identified as Flemish in origin.

PONTEFRACT

8 miles E of Wakefield off the M62/A1

Shakespeare alluded to the town in his plays as 'Pomfret' – a place of influence and power, often visited by kings and their retinues. The great shattered towers of **Pontefract Castle** stand on a crag to the east of the town. Built by Ilbert de Lacy in the 11th century, it was one of the most formidable fortresses in Norman England. In medieval times it passed to the House of Lancaster and became a Royal Castle. Richard II was imprisoned here and tragically murdered in its dungeons on the orders of Henry Bolingbroke who then assumed the crown as Henry IV.

The castle was a major Royalist stronghold during the Civil War, after which it was destroyed by Cromwell's troops. Today it remains as a gaunt ruin with only sections of the inner bailey and the lower part of the keep surviving intact. There is an underground chamber, part of the dungeons where prisoners carved their names so that they might not be utterly forgotten. The unfortunate Richard II may have been incarcerated in this very chamber.

Many of the streets of Pontefract evoke memories of its medieval past with names such as Micklegate, Beast Fair, Shoe Market, Salter Row and Ropergate. Modern development has masked much of old Pontefract but there are still many old Georgian buildings and winding streets.

The town's most famous products, of course, are Pontefract Cakes. Liquorice root has been grown here since monastic times and there's even a small planting of liquorice in the local park. The town celebrates this unique heritage with the five day **Pontefract Liquorice Fayre** in mid-August which includes two days of jousting, archery and battle re-enactments at Pontefract Castle.

188 THE FEATHERSTONE HOTEL

Featherstone

Impressive hotel offering quality food, well-kept ales and comfortable en suite rooms.

see page 326

189 THE LIQUORICE BUSH

Pontefract

Popular town centre inn serving home-made food at very reasonable prices as well as a choice of real ales.

see page 328

190 THE BLUEBELL INN

Wentbridge

Traditional inn in picturesque village offering outstanding cuisine, excellent wine list, real ales and en suite rooms.

see page 329

191 THE CATCHPENNY

Fitzwilliam

Charming early-19th century inn serving tasty home-made food and real ales; patio and garden.

‖ see page 329

192 QUARRY INN

Horbury

Very popular hostelry offering wholesome home-made food, real ales and quality en suite rooms.

‖ ⊨ see page 330

193 THE BREWERS PRIDE

Ossett

Free house with "real ales, real fires and real food"; regular live entertainment and annual beer festival.

‖ see page 331

WINTERSETT

6 miles SE of Wakefield off the A638

Found on the historic estate of Walton Hall, once the home of the famous 19th-century naturalist Charles Waterton, is the **Heronry and Waterton Countryside Discovery Centre**, which provides information and exhibitions about the surrounding country park, which includes two reservoirs and woodland that was once part of the ancient Don Forest. The centre is open Tuesday to Friday and Sundays all year round.

ACKWORTH

8 miles SE of Wakefield off the A628

This village is home to the famous **Ackworth School,** founded by the Quakers in 1779 as a boarding school for Quaker boys and girls in 1779. Today it has 580 boys and girls of many different faiths.

Outside the village a Plague Stone can still be seen beside the road, where villagers would leave money in exchange for food that was brought here when Ackworth was cut off during an outbreak of the Plague.

RYHILL

8 miles SE of Wakefield on the B6428

The village of Ryhill is mentioned in the *Domesday Book* as part of land granted to Robert de Lacy by William the Conqueror. Known as Rihella, in 1124 Robert de Lacy transferred lands including Ryhill to Nostell Priory, where it remained in the control of the Nostell canons until the Dissolution of the Monasteries in 1654. A prosperous London merchant, Sir Rowland Winn, bought the Nostell estate and Ryhill village; the estate has remained in the hands of the Winn family ever since. Ryhill attracts many visitors for its three beautiful reservoirs - popular for fishing, sailing and bird-watching - for its Heronry Centre and for some famous nature walks.

WEST BRETTON

5 miles S of Wakefield on the A637

One of the leading attractions of the area is found conveniently close to junction 38 of the M1. The **Yorkshire Sculpture Park** draws in some 200,000 visitors a year and since you only pay a small charge for parking it represents amazing value for money. Changing exhibitions of sculpture are set in the beautiful 18th-century parkland of Bretton Hall, 200 acres of historic landscape providing a wonderful setting for some of the best sculpture to be seen in Britain today by artists from around the world.

Alongside the programme of indoor and outdoor exhibitions, more permanent features include the YSP collection of works in many different styles (from 19th-century bronzes by Rodin to contemporary sculptures), and a display of monumental bronzes by Henry Moore sited within the adjacent 100-acre Bretton Country Park.

WOOLLEY

6 miles S of Wakefield off the A61

Despite being surrounded by industrial towns, Woolley has managed to retain its rural air and its old hall, now a course and conference centre, standing on land that was originally enclosed as a hunting park during the reign of Henry VII. Just to the northeast lies **Newmillerdam Country Park and Boathouse** which was, in the 19th century, part of the Chevet Estate and a playground for the local Pilkington family. The boathouse, built in the 1820s, has been restored as a visitors' centre while the rest of the 240-acre park offers ample opportunity for walking and viewing wildlife at close quarters. Just to the northwest lies Woolley Edge, from where there are wonderful views out across Emley Moor and, on a clear day, all the way to Barnsley. The discovery of a flint axe as well as flints and scrapers from the Iron Age suggest that there have been settlements here since prehistoric times.

OVERTON

5 miles SW of Wakefield off the A642

A visit to the **National Coal Mining Museum** for England at Caphouse Colliery in Overton includes a guided tour 450 feet underground, indoor exhibitions and videos, outdoor machine displays, a working steam winder, train rides and, for children, an adventure playground and some friendly pit ponies.

194 THE KAYE ARMS

Grange Moor

Former coaching inn with charm and character offering excellent cuisine and extensive wine list.

see page 332

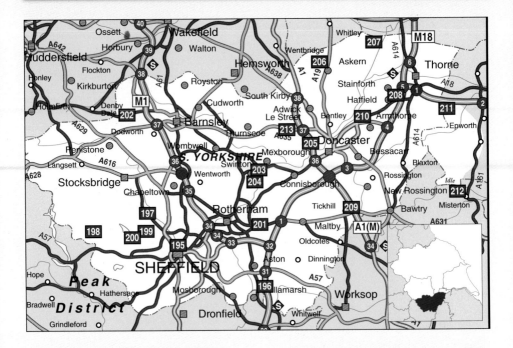

South Yorkshire

South Yorkshire tends to be overlooked as a tourist venue, but this is a region of great age and antiquity and, in many places, real beauty, both natural and man-made. Sheffield, rightly claims to be England's greenest city, and the wild open spaces of the Pennine moorlands of the Peak District National Park roll right up to its western boundaries.

Sheffield's prosperity is founded on steel and, in particular, cutlery, and though there are few ancient buildings in England's fourth-largest city to explore, there is a wealth of museums and galleries. To the north of Sheffield is Barnsley, whose prosperity came from the rich seams of coal that have been exploited in the local area. Meanwhile, to the east lies Rotherham, where iron ore has been mined and smelted since the 12th century. While its wealth is certainly based upon metal, Rotherham is also the home of Rockingham pottery that was once favoured by royalty.

Brodsworth Hall, Brodsworth

Further east again is the charming riverside town of Doncaster, which was established by the Romans and today has the air of a pleasant market town. However, this was once one of the country's most important centres of steam locomotive manufacture and it is famous for having created the *Mallard*, which still holds the record for the top speed attained by a steam train. Today, though, Doncaster is best known as the home of the St Leger, Britain's oldest classic horse race.

Elsewhere in the county visitors can discover the delights of Roche Abbey, a 12th-century Cistercian house, Conisbrough Castle, which boasts the oldest stone keep in England, and the faded Victorian grandeur of Brodsworth Hall.

Burbage, nr Sheffield

SHEFFIELD

In recent years Sheffield has re-invented itself. England's fourth-largest city, it is still busy with its steel, cutlery, engineering and tool-making industries but is also a vibrant, international, multi-cultural city and a world-class centre for sport, headquarters of the government-backed UK Sports Institute and with an impressive array of international venues. There are facilities for ice-skating, dry skiing and two indoor climbing centres. It has also recently overtaken Leeds as the fastest-growing city in Yorkshire, thanks to a forward-looking programme of new housing and public spaces that continue to draw students in their thousands, many of whom choose to stay on in Sheffield after they've finished their studies.

Among the city's many museums is the **Kelham Island Museum** which is located in one of the city's oldest industrial areas and stands on a man-made island that was created more than 900 years ago. Inside the museum buildings visitors can witness the sights and sounds of industrial Sheffield through working machinery, activity areas and event days. A new mezzanine floor has recently been added for the display of the museum's transport collection. This includes the famous Sheffield Simplex car, built in 1920, the Sharron Laycock car, Richardson Light car, Ner-a-car motorcycle and a Rolls Royce jet engine. The museum was badly damaged by the floods of 2007 and forced to close but is expected to re-open by the end of 2008.

Sheffield's industrial heritage is also celebrated at the **Weston Park Museum** (free) which has recently completed a £17 million refurbishment. The animated new displays are specially designed to delight even the youngest visitors and range from Egyptian Mummies, to a traditional butchers shop, from Snowy the polar bear to living ants and bees. The city's collections of beautiful, varied and unusual treasures are brought to life by fascinating histories, incredible facts and hands-on interactives.

Sheffield has several outstanding galleries devoted to the visual arts. The **Millenium Gallery** has helped to establish the city as a cultural force in the north of England. A remarkable building of white columns and striking glass arches, it holds four unique galleries that showcase not only Sheffield's impressive metalware collection but also provide space to show the city's wonderful collection of paintings, drawings and natural history exhibits. One gallery hosts visiting installations from the Victoria & Albert museum and other distinguished collections from throughout the country; another features the very best of contemporary design and technology, while a third houses the fascinating collection formed for the people of Sheffield in 1875 by the Victorian artist, critic and sage John Ruskin. It includes paintings, watercolours and drawings, minerals, plaster casts and architectural details, illuminated manuscripts and books.

Nearby, the **Graves Gallery** (free) has recently been refurbished and repainted, giving prominence to works by legendary artists such as Turner and Cézanne. New displays take visitors on a lavish journey through the collections, spanning the 16th to the 21st century and including works by famous names such as Edward Coley Burne-Jones and Bridget Riley, and local heroes such as George Fullard and Derrick Greaves.

Another gallery of interest, the **Site Gallery** (free), is devoted to photographic and new media exhibitions and events. One of the largest contemporary visual art and media centres in the country, the gallery also offers darkroom and digital imaging facilities, as well as photographic and digital courses in the recently created education suite.

Sheffield's most picturesque museum is undoubtedly the **Bishop's House Museum** (see panel) which dates from around 1500 and is the earliest timber-framed house still standing in the city. Many original features have survived and the bed chamber and great parlour are furnished in the style of the home of a prosperous 17th century yeoman. There are also displays on Sheffield in Tudor and Stuart times, and changing exhibitions on local history themes.

Tucked away in a former church hall on Ecclesall Road is one of Sheffield's best-kept secrets, the **Traditional Heritage Museum.** It is made up of fully reconstructed shops, workshops and offices from 1850-1950, and provides many insights into what Sheffield was like in years gone by.

One of the UK's most interesting and comprehensive collections of nineteenth and twentieth century glass can be seen at the University of Sheffield's **Turner Museum of Glass**. From drinking glasses to contemporary installations the museum celebrates the skill and artistry of glassmakers. Pieces by all the major European and American glassmakers are on display and the collection is unrivalled in its display of work from the 1920s to the 1950s. A museum of a very different nature is the **Sheffield Bus Museum**, housed in the Tinsley Tram sheds on Sheffield Road. The collection includes many types of

195 BISHOPS' HOUSE

Sheffield

Bishops' House is the best preserved timber-framed house in Sheffield.

🏛 *see page 333*

Sheffield Botanic Gardens

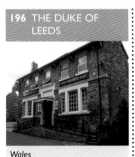

Wales

Traditional 18th century hostelry serving quality food and real ales.

see page 334

bus and other transport-related exhibits such as destination blinds, old timetables and models. The museum also houses the Tinsley Model Railway layout.

Of related interest is the **South Yorkshire Railway** in Meadowbank. As well as displaying more than 60 locomotives, there are vintage carriages and wagons, and a signal box. Plans are under way to run a steam-hauled passenger service on the three-and-a-half miles line from Meadowhall to Chapeltown.

Meadowhall itself is one of Europe's largest shopping centres with more than 270 stores. High street names, designer boutiques and speciality craft stores provide a formidable retail experience. The complex also contains many places to eat, an 11-screen cinema, crèche and an award-winning programme of events.

And if you want to just relax, the city's most peaceful spot has to be the 19 acres of **Sheffield**

Botanical Gardens, first opened in 1836. There are actually 15 distinct gardens featuring plants from all over the world and including the National Collections of Weigela and Diervilla.

AROUND SHEFFIELD

NORTH ANSTON

10 miles E of Sheffield on the B6060

This village, separated from its neighbour South Anston by the main road, is home to the **Tropical Butterfly House, Wildlife and Falconry Centre** where not only can visitors see exotic butterflies, birds, snakes and crocodiles in a tropical jungle setting but also enjoy outdoor falconry displays and, at the baby farm animal area, bottle-feed lambs (depending on the season). This centre, open all year, also has a nocturnal reptile room, nature trail and children's outdoor play area.

RENISHAW

9 miles SE of Sheffield on the A616

This sizeable village gives its name to **Renishaw Hall**, home of Sir Reresby and Lady Sitwell and located about a mile or so to the northwest. The beautiful formal Italian gardens and 300 acres of wooded park are open to visitors, along with an Orangery housing the National Collection of Yuccas, a nature trail, a Sitwell family museum, an art gallery, a display of Fiori de Henriques antique sculptures in the Georgian stables, and a café. The Hall itself is open to group and connoisseur tours by special arrangement only.

WALES

9 miles SE of Sheffield on the B6059

A mile or so to the west of Wales, the **Rother Valley Country Park** provides excellent facilities for water sports including sailing, windsurfing, canoeing and jet skiing, as well as a cable water ski tow. Visitors can hire equipment or use their own, and training courses from beginner to instructor level are available in various water sports. Other attractions include a lakeside golf course, a Craft Centre with craftspeople at work, cycle hire, gift shop, cafeteria – and Playdales, a 'mega play area' for children under 14.

OUGHTIBRIDGE

5 miles NW of Sheffield on the A6102

This pleasing village is set on the west bank of the River Don looking across to the tree-covered slopes of Wharncliffe Wood. The settlement dates back to Saxon times at least but surprisingly there is no church and no evidence of there ever having been one.

WHARNCLIFFE SIDE

5 miles NW of Sheffield on the A6102

Nestling in the valley below Wharncliffe Crags, Wharncliffe Side is a community of some 2000 people and a popular location for commuters to Sheffield and Stocksbridge. An old tradition in the village tells of the Dragon of Wantly which lurked in the recesses of the crags and terrorised the local people until a knight by the name of More did battle with the monster and killed it. A cave up on the crags is still called the Dragon's Den and local children experience an enjoyable frisson of terror by shouting into its depths. Another ancient tradition in the village is the Whitsuntide walk when Sunday school children process around Wharncliffe Side stopping at various points to sing hymns.

PENISTONE

15 miles NW of Sheffield on the A628

Perched 700 feet above sea level, Penistone forms a gateway to the Peak District National Park which extends for some 30 miles to the south of the town. Penistone's oldest building is the 15th-century tower of its parish church which overlooks a graveyard in which ancestors of the poet William Wordsworth are buried. Later centuries added an elegant Dissenters' Chapel (in the 1600s) and a graceful Cloth Hall in the 1700s.

CROSSPOOL

4 miles W of Sheffield on the A57

Intriguingly, it was a fit of pique that led to the building of **The Bell Hagg Inn**. Back in the 1830s a certain Dr Hodgson offered the vicar of Stannington (a village across the River Rivel from Crosspool) a large donation for the church funds. But Hodgson was well known as a gambler and frequenter of pubs so the vicar declined the generous offer. Incensed by this rebuff, Hodgson bought the land directly opposite the church and built the pub there,

197 THE PHEASANT

Oughtibridge

A countryside pub, dating back to 19th century, with a popular Sunday lunch menu

see *page 333*

198 THE STRINES INN

Bradfield Dale

Superb inn with glorious views serving quality traditional English homemade food; en suite rooms with 4-poster beds.

🍴 ⊨ see page 335

199 BARNFIELD HOUSE

Loxley

Outstanding owner-run guest house in lovely rural surroundings and offering luxurious bed & breakfast accommodation.

⊨ see page 335

200 THE ROYAL HOTEL

Dungworth

Welcoming family run guest house on edge of Peak District offering quality cuisine, family room and en suite rooms.

🍴 ⊨ see page 336

a monument to drinking that no one attending Divine Service at Stannington church could possibly overlook. It clings to the cliffside, a defiant piece of architecture obviously intended to make a statement.

ROTHERHAM

The town's most striking building is undoubtedly the **Church of All Saints**. With its soaring tower, pinnacled buttresses and battlements, and imposing porch, it is one of the finest examples of perpendicular architecture in Yorkshire. It dates mainly from the 15th century although there is evidence of an earlier Saxon church on the site.

A church here was listed in the *Domesday Book* and in 1161 the monks of Rufford Abbey were granted the right to prospect for and to smelt iron, and to plant an orchard, and from that day industry has existed side by side with agriculture.

About half the land area of the Borough of Rotherham is actually rural but it was heavy industry that put the town on the map. From the mid-1700s, the Walker Company of Rotherham was famous for cannons, their products serving to lethal effect in the American War of Independence and at the Battle of Trafalgar. They also built bridges, among them Southwark Bridge in London and the bridge at Sunderland. Another famous bridge builder was born here in 1901: Sir Donald Coleman Bailey invented the

Bailey Bridge which proved to be of great military value, especially during the Second World War.

The town also had lighter industries. Rockingham Pottery, produced here in the late 18th and early 19th century, is now highly prized by collectors. There's a fine collection at the **Clifton Park Museum**, a stately building whose interior has changed little since it was built in 1783 for the Rotherham ironmaster, Joshua Walker. The most breathtaking piece is the spectacular Rhinoceros Vase which stands almost four feet high and was the first ever one-piece porcelainn vase cast. In addition, the museum houses a collection of other Yorkshire pottery, English glass, silver and British oil paintings and watercolours. The grounds around Clifton House form the largest urban park in the Borough which has 10 urban parks altogether, along with three country parks, seven golf courses, 10 swimming pools and a leisure centre.

Another museum of interest is the **York and Lancaster Regimental Museum** in the Central Library. The regiment had strong ties with South Yorkshire, its recruits drawn mainly from Barnsley, Sheffield and Rotherham. The displays include historic uniforms, campaign relics and more than 1,000 medals, among them nine Victoria Cross groups. There are also sections on local militia, rifle volunteers and territorials.

Rotherham's latest attraction, opened in 2007, is the **South Yorkshire Transport Museum** which features an interesting collection of vintage buses and commercial vehicles. Various displays and other transport-related artefacts help recall the story of transport in the region. Opening times are limited.

Dramatically set within the former Templeborough steelworks, **Magna** was the UK's first science adventure park. This imaginative exploration of the power of the four natural elements – earth, air, fire and water – offers visitors the opportunity of experiencing the full power of lightning, firing a water cannon, manoeuvring a real JCB digger, getting close to a tornado or blowing up a virtual rock face. In the Living Robots Show predator robots pursue each other in an epic struggle to survive and breed. In the Power Pavilion, after donning overalls and cap for your 'shift', you can shed a few pounds by creating electricity on a giant treadmill, test your strength in a self-lifting chair, attack a target with a giant catapult and discover how much you would weigh on the planets Mars or Jupiter. The site also has a restaurant, cafeteria, picnic areas and shops.

About 6 miles northwest of the town, the palatial 18th-century mansion **Wentworth Woodhouse** boasts the longest frontage in England, some 600 feet long. The house is not open to the public but is clearly visible from its park. Also visible are a number of follies and monuments dating from the 1700s. The most curious of these is the Needle's Eye which consists of a

tower with a stone urn on top and is pierced by a carriageway. Legend says it was built in response to a wager by the Marquis of Rockingham, owner of Wentworth Woodhouse, that he could drive through the eye of a needle. One structure which *is* open (on Sunday afternoons during the season), is the Wentworth Mausoleum which was built in 1788 in memory of the 2nd Marquis.

Also open to the public are the adjacent **Wentworth Woodhouse Gardens** comprising some 16 acres of walled and landscaped areas.

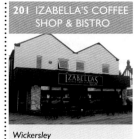

201 IZABELLA'S COFFEE SHOP & BISTRO

Wickersley

Popular eating place serving excellent selection of hot and cold home-cooked dishes.

see page 336

Roche Abbey, nr Rotherham

Cooper Gallery, Barnsley

Cawthorne

Set in 70 acres of historic
parkland and gardens,
Cannon Hall Museum
provides an idyllic and
tranquil setting for a day out.

🏛 *see page 337*

comparatively recent, completed in
1933. Nearby, the **Cooper Gallery**
is a lively centre for the arts which
hosts a varied programme of
exhibitions throughout the year as
well as housing a fine permanent
collection.

The town's most impressive
museum is actually located a few
miles to the west, in the village of
Cawthorne. **Cannon Hall** (see
panel) is a magnificent 18th-
century country house set in
formal gardens and historic
parkland. It offers unique
collections of pottery, furniture,
glassware and paintings, along with
the 'Charge Gallery' which
documents the story of the 13th/
18th Royal Hussars. There's a tea
room open at weekends and a gift
shop.

About a mile to the south of
Barnsley is the **Worsbrough Mill
Museum and Country Park**. The
Grade II listed mill dates from
around 1625. A steam mill was
added in the 19th century and
both have been restored to full
working order to form the
centrepiece of an industrial
museum. Wholemeal flour, ground
at the mills, can be bought here.
The mill is set within a beautiful
200-acre country park, whose
reservoir attracts a great variety of
birds including heron.

Features include a replanted maze, a
bear pit, ornamental and Japanese
gardens, 'hot walls', and a wealth of
stone and water features. The
centre also contains an adventure
playground, craft units and a coffee
shop.

A little further afield, near the
village of Maltby, are the dramatic
ruins of **Roche Abbey** (English
Heritage). The abbey dates from
the 12th century and takes its name
from the rocky limestone of the
riverside site. The majestic remains
of this great abbey stand in a
landscape fashioned by Capability
Brown in the 1770s as part of the
grounds of Sandbeck Park, home
of the Earls of Scarborough.

BARNSLEY

The county town of South
Yorkshire, Barnsley stands on the
River Dearne and derived its
Victorian prosperity from the rich
seams of coal hereabouts. It has an
appropriately imposing Town Hall
although the building is

AROUND BARNSLEY

ELSECAR

5 miles S of Barnsley on the B6097

Situated in the pretty conservation
village of Elsecar, just off the M1

(J36), the **Elsecar Heritage Centre** is located within the former ironworks and colliery workshops of the Earl Fitzwilliam. Restored historical buildings now house an antiques centre, individual craft workshops, and exhibitions of Elsecar's past. The steam railway here is the focus for many events such at Thomas and friends and Elsecar Wartime weekend.

TANKERSLEY

6 miles SW of Barnsley off the A6195

This parish is mentioned in the *Domesday Book*, and the Hall here was used in the now-classic film of the 1970s, *Kes*. During the War of the Roses between the houses of York and Lancaster, Tankersley Park was the site of a battle; it again saw conflict during the Civil War when the Royalists gained victory over Cromwell's troops. In the 14th -century Church of St Peter there are cannon balls and a bullet found after that battle.

WORTLEY

8 miles SW of Barnsley on the A629

This village's name comes from the Saxon meaning 'clearing for growing vegetables' and archaeological investigations on Wharncliffe Chase have indicated that there was a small British settlement here during the time of the Roman occupation. Mentioned in the *Domesday Book*, although it had declined in importance since the reign of Edward the Confessor, in the late 12th century Cistercian monks began to lay the foundations

of the iron industry, and iron-forging began here in the Middle Ages. In the 1700s Sir Thomas Wortley built Wharncliffe Lodge as a hunting lodge and, just over a century later during the Civil War, Sir Francis Whortley raised a private army of 900 to fight for the king's cause.

The ancestral home of the Wortley family, **Wortley Hall,** was built in the late 1500s on the site of an older residence; over the centuries it has been much altered and even left to decay. Restoration work was carried out in the late 18th and early 19th centuries, and it was also around this time that the landscaping and ornamental planning of the grounds and gardens took place.

Back in the village there are the school and schoolhouse built in 1874 by the Wortley family and only closed in 1993, while the oldest house in the village, Tividale Cottage, was practically rebuilt and certainly modernised in 1983. In the early 1700s this was the home of head-master William Nevison, and the cottage is thought to have been the birthplace of his son, the highwayman John Nevison.

Just outside the village are Top and Low Forge, which are said to have been in operation in the 12th century although the earliest documentation dates from 1567. However, by the 17th century these two forges were working ceaselessly, along with many others in the area and, while Top Forge closed in 1912, Low Forge continued production until 1929.

203 ELSECAR HERITAGE CENTRE

Elsecar

The Elsecar Heritage Centre nestles within the beautiful South Yorkshire countryside and dates from the early 1800's

see page 337

204 ELSECAR PARK CAFÉ

Elsecar

Café within spacious park serving honest-to-goodness meals, snacks and drinks.

see page 338

Thurlestones most famous son was Nicholas Saunderson, born in 1682, who was blinded by smallpox at the age of two. He taught himself to read by passing his fingers over the tombstones in Penistone churchyard – 150 years before the introduction of Braille. Nicholas went on to attend grammar school and rose to become Professor of Mathematics at Cambridge University.

THURLSTONE

9 miles SW of Barnsley off the A628

Thurlstone developed when the first settlers realised that the nearby moors provided extensive grazing for sheep and the lime-free waters of the River Don were ideal for the washing of wool. Today the village still has some fine examples of the weavers' cottages which sprang up during the early 19th century, the best of which can be seen on Tenter Hill. Here the finished cloth would have been dried and stretched on 'tenters' – large wooden frames placed outside on the street which gave the road its name.

DUNFORD BRIDGE

15 miles SW of Barnsley off the A628

Located just inside the Peak National Park, the Stanhope Arms is very much a hidden place. The hamlet of Dunford Bridge is only shown on very large scale maps but if you are travelling westwards from Barnsley on the A628, after 13 miles or so you will see a sign for the pub off to the right. It's well worth seeking out this grand old inn, originally built in the 1800s as a shooting lodge for the Cannon Hall Estate. It stands beside the entrance to the Woodhead railway tunnel which runs beneath the moors for more than three miles. When the tunnel opened in 1852 it was twice as long as any other in the world. There's an interesting display of memorabilia regarding the tunnel and the camp built for the Tunnel Tigers (the men who

built it), in the snug of the Stanhope Arms.

SILKSTONE

4 miles W of Barnsley off the A628

The travel writer Arthur Mee dubbed Silkstone's parish church 'The Minster of the Moors' and it is indeed a striking building. Parts of the church date back to Norman times but most of it was built during the golden age of English ecclesiastical architecture, the 15th century. Outside, there are graceful flying buttresses and wonderfully weird gargoyles. Inside, the ancient oak roofs sprout floral bosses on moulded beams, and old box-pews and lovely medieval screens all add to the charm.

The old stocks just outside **The Ring o' Bells** are another sign of the antiquity of this former mining village.

DONCASTER

The Romans named their riverside settlement beside the River Don *Danum*, and a well-preserved stretch of the road they built here can be seen just west of Adwick le Street. The modern town boasts some impressive buildings, notably the Mansion House built in 1748 and designed by James Paine. **The Minster of St George** was rebuilt in 1858 by Sir George Gilbert Scott and it's an outstanding example of Gothic revival architecture with its lofty tower, 170 feet high and crowned with pinnacles. The lively shopping centre is enhanced by a stately Corn Exchange building and a market which takes place every Tuesday, Friday and Saturday.

Doncaster was once one of the most important centres for the production of steam engines. Thousands were built here, including both the Flying Scotsman and the Mallard. The Mallard still holds the record for the fastest steam train in the world, achieving a top speed of 125mph in July 1938. For a further insight into the history of the town and surrounding area, there is **Doncaster Museum** which contains several exciting and informative exhibitions on the various aspects of natural history, local history and archaeology. Housed in the same building is the **Regimental Museum of the King's Own Yorkshire Light Infantry**, which reflects the history of this famous local regiment.

There is no-one connected with the racing fraternity who has not heard of the St Leger, one of the oldest classic races, which has been held at Doncaster since 1776. **Doncaster Racecourse** provides a magnet for all horse-racing enthusiasts and there are a total of 26 meetings each year.

On the north-western outskirts of the town, **Cusworth Hall** is home to the **Museum of South Yorkshire Life.** The Hall is a splendid Georgian mansion built in the 1740s and set in a landscaped park. The interior features varied displays on the social history, industry, agriculture and transport in the area.

205 CUSWORTH HALL TEA ROOM

Cusworth

Tea room in converted stables of a stately home serving delicious home-made fare.

see page 338

Cusworth Hall Country Park, nr Doncaster

206 THE SCHOOL BOY

Norton

Welcoming village hostelry with reputation for good food and well-kept ales; food-themed evenings.

📍 see page 339

207 THE OLD GEORGE

Sykehouse

Hidden gem of a village inn providing excellent cuisine, real ales and a superb beer garden complete with swimming pool.

📍 see page 339

208 HATFIELD CHACE

Hatfield

Spacious traditional inn, very family-friendly and serving excellent food and real ale.

📍 see page 340

209 CASTLEGATES COFFEE SHOP & BISTRO

Tickhill

Stylish eating place offering good choice of wholesome and appetising food.

📍 see page 341

AROUND DONCASTER

NORTON

8 miles N of Doncaster off the A19

This sizeable village is located close to the borders with North and West Yorkshire and was once busy with farming, mining and quarrying. Nowadays it's a peaceful place, a tranquil base for commuters to Doncaster and Pontefract. Its most impressive building is the ancient parish church of **St Mary Magdalene** whose splendid 14th-century west tower is considered by many to be the finest in Yorkshire. Once there was also a priory here, standing beside the River Went, but now only a fragment of wall remains. However, the old water mill has survived.

STAINFORTH

7 miles NE of Doncaster off the A18 or A614

Stainforth was once an important trading centre and inland port on the River Don. It also stands on the banks of the Stainforth & Keadby Canal which still has a well-preserved dry dock and a 19th-century blacksmith's shop. This area of low, marshy ground was drained by Dutch engineers in the 1600s to produce rich, peaty farmland. The place has retained the air of a quiet backwater, a little-explored area of narrow lands and pretty hamlets, the fields drained by slow-flowing dykes and canals. The rich peat resources are commercially exploited in part but also provide a congenial home for a great deal of natural wildlife.

FISHLAKE

10 miles NE of Doncaster off the A614

Set along the banks of the River Don, which is known here as the Dutch River, Fishlake is effectively an island since it is surrounded by rivers and canals and can only be entered by crossing a bridge. It's a charming village with a striking medieval church famous for its elaborately carved Norman doorway, an ancient windmill and a welcoming traditional inn.

THORNE

10 miles NE of Doncaster on the A614

This ancient market town on the River Don has been a port since at least 1500 with ships sailing from here to York, Hull, London and Europe. The waterfront was once busy with boat-builder's yards where vessels of up to 400 tons were built. In 1802, Thorne gained a second waterfront, on the newly constructed Stainforth & Keadby Canal which attracted most of the water traffic from the unpredictable River Don. As late as 1987 there were still boat building yards at work here but in that year they finally closed and the area is being carefully developed in a way that will commemorate the town's heritage.

BRANTON

4½ miles E of Doncaster off the B1396

Surrounded by agricultural land, Brockholes Farm has been a working farm since 1759 and one where the traditional farming skills have been passed down from one

Brockhole Riding and Visitor Centre, Branton

generation to the next. Today, **Brockhole Riding and Visitor Centre** is a combination of working farm, zoo and riding school. It is home to a fascinating collection of animals from small ferrets to rare breeds of farm animals. The pride of place in the farm is given to a herd of pedigree Limousin cattle, powerfully impressive beasts. But there is also a wide range of exotic animals including llamas, wallabies, monkeys and zebra. A "Woodland Walk" reveals red and fallow deer. The riding centre here caters for complete beginners through to experienced riders and, along with professional instructors, has a range of horses and ponies to suit all ages and abilities.

FINNINGLEY
7 miles SE of Doncaster on the A614

A unique feature of this pleasant village close to the Nottinghamshire border is its five village greens, the main one having a duck pond complete with

weeping willows. Finningley is a living village with a well-used Village Hall, originally a barn which later served as the village school. Finningley has a beautiful Norman church with a rectors' list dating back to 1293 and a post office which has been in the same family for five generations. The year 2004 saw the opening of the international **Robin Hood Aiport** outside the village, which utilised the runways from the old RAF base, built just before World War II. This has led to increased development and investment in the area while not disturbing Finningley's traditional appeal.

BAWTRY
9 miles SE of Doncaster on the A614

This pleasant little market town stands close to the Nottinghamshire border and in medieval times it was customary for the Sheriff of South Yorkshire to welcome visiting kings and queens here. In the mid-1500s the then Sheriff, Sir Robert Bowes, accompanied by 200 gentlemen

210 THE BEVERLEY INN AND HOTEL

Edenthorpe
Home-made dishes, quality wines and champagnes, two rotating guest ales, and superb accommodation make this inn a welcoming place to relax.

🍴 🛏 see page 341

211 THE REINDEER

Sandtoft
With three different menus, this inn has classy décor and furnishings and a great atmosphere.

🍴 see page 342

212 THE HAXEY GATE INN

Misterton
Idyllic riverside location for this inn offering good wholesome food, real ales and en suite rooms.

🍴 🛏 see page 343

199

dressed in velvet together with 4000 yeomen on horseback, greeted Henry VIII and – in the name of Yorkshire – presented him with a purse containing the huge sum of £900 in gold.

Today's Bawtry is an upmarket and exciting town with very good shopping in select boutiques, and an impressive selection of excellent and stylish restaurants. As befits a place that can trace its traditions and heritage back to its days as a bustling 12th-century port on the River Idle it has managed to maintain its sense of history and distinct character while keeping up with the times. A happy mix of stunning buildings, small boutiques and sophisticated restaurants, it remains the quintessential English town. Many of the buildings are grand three-storey Georgian affairs that help the town maintain a tranquil and restrained appearance. Once a coaching stagepost along the old Great North Road, it continues its proud tradition of offering great food and drink to

visitors with a range of elegant eateries that are justly popular, so that the town has become a regular evening hot spot, particularly at the weekend. The opening of the Robiin Hood Airport nearby has led to increased investment in the area and Bawtry is set to see more changes and improvements in goods and services on offer while maintaining its traditional attractions.

THORPE SALVIN
14 miles S of Doncaster off the A57

This attractive village is home to the now-ruined Thorpe Salvin Hall, which dates from 1570 and is thought to have been the inspiration for Torquilstone in Sir Walter Scott's *Ivanhoe*.

CADEBY
4 miles SW of Doncaster off the A630

Listed in the *Domesday Book* as 'Catebi', this pleasant little village is surrounded on all sides by prime agricultural land. For centuries Cadeby had no church of its own; parishioners had to travel some two miles to the parish church in Sprotbrough. Then in 1856 the owners of the huge Sprotbrough estate, the Copley family, paid for a church to be built in Cadeby. It was designed by Sir George Gilbert Scott, the architect of St Pancras Station in London, and resembles a medieval estate barn with its steeply pitched roofs and lofty south porch. A century and a half later, Cadeby is again without a church since Sir George's attractive church has recently been declared redundant.

Thorpe Salvin Hall

CONISBROUGH

5 miles SW of Doncaster on the A630

The town is best known for the 11th-century **Conisbrough Castle** (English Heritage) which features prominently in one of the most dramatic scenes in Sir Walter Scott's novel *Ivanhoe*. The most impressive medieval building in South Yorkshire, Conisbrough Castle boasts the oldest circular keep in England. Rising some 90 feet and more than 50 feet wide, the keep stands on a man-made hill raised in Saxon times. Six huge buttresses some 6 feet thick support walls that in places are 15 feet deep. Visitors can walk through the remains of several rooms, including the first floor chamber where the huge open fireplaces give one a fascinating insight into the lifestyle of Norman times. The castle also offers a visual presentation, a visitor centre and a tea room.

Conisbrough Castle

SWINTON

8 ½ miles SW of Doncaster on the A6022

This is the town that is home to the world-famous Rockingham porcelain; the story of the amazing small country pottery which grew to become the king's porcelain manufacturer before falling into bankruptcy is told in a special gallery at Clifton Park Museum, Rotherham. However, here in Swinton itself visitors can still see the secluded Swinton Pottery site where, in beautiful surroundings, the Waterloo Kiln (built in 1815) and the Pottery Ponds are the only surviving landmarks of the renowned Rockingham Porcelain works.

BRODSWORTH

6 miles NW of Doncaster on the B6422

Just outside the village, **Brodsworth Hall** (English Heritage) is a remarkable example of a Victorian mansion that has survived with many of its original furnishings and decorations intact. When Charles and Georgiana Thellusson, their six children and 15 servants moved into the new hall in 1863 the house must have seemed the last word in both

201

grandeur and utility. A gasworks in the grounds supplied the lighting and no fewer than eight water closets were distributed around the house, although rather surprisingly only two bathrooms were installed.

More immediately impressive to visitors were the opulent furnishings, paintings, statuary and decoration. The sumptuous reception rooms have now a rather faded grandeur and English Heritage has deliberately left it so, preserving the patina of time throughout the house to produce an interior that is both fascinating and evocative. A vanished way of life is also brought to life in the huge kitchen and the cluttered servants wing. The Hall stands in 15 acres of beautifully restored Victorian gardens, complete with a summer house in the form of a classical temple, a target range

© John Critchley

Brodsworth Hall, Brodsworth

where the family practised its archery, and a pets cemetery where the family dogs - and a prized parrot with the unimaginative name of Polly - were buried between 1894 and 1988. There is also a fascinating exhibition illustrating the family's obsession - yachting.

Accommodation, Food & Drink and Places of Interest

The establishments featured in this section includes hotels, inns, guest houses, bed & breakfasts, restaurants, cafes, tea and coffee shops, tourist attractions and places to visit. Each establishment has an entry number which can be used to identify its location at the beginning of the relevant chapter or its position in this section.

In addition full details of all these establishments and many others can be found on the Travel Publishing website - www.travelpublishing.co.uk. This website has a comprehensive database covering the whole of Britain and Ireland.

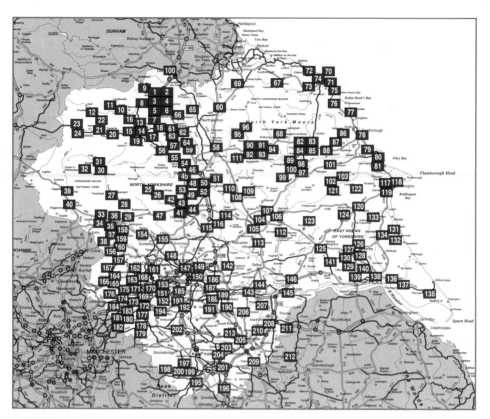

ACCOMMODATION

2   The Holly Hill Inn & Ivy Restaurant, Richmond
3   The Talbot Hotel, Richmond
6   The Castle Tavern, Richmond
11   The Kings Arms Hotel, Reeth
15   The Golden Lion Hotel, Leyburn
16   The Cross Keys, Bellerby, Leyburn
17   The Wyvill Arms, Constable Burton
18   The Countrymans Inn, Hunton
19   The Black Swan Hotel, Middleham
22   The White Rose Hotel, Askrigg
24   The White Hart Inn, Hawes
26   The Birch Tree Inn, Willsill, Harrogate
30   Blue Bell Inn, Kettlewell, Skipton
31   The Buck Inn, Buckden, Skipton
32   The Queen's Arms Inn, Litton
36   The Masons Arms Inn, Eastby, Skipton
37   White Lion, Kildwick, Keighley
40   The Boars Head Hotel, Long Preston
42   The New Inn, Burnt Yates, Harrogate
46   Station Hotel, Ripon
49   The Crown Inn, Roecliffe
50   The Black Bull Inn, Boroughbridge
52   The Grantham Arms Hotel, Milby
54   Staveley Arms, North Stainley, Ripon
55   The Bull Inn, West Tanfield, Ripon
59   The Woodman Inn, Burneston, Bedale
61   The Three Coopers, Bedale
62   The Waggon & Horses Inn, Bedale
63   The Green Dragon, Bedale
64   The Green Dragon, Exelby, Bedale
65   The White Swan, Danby Wiske
66   The Angel Hotel, Catterick Village
72   Estbek House, Sandsend, Whitby
73   Dunsley Hall Country House Hotel, Dunsley, Whitby
74   Raithwaite Hall Luxury Holiday Cottages, Raithwaite, Whitby
76   Flask Inn, Robin Hood's Bay
79   Lingholm Court Holiday Cottages, Lebberston, Scarborough
84   17 Burgate, Pickering
85   The Old Manse, Pickering
86   The Everley Country Hotel, Hackness
87   The Anvil Inn, Sawdon, Scarborough
88   The Cayley Arms, Allerston
94   The Pheasant at Harome, Harome
95   The Inn at Hawnby, Hawnby, Helmsley
96   Laskill Grange, Hawnby, Helmsley
100   The Cresswell Arms, Appleton-le-Street, Malton
103   Blue Bell Inn, Weaverthorpe
110   The Bluebell Country Inn, Alne, York
113   The Black Bull Inn, Escrick, York
114   The Chequers Inn, Bilton-in-Ainsty
119   Manor Court Hotel & Azzurro Restaurant, Carnaby, Bridlington
122   The Old Mill Hotel & Restaurant, Langtoft, Driffield
130   The Ferguson Fawsitt Arms & Country Lodge, Walkington
144   The Royal Oak Inn, Hirst Courtney
154   The Dalesway Hotel, Ilkley
156   Park Top House, Haworth
160   The Eastburn Inn, Eastburn, Keighley
164   White Lion Hotel, Hebden Bridge
166   White Lion, Heptonstall, Hebden Bridge
167   Grain Farm, Pecket Well, Hebden Bridge
180   Wharfeside Inn, Slaithwaite, Huddersfield
184   The Turnpike Inn, Rishworth, Halifax
188   The Featherstone Hotel, Featherstone
190   The Bluebell Inn, Wentbridge
192   The Quarry Inn, Horbury, Wakefield
198   The Strines Inn, Bradfield, Sheffield
199   Barnfield House, Loxley, Sheffield
200   The Royal Hotel, Dungworth, Sheffield
210   The Beverley Inn & Hotel, Edenthorpe, Doncaster
212   The Haxey Gate Inn, Misterton

FOOD & DRINK

1   Seasons, Richmond
2   The Holly Hill Inn & Ivy Restaurant, Richmond
3   The Talbot Hotel, Richmond
4   Cross View Tea Rooms & Restaurant, Richmond
5   Sip Coffee, Richmond

PLACES OF INTEREST

The Station, Station Yard, Station Road,
Richmond, North Yorkshire DL10 4LD
Tel: 01748 825340
e-mail: book@restaurant-seasons.co.uk
website: www.restaurant-seasons.co.uk

Richmond's now disused Victorian railway
station is a striking stone building with a
cloister-like frontage that gives it a vaguely
ecclesiastical appearance. For many years, it
was occupied by a variety of businesses,
including a garden centre, but has now been
completely redeveloped. The complex now
contains a two-screen cinema, half a dozen
artisan food producers, a gallery, offices,
several meeting rooms and, most importantly,
Seasons café/restaurant. Owners Ian and Jane, who both have more than 20 years experience in
the hospitality trade, opened here in November 2007 after carrying out a complete refurbishment.
Their restaurant has a stylish modern décor with old features blending perfectly with modern
facilities. The menus are designed around a modern British theme with Mediterranean influences.
Fresh locally sourced produce wherever possible and, of course, all the menus are based on
seasonal ingredients.

Ian and Jane pride themselves on an innovative approach to everything they do and they
believe that their customer service is second to none. The day at Seasons begins at 9am when a
Breakfast and Brunch menu is available until noon. In addition to a full English breakfast, or its
vegetarian version, there's a choice of toasted English muffins with fillings such as Eggs Benedict
or Scrambled egg and bacon. From noon until 10pm, the Café Menu is available, offering a huge
choice that includes home-made soup, nachos, burgers, pizzas, hot and cold sandwiches, salads and
desserts, as well as main meals like the real ale battered Whitby haddock and chips with mushy
peas, or Chicken Strips in a white wine and tarragon sauce served with cous cous.

The restaurant proper opens at 5.30pm with last food orders at 10pm. Naturally, the menu
varies according to the season but typically you might find a Carpaccio of seared Dales beef with a
marinated bean salad amongst the starters, along with an Asparagus and Parmesan filo tart topped
with a poached quails egg. As your main course, how about a whole char grilled black bream
served with a dill-marinated cucumber and potato salad? A vegetarian option might be the Nettle &
Potato Gnocchi in sauce of sage, walnuts and sheep's cheese. To accompany your meal, there's a
good selection of wines, bottled beers, spirits and real ale from the Richmond Brewing Company
next door.

2 THE HOLLY HILL INN & IVY RESTAURANT

Holly Hill, Richmond,
North Yorkshire, DL10 4RJ
Tel: 01748 822192
e-mail: holly.hill.hotel@btconnect.com
website: www.hollyhillinn.co.uk

Situated on the outskirts of the historic market town of Richmond (gateway to the Dales) and directly on the Coast to Coast route, **The Holly Hill Inn** has so much to offer the weary traveler: A selection of Real Ales, a hot home-cooked meal and a comfortable and spacious en-suite room for the night.

The traditional medieval style of the Inn, including the lounge with feature brick-built fireplace, makes it a very warm and cosy atmosphere indeed. Formerly an old coaching inn dating back to the mid 18th century, it stands next to the old toll house on an old Drovers Road into Richmond.

Awaiting lucky visitors is a warm, friendly welcome from staff and locals alike. All modern facilities are at hand but one still has the feeling of a bygone age. Whether summer or winter, the panoramic view of Richmond with its castle on the skyline, sets the scene of a picture of 'Merry England' and the traditions of many past generations.

Richmond town is smothered in history, being in the heart of Swaledale, with Wensleydale, Teesdale and the North Yorkshire Moors only a short drive away. Richmond has itself spectacular views and offers a variety of things to do - ranging from walks, to visiting castles or museums. The Holly Hill Inn is well situated and is on the road to Leyburn, another Market town with its own museums and coffee shops.

Whether on holiday with the family or travelling on business, all rooms are en-suite (showers) - spacious, clean and modern. The rooms were re-furbished in August 2006 and all have views that will take your breath away.

The Ivy Restaurant serves a tempting menu of hot and cold home-cooked food for lunchtimes and evenings. Old favourites, such as Homemade Pie of the Day, Fish & Chips, and Chef's Homemade Beef Lasagne, as well as some international classics are very popular. The pork and lamb used couldn't be more local- from the farm adjacent to the inn, and the head chef also specializes in fish dishes, which is purchased on a daily basis.

Open all day every day, the inn offers 2 regular ales: Theakstons and Black Sheep, and have the occasional guest ale. Food is available Mon-Fri (12-2pm and 6-9pm) Saturdays 12 - 9pm and Sundays 12-8pm there are some seasonal variations so please call to avoid disappointment. Children welcome and most credit cards are taken. There is disabled access and facilities and one ground floor bed and breakfast room.

Although The Holly Hill Inn is hidden to many, once found, you'll be back- it is superb in every department, and loved by all who visit here.

207

3   THE TALBOT HOTEL

33 Market Place, Richmond,
North Yorkshire DL10 4QG
Tel: 01748 829734

Situated in the heart of popular Richmond, overlooking Richmond's cobbled Market Square, **The Talbot Hotel** is a handsome Georgian

building where mine hosts, Tony and Linda Hughes, offer their guests a warm welcome. Good food and comfortable accommodation is promised here.

Linda is an accomplished cook and her menu offers wholesome and appetising food based on top quality fresh local produce cooked to order. The Talbot is open all day, everyday for ale, offering two real ales (some possibly brewed in Yorkshire) and food is available every lunchtime and evening.

Tony and Linda who both have 2 years experience in the trade, took over here in the spring of 2008 and as we go to press are completing a major refurbishment programme. This includes the 4 guest bedrooms, 3 of which have en suite facilities; the fourth has its own private bathroom.

Children are welcome; all major credit cards are accepted; and there is good disabled access to the bar and dining areas but the bedrooms are upstairs.

4 CROSS VIEW TEA ROOMS & RESTAURANT

38/39 Market Place, Richmond,
North Yorkshire DL10 4QL
Tel: 01748 825897

Offering traditional home baking and cooking, **Cross View Tea Rooms & Restaurant** occupies a prominent position on Richmond's spacious market place. Through its picture windows, customers get a grand view of the market, the old church and the Cross from which the tea rooms take their name, although the Cross is actually an obelisk.

Cath and Ian Muir have owned the tea rooms since 2003 and they now enjoy a glowing reputation for excellent home-cooked fare based on fresh local produce wherever possible. Service by the friendly and efficient staff, led by the long-serving team of Di and Sheila, is excellent.

Everything on the menu is prepared and cooked here, from the hearty breakfasts to the delicious scones and wonderful cakes and puddings. Dishes such as the Herb-crusted Salmon in Butter Spinach are particularly popular but you can order anything on the menu with confidence that you are going to receive a dining treat. On Sundays, roasts are added to the regular menu.

The tea rooms are open from 9am to 5pm, Monday to Saturday; and from 10am to 5pm on Sunday. Children are welcome; payment by cash or cheque only. There is good disabled access.

5 SIP COFFEE ¶

**18 King Street, Richmond,
North Yorkshire DL10 4HP
Tel: 01748 822877**

Located in the heart of historic Richmond, **Sip Coffee** was created in 2006 by owner Chris Pugh and has quickly become very popular with both locals and visitors. As you might

expect from the name, there's an excellent choice of coffees but the menu also offers a wide variety of teas and other hot and cold drinks. The freshly baked paninis with a wide choice of fillings are both tasty and good value for money. Sip Coffee is open Monday to Saturday from 9am to 3pm, (4pm in the summer).

HIDDEN PLACES GUIDES

Explore Britain and Ireland with *Hidden Places* guides - a fascinating series of national and local travel guides.

Packed with easy to read information on hundreds of places of interest as well as places to stay, eat and drink.

Available from both high street and internet booksellers

For more information on the full range of *Hidden Places* guides and other titles published by Travel Publishing visit our website on

www.travelpublishing.co.uk
or ask for our leaflet by phoning
01752 276660 or emailing
info@travelpublishing.co.uk

6 THE CASTLE TAVERN ¶ ⊢

**3-4 Market Place, Richmond,
North Yorkshire DL10 4HU
Tel: 01748 823187**

Located centrally in Richmond's spacious Market Place, **The Castle Tavern** is a fine old English inn dating back to the mid-1700s when it served as a coaching inn. Since the autumn of 2007 mine hosts at the Castle have been Diane and Paul, a friendly and welcoming couple for whom the inn was their first venture in the hospitality business. They have succeeded admirably and have quickly established a glowing reputation for quality food, ale and accommodation.

Diane and Paul share the cooking and their menu is available from 11am to 3pm, Monday to Saturday, and from noon until 4pm on Sunday. During the season, food is also served from 5.30pm to 8.30pm. Dishes are based on local produce wherever possible and include old pub favourites such as Fish & Chips, Burger & Chips, jacket

potatoes and toasties. Kids meals are also available. Lovers of real ales will find a choice of Black Sheep and a guest ale.

The Castle also offers comfortable accommodation with 6 variously sized rooms available, one of which has en suite facilities, and 2 are family rooms. Payment at The Castle is by cash or cheque only.

7 ARCHER'S JERSEY ICE CREAM

The Station, Station Yard, Richmond,
North Yorkshire, DL10 4LD
Tel: 01748 828263
e-mail: susan@newmoorfarm.co.uk
website: www.archersjerseyicecream.com

The ice cream parlour at New Moor Farm sells some of the finest ice cream you'll ever taste. The Archer family has farmed at Walworth Gate since 1976, but in 2001 their entire herd of Holstein Friesians was wiped out by

foot and mouth. John, Susan and their three children started again with a herd of some 300 Jersey cows producing the very best milk and in 2004 they diversified by setting up **Archer's Jersey Ice Cream** as a way of adding value to the milk. They converted two garages and an old forge to make the parlour selling their marvellous product between 10am and 6pm (to 5 in winter).

Besides the creamy, delicious main attraction, with flavours ranging from classic vanilla to banana, liquorice, honey & ginger, strawberry, champagne rhubarb, hokey pokey and Christmas pudding, the parlour sells home-made cakes and pastries, special occasion ice cream cakes, coffees, teas, smoothies and fresh fruit juices – and, naturally, full-fat and semi-skimmed Jersey milk and cream. There are seats inside and outside, a children's play area and a two-mile farm walk with sweeping views of the surrounding countryside. The Archers' at The Station, Richmond, open from 10.30am to 7.30pm (winter 11.30am to 6.30pm).

8 THE GEORGE & DRAGON

Hudswell, nr Richmond,
North Yorkshire DL11 6BL
Tel: 01748 823082
e-mail: georgeanddragon7@btconnect.com

Located in the picturesque village of Hudswell, a couple of miles west of Richmond, **The George and Dragon** commands spectacular countryside views from the rear of the premises. This welcoming village hostelry is owned and run by Alan and Ann Garside who in the relatively short time they have been here, have made their inn a destination pub noted for its good food, well-kept ales and hospitality.

Alan is in charge of the kitchen and he offers an enticing selection of quality dishes based on produce sourced within the county and freshly cooked to order. Specialities of the house include home-made Steak & Guinness Pie and Large Yorkshire Puddings with various fillings. Meals can be enjoyed either in the 20-seater restaurant overlooking the garden and patio, or in the garden itself. There's no food on Mondays but for the

rest of the week it is served from noon until 2.30pm, and from 6pm to 9pm. On Sundays the regular menu is replaced by a traditional roast with vegetarian options which are served from noon until 3pm.

Booking is strongly advised at the weekends. The bar offers 3 real ales on tap along with a comprehensive selection of other beverages.

9 THE ANGEL INN

**62 The High Street, Gilling West,
nr Richmond, North Yorkshire DL10 5JW
Tel: 01748 823811
e-mail: angel-inn@hotmail.co.uk**

Located in the pretty village of Gilling West, just a short drive from Scotch Corner and the A1, **The Angel Inn** is a well-known and popular hostelry which is owned and run by Robert Bruce and his business partners, Jim and Claire Pearson. They took over in the summer of 2007 and since then the place has gone from strength to strength and is now a 'destination property' for all who enjoy good food and well-kept ales.

The building itself dates back in parts to the 13th century and the interior has all the charm and character one could hope for in a village inn.

Jim is an accomplished cook - he has been a chef for more than 20 years - and his menu offers a very wide choice of dishes. Amongst the starters are Royal Thai Dim Sum and Mushroom Cassalinga - mushrooms and prawns in a creamy garlic sauce topped with cheese and served with garlic bread. For main courses, old favourites such as Steak & Ale Pie, steaks, gammon and fish & chips are all there, but you'll also find international dishes such

as Italian-style Chicken, Beef in Black Bean with Peppers, and The Angel Special Kung Po - stir-fried chicken, beef and prawns with cashew nuts and vegetables in a special kung po sauce. Vegetarians are well served with a choice that includes Roast Tuscan Red Pepper and a Three Cheese Pasta & Broccoli Bake. Children have their own "Little Angels" menu. On the last Saturday of each month, the Angel hosts a themed night, usually related to food.

To accompany your meal, the choice of beverages includes 3 real ales with Black Sheep as the regular brew. Meals can be enjoyed either in the 20-seater restaurant, in the bar areas, in the beer garden, or at the tables in front of the inn. Food is served from noon until 2pm, and from 6pm to 9pm, Wednesday to Friday; from noon until 3pm, and from 5pm to 9pm on Saturday; and from noon until 3pm on Sundays when a traditional roast lunch replaces the regular menu. Booking is strongly recommended for weekend evenings and Sunday lunchtimes. All major credit cards except American Express and Diners are accepted, and the inn is disabled friendly.

10 SWALEDALE FOLK MUSEUM

The Green, Reeth,
North Yorkshire DL11 6QT
Tel: 01748 884118
website: www.swaledalemuseum.org

The **Swaledale Folk Museum** was opened in 1974, and is based in the old Methodist School, which took its first pupils in 1836. It is a fascinating repository of over 1,000 objects connected with living and working in the Dale. If you want to learn about lead miniing this is the place for you, where lead and its associated rocks, minerals and fossils were yielded up by the hard labour of the miners. You can see the tools they used, trace their progress through the landscape via nineteenth century maps, and imagine what it must have been like to work underground with only candlelight for a guide.

Sheep farming has been the mainstay of Swaledale agriculture since Tudor Times. As a thriving community the Dale was also home to many skilled trades and crafts; tinsmithing, joinery and stonemasonry, all represented in the Museum. While work was hard outside, it was no less easy inside. There are displays of domestic equipment from washing tubs and dollies to early electric irons.

Keeping the house clean, and the family fed was a labour intensive job, but did not preclude time for entertainment. The strange iron spring with a spike is for playing knurr & spell. There are nineteenth century quoits, and a whole section on the local brass and silver bands. There are many old photographs, which show Reeth as it was in the early twentieth century, and faces that are still familiar.

213

11 THE KINGS ARMS HOTEL

High Row, Reeth,
North Yorkshire DL11 6SY
Tel: 01748 884259
e-mail: info@kingsarms.com
website: www.thekingsarms.com

Located in the centre of the pretty village of Reeth, capital of Swaledale, and overlooking the village green is the perfectly situated **Kings Arms Hotel,** "Swaledale's Inn on the Green". Dating back to 1734 and affectionately known as the "Middle House" because of its position, the hotel has everything the travelling tourist could desire. There is an extensive menu, an olde worlde bar and dining room with an imposing log fire and, in keeping with modern day standards, comfortable en-suite guest bedrooms.

After parking in the village square, the visiting guest is impressed by the warm and friendly welcome, an atmosphere that will persist throughout your stay. The Inglenook Bar and Dining Room provide a popular and convivial meeting place for locals and visitors alike and this atmosphere is further enhanced as the result of the large log fire burning in the inglenook fireplace.

The Vogel family, Jacqueline, Bernard and their daughter Hannah, took over here in June 2007 and the hotel swiftly became very popular - a development not unconnected with the fact that Bernard is a Master Chef with more than 40 years experience in catering. His extensive menu offers a wide variety of dishes - cold platters, giant Yorkshire puddings, traditional dishes such as Beef & Guinness Pie or Gammon Steak with fried egg, chips and onion rings, as well as vegetarian dishes. The regular menu is supplemented by daily specials. At lunchtimes, a selection of hot and cold sandwiches is also available. Food is available every day from noon until 2.30pm, and from 6pm to 9pm. At Sunday lunchtimes, a traditional roast replaces the regular menu. Booking is essential at weekends.

The well-stocked bar offers a comprehensive choice of drinks, including up to 5 real ales - Black Sheep, Theakston's Best, Olde Peculier, Black Bull and a rotating guest ale.

The hotel also offers comfortable accommodation in 10 recently refurbished guest bedrooms, all of them with en suite facilities. They include doubles, singles, a family room and a honeymoon suite that comes with a complimentary bottle of bubbly.

The Kings Arms welcomes children and dogs (in the bar); accepts all major credit cards apart from American Express and Diners; and has good disabled access to the bar and restaurant, but the guest bedrooms are upstairs.

12 SWALEDALE WOOLLENS

Strawbeck, Muker in Swaledale, Richmond,
North Yorkshire DL11 6QG
Tel: 01748 886251
e-mail: mail@swaledalewoollens.co.uk
website: www.swaledalewoollens.co.uk

Swaledale Woollens was founded in Muker in Swaledale more than 30 years ago by villagers reviving the old cottage industry of knitting. Here in one of the most beautiful areas of Northern England the tradition of hand knitting in local wool goes back over 400 years to the days of Queen Elizabeth I. It was Elizabeth who set a new fashion by wearing hand knitted stockings and, with demand increasing, every family in the Dale - men, women and children - became involved in knitting woollen stockings. By the end of the 19th century however, changes in fashions together with the arrival of knitting machines ended most of the Dales hand knitting trade.

Swaledale Woollens is now owned and run by Kathleen Hird who carries on using local Swaledale and Wensleydale wool for the knitwear. There are more than 30 people knitting from their homes and producing a unique range of quality woollen knitwear. The wool provided for the knitters is mainly from Swaledale sheep, but use is also made of the different shades and textures provided by the nearby Wensleydale breed and Welsh hill sheep. The Swaledale, Wensleydale and Welsh wools are spun at the only remaining traditional worsted Woollen Mill in Bradford. Then it is dyed in to soft country colours and delivered to Muker. Real horn buttons are used on many of the garments. Kathleen takes it to her team of conscientious knitters then collects it when the ladies and gentlemen have knitted or crocheted it into garments.

The shop stocks a wide range of high quality knitwear, including sweaters, cardigans, hats, gloves, rugs, hangings, shawls, scarves, slippers and socks. It also stocks sheepskin slippers, gloves and rugs. What better choice could there be for a quality and unique, hand-crafted gift for yourself, friends and family? And you can also place your order online from the comfort of home!

Swaledale Woollens is open from 10am to 5pm every day except Christmas Day and Boxing Day. The shop closes at 4pm during November, December, January and February.

215

Market Place, Leyburn,
North Yorkshire DL8 5BW
Tel: 01969 623327   Fax: 01969 624927

A striking 3-storey building, **The Bolton Arms** occupies an elevated position overlooking Leyburn's spacious Market Place with its cobbled paving and 18th century shops, inns and houses. The Bolton Arms is itself late 18th century and was built as a coaching inn. It took its name from local landowner Lord Bolton of nearby Bolton Hall where his descendants still live.

Today, the inn is still a traditional pub but with a modern touch. With its magnificent open fire and comfortable leather sofa, it provides a warm welcome on a cold winter's day. In summer, the patio to the side of the inn is blooming with flowers set in hanging baskets and window boxes. The patio is furnished with bistro style tables, chairs and picnic tables - perfect for dining alfresco or relaxing with a cool drink on a warm summer's day. The bar stocks a range of well-kept ales,

including John Smith's Cask, Black Sheep and changing guest ales, along with a good selection of draught bitters, lagers, cider, stout, and wine by the glass or bottle.

At lunchtimes, the offers lite bites ranging from delicious paninis, pastas, salads, sandwiches, baguettes and all the good old pub favourites. On Thursdays an OAP special 2-course lunch is available; and on Fridays - Market Day - a similar deal is open to all.

In the evenings, an Early Bird 2 or 3 course dinner is served from 5.30pm in the bar or bistro. The evening menu proper offers a choice of hearty dishes such as the home-made rich steak and cask ale pie with a short crust top, or the very popular home-made Beef Lasagne. Vegetarian dishes are also available. Children are well-catered for with their own kids menu including novelty ice creams and fun colouring packs. Booking is essential for Friday and Saturday evenings, and for the popular Sunday Carvery.

The Bolton Arms has a first floor function room equipped with its own bar. It's an ideal venue for all kinds of functions from weddings and birthday parties to dinner dances and meetings. The room can accommodate up to 80 people for a sit down meal; up to 150 for dances, finger buffets and so on. For any of these events, tailor-made menus can be arranged to suit your needs.

14 MRS PUMPHREYS

High Street, Leyburn,
North Yorkshire DL8 5AH
Tel: 01969 623815

Located just around the corner from Leyburn's large cobbled market place, **Mrs Pumphrey's** is a very popular coffee shop that has been serving wholesome fare here since 1993. The business is run by the mother and daughter team of Jackie and Susanne Schollar, aided by their long-time employee, Elaine. The extensive sit-down menu offers a choice that ranges from a full English Breakfast to sandwiches, paninis, melts, burgers and jacket potatoes. Almost all the items are also available to takeaway. The coffee shop is open from 9am to 4pm-ish, Monday to Saturday. Payment is by cash only.

217

15 THE GOLDEN LION HOTEL

Market Place, Leyburn,
North Yorkshire, DL8 5AS
Tel: 01969 622161

Noted for its fine en-suite accommodation, with a lift to all floors and full disabled facilities, splendid food and a wine cellar to match, **The Golden Lion Hotel** is a true home from home. Situated in the heart of the market town of Leyburn, overlooking the huge Market Square at the 'Gateway to Wensleydale'.

This fine hotel has been dispensing hospitality for over 240 years, and has recently changed hands, with the Collins family taking over- son Jonathon is a professional chef, while daughter Jenna has lots of experience running front of house. The family are already getting excellent comments from the locals, and have a lot planned for the place in the near future.

Traditional ales are just one of the many draws here, where the accent is firmly on quality home-cooked food served at breakfast, lunch and dinner. Renowned for its freshly cooked food of local origins, excellent cuisine is served in the 70-seat restaurant, decorated with Dales murals painted by local artist Lynn Foster.

An A La Carte menu offers a good choice of delicious dishes including sirloin steaks, braised lamb steak, local cured gammon, beef-and-ale pie, grilled salmon steak, haddock, chicken and a vegetarian dish of the day. Open all day every day, there are three real ales (Black Sheep, Timothy Taylor

Landlord, and a rotating guest ale) together with a good complement of lagers, cider, stout, wines, spirits and soft drinks in the oak-panelled bar, where light snacks and cream teas are also available. Food is served for breakfast at 8-9.30am, lunch at 12.30pm, and dinner from 6.30pm.

The hotel also has banqueting facilities for special occasions or conferences, with space for 80 seated guests or 150 served buffet style. The 13 tastefully furnished en-suite guest bedrooms all have telephone, TV, radio and tea-and-coffee making facilities, and boast views over Leyburn and across to the racehorse training gallops of Middleham. Room tariff includes breakfast.

Mid-Wensleydale is an exceptionally scenic area where people are known for the genuine warmth of their hospitality. The small attractive towns of Middleham and Leyburn are at the centre of Yorkshire's best known Dale, making The Golden Lion Hotel a natural base for exploring the villages and enjoying the scenery of Wensleydale and the whole of the Yorkshire Dales. Local attractions such as Bolton Castle, Jervaulx Abbey, Masham (with its Brewery Centres) and Richmond, York, Harrogate and Ripon are also within easy reach.

Bellerby, Leyburn,
North Yorkshire DL8 5QS
Tel: 01969 622256
e-mail: crosskeys.bellerby@yahoo.co.uk
website: www.crosskeysbellerby.co.uk

Located in the heart of Wensleydale, Bellerby is a delightful spot that is known locally as the village of many bridges. Overlooking the spacious village green, the **Cross Keys Inn** is an 18th Century traditional family inn that is popular with locals and tourists alike and offers many fine facilities. The inn is open throughout the year and you can rest assured of a warm welcome from mine hosts, Sue and Richard Haworth, who took over here in 2007 and have created a relaxed and friendly environment.

This is a truly family-friendly inn. Children can enjoy the well-equipped outside play area while parents can watch over them from the nearby beer garden, weather permitting! Sue and Richard

have introduced Family Weekends with lots of children's playground attractions which have proved very successful. There's plenty of entertainment for adults too. Various events are held throughout the year that appeal to young and old alike and Quiz nights (normally on a Monday evening) are extremely popular with prizes for the winning (and worst) teams. Full details can be found on the inn's web site.

The inn also hosts frequent live entertainment on Saturday evenings by local acts including comedians and singers (or even singing comedians!), and of course Karaoke events allow patrons to exhibit their exceptional hidden abilities. Fortunately, the guest accommodation is on the opposite wing of the inn so that this wonderful raw talent cannot be heard! This accommodation comprises 1 family sized en suite room which is available all year round.

The Cross Keys is also noted for the appetising home-made food on offer, based wherever possible on fresh local produce. Theme-based food events take place regularly including popular Steak Nights. Food is available at all opening times except on Wednesdays and Sunday evenings. To accompany your meal, the well-stocked bar offers a comprehensive range of beverages, including 4 real ales - John Smiths as the regular brew; an ale from the Copper Dragon brewery, plus two rotating guest ales.

Also part of the inn's amenities is a separate tea room which is open from 10am to 4pm, Monday to Saturday. The inn itself is open from noon during the summer months, and from 5pm in the winter. And for those who enjoy the outdoor life, the inn has a small number of camping pitches within the spacious garden area.

Constable Burton,
North Yorkshire DL8 5LH
Tel: 01677 450581

The gardens of Constable Burton Hall are one of the major visitor attractions in this area but the gardens at **The Wyvill Arms** are also pretty impressive and beautifully maintained. So too is the building with its creeper-clad walls. The inn was built in 1920 but the dry stone walls covered in ivy make it look much older. The Wyvill Arms is owned and run by the Stevens family whose various members have owned a number of top class establishments in this corner of North Yorkshire. At the Wyvill, Nigel Stevens is aided by his mum Theresa and father Roger.

Nigel is a professional chef and his food is, in a word, superb. He uses only the finest, fresh produce for his dishes and 99% of the ingredients have been sourced in the county with the fish coming from either Whitby or Hartlepool. The menu changes with the seasons so at the appropriate time you might find amongst the starters home-grown Asparagus drizzled with crustacean oil, or a harlequin terrine of smoked ham, Wensleydale cheese and duck mousse with a pear and apple chutney. Main courses range from a roasted barracuda on candied aubergines Andalucian style, through a choice of steaks, to local roast lamb fillet and a selection of vegetarian dishes. In addition to the regular menu, there are also weekly changing special dishes. The restaurant seats up to 50 and there are also picnic tables in the spacious garden. Food is served from noon until 2.15pm, and 6pm to 9pm, Tuesday to Sunday. At Sunday lunchtimes only roasts and a vegetarian option are available. To accompany your meal, the bar stocks a comprehensive range of beverages, including 3 real ales - Black Sheep, a Theakston's brew and a guest ale.

The Wyvill also offers quality accommodation in 2 attractively furnished and decorated guest rooms. One room can be either a family, double or twin; the other is a double.

Children are welcome at The Wyvill; there's good disabled access to the bar and dining areas; all major credit cards except American Express and Diners are accepted; and there's ample off road parking.

18 THE COUNTRYMAN'S INN

Hunton, nr Bedale,
North Yorkshire DL8 1PY
Tel: 01677 450554
e-mail: tony@countrymansinn.co.uk
website: www.countrymansinn.co.uk

The Countryman's Inn is a traditional village country pub in the village of Hunton where visitors will find a warm welcome and a relaxed and friendly atmosphere. In the bar with its beamed ceilings and seasonal log fire, you'll find a well-kept selection of 4 cask-conditioned ales, 3 of which are brewed within 10 miles of the pub - and a guest ale from as far as 30 miles away! There's also a wide selection of other beers, lagers and wines to suit all occasions.

The Countryman's restaurant has a deserved local reputation for its range of foods offering good value fixed priced lunches and dinners, a must in Yorkshire! Amongst the starters are Steamed Bantry Bay Mussels with white wine, garlic, parsley and cream, and an interesting Squid & King Prawn Salad. As a main

course, how about Roast Breast of Chicken stuffed with Stilton and served on a bed of creamed leeks. Or pan-fried Fillet of Sea Bass served on a bed of garlic and lemon wild mushrooms. The menu also offers a selection of stir frys, grills and vegetarian options such as Spring Vegetable Risotto with Parmesan cheese and onion rings. To complete your dining pleasure, try one of the delicious home-made desserts - Blueberry Pavlova, perhaps. The inn also offers "Value" Lunch & Early Dinner menus. Food is served from noon to 2.30pm, Wednesday to Sunday; and from 6pm to 9pm, Wednesday to Saturday. During the summer months, customers are welcome to enjoy the hospitality 'alfresco' in the attractive beer garden and patio area. To accompany your meal, there's a comprehensive selection of beverages, including an excellent wine list and a choice of 4 real ales.

If you are lucky enough to be able to enjoy a stay in the Dales, whether on business or pleasure, you could make use of one of the inn's three comfortable and well-equipped, en-suite bedrooms. One of the rooms is large enough to serve as a family room.

A fairly recent innovation at the Countryman is its Musical Evening, held every other Monday. Every one is welcome so, if you play an instrument, or sing, go along and join in.

221

19 THE BLACK SWAN HOTEL

Market Place, Middleham,
North Yorkshire DL8 4NP
Tel: 01969 622221
e-mail: blackswan_middleham@tiscali.co.uk
website: www.blackswan-middleham.co.uk

The Black Swan Hotel is located in the heart of the captivating small town of Middleham, famous for its Castle, once the home of Richard III, and for its many horse studs and race horses. The hotel occupies a delightful 17th century Grade II listed building, replete with ancient oak beams and with an open log fire. Ian, a Yorkshireman, and his wife Sally, took over here in January 2008 and very quickly were receiving rave reviews for the friendly atmosphere and cosy feel and the quality of the food on offer.

The menus, which change regularly, are based on top quality fresh locally sourced produce, sirloin steaks, home-made pies and Beef in Old Peculier Ale Casserole all particularly popular. You'll also find vegetarian dishes such as the Wild French and Japanese Mushroom Stroganoff with

rice and salad. There's a separate menu for the bar meals which include Local Masham Pork Sausages on Creamy Mash with Rich Gravy and Peas. And amongst the desserts, there's a wonderful home-made Apple Crumble or Sticky Toffee Pudding served with cream, ice cream from a local prize winning producer. Food is served every day from noon until 3pm, and from 7pm to 9.30pm; booking at the weekend is strongly advised. In good weather, meals can be enjoyed in the attractive south-facing Beer Garden which backs almost onto the Castle. On summer evenings, the garden is lit so that meals can be served 'al fresco'. To accompany your meal, the well-stocked bar offers a comprehensive range of beverages, including up to 5 real ales - John Smith's, Black Sheep, Theakston's Old Peculier, Theakston's Best and a further Theakston's guest ale.

The hotel also offers quality accommodation in attractive en suite rooms with a choice of single, twin, double, 4-poster and family room which will sleep up to 5. All the rooms are equipped with television, direct dial phone and hospitality tray. The family and 4-poster rooms also have Televideo with a large selection of videos.

Middleham itself is an excellent centre for touring the Yorkshire Dales and James Herriot Country. Hawes, the home of Wensleydale cheese; Richmond with its fine Castle and market; Masham, where both Black Sheep and Theakston's Breweries are based; and scenic Aysgarth Falls are all within easy reach, while York with its manifold attractions is only an hour's drive away.

20 THE COPPICE COFFEE SHOP

Aysgarth Falls, nr Leyburn,
North Yorkshire DL8 3TH
Tel: 01969 663763
e-mail: ryderscoppicekc@aol.com
website: www.thecoppiceaysgarthfalls.co.uk

Located just a short walk from the famous Aysgarth Falls, **The Coppice Coffee Shop** is a family-run business which opened in 1997. The Falls and woodland at Aysgarth have been attracting visitors since the 18th century. Artists such as JMW Turner painted here and William Wordsworth and his sister Dorothy wrote about their visit here in 1812. More recently, Kevin Costner made the Falls even more famous by filming the fight scene between Robin Hood and Little John at the Upper Falls.

Karen and Richard Chapman's menu at The Coppice offers an extensive choice that includes home-made soups, cakes and puddings (including gluten and dairy-free), well-filled rolls such as the tasty best back bacon

smothered in Wensleydale cheese, piping hot jacket potatoes served with a bowl of fresh salad and a selection of daily specials. The flexibility of the menu works well: smaller portions for smaller appetites; the good value children's menu and the special diet menu are all part of the service along with facilities for the disabled. The Coppice is open daily, closed on Christmas day.

21 THE KINGS ARMS

Askrigg, Leyburn,
North Yorkshire DL8 3HQ
Tel: 01969 650817   Fax: 01969 650927

The Kings Arms in the pretty Wensleydale village will be very familiar to devotees of BBC-TV's 1970s drama series *All Creatures Great and Small*, where it appeared frequently as The Drovers Arms. James Herriot's surgery was (and still is) in Thirsk but the producers decided that Thirsk looked too modern. Unspoilt Askrigg, they felt, could easily pass for a 1930s/1940s Yorkshire village.

Mine hosts at The Kings Arms, Craig and Tilly Smith, took over here in the spring of 2008, although Craig had worked here for the previous 14 months. An accomplished Head Chef he has more than 7 years experience in a number of well-known local establishments. His menu is based on top quality, fresh local produce, all sourced within the county,

skilfully prepared and attractively presented. To complement your meal, there are up to 7 real ales on tap at any one time. Food is available from noon until 2.30pm, and from 6pm to 9pm, every day.

Children are very welcome; all major credit cards except American Express and Diners are accepted; and there is good disabled access.

22 THE WHITE ROSE HOTEL

Main Street, Askrigg,
North Yorkshire DL8 3HG
Tel: 01969 650515 Fax: 01969 650176
e-mail: stay@thewhiterosehotelaskrigg.co.uk
website: www.thewhiterosehotelaskrigg.co.uk

The attractive Wensleydale village of Askrigg lies within the Yorkshire Dales National Park and provides an excellent base for exploring the superb natural beauty of this scenic area. And if you are staying in Askrigg, **The White Rose Hotel** is *the* place to stay. It offers superb accommodation, excellent facilities and warm hospitality. Built in 1840, the exterior displays much olde worlde charm, whilst the interior has recently undergone extensive renovation and redecoration.

The hotel has a cosy and comfortable bar and characterful restaurant open to non-residents and residents alike. There are always three to four real ales, and a wide range of tasty bar meals. The hotel restaurant is full of character and a splendid venue in which to sample the excellent cuisine. The adjacent Conservatory dining area provides a very pleasing environment in which to enjoy the outstanding food on offer. Lunch is served from noon until 2pm, and dinner from 6pm to 9pm with dishes based on locally-sourced produce. Among many specialities of the house, there are roast dinners served every day.

Open all year round, the hotel has 12 attractively furnished and decorated guest bedrooms - 5 doubles; 4 king size; 2 superior doubles and 1 twin. All the rooms have en suite facilities and are equipped with television and tea/coffee-making facilities.

Sightseeing opportunities within a few miles include the magnificent Hardraw Force (England's highest waterfall) and Aysgarth Falls (England's most impressive series of powerful falls) as well as the breathtaking scenery of the region. Wensleydale provides excellent walking and several of Yorkshire's most impressive and interesting historic sites including Bolton Castle, Middleham Castle, Richmond Castle and the beautiful abbey ruins at Jervaulx, Fountains and Easby Abbeys. Add to this visitor attractions such as the Dales Countryside Museum and Wensleydale Creamery, both in Hawes, the intriguing Forbidden Corner near Leyburn, and the historic city of York with its manifold attractions.

Furthermore, there is a wide range of day tours that can take in the splendour of Cumbria's Lake District, the North York Moors National Park, amazing Upper Teesdale and the North Pennines Area of Outstanding Natural Beauty. And for a shopping extravaganza, Leeds and Harrogate are both within easy reach.

23 DALES COUNTRYSIDE MUSEUM

Station Yard, Hawes,
North Yorkshire, DL8 3NT
Tel: 01969 666210
e-mail: dcm@yorkshiredales.org.uk
website: www.yorkshiredales.org.uk

Visit the **Dales Countryside Museum** and see for yourself how our ancestors survived in this beautiful, but some-times harsh, environment. This award winning museum brings alive the past of the Yorkshire Dales, with interactive exhibits, exciting displays, video and CD Rom. The museum has several galleries, the largest one being in the Victorian goods shed that once housed the goods waiting for collection by the steam engines of the Midland railway. Adjoining the goods shed exhibition hall is the purpose built museum which houses a gift shop and information centre, public toilets, education & study rooms, an outside amphitheatre and the John Baker Exhibition Hall. The Museum's time tunnel will then take you onto the platform of the old station, where a series of railway carriages house the video and artefacts from Dales life throughout the centuries.

The museum showcases local craft workers and craft demonstrations are held throughout the year. For details of opening time, how to get there, exhibitions and events, please telephone the information desk on 01969 667450, or visit the Authority's award winning website. Fully accessible by wheelchair the Dales Countryside Museum is situated in side Station Yard, just off the main A684 at the eastern end of Hawes, Wensleydale. Opening times: 10am until 5pm daily (except Christmas Holidays)

24 THE WHITE HART INN

Main Street, Hawes,
North Yorkshire DL8 3QL
Tel: 01969 667259

Located in the heart of the popular market town of Hawes, **The White Hart Inn** has been refreshing tired and thirsty travellers since the 1600s. Mine hosts at this gem of a tavern are the daughter, mother and father team of Michelle, Neil and Judith.

Michelle is a talented cook and her extensive menu ranges from old favourites such as home-made Meat & Potato Pie, through a vegetarian Aubergine parmigiana, to a tasty Caribbean Coconut Chicken. The Children's Menu offers an unusually wide choice. At lunchtimes a good selection of sandwiches and crusty baguettes are available. Food is served from noon until 2pm, and from 6.30pm to 8.30pm, daily, and on Sundays a choice of roasts is added to the menu. Booking is essential at weekends, especially

during the season. Real ale lovers will be pleased to find a choice of 3 brews - John Smiths, Black Sheep and a rotating guest ale.

The White Hart also offers comfortable accommodation in 7 standard rooms with a choice of double, twin or single. The inn accepts all major credit cards apart from American Express and Diners; and there is disabled access to the bar and dining areas.

25 WILDINGS OF PATELEY BRIDGE

**Nidd Walk, Pateley Bridge,
North Yorkshire HG3 5NA
Tel: 01423 711152**

Housed in what used to be a pumping house, **Wildings of Pateley Bridge** occupies a lovely position beside the River Nidd in the heart of this popular little town. Owned and run by Alan and Jane Measham, this outstanding traditional tea room offers a huge choice of appetising food. Breakfast baguettes are available throughout the day along with warm ciabattas, baps, jacket potatoes, home-made pâté flavoured with brandy and garlic, hot or cold sandwiches, and sweet or savoury pancakes served with a side salad. Also available are poached eggs on a bed of locally cured ham and cream cheese, and salad platters. Sweets and puddings include old favourites such as Spotted Dick and Treacle Pudding as well as a fresh fruit salad and Apple & Blackberry Crumble.

From 3pm, Riverside Cream Teas are served and

throughout the winter months, the Winter Warmer offers the soup of the day together with your choice of cake. Teatime treats also include a wide selection of freshly baked scones and a variety of delicious cakes. To accompany your meal, there's a vast range of coffees, teas and soft drinks to choose from. Wildings has a large open terrace overlooking the beautiful river Nidd, where diners can sit & relax with their meals and drinks. Wildings is open from 10am to 5pm, Tuesday to Sunday; all major credit cards apart from Diners are accepted.

26 THE BIRCH TREE INN

**Willsill, Harrogate,
North Yorkshire HG3 5EA
Tel: 01423 711131**

Enjoying a lovely rural location in the village of Willsill near Pateley Bridge, **The Birch Tree Inn** is a fine old country inn with a reputation for excellent food. Mine hosts, Paul and Sue, took over here in the spring of 2008, their first venture as landlords although Paul has been in the hospitality business for some 30 years.

Paul is an accomplished chef who counts amongst his awards the prestigious title of 'Associate Culinaire Francaise'. Not surprisingly his menu has a distinct Continental flavour although the ingredients are locally sourced wherever possible; you'll find Nidderdale lamb on the menu, for example, along with other meats from local farms. Paul's fresh fish dishes are also popular with Grilled Swordfish and Grilled Salmon

with Whiskey amongst the choices. Food is served from noon until 2pm, Tuesday to Sunday, and from 6.30pm to 9pm daily.

The bar is stocked with a comprehensive range of beverages, including 2 real ales - Timothy Taylor Landlord and Black Sheep. If you are planning to stay in this pleasant part of the county, the inn has 3 attractively furnished and decorated guest rooms, all of them en suite.

27 THE YORKSHIRE LASS CAFÉ

Main Street, Grassington,
North Yorkshire BD23 5AP
Tel: 01756 751835
e-mail: dalescrea8@hotmail.co.uk
website: www.yorkshirelasscafe.co.uk

At **The Yorkshire Lass Café** you can not only enjoy hearty home-cooking but also create your own pot. The food first. Using only the finest and freshest local ingredients, owner Lindsay Hobbs has created a traditional menu with something for every taste and budget; from toasted paninins to home-baked delights. The café is open every day during the season from 9am to 5pm, and on Friday and Saturday evenings it stays open supplying Grassington with tasty pizzas to eat-in or take-away. If you are celebrating a special occasion, holding a meeting or require catering for any event, The Yorkshire Lass will work with you to create a menu that matches your needs and budget. The same wonderful home-cooking and fresh local ingredients are a part of all that they do.

For surfers of the net, the café has three speedy broadband stations for those using our computers, for which there's a small charge, and there's free Wi-Fi with their Wireless Hotspot connectivity.

Now for the pots. Whenever the café is open you can decorate a pot, mug or plate "and CRE8 a lasting memento of your visit to The Yorkshire Lass and Grassington!" When glazed and fired - you can collect the pot, or they will post it to your home.

Appletreewick, nr Burnsall, Skipton,
North Yorkshire BD23 6DA
Tel: 01756 720270
e-mail: info@craven-cruckbarn.co.uk
website: www.craven-cruckbarn.co.uk

Set beside a former drovers road and surrounded by miles of unspoilt National Park, **The Craven Arms and Cruck Barn** is the kind of traditional Yorkshire Dales inn that you always hoped to find. Original oak beams, flagged floors, gas lighting and open fires all combine to create a captivating atmosphere.

Dating back to the 1600s, the inn once belonged to Sir William Craven who was born to a farmer's family in Appletreewick and went on to become Lord Mayor of London. He returned to the area as a great benefactor and is now regarded as the 'Dick Whittington of the Dales'.

Today this lovely old hostelry is owned and run by the father and son team of David and Robert Ainsworth who arrived here in 2004. They then embarked on an astonishing venture, nothing less than building a restaurant at the rear of the inn that is a genuine yorkshire, heather thatched cruck barn and is believed to be the first of its kind to be built in the Dales since Henry VIII was on the throne. "Cruck barns are constructed around an 'A' frame of green, unseasoned oak" says Rob. "Once dry they contort to take on a character not possible using modern materials." Completed by the end

of 2006 with the help of family and local traditional craftsmen, the barn was built using local stone and wood, and even the heather thatching came from a field only two miles away.

The interior, which has a minstrel's gallery, provides a superb setting for fine dining and special functions. The Ainsworths pride themselves on the wholesome, home-cooked food based on locally sourced produce that is served in this very special restaurant. As well as an ever-changing extensive menu that has something to suit everyone's taste, there's also an À La Carte menu for anyone desiring an extra special dining experience.

Food is also available in the bar where there's a good choice of bar meals and home-made children's meals and, at lunchtime, jacket potatoes and hot and cold sandwiches. To accompany your repast, the inn offers a choice of no fewer than 8 cask ales, including Dark Horse Best, Black Witch, Theakston's Best, Tetley's and regulary changed guest ales from the local Yorkshire breweries, all lovingly cask conditioned in their own cellar by the pubs dedicated cellarman.

29   BOLTON ABBEY

Bolton Abbey Estate Estate Office,
Bolton Abbey, Skipton,
North Yorkshire BD23 6EX
Tel: 01756 718009
website: www.boltonabbey.com

Bolton Abbey near Skipton is the Yorkshire Estate of the Duke and Duchess of Devonshire. Situated in Wharfedale, in the Yorkshire Dales National Park this historic estate is a magnet for visitors drawn to its breathtaking landscapes and excellent facilities.

Visitors have flocked to Bolton Abbey for over one hundred years. On an August Bank Holiday in the 1890's the railway brought 40,000 people to Bolton Abbey; nearly as many people now visit York in a week. After the First World War visitors arrived by train in their "Sunday Best" with the children carrying buckets, spades and fishing nets. Some fathers never got much further than the Devonshire Arms' Refreshment Room, but many removed their boots and rolled up their trousers to paddle with their children by the sandy river bank. Little has changed over the years; visitors still come to see the landscape that inspired artists like Turner and Landseer, and poets such as Wordsworth.

As the name suggests Bolton Abbey was originally a large monastic Estate, based around the 12th century priory. Legend has it that the Priory was established in 1120 by Cecily de Romille as an expression of her grief following the drowning of her son in the nearby Strid. Today, the ruins of the Priory set in an incomparable position overlooking the river Wharfe will evoke the past glories of the Estate whilst the restored and thriving parish church shows that the Estate is still very much a living community.

30   BLUE BELL INN

Middle Road, Kettlewell, Skipton,
North Yorkshire BD23 5QX
Tel: 01756 760230
websites: www.copper dragon.co.uk
or www.bluebell inn.co.uk

If you're looking for excellent cask ales, tasty home-cooked food and comfortable accommodation, look no further than the **Blue Bell Inn.** Established in 1680, this lovely old hostelry is full of character, with some very handsome features such as the large brick-built fireplace and a wealth of warm wood panelling. The Blue Bell began life as a coaching inn on the Dales Way and the route of that famous walk, and the popular Inn Way, pass directly through Kettlewell, making it an ideal touring base.

The inn is noted for its appetising food with an extensive menu that ranges from a hearty Steak & Copper Dragon Ale Pie, through award-winning locally-made Cumberland Sausages, to a delicious home-made Fish Pie. Vegetarians are well-catered for

and there's also a children's menu. To accompany your meal, the bar offers a comprehensive choice of beverages, including 4 real ales from the Copper Dragon Brewery in Skipton.

The Blue Bell also offers comfortable en suite accommodation in 6 en suite bedrooms. One of these is a family room; two are on the ground floor, and all rooms command marvellous views over the surrounding countryside.

Buckden, Skipton,
North Yorkshire BD23 5JA
Tel: 01756 760228 Fax: 01756 760227
e-mail: info@thebuckinnbuckden.co.uk
website: www.thebuckinnbuckden.co.uk

The very impressive **Buck Inn** stands in the heart of the Yorkshire Dales, surrounded by the breathtaking beauty of this National Park. But it's not just the scenery that has made this inn internationally renowned. A traditional Georgian coaching inn with every modern comfort, The Buck is widely acclaimed for its culinary expertise and has a personally compiled wine list with comprehensive coverage of all the wine regions of the world.

The dining room is spacious, tasteful and encourages you to linger long and enjoy the atmosphere, aromas and flavours. Crystal glasses, lace napkins, and top of the range crockery all add to the pleasure of dining here. An extensive menu is available and offers everything from a satisfying pub snack to a full selection on the A La Carte menu and Specials Board; all served in the comfortable and welcoming bar or Courtyard Restaurant. All the food is locally sourced from the finest growers and farmers in the region - dining here is treated as an experience to be savoured to

the full. The menu is varied and meals served to the highest of standards with flair and stylish imagination. The restaurant is open every day from 6pm until 9pm. Real ale lovers will be pleased to find that the bar offers 6 real ales with Black Sheep, Timothy Taylor Landlord and Dark Mild, and the locally brewed Aysgarth Buckden Pike (only available here) as the regular brews.

The accommodation offers a choice of 12 divine rooms with four poster beds available, all en suite and equipped with all you could need. All bedrooms include a colour television, direct dial telephones and beverage making facilities. Every care has been taken in individually designing and furnishing each room in a comfortable and gracious style in keeping with The Buck's exacting

standards. Two of the rooms are on the ground floor and many of the bedrooms command magnificent views of the Yorkshire Dales and the River Wharfe, including the Wharfedale Suite. Breakfast is of course a sumptuous delight - indeed, every meal, service, amenity and facility here at The Buck Inn will exceed your expectations.

From the Buck Inn, picturesque villages, fells and other natural beauties are easily reached on foot or by car, and the area also boasts a wealth of museums, galleries and historic homes and buildings.

Litton, North Yorkshire BD23 5QJ
Tel: 01756 770208
e-mail: info@queensarmslitton.co.uk
website: www.thequeensarmslitton.co.uk

Tucked away in the heart of the Yorkshire Dales National Park, you'll find **The Queen's Arms Inn** which is the kind of authentic rural free house that many feared may have disappeared forever.

Littondale's visitors and locals have been regulars at The Queen's Arms since its beginnings as an 18th century drover's inn, "and we sometimes think some of them may never have left!" say mine hosts Jayne and Douggie.

The welcome today is as warm as ever, with a real fire, real oak-beamed ceilings and real, home-cooked local food cooked by a professional chef and served by real people. The menu offers an extensive choice that includes grills, fish dishes such as fresh Wharfedale trout, home-made pies, roasts and a good choice of vegetarian dishes such as Quorn in Red Wine. Snacks and sandwiches are also available. Food is served from noon until 2.30pm, and from 6.30pm to 9pm, every day. Booking ahead is strongly advisable at weekends.

Lovers of real ales will be delighted to find that the inn has had its own micro-brewery since 2001. Head Brewer Alan Rogers produces several tasty brews including Litton Ale, Leading Light, Potts Beck, Dark Star and Goldcrest. The bar is also well stocked with a comprehensive range of beverages, including fine wines. This is a genuine, proper pub!

If you're just passing through the Dales, or are here for a longer visit, the inn has 5 excellent en suite bed and breakfast accommodation available throughout the year. Four of the rooms are doubles; one is a family room. All are comfortably and tastefully furnished with tea and coffee-making facilities and a TV, VCR and a small selection of videos. All the rooms enjoy

fabulous views across Littondale. A hearty Dales breakfast is included in the tariff and there are flexible hours for the meal.

The Queen's Arms Inn is ideal for those on a walking or caving holiday, or if you're just looking for a comfortable, friendly rural retreat with nothing to disturb your sleep but the occasional barn owl. Or simply call in for a drink, settle in by the fire and get chatting to whoever happens to be around - be they residents, passers-by or a local farmer. The inn is child-friendly and dogs are welcome.

231

33 SKIPTON CASTLE

Skipton, Yorkshire BD23 1AQ
Tel: 01756 792442
e-mail: info@skiptoncastle.co.uk
website: www.skiptoncastle.co.uk

Guardian of the gateway to the Yorkshire Dales for over 900 years, this unique fortress is one of the most complete and well-preserved medieval castles in England. Standing on a 40-metre high crag, fully-roofed **Skipton Castle** was founded around 1090 by Robert de Romille, one of William the Conqueror's Barons, as a fortress in the dangerous northern reaches of the kingdom.

Owned by King Edward I and Edward II, from 1310 it became the stronghold of the Clifford Lords withstanding successive raids by marauding Scots. During the Civil War it was the last Royalist bastion in the North, yielding only after a three-year siege in 1645. 'Slighted' under the orders of Cromwell, the castle was skilfully restored by the redoubtable Lady Anne Clifford and today visitors can climb from the depths of the Dungeon to the top of the Watch Tower, and explore the Banqueting Hall, the Kitchens, the Bedchamber and even the Privy!

Every period has left its mark, from the Norman entrance and the Medieval towers, to the beautiful Tudor courtyard with the great yew tree planted by Lady Anne in 1659. In the castle grounds visitors can see the Tudor wing built as a royal wedding present for Lady Eleanor Brandon, niece of Henry VIII, the beautiful Shell Room decorated in the 1620s with shells and Jamaican coral and the ancient medieval chapel of St. John the Evangelist. The Chapel Terrace, with its delightful picnic area, has fine views over the woods and Skipton's lively market town.

34 THE ROYAL SHEPHERD

Canal Street, Skipton,
North Yorkshire BD23 1LB
Tel: 01756 793178
e-mail: tonyhodgson/royalshepherd@hotmail.co.uk

The Royal Shepherd occupies a superb canalside location and has a well-established reputation for excellent food which is served all day, every day - and at very reasonable prices. The outdoor patio area overlooks the canal while the interior provides great comfort in traditional surroundings.

The inn's extensive menu offers a huge choice of traditional favourites such as Yorkshire Pork Pie & Pies, home-made Steak Pie, a famous Royal Fish Supper, and roast dinners which are served daily until 3pm. After 3pm, a choice of dishes from the grill are served, including a huge Mixed Grill. Vegetarians are well-catered for with a selection of dishes that includes Spinach & Feta Goujons, and Thai Red Vegetable Curry. For lighter appetites, there's also a good choice of

salads, sandwiches, baguettes, toasties, baps, jacket potatoes and, amongst the starters, a trio of Yorkshire puddings filled with onion gravy.

Amongst the beverages served at the well-stocked bar are 3 real ales, two of which are from the local Copper Dragon Brewery, along with Timothy Taylor's Landlord. The inn accepts all major credit cards apart from American Express.

35 THE CRAVEN MUSEUM

Town Hall, High Street, Skipton,
North Yorkshire BD23 1AH
Tel: 01756 706407 Fax: 01756 706412
e-mail: museum@cravendc.gov.uk
website: www.cravendc.gov.uk

Crammed full of fascinating exhibits, the
Craven Museum is a great place to explore
the history of Skipton and the Craven Dales.
The museum displays collections of local
history,
archaeology,
natural
history, art
and geology
in a small
but very
popular
museum
situated in
the Town

Hall at the top of Skipton's busy market
place. Temporary exhibitions vary from
community projects to items on loan from
other museums. Admission is free and the
museum is open all year round.

36 THE MASONS ARMS INN

Eastby, nr Skipton,
North Yorkshire BD23 6SN
Tel: 01756 792754
e-mail: isobel.crocker@btinternet.com
website: www.masonsarmseastby.co.uk

A traditional Dales inn surrounded by beautiful
views, **The Masons Arms Inn** was originally built
to accommodate the needs of stonemasons
working in the nearby quarry. The landlady was a
formidable lady who refused to serve any navvy
on pay day who could not prove that he had sent
home money to his wife and children. And if they
were too over indulgent they spent the night in the
tiny jail house which still stands opposite the pub
today.

Inside the inn, you'll find that the lounge and
games rooms have real open fires and, keeping up to
date, snuggled in the corner of the cosy tap room in
between the fireplace and the cribbage board, there's
Internet access freely available to all on 4 computers.

Excellent
traditional food,
professionally
cooked, is served

in the restaurant or in the more informal surroundings of
the lounge and bar which offers a choice of 4 real ales. The
accommodation at the inn comprises one twin and one
double room, both en suite and with great views. Also
available are 2 self-catering cottages sleeping up to 5 and
located in the nearby village of Embsay.

Kildwick, nr Keighley,
North Yorkshire BD20 9BH
Tel: 01535 632265
e-mail: nicjwheel@yahoo.co.uk

A large and impressive building, **The White Lion** stands opposite the church in the picturesque village of Kildwick on the north bank of the River Aire. New owners, Nicola and Simon, ably assisted by chef Richard, have made this a superb place to dine, drink or stay.

Behind the handsome stone frontage of the inn, the look is charmingly traditional with old beams, exposed stone, dark wood panelling and rustic furniture all contributing to the inviting atmosphere. In the restaurant, where horse brasses, pewter tankards and old prints adorn the walls, diners have a plentiful choice of dishes. At lunchtime there are main dishes such as slow-cooked shoulder of local beef, pasta dishes, bar meals and sandwiches. In the evening, amongst the starters are grilled green lip mussels with a garlic crumb topping, and a vegetarian grilled halloumi with baked blue cheese mushrooms. For the main course, how about local calf's liver with crispy bacon, a tasty sea bass fillet with stir-fried green vegetables and an oriental dressing, or a vegetarian grilled Yorkshire goat's cheese with a roast vegetable tart and a pesto dressing? Food is served from noon until

2.30pm, and from 6pm to 9pm, Monday to Saturday. On Sundays, food is served between 12 - 8 where there is a different menu offering Sunday Roasts, Fish and Veggie alternatives. Booking ahead is strongly recommended at weekends.

To accompany your meal, the bar stocks a comprehensive range of beverages, including 4 real ales with Timothy Taylor Landlord, Tetley Mild and Black sheep as the regular brews. In good weather, customers can enjoy their refreshment at tables and benches in the spacious terrace and garden at the front of the inn which has a sheltered area for smokers. This friendly hostelry hosts a Quiz Night on Thursday evenings from 9.30pm - all are welcome and free nibbles are provided.

If you are planning to stay in this scenic corner of the county, close to the Yorkshire Dales National Park and Brontë Country, the White Lion has 3 attractively furnished and decorated guest bedrooms, 1 double and 2 family rooms, all upstairs and all with en suite facilities. A hearty Yorkshire breakfast is included in the tariff. The White Lion accepts all major credit cards apart from Diners; there's good disabled access to the bar and restaurant; and ample parking.

Colne Road, Malsis, Sutton-in-Craven,
Keighley, North Yorkshire BD20 8DS
Tel: 01535 633855
e-mail: dogandguninn@btopenworld.com
website: www.dogandguninn.net

The tiny hamlet of Malsis features on very few road maps but it's well worth seeking out in order to visit **The Dog & Gun,** an outstanding hostelry run by the Walker family, Anita and Ross and their children Aaron, Rickki and Amy. The inn is an

attractive old building which has been beautifully restored using traditional timbers and materials. The old atmosphere is today preserved with its thick walls, raised wooden floor, real fire stove and its library corner. To further enhance the atmosphere, the Walkers have added another real fireplace, new toilets and a new kitchen and patio area. The inn is open 7 days a week and it's a great place as somewhere to meet, somewhere to eat, somewhere to enjoy your favourite tipple or a place to escape from the stresses of daily life.

Good food is a priority here. Ross is a Master Chef and his menu, based on locally sourced produce, includes house specialities such as charcoal-grilled steaks, home-made steak pie, rack of lamb, poached chicken, curry of the day, pasta dishes, salads and more. The puddings alone make the trip worth while - home-made bilberry pie, hot chocolate fudge cake and raspberry pavlova are just some of the treats on offer. And why not complement them with a glass of dessert wine, Muscat de Rivesaltes or Aleatico di Puglia perhaps. Food is served from noon until 9pm, Monday to Saturday; from noon until 4pm on Sundays when traditional roasts are on offer, and again from 4pm to 9pm on Sunday evening. During the week, Cream Teas are available from 3pm to 5pm.

At least 5 real ales are on tap - Timothy Taylor's award-winning hand pulled fine ales, expertly served with a smooth creamy head that lasts all the way down the glass. The bar also stocks a full

range of wines, spirits and soft drinks. In good weather, customers can enjoy their refreshments in the patio area overlooking the quiet road.

Recently, the Walkers have started smoking their own fish and other products and making their own sauces and mustards. These are available on the menu and also to buy in vacuum-packed packets to take away.

Children are welcome at the Dog and Gun; all major credit cards apart from Diners are accepted; there's good disabled access throughout and ample parking.

39 SETTLE DOWN CAFÉ

11 Duke Street, Settle,
North Yorkshire BD24 9DU
Tel: 01729 822480
e-mail: settledowncafe@tiscali.co.uk

Just a short stroll from Settle railway station,
the **Settle Down Café** is a charming eating
place serving
quality home
cooking with a
varied menu,
supplemented
by daily specials.
Peter Jones who
together with
his wife Julie,
owns and runs
the café is a
talented cook
and his dishes
are much

appreciated by local people who return time
and again to enjoy them. The café is open
from 9-ish to 5-ish, daily except for
Thursdays. Payment is by cash or cheque
only.

40 THE BOARS HEAD HOTEL

9 Main Street, Long Preston, Skipton,
North Yorkshire BD23 4ND
Tel: 01729 840217
e-mail: darrenjmonks@hotmail.co.uk
website: www.hotelyorkshiredales.co.uk

Run by brothers Paul and Darren Monks,
The Boars Head Hotel is a fine old
hostelry with a history dating back to the
16th century. Darren is an experienced chef
and his
extensive
menu
ranges from
old
favourites
such as
steaks,

Shepherd's Pie, and Beef Lasagne to specials
such as the Hickory Chicken and the
vegetarian freshly cooked watercress pancake.
Lovers of real ales will find a choice of 4
different brews. The hotel also offers quality
bed & breakfast accommodation with 5 en
suite rooms available. All major credit cards
are accepted.

41 MERCER ART GALLERY

Swan Road, Harrogate,
North Yorkshire HG1 2SA
Tel: 01423 556188 Fax: 01423 55613

Situated 100 yards from the entrance to the Valley
Gardens and Royal Pump Room Museum, the
Mercer Art Gallery is home to the district's
collection of
fine art, which is featured throughout the year as part of an
exciting and diverse exhibition programme.

2007 is an exciting year when Harrogate's most famous
artist, William Powell Frith, is celebrated with a blockbuster
exhibition of works by this great Victorian painter from March

to July. This is the first
exhibition of his work for over
50 years and the first time over
60 of his paintings, prints and
drawings have been brought
together.

Other exhibitions include:
Treasures of the Mercer, a chance
to see some highlights from
the permanent collection;
pastel and charcoal drawings
by Knaresborough Castle's 2006 artist in residence, Andrew
Cheetham; and art from Turkmenistan.

Watch out for special events and activities for families, adults,
and children. Open: Tuesday to Saturday and Bank Holiday
Monday 10-5, Sunday 2-5. Admission is free.

Burnt Yates, Harrogate,
North Yorkshire HG3 3EG
Tel: 01423 771070 Fax: 01423 772360
e-mail: newinnharrogate@btconnect.com
website: www.thenewinnburntyates.co.uk

Superbly situated in the village of Burnt Yates, on the edge of the Yorkshire Dales, is **The New Inn**, a beautifully maintained, traditional hostelry that first opened its doors in 1810. Today, owned and meticulously run by Tim and Pauline King, this Free House combines the perfect ingredients for an enjoyable lunch or evening out - a genuinely warm welcome, expertly kept real ales, fine wines and delicious food, all home-cooked using high quality local produce. During the winter months you have the choice of relaxing in front of a roaring fire in the cosy bar, or savouring your meal in the stylish restaurant; when the weather is warmer, sip a chilled drink on the private patio area.

The New Inn is noted for its excellent food prepared by a professional and talented chef. Amongst the starters you'll find his own soup of the day, an Italian style selection, and creamy garlic mushrooms topped with grilled Cheddar cheese. As a main course, the choice includes a delicious Creamy Fish Pie, Roast Gressingham Duck Breast, Rib Eye or Sirloin Steaks. The steaks are of the highest quality and are supplied by a Summerbridge butcher who sources them from local Dales farms. For vegetarians, the choice includes a grilled vegetable and tomato bake topped with mozzarella cheese. The regular menu is supplemented by daily specials and for lighter appetites a selection of sandwiches, baguettes, wraps and salads is available. Food is served every lunchtime and evening except Monday lunchtime. On Sundays, there's a choice of 2 roasts of the day. Due to the popularity of restaurant, booking is strongly advised at weekends. To accompany your meal, the well-stocked bar offers an extensive selection of beverages, including 3 real ales - Tetleys, Rudgate Viking and Theakstons.

Whether you are visiting for business or pleasure, The New Inn's comfortable, fully-refurbished en suite bedrooms make an ideal base for a truly memorable stay. Each of the hotel's eight 4-star rated bedrooms provide that 'home from home' feeling. They were all refurbished in the spring of 2007 to very exacting standards. All rooms are en suite with tea/coffee making facilities and colour television. A full English breakfast is included in the price of the room.   '

43 RIPLEY CASTLE

Estate Office, Ripley, Harrogate,
North Yorkshire HG3 3AY
Tel: 01423 770152
website: www.ripleycastle.co.uk

For almost 700 years the Ingilby family has loved their castle and no wonder, given its fabulous treasures, and glorious grounds. The first clue to the magnificence of **Ripley Castle** lies in its impressive 15th Century arched gatehouse at the entrance to its 1,000 acres of land. The estate - which today includes a stately home, complete with paintings and furniture that would grace a royal palace, as well as grounds containing a glorious lake and deer park - has been in the possession of the Ingilby family since the marriage of Sir Thomas Ingilby to Edeline Thweng in 1308.

Ripley Castle's grounds contain some of Britain's largest herbaceous borders, interspersed with fountains and lawns. There are walled gardens that are a pleasure to visit at any

time of year, and the National Hyacinth Collection which creates a delightful pastiche of colours and fragrances, especially in early summer. The kitchen gardens, meanwhile, contain rare collections of herbs, spices, fruit trees and vegetables. A walk around the wooded pleasure grounds leads to the lakeside path, where herds of Fallow and Red Deer graze peacefully under ancient oak trees.

44 HANNAH'S HOUSE

10 Castlegate, Knaresborough,
North Yorkshire HG5 8AR
Tel: 01423 868828

Standing close to the ruins of Knaresborough Castle, **Hannah's House** is a delightful old building dating in parts to the 1600s. It

started life as an ale house but is now a superb, fully licensed restaurant serving traditional Yorkshire food and providing traditional Yorkshire value. This outstanding restaurant has been owned and run since 1995 by Doris and Lawrence Lawford. Lawrence is an Executive Chef with some 40 years experience and his menu offers an extensive choice with meat and poultry dishes amongst the specialities of the house.

HIDDEN PLACES GUIDES

Explore Britain and Ireland with *Hidden Places* guides - a fascinating series of national and local travel guides.

Packed with easy to read information on hundreds of places of interest as well as places to stay, eat and drink.

Available from both high street and internet booksellers

For more information on the full range of *Hidden Places* guides and other titles published by Travel Publishing visit our website on

www.travelpublishing.co.uk or ask for our leaflet by phoning **01752 276660** or emailing **info@travelpublishing.co.uk**

45 MADISON CENTRAL

The Arcade, Ripon,
North Yorkshire HG4 1NZ
Tel: 01765 698368

A real magnet for lovers of home cooking, **Madison Central** is owned by Joanne Bowes but she did work here for 5 years before buying the premises in the autumn of 2006.

Everything on the menu here is really appetising and wholesome but Joanne is renowned throughout the country for her wonderful muffins. Her repertoire includes more than 25 different varieties of muffin and on any one day you'll find up to 12 different flavours on offer. All Joanne's dishes are freshly made and prepared with local produce wherever possible. The choice includes an All Day Breakfast, salads, a hearty Club Wrap, baked potatoes, ploughmans, toasties and sandwiches which are available on white or brown

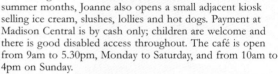

bread, or on genuine Italian ciabatta or genuine French baguette.

During the

summer months, Joanne also opens a small adjacent kiosk selling ice cream, slushes, lollies and hot dogs. Payment at Madison Central is by cash only; children are welcome and there is good disabled access throughout. The café is open from 9am to 5.30pm, Monday to Saturday, and from 10am to 4pm on Sunday.

47 THE SUN INN

Brame Lane, Norwood, Harrogate,
North Yorkshire HG3 1SZ
Tel: 01943 880220
e-mail: thebar@thesun-inn.co.uk
website: www.thesun-inn.co.uk

A fine old country hostelry, **The Sun Inn** at Norwood dates back to the 1700s when it was a coaching inn complete with stables and a smithy. Inside, wooden floors, ancient beams and wood-burning stove all add to the appeal. From the bar area, customers look down to the dining area which in turn looks out onto the spacious patio and beer garden which enjoys spectacular countryside views.

Neal and Fiona Walkinshaw took over here in early 2008 - Fiona already knew the pub well as she was born and bred in the village. She is also an accomplished chef and her menu offers a tasty selection of home-made dishes based on local produce wherever possible, especially the meat. Fiona's home-

made Steak Pie, home-made lasagne and steaks are particularly popular. Vegetarians are also well-catered for with dishes such as the Cheesy Leek & Potato Bake. Real ale lovers will be delighted to find a regular choice of 4 real ales, with as many as 10 different brews on tap in the height of the season.

Children are welcome at The Sun; there's good disabled access throughout, and all major credit cards apart from American Express and Diners are accepted. The Sun Inn also provides regular live entertainment.

46 STATION HOTEL

North Street, Ripon,
North Yorkshire HG4 1JP
Tel: 01765 690502
e-mail: xsara1984@aol.com

A warm and friendly hostelry, **The Station Hotel** stands close to Ripon's city centre and within easy walking distance of the famous Minster. Mine hosts, Sara Jones and her family, who took over here in the spring of 2008 are well known in the city as they also run the private Ripon Bowling Club.

The hotel is open every lunchtime and evening, and all day on Friday, Saturday and Sunday. Food is served from 5pm to 8pm, Monday to Saturday; and from noon until 3pm on Sunday when a Carvery replaces the regular menu - booking ahead is for this strongly recommended. This offers wholesome honest-to-goodness food with dishes such as home-made lasagne and cottage pie, all at very competitive prices. There are occasional daily specials. At weekends, breakfasts are served between 9am and 12 noon. Children are welcome and have their own little menu. The bar is stocked with a good selection of draught keg ales, lagers, cider and stout as well as one real ale - Tetleys.

The hotel also offers comfortable accommodation in 5 upstairs rooms, all of them attractively furnished and decorated, and with en suite facilities. The room prices include a hearty breakfast. All major credit cards apart from American Express and Diners are accepted, and the hotel has its own private car park at the rear.

49 THE CROWN INN

Roecliffe, North Yorkshire YO51 9LY
Tel: 01423 322300 Fax: 01423 322033
e-mail: info@crowninnroecliffe.com
website: www.crowninnroecliffe.com

The picturesque conservation village of Roecliffe near Boroughbridge is of Norse origin - 'rauthr' 'klif' meaning red cliff or bank and referring to the right bank of the river Ure on which it sits. In the heart of the village, **The Crown Inn** is a lovely old 16th century coaching inn, that has been brewing and serving ale to travellers on this site since the 14th century. Owner Karl Mainey arrived here in June 2007 and carried out a major refurbishment which has retained such historic features of the inn as the stone flag floors, crackling open log fires and ancient oak beams.

Karl has been a professional chef for some 18 years and insists on utilising all small local suppliers to acquire the finest Yorkshire produce - some 90% of the produce used here is sourced locally. Karl changes the whole menu weekly to reflect the best quality seasonal ingredients available. You will find the extensive menu listed on the chalk boards in all three rooms. Typical dishes include fresh Whitby Crab Cake with fresh ginger and lemon; gorgeous Pollack from the East Coast of Yorkshire served with crisp beer batter, home-made tartare sauce and organic tomato sauce; Galloway rare breed rib eye steak from a farm at nearby Sutton Bank; and local Venison Loin roasted with gin and juniper. Vegetarians are well-catered for with dishes such as Ribblesdale Goats Cheese Croquettes or Tadcaster Organic Vegetable Pie.

At The Crown, it's very important to save room for a dessert because Annette, the pastry chef, holds the honour of being National Pub Pastry Chef of the Year, 2008. And if you prefer a savoury, The Crown offers a board of hand-made Yorkshire cheeses which are served with Annette's home-baked biscuits and home-made Christmas cake. To accompany your meal, the well-

stocked bar has a complete range of beverages that includes real ales, spirits and fine wines.

Food is served from noon until 2.30pm, and from 6pm to 9.30pm, Monday to Saturday; and from noon until 7pm on Sunday. It is essential to book at weekends, and advisable at all times.

If you are planning to stay in this pleasant part of the country, The Crown has 10 well-appointed and comfortable guest bedrooms, all with en suite facilities. Three of the rooms are on the ground floor.

241

6 St James Square, Boroughbridge,
North Yorkshire YO51 9AR
Tel: 01423 322413 Fax: 01423 323915

Yorkshire abounds in ancient hostelries but **The Black Bull Inn** in the heart of Boroughbridge is one of the most venerable with a history going back to 1262. For many years it provided hospitality for travellers on the stage coaches running between Thirsk and Harrogate. Lots of traditional features remain inside, complemented by an up-to-the-minute décor and furnishings.

The inn is notable for the quality of the food it serves. There's an extensive bar snacks menu with a choice of dishes ranging through chargrilled dishes to traditional favourites such as Haddock & Chips, curry and a home-made pie of the day. The regular choice is supplemented by seasonal specials and fresh seafood dishes. If you choose from the à la carte menu, you'll find a tasty dish of King Prawn Tails and Queen Scallops amongst the starters; steaks, char grilled dishes, a

selection of 'Sizzlers', and dishes such as Tenderloin of Pork with a pink peppercorn and Calvados sauce as main courses. Round off your meal with one of the wonderful desserts - Lemon Heaven perhaps, or Baked Jam Sponge, Dark Chocolate Truffle Torte, or a Banoffee meringue roulade. If you prefer a savoury, a selection of English and Continental cheeses is available. Food is served every day from noon until 2pm, (2.30pm on Sunday); and from 6pm to 9pm. Booking a table at weekends is strongly recommended. The inn itself is open from 11am to 11pm.

To accompany your meal, the bar offers an extensive choice of beverages, including 3 real ales - John Smiths, Timothy Taylor Bitter and a rotating guest ale.

The Black Bull also offers comfortable accommodation in 4 well-appointed double bedrooms, all with en suite facilities. The very reasonable tariff includes a hearty English breakfast.

Children are welcome at the Black Bull; all major credit cards are accepted; there's off road parking; and the inn has good disabled access to the bar and restaurant but the accommodation is upstairs.

Within easy reach of the inn are some of Yorkshire's major visitor attractions. The World Heritage Site of Fountains Abbey; the magnificent Studley Royal Gardens, Ripon with its great cathedral; and the spa town of Harrogate are all just a short drive away.

48 NEWBY HALL & GARDENS

near Ripon, North Yorkshire HG4 5AE
Tel: 0845 4504068
website: www.newbyhall.com

Newby Hall and Gardens, near Ripon in North Yorkshire, is one of England's renowned Adam Houses, and home to spectacular treasures and antiques as well as 25 acres of stunning landscaped gardens. Acclaimed as one of the Historic Houses Association's most visited properties, Newby Hall has an enviable position as one of Yorkshire's best-loved historic properties.

Collections inside Newby Hall itself include a set of 18th Century Gobelins tapestries, fine Chippendale furniture, classical statuary and even an unusual selection of European and Far-Eastern chamber pots!

Newby Hall and Gardens remains a firm favourite with families, gardening enthusiasts and heritage lovers who come to experience the many attractions this beautiful estate has to offer.

Newby's miniature railway is ever-popular with children and adults alike, and the Adventure Garden will amuse children for hours. The Sculpture Park takes in many pieces of contemporary work from a variety of artists, all of which are for sale, while the Woodland Walk is a delightful stroll through Bragget Wood and the adjacent orchard.

51 THE GOLDEN LION

Main Street, Helperby, York YO61 2NT
Tel/Fax: 01423 360870

Tucked away in scenic countryside northeast of Boroughbridge, the picturesque village of Helperby is fortunate in having a quality pub complete with inglenook fireplace, and lots of horse brasses and gleaming copper.

Mine hosts at **The Golden Lion,** Paul and Denise, took over here early in 2006 and have built up a loyal local following with visitors also being drawn in to enjoy good company, well-kept ales and appetising food based on fresh local produce as far as possible. Food is served from noon until 9pm, Monday to Saturday. The regular menu is supplemented by daily specials. On Sundays, roasts replace the regular menu and are

served from noon until they have sold out. Three real

ales are on tap to complement your meal which in good weather can also be enjoyed at picnic tables at the front of the inn.

The Golden Lion is also well-known for its live entertainment which takes place every Sunday from 6pm to 9pm. Children are welcome; there is good disabled access throughout, and the inn accepts all major credit cards except American Express and Diners.

52 THE GRANTHAM ARMS HOTEL

Milby, Boroughbridge,
North Yorkshire YO51 9BW
Tel: 01423 322261
e-mail: simon@lorimer.eclipse.co.uk
website: www.granthamarms.com

Located in the small village of Milby, **The Grantham Arms Hotel** is a fine old hostelry noted for its fine ales and excellent food served daily apart from Monday lunchtimes. The hotel's Sunday Carvery is justly famous (booking is strongly advised) and the atmosphere here is always friendly and welcoming. The hotel is centred near 8 major racecourses and offers special race day rates for coaches booked in advance. It also offers quality accommodation in 8 well-appointed guest rooms, all with en suite facilities. All major credit cards are accepted apart from American Express and Diners.

HIDDEN PLACES GUIDES

Explore Britain and Ireland with *Hidden Places* guides - a fascinating series of national and local travel guides.

Packed with easy to read information on hundreds of places of interest as well as places to stay, eat and drink.

Available from both high street and internet booksellers

For more information on the full range of *Hidden Places* guides and other titles published by Travel Publishing visit our website on

www.travelpublishing.co.uk
or ask for our leaflet by phoning
01752 276660 or emailing
info@travelpublishing.co.uk

53 MASONS ARMS

St John's Road, Bishop Monkton, Harrogate,
North Yorkshire HG3 3QU
Tel: 01765 676631
e-mail: masonsarmsbishopmonkton@btconnect.com
website: www.masonsarmsbishopmonkton.org.uk

In the picturesque village of Bishop Monkton, just off the A61 south of Ripon, **The Masons Arms** stands across the road from the village stream in a truly picture-postcard setting. Dating back to the mid-1700s, this fine old inn is run by Niki and Matt who took over here in February 2008. They carried out a major refurbishment and opened for business in April. Local people love the place and word of mouth has brought a steady stream of new visitors.

The food on offer has proved particularly popular. There are different menus for lunchtimes (noon until 2pm, Monday to Saturday; and noon until 4pm on Sunday), and evenings (6.30pm to 9pm, Monday to Saturday). At lunchtimes the blackboard menu lists appetising dishes such as Crayfish and Crab Salad, or

Thick-cut Yorkshire Gammon with mustard mayo, as well as sandwiches and lite bites. In the evenings, the printed menu

offers old favourites such as beer-battered haddock and chips, and Steak & Ale Pie as well as steaks, and a vegetarian seasonal vegetable pasta. There are 3 real ales on tap - Tetleys, a brew from the Daleside Brewery and a rotating guest ale. All major credit cards are accepted.

North Stainley, Ripon HG4 3HT
Tel/Fax: 01765 635439
e-mail: info@staveleyarms.co.uk
website: www.staveleyarms.co.uk

QUALITY IN TOURISM

FOUR STAR
★ ★ ★ ★

The Staveley Arms 'a hidden gem' enjoys a glowing reputation for its fine food, real ales, excellent Carvery and friendly service. The building is believed to date back to the early 1600s and it still retains its traditional stone floors, oak beams and welcoming log fires. Mine hosts, Mike and Elaine, arrived here in February 2004 and have presided over a steadily growing success story.

The bar boasts an open fire, stone floor and high beamed ceiling providing a cosy atmosphere. At the bar you will find Extra Cold Kronenberg, Fosters Chilled and Strongbow as well as Guinness and John Smiths Extra Smooth. Mike and Elaine take pride in their beers and feature Theakston Best, Theakstons XB and a regular guest ale such as Theakston OP, Leveller Ale and many others. At the bar a selection of meals is available including such favourites as Theakstons Battered Fresh Haddock and home-made chips, home-made Theakstons Steak & Ale Pie and

Chargrilled Gammon Steak. A Chef's Roast of the Day, a vegetarian option and junior meals are also available. In good weather, refreshments can be enjoyed in the beautiful and spacious beer garden.

An à la carte menu of fresh, locally sourced meals cooked with care by our experienced team of chefs is available in the restaurant where the culinary delights include the Chef's Thai Fishcakes or Creamy Garlic Mushrooms amongst the starters; fresh local steaks, a traditional fresh 16oz Cumberland Sausage Spiral, and a vegetarian home-made lasagne as main courses. Desserts include a home-made individual fresh cream Pavlova and fresh Apple Pie. Food is served from noon until 2pm-ish, and from 6pm to 9pm. On Sundays a popular Carvery is served with a choice of 4 different roasts available from noon until 2.45pm. All our meat is sourced from award winning butchers 'Weatherheads' in Pateley BridgeA Carvery is also available on the first Friday of every month from 7pm until 8.30pm. Booking ahead for the Carveries is strongly recommended.

The Staveley Arms has been host to many successful wedding receptions and other special events. The Bread Board Restaurant can seat up to 60 people for meals or more for buffets, while the Old Bar Restaurant can cater for smaller parties of up to 26 people.

Reasonably priced, 4 Star accommodation at the Staveley Arms comprises of two recently decorated double en suite bedrooms. Each room has colour TV, coffee facilities and king size comfort beds. A full English breakfast is included in the tariff.

55 THE BULL INN

Church Street, West Tanfield, Ripon,
North Yorkshire HG4 5JQ
Tel: 01677 470678

The delightful village of West Tanfield sits beside the River Ure and is perhaps best known for its impressive Tudor gatehouse, the Marmion Tower.

But the village has another impressive amenity in the form of **The Bull Inn**, a charming former coaching inn that stands close to the ancient bridge over the Ure. Owners Jules and David Sandford arrived here in the spring of 2008 and have carried out a complete refurbishment of the premises while retaining its olde worlde flavour.

David is an accomplished and classically trained chef with more than 30 years experience and

his menu offers appetising dishes based on the best of fresh local produce wherever possible. Food is available every lunchtime and evening, except Tuesday when the pub is closed and food is served until 4pm on Sundays. There are real ales on tap and in good weather customers can enjoy their refreshments in the riverside garden. Children are welcome and dogs can be taken into the gardens.

The Bull also offers comfortable accommodation in attractively furnished and decorated en suite rooms, one of which is a single.

A friendly welcome from Jules, David & their team awaits you.

246

56 BLACK SHEEP BREWERY BISTRO AND VISITORS CENTRE

Wellgarth, Masham, Ripon,
North Yorkshire, HG4 4EN
Tel: 01765 689227
website: www.blacksheepbrewery.co.uk

Established in the early nineties by Paul Theakston, 6th generation of Masham's famous brewing family, the brewery has grown from strength to strength and in early 2007 it was proudly awarded Brewery of the Year by the Good Pub Guide for the second year running. In addition Black Sheep Best Bitter was chosen as the North East's favourite cask ale in the recent Best of British Beer Awards hosted by Cask Marque and the Daily Telegraph.

The Black Sheep Brewery Visitor Centre is a major year-round attraction with regular 'shepherded' tours of the brewery involving a fascinating trip around the traditional brew house and fermenting room. Visitors experience the traditional brewing process and sample the award-winning ales.

The spacious split level Bistro and Baa...r, with beautiful views over the river Ure provides a variety of culinary delights throughout the day and into the evening. Also, if you're looking for that special gift, the Black Sheep Shop is full of 'ewe-nique' gifts for all occasions including our full range of Black Sheep beers.

The Black Sheep Brewery Visitor Centre is a great venue for corporate entertaining, product launches, parties and weddings, as well as hosting many special events throughout the year. Groups and parties are very welcome and a car and coach park is available on-site.

57 THORP PERROW ARBORETUM, WOODLAND GARDEN AND FALCONRY CENTRE

Thorp Perrow, Bedale,
North Yorkshire DL8 2PR
Tel: 01677 425323
website: www.thorpperrow.com

Thorp Perrow Arboretum is one of the finest private collections of trees and shrubs in the country. This 85 acre arboretum is unique to Britain, if not Europe, in that it was the creation of one man, Colonel Sir Leonard Ropner (1895 – 1977) and is now owned and managed by Sir John Ropner.

Situated in the peaceful and unspoilt Yorkshire Dales, not far from the historic town of Bedale, Thorp Perrow is an exciting place to explore offering something for everyone. This tranquil and peaceful haven is home to some of the largest and rarest trees and shrubs in England. A treasure trove of specimen trees and woodland walks.

The Falcons of Thorp Perrow is the ultimate family day out, incorporating the opportunity to learn more about

birds of prey and associated wildlife, with the enjoyment of hands on experience for all the family. Combined with the beautiful and historic Arboretum, a full and spectacular day in the Yorkshire countryside is complete. The regular flying demonstrations will not only give the opportunity to witness the breathtaking ability of eagles, falcons, hawks, vultures and owls from all five continents of the world, but also an opportunity to participate.

58 THE WORLD OF JAMES HERRIOTT

23 Kirkgate, Thirsk,
North Yorkshire, YO7 1PL
Tel: 01845 524234 Fax: 01845 525333
e-mail: wojhemails@hambleton.gov.uk
website: www.worldofjamesherriott.org

Celebrating the world's best-known vet, **The World of James Herriott** opened in the spring of 1999, since when it has welcomed more than 400,000 visitors. The setting is Skeldale House, now a Grade II listed building, where James Herriott lived

and worked. The house has been lovingly restored to how it was in the 1940s and 1950s, with many original pieces of furniture donated by the author's family. Beyond the famous red door, visitors enter the dining room, which doubled as the practice office. Then on to the cosy family room where the vet's favourite music – Bing Crosby – plays. Further down the corridor is the dispensary where he made up the prescriptions and the little surgery where he would treat domestic animals.

Skeldale houses the only veterinary science museum in the

country and a new interactive surgery and farm. The World of James Herriott moves with the times with audio tapes escorting visitors round the house and a short film of the vet's life story narrated by Christopher Timothy. The garden has also been taken back in time, and other attractions include studio sets from *All Creatures Great and Small*, some 70s' cameras and equipment and the original Austin Seven tourer AJO 71. This fascinating, family-friendly place is open throughout the year.

HERRIOT
Museum I Attraction I Historic Site
www.worldofjamesherriot.org

59 THE WOODMAN INN

Burneston, nr Bedale,
North Yorkshire DL8 2HX
Tel: 01677 422066

Dating back to the late 1600s, **The Woodman Inn** is everything you'd hope for in a traditional country inn. Mine hosts, Jon

and Jacqui Cook, took over here in November 2007 and have carried out a complete interior makeover while retaining the inn's charm and character.

Jon is an accomplished chef and his menu includes many old favourites, such as the home-made Steak & Ale Pie or the Fish 'n' Chips, along with less familiar dishes like the Smoked Haddock Rarebit (grilled haddock topped with melted cheese), and the Stir Fry Vegetables topped with Goat's Cheese. A selection of Light Bites is also

available. Food is served from 12 noon until 2pm, and from 6pm to 9pm.

The bar offers 3 real ales on tap - Cumberland Ale, Marstons Pedigree and a guest ale - as well as a good range of lagers, cider, stout, wines, spirits and soft drinks.

The Woodman also has accommodation available all year round in converted barns to the rear of the main building. There are 3 rooms, (1 family; 1 double), all en suite and available on a room only or B&B basis.

61 THE THREE COOPERS

Emgate, Bedale, North Yorkshire DL8 1AL
Tel: 01677 422153
e-mail: threecoopers@tiscali.co.uk
website: www.thethreecoopers.co.uk

Hidden away just off Bedale's handsome main street and market place, **The Three Coopers** is a lovely 17th century village pub. Pristine and delightful inside and out, this convivial pub is always warm and welcoming. The décor is traditional, with several original features still in place, including the large open fires and a wealth of warm woods throughout. Mine host at The Three Coopers is Jane Steenson, a friendly and welcoming lady who took over here in 2005.

Jane is also an accomplished cook and her menu offers a good choice of wholesome, home-made dishes based mostly on fresh local produce. Food is served at lunchtimes, Tuesday to Saturday, and from 5pm to 8pm, Friday and Saturday. Specials are added to the regular menu on the Friday and Saturday. In good weather, customers can enjoy their refreshments in the delightful secluded beer garden.

The Three Coopers features in both the *Good Pub Guide* and the *Good Beer Guide* so the quality of the ales served here will come as no surprise. The bar offers a choice of quality cask ales from the Jennings and Marstons Breweries, including Cumberland Ale, Snekuiter and Marstons Burton Ale, and an ever-changing range of guest ales. These are served all day along with a selection of lagers, ciders, stouts, fine wines, and a small but interesting range of malt whiskeys.

If you are planning to stay in this scenic part of the county, The Three Coopers offers a wonderful selection of 5 high quality en suite rooms, furnished and finished to a very high standard. All rooms have a superb hospitality tray, which includes a wide choice of teas, coffees etc and complimentary wine and mineral water. Hairdryers, flat screen TVs and luxury toiletries come as standard. In the morning, enjoy a traditional Yorkshire breakfast and sample some of the wonderful locally produced sausages, black pudding and bacon that are available. Jane has plans for further expansion which includes a complete make over and extension of the existing sheltered beer garden to include a sun terrace, barbeque area and covered smoking area.

At the moment, payment at The Three Coopers is by cash or cheque, but credit cards will be introduced soon. Children are welcome and there is good disabled access to the bar and dining areas but the guest rooms are upstairs.

62 THE WAGGON AND HORSES INN

20 Market Place, Bedale,
North Yorkshire DL8 1EQ
Tel: 01677 425235

A handsome and welcoming 17th century coaching inn, the impressive **Waggon and Horses** is run by David and Christine Hooley, who bring a wealth of experience to the venture. They arrived here in 2006 and have carried out a major refurbishment and upgraded the inn's facilities to a very high standard. They have also created a charming patio/beer garden to the rear of the inn.

Christine is an accomplished cook and her menu offers an extensive choice of superb home-made food. All the old favourites are there - Steak Pie, Chicken Curry and Battered Haddock - along with a selection of grills, a *really* Full English Breakfast, burgers and, of course, Giant Yorkshire Puddings. For lighter appetites there are jacket potatoes, baguettes,

sandwiches and salads. Food is served from midday to 7pm, Monday to Saturday; and from noon until 4pm on Sunday. To accompany your meal, the bar offers a comprehensive range of beverages, including 3 real ales.

The inn also offers accommodation in three spacious and attractive en suite guest bedrooms comprising 1 double/twin; 1 single, and 1 family room.

63 THE GREEN DRAGON

Market Place, Bedale,
North Yorkshire, DL8 1EQ
Tel: 01677 425246
e-mail: enquiries@greendragonbedale.co.uk
website: www.greendragonbedale.co.uk

A handsome town centre inn in the heart of Bedale, **The Green Dragon** is elegant and charming inside and out. It's been refurbished several times over the years - but still friendly and popular with young and old alike. Bed and breakfast is available; with 6 en-suite upstairs rooms.

The newly constructed restaurant to the rear of the premises looks down over the patio area, and serves some delicious meals. The restaurant opens Wed - Sat from 6-9pm and for their popular Sunday Lunch, but quality food is still available Wed - Sat in the bar areas. The restaurant seats 28, and it's an advantage to book at all times to avoid disappointment. Some exquisite Starters are available (including Chicken Liver Pate and Deep Frid Brie), and a range of Main Courses (including Steak & Ale Pie, Pan Fried Salmon and

Pork Medallions in Brandy & Cream Sauce).

Three Real ales (John Smiths Cask, Banks Bitter, John Smiths Magnet) are served alongside a good range of lagers, wines and spirits. The pub was much frequented by the Canadian Air Force during the last war, and there are a handful of interesting photographs from this time on the walls. Children are very welcome. Credit cards taken (except Diners). Bedale golf club nearby.

251

High Row, Exelby, Bedale,
North Yorkshire DL8 2HA
Tel: 01677 422233
e-mail: chris@thegreendragonexelby.co.uk
website: www.thegreendragonexelby.co.uk

Just a few minutes drive from the A1, **The Green Dragon** in the attractive little village of Exelby is surely one of the finest inns in Yorkshire. The inn dates back to the early 18th century and boasts an excellent restaurant, comfortable, well appointed accommodation and a large car park. The Green Dragon is a family run, independent country inn taking pride in its friendly welcoming service. In winter the open log fires provide a warm cosy atmosphere, whilst in the summer visitors and guests can enjoy the larger decked area with gas heaters for sheltered alfresco eating. Beyond the beer garden is a large field where children can play.

Inside the recently refurbished inn, you can enjoy bar meals such as home-made Steak Pie made with tender local beef, or choose from a range of sandwiches and hot baguettes. Amongst the starters, look out for the tasty Black Pudding Stack with Wensleydale & Bacon Sauce. An à la carte menu is available in the spacious and attractive restaurant which seats up to 60. Here the menu offers an enticing range of roasts, grills, fish and poultry dishes as well as vegetarian options. Daily

specials are also available every lunchtime and evening. Whatever you choose, you can be sure that the food is home cooked and locally sourced wherever possible. Food is served every day from noon until 2pm; and from 6pm to 9.30pm. On Sunday lunchtimes, the regular menu is replaced with choice of roasts plus a vegetarian and fish option.

To accompany your meal, there's a good selection of fine wines and mine host, Chris, is renowned for his excellent real ales. There are up to 3 of them on tap at any one time with Black Sheep Best Bitter and Theakston's Black Bull as the

regular brews, plus a rotating guest ale - in his first year, Chris offered his customers no fewer than 60 different real ales.

The accommodation at The Green Dragon comprises 4 tastefully decorated and furnished rooms, (2 doubles; 1 twin and 1 single). All the rooms have en suite facilities and are equipped with colour television and hospitality tray.

Exelby village is approximately 2 miles from the delightful market town of Bedale, the "Gateway to Wensleydale", which boasts a good range of shops, pubs, restaurants and a leisure centre.

Danby Wiske, Northallerton,
North Yorkshire DL7 0NQ
Tel: 01609 770122

The White Swan Inn, a friendly, family-run business of Shaun and Val Bennett overlooks the village green in the small idyllic village of Danby Wiske which is on the route of the Coast to Coast walk and just 5 miles from the historic market town of Northallerton. Many of the walkers along route have sampled the warm welcome, generous hospitality and the delicious home made food on offer, cooked from fresh, local produce. Particularly popular are homemade soup, steak & ale pie, bangers & mash and seasonal game dishes – the sort of hearty fare walkers appreciate.

The bar offers a wide range of beverages including three real ales all of which are locally brewed. Gentle back-ground music plays whilst customers sit in the homely atmosphere and give their tired feet a rest. The inn is also a popular meeting place for local farmers and residents of the village and is frequented by the local "shoots".

The White Swan offers bed and breakfast accommodation in four comfortable rooms one of

which is a double en suite with balcony. There are also two twin rooms and one family room sleeping four.

Camping space is provided in the large rear beer garden with washing and shower facilities.

Several annual events take place including the scarecrow trail, Morris dancing and vintage car rallies to name but a few.

Children are welcome and during the lifetime of this book credit cards will be accepted.

The village dates back over 1,000 years and of particular note is the parish church, parts of which date back to Norman times. It has a large 15th century bell tower which is still rung on Sundays and special events. One of its treasures includes a Norman tympanum and font of which there is only two of its kind in the country. There are also Jacobean pews and a life-size effigy of Matilda, widow of Brian Fitz Alan of Beadale, which dates to around 1340.

Whilst being off the main track Danby Wiske is an ideal retreat yet close to horse racing, motor cross, fishing and exploring local historical towns.

253

66 THE ANGEL HOTEL

19 High Street, Catterick Village, Richmond,
North Yorkshire DL10 7LL
Tel: 01748 818490

Located just a stone's throw from the well-known Catterick Racecourse, **The Angel Hotel** is a very busy and popular hostelry enjoyed by locals and visitors alike. Mine hosts, Claire and Beau, provide a warm welcome to all.

Claire is an accomplished cook and her menus, which change seasonally, offer a good choice with something to suit every palate. But if you don't see anything you like, just ask and they will try to accommodate all tastes. The summer menu presents an enticing selection that ranges from popular favourites such as jacket potatoes, beef burgers, ploughman's and omelettes, as well as Bacon & Cheese Tortilla, Quesadillas, Tikka Pitta

and Chili con Carne. There's a regularly changing real ale to enjoy as well as a choice of keg ales. Food is served from noon until 2pm, Tuesday to Thursday; from noon until 4pm on Friday and Saturday; and from noon until 2.30pm on Sunday when roasts replace the regular menu.

The Angel also offers comfortable accommodation in 6 guest bedrooms (3 twins; 3 singles). These are currently standard rooms with shared bathrooms but en suite rooms will be available from August 2008.

68 RYEDALE FOLK MUSEUM

Hutton le Hole, York,
North Yorkshire YO62 6UA
Tel: 01751 417367
e-mail: info@ryedalefolkmuseum.co.uk

Ryedale Folk Museum is a wonderful working museum insight into bygone eras. Here you will find the finest collection of thatched buildings in Yorkshire - the rescued and restored houses chart the changes in rural life, from the simplicity of the early Tudor crofter's cottage to the cosy Victorian clutter of the White Cottage.

There were mines and railways in nearby Rosedale, bringing a completely different way of life to the moors - explore the story behind these and the Elizabethan glass furnace and other moorland industries. Rural workers such as tinsmith, wheelwright, blacksmith, saddler, shoemaker and joiner each have a workshop with the tools of their trade on display and regular demonstrations take place including weaving, spinning, woodwork and cane and rushwork. An outstanding collection of tools also records the extraordinary changes in agriculture over the last 300 years, from wooden pitchforks onwards.

In the growing gardens, there are the medicinal herbs of the crofter's garth and the more recent cottage garden flowers, whilst the Victorian vegetable garden contains old varieties of vegetables as they used to be. The working landscape explores the way it was once used and how the way of life has altered it over the years. Farm animals, rare wild flowers and historic crops are sights to be seen here and a project is underway to help conserve the vanishing cornfield flowers. Over 40 varieties are growing here.

A gift shop sells a selection of books, maps and souvenirs. Open March to November - ring for details.

254

67 THE MOORS TEA ROOM

Lodge Lane, Danby,
North Yorkshire, YO21 2NB
Tel: 01963 240600

The evocative name of **The Moors Tea Room** says it all: picture a charming, pristine tea room set amid some breathtaking North Yorkshire Moors scenery and this is indeed what awaits you at this excellent establishment. Located adjacent to the Moors Visitor Centre, it's the perfect place to enjoy a relaxing cuppa and some excellent food while you soak up the marvellous atmosphere.

This handsome stone building is tastefully decorated and furnished in colours, fabrics and furnishings that create a cosy, homely feel and provide great comfort. Choose from a menu of home-made dishes based on the best of locally-sourced produce. Yorkshire Roast Ham with Wensleydale cheese & pickle is one speciality and a small sample from the menu includes tempting items such as sandwiches filled with free range chicken and tarragon mayonnaise, dry-cured bacon with free range fried egg, fresh prawns, goat's cheese with caramelised peppers, together with specials such as the Yorkshire 3-cheese ploughman's, a choice of hearty soups, or prawn, red pepper and tomato frittata. The cakes are nothing short of 'out of this world' - well worth the trip to Danby on their own - and there's a special children's menu with favourites such as macaroni cheese with garlic bread, boiled egg and soldiers, tuna, egg, or ham and cheese sandwiches, and more. To drink, there's a comprehensive range of beverages including coffees, teas, fruit juice, milk and soft drinks.

The tea room has seating for 40 indoors and another 32 outside on the patio - booking at this popular and welcoming place is advised for larger parties and on Bank Holidays. Danby makes a convenient stopping-off point when touring the many sights and attractions of the region.

The tea room is open from 10am to 5pm, April to November, and from 11am to 4pm at other times of the year.

69 THE QUEENS HEAD

49 The High Street, Stokesley,
North Yorkshire TS9 5AD
Tel: 01642 713032

Overlooking the spacious market square of this appealing little town, The Queens Head is a satisfying traditional hosterly serving wholesome food and well-kept real ales. The menu offers a good choice of popular pub favourites such as Steak & Ale Pie, steaks, fish & chips, curry and ham, egg and chips all at reasonable prices. For lighter appetites there's a selection of sandwiches, jacket potatoes and burgers. Food is served from noon until 8pm, Monday to Saturday, and from noon until 5pm on Sunday. Friday is karaoke night and the inn hosts occasional discos and light entertainment.

71 WHITBY ABBEY

Whitby, North Yorkshire YO22 4JT
Tel: 01947 603568
website: www.english-heritage.org.uk

The stark and magnificent ruins of Whitby Abbey are much more than a spectacular cliff-top landmark. Since prehistory, successive generations have been drawn to this dramatic headland as a site of settlement, religious devotion and even literary inspiration.

70 THE STATION INN

New Quay Road, Whitby,
North Yorkshire YO21 1DH
Tel: 01947 603937
e-mail: stationinn@btconnect.com
website: www.beerintheevening.com

A charming, relaxed town pub with a warm and friendly atmosphere, **The Station Inn** offers a wide variety of beers, lagers, wines, coffee and food daily, in surroundings full of character in the heart of Whitby.

The Station Inn hosts a minimum of 8 real ales at a time, usually with 2 rotating guest ales as well. Regular Real Ales include Whitby's Black Dog Abbey Ale, Copper Dragon Challenger IPA, Daleside Blonde,

Timothy Taylor Golden Best, Courage Best Bitter, Hopback Summer Lightning, Courage Directors, and Theakston Black Bull. Sandwiches, pies and snacks are available. Opening times: Mon-Sat (10am – midnight) and Sundays (10am – 11.30pm).

With a good live music line up and the "best kept selection of real ales in the area", this pub is nothing less than "a gem in the centre of town". Events include Open Folk night (Sundays, 9pm-close), Quiz night (Thursdays from 9pm, first prize is a gallon of ale!), and every Friday live bands play.

East Row, Sandsend, Whitby,
North Yorkshire YO21 3SU
Tel: 01947 893424   Fax: 01947 893625
e-mail: reservations@estbekhouse.co.uk
website: www.estbekhouse.co.uk

On the edge of the North Yorkshire Moors coastline, with the Cleveland Way in front and the National Park boundary to the rear, **Estbek House** enjoys a glorious setting in one of England's prettiest seaside villages. The house is Georgian, built around 1750, and hands-on owners David Cross and Tim Lawrence have made it one of the finest restaurants with rooms in the whole county. On arrival, Estbek offers guests the chance to relax with a glass of Champagne in the bar, with time to look and discuss the evening's menu and wine selection. The food here is absolutely outstanding - it's no surprise to find that the restaurant has held an AA rosette since September 2004. The daily changing menu is focused on the very locality of Estbek, with the sea and moorland at the door, it is hard not to enjoy the best of this beautiful corner of the world. The finest of fresh local ingredients are skilfully prepared to create dishes which are based on the natural flavour, a flavour which is all too often lost in a modern world.

Amongst the starters you might find fresh monk fish goujons cooked in a lemon pepper batter and served with tartare sauce and a salad garnish, or Littlebec Goats Cheese Salad made with cheese from the small craft dairy of Littlebec located in Littlebeck, not more than 5 miles from Estbek.

Main course choices might include Lobster Thermidor, made with a locally caught lobster; Gressingham Duck with figs and a balsamic reduction; or a vegetarian Pinenut and Wild Mushroom Ravioli with home-made pasta.

The desserts at Estbek are to die for, whether it's the Preserved Pear with Wensleydale Cheese & Wensleydale Ice Cream; the Wild Berry Compote with Vanilla Pod Ice-Cream; or the Old English Rhubarb & Stem Ginger Trifle.

They are as passionate at Estbek about wine as about food and the selection includes a connoisseur list and a range of excellent quality wines by the glass.

The guest accommodation at Estbek is also top class, comprising 3 doubles and a twin, all equipped with flat screen TV, CD player, alarm clock, hairdryer, hospitality tray and a complimentary bathroom guest pack. The double rooms have en suite showers, while the twin is fitted with a whirlpool spa bath.

73   DUNSLEY HALL COUNTRY HOUSE HOTEL

Dunsley, Whitby,
North Yorkshire YO21 3TL
Tel: 01947 893437
e-mail: reception@dunsleyhall.com
website: www.dunsleyhall.com

Stylish and original, **Dunsley Hall Country House Hotel** retains the quality and unique character of the Victorian period. With the feel of a country house, its comfortable furniture, books, memorabilia, open fires in the winter and traditional

standards of excellence are part of the welcoming Yorkshire hospitality that has become the hallmark of this independent and family-run hotel.

Set in the quiet hamlet of Dunsley, in four acres of superb gardens complete with resident peacocks, Dunsley Hall offers the best of both worlds. It is both an elegant country house of quality in a peaceful rural setting, yet is only five minutes from one of Britains most dramatic coastlines and historic seaports.

Rated a 3 star hotel (82%), each of the bedrooms (26 en-suite rooms) is individually furnished, some with four poster-beds. They offer views of the grounds, the countryside, or the North Yorkshire coastline. Quality cuisine is available for breakfast, lunch from

12pm, and dinner from 7pm. The restaurant serves an award winning menu where seafood is a speciality. It's better to book at all times to avoid disappointment. Children under 5 are not allowed in the Evening Dining Room, but a children's menu is available in the bar from 6.30pm.

The choice of dishes is prepared with local produce from a seasonally varied menu. The atmosphere, attention to detail, friendly service and interesting wine cellar combine to create a very special dining experience. For relaxation, the hotel grounds include a nine-hole putting course, croquet lawn and tennis court. Marquees can also be arranged in the grounds for outdoor events.

For celebrating a special occasion, Dunsley Hall is a memorable location, and provides a choice of suites for different types of event, to a maximum of 120. Special menus can be arranged and personal attention is always part of the service.

Dunsley Hall is perfectly located for exploring North Yorkshire's National Park and Moors, the historic seafaring town of Whitby, Castle Howard of Brideshead Revisited fame and TVs' Heartbeat country. Bring your wellingtons and a warm coat to experience Dunsley's working farm at nearby Ramsdale. The hotel has almost 50 acres of farmland available for outdoor pursuits and team building events, or to experience a small working farm first hand.

Dunsley Hall Country House Hotel is the 'jewel in the crown' for this area, a mellowed stone hideaway nestling not far from the sea in four acres of landscaped gardens.

74 RAITHWAITE HALL LUXURY HOLIDAY COTTAGES

Raithwaite Hall Estate, Sandsend Road,
Whitby, North Yorkshire YO21 3ST
Tel: 01947 893284
e-mail: admin@raithwaite.co.uk
website: www.raithwaite.co.uk

Just 500 yards from one of the finest stretches of sandy beach on the **Yorkshire coast**, **Raithwaite Hall Luxury Holiday Cottages** nestle in a secluded estate. Raithwaite Hall has **60 acres** of shared grounds which include mature **woodland,** rare plants, tumbling streams, a **lake** and a wide variety of wildlife such as deer, badgers, swans and herons. **Raithwaite,** Celtic for ' a hill in the water', aptly describes the estate of seven stone built **cottages** that have been recently converted to the highest standards, offering well-equipped modern facilities. They each enjoy peaceful and secluded locations making the perfect escape for a relaxing **holiday.**

All the cottages (including 3 new cottages available very shortly) have either 4 or 5 star ratings and range from 2 person properties to a very spacious 9 person family cottage. They are available all year round, and short breaks (2 nights minimum) are available out of season. All cottages are fully equipped with; fridge-freezers, microwaves, dishwashers, washing machines and drying facilities; LCD TVs with Sky and DVD players; gas central heating and electricity included; all bed linen provided; and each cottage has a payphone.

The Fruit House and Jasmine Cottage are luxurious detached properties for 2 people, each with a conservatory style dining area and private terrace, as well as a large bedroom with en-suite bathrooms. The Rambling Rose and Clematis Cottage are for 4-5 people, with their own patio area, shared courtyard and spacious beamed living rooms, making them ideal for families. The Woodcutters and Gamekeepers cottages each house 6 people, are just 200 yards from the beach and have private gardens, lawns and patio areas.

Whitby is dominated by the cliff-top ruins of a beautiful 13th century abbey. This quaint maritime town, with its old cobbled streets, picturesque houses and **sandy, blue flag beach**, is set among fine stretches of coast with spectacular cliffs and bays. A selection of diverse **attractions** includes the **Captain Cook Memorial Museum, Victorian Jet Works**, the **Dracula Experience** and **Whitby Museum** which offers a cabinet of curiosities from geology to jet carving, birdlife to bygones and costumes to clocks. For food connoisseurs, Whitby has it all. Award-winning **seafood restaurants**, continental delights, traditional sea-shanty inns preparing locally cooked produce and olde worlde English tea rooms serving freshly backed pastries and **Yorkshire** teas.

Guests from all over the world return time and time again to this "little piece of paradise".

75 THE HARE AND HOUNDS

High Hawsker, Whitby,
North Yorkshire, YO22 4LH
Tel: 01947 880453
email: hare-and-hounds@hotmail.co.uk

Harry and Lisa Hansell took over **The Hare and Hounds** in May 2007. They have introduced a new menu, and three real ales are hosted here, including Theakstons Best, John Smiths Magnet, and a rotating guest ales. It is a traditional country pub and families are welcome. Open all day, everyday most of the year, but they close during afternoons in the winter

months. Quality food is available daily between  12-2pm and 6.30-9pm, and snacks are available between 2pm - 6.30pm. All meals are cooked to order, using local produce. Advisable to book Fri/Sat evenings and Sunday lunchtime. A beer garden and off-road parking are both available.

HIDDEN PLACES GUIDES

Explore Britain and Ireland with *Hidden Places* guides - a fascinating series of national and local travel guides.

Packed with easy to read information on hundreds of places of interest as well as places to stay, eat and drink.

Available from both high street and internet booksellers

For more information on the full range of *Hidden Places* guides and other titles published by Travel Publishing visit our website on

www.travelpublishing.co.uk
or ask for our leaflet by phoning
01752 276660 or emailing
info@travelpublishing.co.uk

76 THE FLASK INN

Nr Robin Hood's Bay, Whitby,
North Yorkshire, YO22 4QH
Tel: 01947 880305
e-mail: info@theflaskinn.com
website: www.theflaskinn.com

Surrounded by thousands of acres of unspoiled countryside and a short drive or walk to the coast, the famous **Flask Inn** has been a popular 'stop-off' and 'stop-over' premises for many years, because of its friendly pub atmosphere, delicious home cooked meals and quality accommodation available. Originally a traditional moorland 17th century coaching Inn overlooking the North Yorkshire Heritage coast, The Flask Inn is ideally situated for the exploration of some of the most beautiful landscape in England. It provides the perfect setting for you to take time-out for a leisurely rest or an activity break.

Dave and Diane Webster have been the owners for nearly 2 years, and remark how popular The Flask Inn is with locals and visitors alike. Food is served 12 - 2pm and 6 – 9pm from a comprehensive menu, including a

Specials board. Friday evenings and Sunday lunch times are when you can taste their delicious carvery; freshly cooked roast meats, heaps of fresh vegetables and tasty deserts (booking is advisable). They employ a professional cook and chef, but Diane is also an ace in the kitchen!

Three real ales are available, including Tetleys and Black Sheep, plus a rotating guest ale. There are 6 comfortable en-suite rooms (full Yorkshire breakfast included in price), as well as an off-road car park, patio area and quality family room.

77 STAINTONDALE SHIRE HORSE FARM 🏛

Staintondale, Scarborough,
North Yorkshire YO13 0EY
Tel: 01723 870458
website: www.shirehorsefarm.co.uk

If you are a smitten horse and pony lover, enjoy the countryside and a happy relaxing environment - this is the place for you. In total there are 18 horses and ponies, from tiny Shetlands to massive Shire Horses. In between, a variety of all shapes and sizes. A Shire stallion called Mascot is the oldest at 22 and like many of the others he was born at the farm. In his younger days he could jump a five bar gate!

It really is about family fun and you can enjoy watching various live shows with both the Shires and the ponies. A pair of matched Shetlands are harnessed to a wagonette and the highlight of the day is possibly the fun and photo Western show. Tony Jenkins, the owner, has a magnificent golden Palomino which he has trained to be a western horse. He has a stunning silver mounted saddle and matching bridle. He also does a few tricks and can see-saw on a rocking bridge.

The farm is idyllicly set in 40 acres of North Yorks National Park coastline and offers excellent facilities for a truly relaxing day out. There are picnic and play areas in safe amenity enclosures and some pretty farm walks to elevated fields where you can enjoy the magnificent coastal and sea views. Seats are provided and at various points you can access the horses in their natural environment.

A timeless flagged floor café and gift shop complete the picture, with tea made from the farm's own fresh spring water. Open Sunday, Tuesday, Wednesday, Friday and Bank Holiday Mondays from mid May to mid September.

78 CENTRAL TRAMWAY COMPANY LTD 🏛

Marine Parade, Scarborough,
Yorkshire YO11 2ER
Tel: 01723 501754
website: www.funimag.com

The **Central Tramway Company** Scarborough Limited was created and registered in 1880 and still operates in its original corporate form. The lift was designed for steam operation and first opened to the public in August 1881. Located in the real centre of the South Bay to link the city to the shore just beside the Grand Hotel.

Below the track and about 60 feet from the top station the steam operated winch gear was housed. The driver of the lift had no view of the cars and relied on an indicator with other visual aids such as string tied on to the

haulage rope, and chalk marks on the winch drums to indicate the arrival of the cars at the top and bottom stations. In 1910 the steam was abandoned and the gear converted to electric drive. In 1932 the cars were replaced and the motor placed under the top station. Control was from a driving position at the top of the station with full view of the cars. For emergency use each car is fitted with a screw on and wedge safety brake which operates on a safety rail down the center of each track and the rail also carries the rollers for the support of the cables.

79 LINGHOLM COURT HOLIDAY COTTAGES

Lingholm Farm, Lingholm Lane,
Lebberston, Scarborough,
North Yorkshire, YO11 3PG
Tel: 01723 586365
e-mail: info@lingholm.co.uk
website: www.lingholm.co.uk

Combining both a countryside and a seaside holiday, these 4* award winning self catering holiday cottages are ideal family holiday accommodation or a relaxing weekend getaway. **Lingholm Court Holiday Cottages** are situated in a peaceful location between Scarborough (5 miles) and Filey (3.5 miles) down a country lane on a 1200 acre working arable farm.

Available all year round with shorter breaks out of season, these three farm barn conversions are charming and comfortable, with fully equipped kitchens, spacious and attractive bedrooms and marvellous views over the surrounding open countryside. All sleeping four people, each cottage has its own washing machine and tumble drying facilities, and are attractively furnished to a very high standard, yet retain many original features. In each cottage, guests are also provided with books, games, DVDs, local brochures, tourist map and local map. The games room has a pool table and table football, and all cottages have their own BBQ and patio furniture.

Lebberston has a country inn serving food whilst the neighbouring village of Cayton has everyday shopping. It is also the home of Lebberston Market, an outdoor Sunday market, which takes place each year throughout the summer season.

2006 Winners of Discover Yorkshire Coast tourist awards "Self Catering Property of the Year".

80 THE HORSESHOE INN

89 Stonegate, Hunmanby, Filey,
North Yorkshire, YO14 0PU
Tel: 01723 890419

Situated in the village of Hunmanby, **The Horseshoe Inn** dates back to the mid 19th century. This traditional looking inn has recently been taken over by new tenants / licensees, Ken Porter and Lee Griffiths, and they are very eager to get the place running as they want. They have already persuaded locals to return and visitors are taking more and more of an interest.

Ken is a qualified chef who's been in the trade 27 years, but this is their first venture into this type of business together. Open all day, everyday with two rotating real ales to enjoy, and quality food available Mon-Sat (11.30 – 2pm and 5.30 – 8.30pm) and Sundays (12 - 5.30pm). Choose from the printed menu, or the extensive Specials board including; steak & ale pie, smothered chicken breast, lasagne

and gamon/ sirloin steak to name but a few. Produce is bought locally where possible.

Entertainment comes in the form of Kareoke on Fridays (from 9pm), and there is a popular Annual Beer Festival held in September (ring for details). Families are welcome here and off-road parking is available. Pay by cash/cheque only. No problems for disabled people.

81 THE BUCK INN

8 Bridlington Street, Hunmanby, Filey,
North Yorkshire YO14 0JR
Tel/Fax: 01723 891559

The Buck Inn is a spacious and distinctive traditional inn located in the village of Hunmanby, a short drive from the coast and the popular resorts of Filey, Bridlington and Scarborough. Set in the heart of the village, the inn dates back to the early 1800s.

The Dunn family took over hear in the spring of 2008 with Neil and Allison, and Neil's mum and dad, Christine and Bob, all involved in the enterprise. Neil is an experienced chef and his menu offers an enticing choice of wholesome and appetising dishes based on locally sourced produce. Amongst the starters you'll

find Cullen Skink soup, and vegetable goujons, whilst the main courses include perennial pub favourites such as home-made Steak & Ale Pie and beer-battered haddock, as well as Whitby whole-tailed scampi, and a choice of steaks. On Sundays, roasts are added to the regular menu. Try not to pass on Neil's desserts which include an indulgent Chocolate Hanky Panky and a traditional Apple and Cinnamon Crumble. Beverages available include 2 real ales - John Smiths and a rotating guest ale. Booking ahead is strongly advised at weekends.

82 THE SUN INN

136 Westgate, Pickering,
North Yorkshire YO18 8BB
Tel: 01751 472797
e-mail: annekirk4@hotmail.com

Located on the A170, just a 5-minute walk from Pickering's town centre, **The Sun Inn** occupies what was once a farmhouse. The building dates back to the early 1700s but became a public house in 1831. Mine hosts, Dave and Anne Kirk, took over here in November 2006 bringing with them a wealth of experience in the hospitality business.

Anne is an accomplished cook and during the summer months offers a menu of honest-to-goodness pub fare. This includes a Pie of the Day, Lasagne, chips and salads, Chicken Curry as well as sandwiches and toasties. Food is available from opening time until around 8pm. To accompany your meal, there's an extensive choice of beverages including up to 3 real

ales, with Tetleys and John Smith's as the regular brews.

During the summer, the inn is open all day, every day; in winter it is open from 4pm, Monday to Thursday; from 1pm on Friday, and from midday on Saturday and Sunday. From time to time, the inn hosts live entertainment and in August a Band Festival is held in the spacious garden to the rear which is full of flowers, fruit bushes and fruit trees.

83 PICKERING CASTLE

Castlegate, Pickering,
North Yorkshire YO18 7AX
Tel: 01751 474989
website: www.english-heritage.org.uk

Set in an historic moors-edge market town, this splendid 13th century castle and royal hunting lodge makes a fascinating visit for all ages. Explore the walls and towers overlooking deep moats. Take the steps up the man-made mound to the shell-keep, for wonderful views of the North York Moors.

85 THE OLD MANSE

Middleton Road, Pickering,
North Yorkshire, YO18 8AL
Tel: 01751 476484
e-mail: info@oldmansepickering.co.uk
website: www.oldmansepickering.co.uk

Situated in the heart of Pickering, **The Old Manse** is a fine Edwardian North Yorkshire 2* Hotel with many original features and a large garden and orchard.

It offers 10 en-suite bedrooms two of which are on the ground floor and one has been partially adapted for disabled access. Bedrooms are pleasantly decorated and thoughtfully equipped. Wireless broadband available. The pleasant and comfortable dining room offers both dinner and bar menu of the highest quality cuisine. Open all year round with special package deals available in Autumn. Children welcome, off-road parking available and all major credit cards taken.

84 17 BURGATE

17 Burgate, Pickering,
North Yorkshire, YO18 7AU
Tel: 01751 473463
e-mail: info@17burgate.co.uk
website: www.17burgate.co.uk

An elegant award-winning Georgian Market Town House situated in the heart of the market town of Pickering between the town centre and the castle, offering deluxe individually designed and furnished en-suite accommodation.

17 Burgate is more than a B&B, it was designed for relaxing. Savour a bottle of chilled Chablis or house cocktail, in the courtyard with its perfume of summer flowers and day long sun. Alternatively, enjoy a glass of vintage armagnac or a local beer, within the depths of a soft leather sofa in the lounge bar in front of the log burning stove.

17 Burgate has been sympathetically renovated to retain the features and charm of its long history dating back to the 17th Century, whilst at the same time all the requirements of the discerning modern traveller have been included.

The location has been instrumental in helping customers choose '17' as the place to stay. The North Yorkshire Moors Railway across the road, Whitby and Scarborough, Heartbeat Country, York and many other attractions are all close-by.

17 Burgate provides great breakfasts and simple suppers using delicious local produce and there is a great selection of places to eat in the surrounding area-from Michelin Stars to fish and chips and traditional afternoon teas.

86 THE EVERLEY COUNTRY HOTEL

Hackness, Scarborough,
North Yorkshire YO13 0BT
Tel: 01723 882202
website: www.everleycountryhotel.co.uk

No matter what the weather, the views are spectacular at **The Everley Country Hotel**. It is set in one of the most beautiful valleys of the North York Moors National Park, an ideal location for families, walkers, cyclists, bird watchers and tourists who will appreciate the local scenery and wildlife.

This tastefully converted traditional farmhouse, originally built in 1754, is approximately a 15 minute scenic drive from Scarborough. The view from the garden terrace is simply stunning. The interior of the hotel has a lovely atmosphere, and is both comfortable and welcoming, with many traditional features including carved panels and furniture by a local craftsman.

Specialising in offering good quality food both in the restaurant and bar, and using fresh local ingredients whenever possible, an extensive menu is available including a "From the Grill" section. Food is served Tues-Sun (12-2pm and 6-9pm), and booking is advisable on weekends. No children allowed in Restaurant in the evenings and Sunday lunchtime. Over 10's allowed to dine in bar area.

Accommodation is available all year round, including three en-suite guest rooms (soon four), and a 5 star Holiday Cottage (sleeps 4 + 1 child) attached to the main premises. Owners Steven and Heather Baxter have been here since 2006, upgrading this property to the highest of degrees. It had always been a popular place, but since they took over it has been drawing visitors like a magnet.

87 THE ANVIL INN

Main Steet, Sawdon, Nr Scarborough,
North Yorkshire, YO13 9DY
Tel: 01752 859896
e-mail: info@theanvilinnsawdon.co.uk
website: www.theanvilinnsawdon.co.uk

Sit yourself down on the old pew and enjoy a pint of real ale or a glass of wine after a walk through the dale with its beautiful springtime rhododendrons, or relax in the pretty beer garden, and enjoy a glorious Sawdon sunset. **The Anvil Inn** is a traditional stonebuilt inn, a former blacksmith's forge, and now the bar retains almost all of its original features.

With a renowned and well known professional chef on board, Mark Wilson uses only the freshest, finest ingredients from local sources. Open every session apart from Mondays, with food being served Tues-Sat (12-2pm and 6:30-9pm) and Sundays (12-3pm). Booking is advisable. Two popular main courses include the 'Outdoor reared belly pork, sticky Chinese

glaze with stir fried pak choi', and the 'Pan roasted supreme of free range chicken'. The fresh fish menu is also popular.

Two luxurious self-catering cottages adjacent to The Anvil Inn are available for short breaks (minimum 3 nights), beautifully decorated in contemporary style and kitted out with top of the range fittings.

All this combines to make it a character-full and atmospheric place to come for a drink or a meal – candlelit at night and warmed by the log burning stove.

265

88 THE CAYLEY ARMS

Allerston, North Yorkshire YO18 7PJ
Tel: 01723 859338

A spacious village inn, **The Cayley Arms** is found in the village of Allerston, a couple of miles east of Pickering. Mine hosts, Sue and Dickie Ward, took over here in the spring of 2008 and have quickly established a glowing reputation for Sue's delicious home cooking. Food is served every evening except Tuesdays, and at lunchtime on Friday, Saturday and Sunday. The Cayley Arms also offers quality en suite accommodation in 5 comfortable guest bedrooms. The inn has a pleasant beer garden and large off road car park; payment is by cash or cheque only.

91 HELMSLEY WALLED GARDEN

Cleveland Way, Helmsley,
North Yorkshire YO62 5AH
Tel: 01439 771427
e-mail info@helmsleywalledgarden.org.uk
website: www.helmsleywalledgarden.org.uk

Helmsley Walled Garden is a 5 acre walled garden built in 1758 and set beneath Helmsley Castle. The garden produced fruit and vegetables for Duncombe park until it fell into ruin. The garden fell derelict until 1994 when a charity was established to restore the garden and provide horticultural therapy. This is a plantsman's garden including 350 varities of Clematis, 52 Yorkshire apples and 34 Victorian vines as well as Victorian glasshouses, a Paeonia Garden, a dipping well, rainbow border etc. Open daily from 1st April to 31st October 10.30 - 5pm. Dogs welcome on leads. Full wheelchair access.

90 THE FOUNTAIN AT DUNCOMBE PARK

The Parkland Centre, Duncombe Park Estate,
Helmsley, North Yorkshire YO62 5EA
Tel: 01439 771115
e-mail: mark.the fountain@btconnect.com
website: link from www.duncombepark.com

The Fountain at Duncombe Park lies within the glorious estate of Duncombe Park, a magnificent early 18th century mansion which is the home of Lord and Lady Feversham. The Fountain occupies what used to be the kennels where an earlier Lord Feversham kept his own pack of hounds. The kennels have been imaginatively converted and now offer an appetising choice of wholesome, home-made food.

The tearoom is owned by Mark and Tabitha Harrison who between them have some 30 years experience in the catering business. Tabitha's home baking is a major attraction here and there is always an enticing selection of cakes, scones and teacakes on offer. More substantial meals are listed on the blackboard - dishes such as Steak & Yorkshire Ale Pie, warm chicken Caesar or a vegetarian sun-dried pepper risotto. The filled giant Yorkshire puddings are especially popular. All the meat used here is sourced in Britain, and whenever possible in Yorkshire. Also available is a choice of filled paninis, jacket potatoes and fresh sandwiches.

The Fountain is licensed and offers a selection of wines from around the world. The restaurant is open from Sunday to Thursday, Easter to late October.

89 THE GOLDEN LION INN

Barugh Lane, Great Barugh,
North Yorkshire YO17 6UZ
Tel/Fax: 01653 668242
e-mail: i.boyington242@btinternet.com

The Golden Lion Inn is a traditional country pub situated in the picturesque village of Great Barugh in the heart of the North Yorkshire countryside. A Free House, the inn is owned and run by the Boyingtons - Gillian, Ian and their family. They arrived here in the summer of 2007 after several years working in the hospitality business in Yorkshire.

Parts of their fine old hostelry date back to the early 1600s - when renovations were carried out, original stonework of around 1600 was exposed. Today, traditional features such as flagstone floors and brick built open fires are married happily to fresh modern elements.

The inn has a well-established reputation for good home-cooked food. Gillian is an accomplished chef and her menu offers an enticing range of wholesome and appetising food. You could start perhaps with Mackerel Fillets served on a mixed salad with home-made gooseberry sauce. Amongst the main courses you'll find old favourites such as a hearty Mixed Grill, a very popular Steak & Ale Pudding, and fresh home-battered fish and chips. Other options include home-made curry, home-made Spaghetti Bolognese, omelettes and a large Beef Lasagne. Vegetarians have their own menu and there are special dishes for children. In addition to the regular menu, there's also a choice of daily specials. The menu of home-made desserts is particularly appealing with its selection of traditional dishes such as Spotted Dick, Jam Sponge or Apple Pie. Food is served from 5pm until 9pm, Monday to Friday. On Saturday light lunches are available from noon until 2pm; tea/coffee and cakes from 2pm to 3.30pm, and evening meals from 5pm until 9pm. On Sundays, lunch is served from noon until 2pm; evening meals from 6pm to 9pm.

To accompany your meal, a wide choice of beverages is available, including 3 real ales - Jennings, Marstons Pedigree and a guest ale. In good weather, you can enjoy your refreshments in the pleasant beer garden to the rear which commands stunning views of the Moors.

The Golden Lion can be found by driving west out of Malton on the B1257- pass through the village of Swinton and then turn right at the signpost for Kirkbymoorside and follow this road for about 3 miles. The inn is on the right as you turn left into the village.

92 HELMSLEY WALLED GARDEN CAFÉ

Helmsley, North Yorkshire, YO62 5AH
Tel: 01439 771194
e-mail: monicagripaios@hotmail.com
website: www.helmsleywalledgarden.org.uk

Helmsley Walled Garden is a beautiful five
acre garden in the heart of North Yorkshire.
The Vinehouse Café is situated in the newly
restored Victorian Vinery- Exclusively
vegetarian, offering a selection of delicious
and unusual fresh salads, home made pates
and soup
with a hot
dish of the
day too (we
use as much
produce as
possible
from the
garden).

Scrumptious
homemade cakes, fairtrade tea and coffee and
a selection of chilled organic drinks. Open
every day from April - 31st October, 10.30-
5pm. Dogs are welcome on a lead in the 1st
bay of the vinehouse.

93 THE OLD POLICE STATION CAFÉ

17 Market Place, Helmsley,
North Yorkshire, YO62 5BL
Tel: 01439 770413

Situated in a prominent position, overlooking
the Market Square in the popular, unspoilt
market town of Helmsley, **The Old Police
Station Café** has
been in business
for over 40 years.
Both tourists and
locals alike are
attracted to what's
on offer here: tasty
food is made on
the premises by
dedicated staff,

with hot breakfasts, homemade cakes and
pies being extremely popular choices. A
variety of beverages, hot & cold sandwiches,
jacket potatoes, baguettes, paninis, and snacks
are available, as well as a Specials Board.

Open every day except Christmas Day,
8.30-5pm in the summer months and 9-4pm
in the winter.

94 THE PHEASANT AT HAROME

Harome, Helmsley,
North Yorkshire YO62 5JG
Tel: 01439 771241
Fax: 01439 771744
e-mail: reservations@thepheasanthotel.com
website: www.thepheasanthotel.com

The Pheasant at Harome began life as the village
blacksmith's, plus two cottages and a shop. These
varied properties have been renovated and
extended to
create a very
comfortable
Country

Hotel with a wealth of amenities. There's a small oak-
beamed bar with a log fire, an Orangery, and a large drawing
room which, together with the conservatory dining room
and the stone-flagged terrace, overlook the mill stream.
Luxury is provided in the shape of the superb indoor heated
swimming pool.

Good food is taken very seriously here. Wherever possible the produce is sourced locally, with
fish from Whitby and Scarborough, local game and poultry, and Yorkshire lamb and beef. Bar
snacks are served at lunchtime, with an à la carte menu in the evenings. Typical dishes include
Smoked Trout with Horseradish Sauce or a Grape, Kiwi and Melon Cocktail amongst the starters,

with Roast Breast of Fresh Guinea Fowl,
Boeuf Bourguinonne made with local beef,
and various salads amongst the main courses.
The hotel has 12 attractively furnished and
decorated bedrooms, all en suite and
equipped with TV, direct dial telephone, and
hospitality tray. Some overlook the village
pond and mill stream; the remainder look out
over the courtyard and walled garden.

95 THE INN AT HAWNBY

Hawnby, Helmsley,
North Yorkshire YO62 5QS
Tel: 01439 798202
e-mail: info@innathawnby.co.uk
website: www.innathawnby.co.uk

Set in the heart of the North York Moors National Park, one of the most beautiful parts of Yorkshire, **The Inn at Hawnby** is a welcoming and appealing hotel in a peaceful rural setting reached via the B1257 from Helmsley. Mine hosts at this former drovers inn dating back to the early 1800s are Dave and Kathryn Young who took over here in 1999 and have established a glowing reputation for this fine country hotel which enjoys a 4-Diamond rating from the English Tourism Council.

The recent arrival of head chef Nick Poole has heralded a fantastic new menu which guests can enjoy either in the handsome restaurant or in the delightful, well-kept gardens. A typical menu might offer Cold Smoked venison & Salmon amongst the starters; the

choice for main courses might include local ribeye steak, a Rosemary & Garlic Chicken; or a

vegetarian Tomato & Vegetable Ragout with a Creamy Cheddar Mash. To accompany your meal, there's a choice of 3 real ales, usually from Yorkshire breweries.

The Inn has nine superb guest bedrooms, all of them en suite; six of them are located in the main building, while the other three are in the imaginatively converted stables opposite.

96 LASKILL GRANGE

Laskill Grange, Hawnby,
North Yorkshire YO62 5NB
Tel: 01439 798268
Evening Tel: 01439 772003
e-mail: laskillgrange@tiscali.co.uk
website: www.laskillgrange.co.uk

Set on a 600-acre farm with its own natural spring water, the outstanding **Laskill Grange** offers truly idyllic holiday accommodation with a 4-Diamond Silver Award from the AA. At the gracious and elegant farmhouse, Laskill Grange, bed and breakfast accommodation comprises 3 doubles, 2 twins and 1 single guest bedrooms, all with en suite facilities. Each room has fine traditional features, complemented by elegant and stylish décor and furnishings. All rooms are lovingly cared for and well-equipped. The spacious guests lounge boasts an open fire while the superb grounds contain a lovely garden with lake, stream and summerhouse.

Laskill Grange also offers excellent self-catering accommodation in 7 superior barn conversions. Reached just

across a courtyard from the main farmhouse, the properties have oak beams, stone fireplaces with living flame fires or stoves, colour TV, and well-equipped kitchens. They can sleep from 2 up to 6 guests. Two of them, The Granary and Coach House, are suitable for guests with disabilities. Pets are allowed in some cottages. Outside, each cottage has a barbecue and patio area, and there is also a shared walled garden.

3/5 Castlegate, Malton,
North Yorkshire YO17 7DP
Tel: 01653 692365

Regarded by many as the best tearoom in the county, the **Yorkshire Tea Rooms & Restaurant** offers a huge choice of appetising home-made fare. This is very much a family-run business with owner Tracy Cuthbertson supported by her partner Ian, her daughter Sophie, her mum Ann and sister-in-law Dawn. Tracy worked here as the chef for 6 years before taking over as the owner in early 2007.

The family's day starts at 8am with a breakfast menu, served until 11.30am, that includes a Full English, lighter bites such as Scrambled Egg on Toast, but for the really hearty appetite there's the 'Massive Breakfast' which consists of 2 bacon slices, 2 sausages, 2 fried eggs, baked beans, tomato, fried bread, 2 hash browns, black pudding, mushrooms, toast and marmalade, and either a pot of tea or a cup of coffee.

Throughout the day, a wide choice of starters and main courses is available. Amongst the starters are a soup of the day, Yorkshire pudding and onion gravy, and Japaleno Peppers. As a main course, how about the home-made Steak & Kidney Pie, the home-made chicken curry, or a vegetarian home-made quiche? Various salads are available as well as hot or cold sandwiches, baked potatoes and paninis, and children have an unusually wide choice of meals specially for them. All the produce used here is sourced locally. Desserts include traditional favourites such as Spotted Dick, Jam Roly Poly, Sherry Trifle and Fruit Crumble.

To accompany your meal, there's a wide choice of tea, coffees, soft dinks, beers and wine by the glass or bottle. The restaurant seats up to 46 diners but in good weather you can also enjoy your meal in the secret, hidden garden to the rear of the restaurant.

On Sundays beef, pork and chicken roasts are served until they run out and the regular menu is re-instated. Such is the popularity of the restaurant, that booking at weekends is strongly recommended.

The restaurant is open every day from 8am to 8pm, later in summer; children are welcome; and disabled access is good. Please note that payment at the Yorkshire Tea Rooms is by cash only.

Old Malton, Malton, Ryedale,
Yorkshire YO17 6SD
Tel: 01653 697777
e-mail: admin@edencamp.co.uk
website: www.edencamp.co.uk

Housed in the grounds of an original Prisoner
of War Camp, a visit to **Eden Camp** will
allow you to experience the sights, sounds and
even the smells of life on both the Home
Front and Front Line during World War Two.

The award winning museum also covers
the First World War, and the military conflicts
around the world in which British Military
Forces have been involved since 1945.

A visit to Eden Camp provides both an entertaining and
educational day out for all ages. Open 7 days a week, 50
weeks of the year (closed 24th Dec - until the second
Monday in January.)

Disabled and dog friendly, free parking and full catering
is available on site.

Castle Howard, York,
North Yorkshire YO60 7DA
Tel: 01653 648333
e-mail: house@castlehoward.co.uk
website: www.castlehoward.co.uk

Castle Howard, winner of York Tourism Bureau's 'Out of Town Attraction of the Year' award, is now so much more than a magnificent 18th century house with extensive collections and breathtaking grounds featuring temples, lakes and fountains.

Historical characters, such as the original architect, Sir John Vanbrugh and the 6th Countess, Lady Georgina provide a first person observation of what life was like at Castle Howard. Other characters include Widow Etty, whose husband was killed in an accident during the construction of Castle Howard; the 18th century Governess awaiting the next generation, busying herself with the tutorage of the young visitors; the 5th Earl's Butler, who is a fountain of knowledge and good sense - just what is needed to curb the rash spending of the Earl; the School Mistress, helping to run the school relocated to

Castle Howard during the Second World War, who can be spotted covering 'indecent' statues and ensuring the girls do not run down the corridors.

The range of tours around the house and gardens are very popular and include restoration and renovation; the great fire of 1940; the haunts of *Brideshead Revisited*; the history of the Roses and many more. There are various places to stop and enjoy refreshments and a plant centre and

tree nursery, both open for sales to the public. A varied programme of events takes places throughout the year, including the Proms Spectacular and Archaeology Weekends.

Open daily between February and November, a land-train is available to transport visitors from the car park to the house and there is disabled access to many parts.

100 THE CRESSWELL ARMS

Appleton-le-Street, Malton,
North Yorkshire YO17 6PG
Tel: 01653 693647 Fax: 01653 695920
website: www.cresswellarms.co.uk

The Cresswell Arms is a classic stone-built inn dating back to the 1800s when it was flanked by a blacksmith and a butcher. All are now incorporated within this spacious old inn. Mine host is Liz Gibson who is ably assisted by her right-hand lady, Debbie, and the excellent chef, Andrew.

The last few years have seen a complete makeover of the interior of the inn. The bars, dining room and kitchen have been completely renovated, a new function room has been built, and in April 2007 eight new en suite bedrooms, a patio area and extra car parking spaces were added.

The inn has 3 dining rooms: the Pool Room seats 12 comfortably for a private party; the Dining Room seats up to 24, and the Function Room can hold 65 seated guests or up to 90 buffet guests. It is perfect for weddings, particularly in the summer when the doors can be opened onto the patio.

Food is also served in the bar where the extensive menu includes old favourites such as ham, egg and chips, along with less familiar dishes like the Gnocchi with a bacon, blue cheese and spinach sauce. At lunchtimes only, a variety of sandwiches is available. In good weather, refreshments can be enjoyed on the attractive patio to the rear of the inn.

The dining room menus offer traditional English cooking with a slight twist and all the dishes are freshly prepared to order using locally sourced ingredients. There's a comprehensive wine list to suit all tastes and budgets. Reservations are advised, especially for larger parties.

Accommodation at the Cresswell comprises 10 en suite bedrooms, all individually decorated to a high standard and positioned around the courtyard and patio area. There are 4 double rooms, 5 twins, and 1 family room which can sleep up to five. The rooms offer many facilities, including TV/DVD, digital radio, telephone, broadband, and hospitality tray. One room has disabled access and disabled facilities.

The inn has ample parking and all major credit cards are accepted. Well-behaved dogs are welcome although not in the public areas. The Cresswell Arms is open for business all-year round, with its open fires offering a warm welcome in the colder weather. It is easily found on the B1257, a couple of miles west of Malton.

273

Church Street, West Heslerton, Malton,
North Yorkshire YO17 8RQ
Tel: 01944 728365
e-mail: r.shaul@btinternet.com

Conveniently located just off the main A64 Malton to Scarborough road at West Heslerton, **The Dawnay Arms** is a traditional Yorkshire Wolds village inn which dates in parts to the 1700s. Many inns in this area were named after local landowners and this is no exception, being named after the Lord of the Manor, Payan Dawnay in the mid-1800s. Before that it was known as the Bay Horse and was a popular venue for their lordships after hunting.

Roger and Helen Shaul took over here in December 2007 and with the help of their talented chef, Angie, have attracted discerning diners from across the county and even further afield. Angie's enticing menu offers dishes based mostly on locally sourced ingredients. Amongst the starters you'll find dishes such as Pan-fried Bruschetta with melted goat's cheese and red onion marmalade, and a King Prawn Skewer with either garlic or chilli dip. For the main course, there's a choice of steaks, a fish and seafood selection, and various Chef's Specials such as the Chicken breast fillet stuffed with smoked Applewood cheese, wrapped in bacon and served in a white wine sauce. Particularly popular is Angie's delicious home-made Steak Pie. The regular menu is supplemented by daily specials - home-made wild mushroom

Stroganoff perhaps, or a baby brisket joint with horseradish. Food is served from noon until 2pm, and from 6pm to 9pm, Tuesday to Friday; from noon until 9pm on Saturday; and from noon until 7pm on Sunday.

To accompany your meal, why not sample one of the finest hand-pulled ales in the Wolds. John Smiths and Tetleys are the regular brews, plus an occasional guest ale. In good weather, you can enjoy your refreshment in the sun trap beer garden and patio to the rear of the inn.

The Dawnay Arms welcomes children until 9pm; all major credit cards are accepted, and there is good disabled access throughout.

274

103 THE BLUE BELL INN

Weaverthorpe,
North Yorkshire YO17 8EX
Tel/Fax: 01944 738204
e-mail: bluebellinn@hotmail.co.uk
website: www.bluebellinnweaverthorpe.co.uk

The Blue Bell Inn is a handsome village hostelry resting on the North Yorkshire / Wolds border in the picturesque village of Weaverthorpe, overlooking the village green and surrounded by glorious countryside. At this friendly, family-run inn guests can relax in an oak beamed bar beside a welcoming open fire, dine in the elegant restaurant or private dining room, both of which offer excellent food and wine. And to finish, why not stay in one of the 12 en suite rooms.

The restaurant is well known in the area for serving excellent food, which concentrates on modern English cuisine using locally sourced produce where possible. The cosy ambience of the restaurant and bar provide the perfect start to your evening and with great food and fine wine, it just gets better! The private dining room can seat from 8 to 12 guests for a special occasion or just a get-together with friends. Some sample signature dishes amongst the starters are a bell tower of local black pudding and flat mushrooms with a soft poached egg and mustard sauce or Fishers Fishcakes - smoked haddock and salmon fishcakes complemented by a light horseradish cream sauce.

Amongst the main courses, how about a Fillet of Burdass lamb served on minted mushy peas with roasted shallots accompanied by a rosemary and mint reduction? Or Belly of prime rare breed saddle back pork with mustard seed mash, crisp green cabbage and a light pork jus. For fish lovers, there are dishes such as a Fillet of sea bass on a bed of vine tomatoes, red onion and basil leaves with a pesto dressing. Food is served from noon until 2pm, Wednesday to Sunday; and from 6.30pm to 9.30pm, Tuesday to Saturday. To accompany your meal, the extensive choice of beverages includes 2 real ales - Tetleys and Timothy Taylor Landlord.

If you are planning to stay in this scenic part of the county, The Blue Bell has six rooms within the main building, all tastefully decorated and well appointed with en-suite shower rooms. Alternatively, next to the inn is the Champagne House, built in 2006. This offers 6 luxury rooms all individually designed, each influenced by different champagne houses. Verve Clicquot, Bollinger, Laurent Perrier and Pol Roger are superior rooms and the Krug and Dom Perignon are two luxury rooms.

275

102 THE THREE TUNS INN

West Lutton, Malton,
North Yorkshire YO17 8TA
Tel: 01944 738200

Located in the picturesque village of West
Lutton, near Malton, **The Three Tuns Inn**
is a traditional village hostelry where mine
host is Jacqui Vickers who has some 25 years
experience in the hospitality business. The inn
has a well-stocked bar where there's a choice
of 3 real ales with Tetley's as the regular
brew. There's also a pool room and a spacious
beer garden. At present only cold snacks are
available but as soon as the new kitchen is
fitted, hot food will be on offer. The inn is
open every evening and all day Saturday and
Sunday.

105 CLIFFORD'S TOWER

Tower St, York, North Yorkshire YO1 9SA
Tel: 01904 646940
website: www.english-heritage.org.uk

In 1068-9, William the Conqueror built two
motte and bailey castles in York, to
strengthen his military hold on the north.
Clifford's Tower, an unusual four-lobed keep
built in the
13th century
atop the
mound of
William's
larger fortress,
is now the
principal
surviving
stonework
remnant of
York's

medieval castle. The sweeping views of the
city from the tower still show why it played
such an important part in controlling
northern England. On summer weekends a
costumed interpreter brings to life key events
in the history of York and the Tower.

104 JORVIK VIKING CENTRE

16 Coppergate Walk, York,
North Yorkshire YO1 9NT
Tel: 01904 643211

The world famous **JORVIK** centre in York
transports visitors back in time to experience the
sights, sounds and - perhaps most famously - the
smells of 10th century York. Over 20 years of
archaeological research led to the new re-creation of Viking
Age York in JORVIK, which re-opened to wide acclaim in April
2001. The new JORVIK now presents a far broader view and
more detailed depiction of life in the Viking Age.

Visitors to the centre are shown that, in AD 975, York was
a bustling commercial centre where 10,000 people lived and
worked. Travelling in state-of-the-art time capsules, visitors are
carried past and through two storey dwellings, enjoying views
over backyards and rooftops, and even glimpsing the Viking
Age equivalent of today's Minster.

February 2002 saw the
launch of the new 'Viking
Voyagers' exhibition. Visitors
can get the low-down on all
aspects of sea-faring from
trading in the Far East and
raiding in the North East, to
life on board and the technicalities of mastering the ocean waves.
The year-long exhibition features hands-on activities, artefacts and
new academic research around the theme of Viking ships and is
not to be missed.

106 THE DUKE OF YORK

Gate Helmsley, York,
North Yorkshire YO41 1JS
Tel: 01759 373698
e-mail: hillierdee@tiscali.co.uk

Standing beside the York to Stamford Bridge road, the A166, **The Duke of York** began life as three country cottages and dates back to the late 1700s. The very attractive premises are adorned at the front with hanging baskets and other floral displays. The interior is equally appealing, a striking mix of traditional and modern with a wealth of exposed woodwork and brickwork, a polished oak bar and comfortable seating. Leaseholders Chris and Joanne McDonough arrived here in the autumn of 2003, joining Joanne's mum, Dee, who has been here since November 2001. They have worked hard to build on the inn's reputation for great food, well-kept ales and friendly hospitality.

The food served here attracts discerning diners from near and far. The kitchen is striving to achieve the status of serving only produce sourced in Yorkshire - already they use only Yorkshire meat, fish, ice cream, milk butter and cream. The lunchtime menu offers a good selection of Hearty Bites, including a Full House Breakfast, Light Bites, sandwiches and hot baguettes as well as the main menu. In the evenings, the extensive menu ranges from a generous Steak, Guinness & Mushroom Pie, through grills and fish dishes, to vegetarian classics such as the Mozzarella Cheese Melt. Kids are unusually well-served with a choice that includes scampi and sizzling sausages with home-made chips or a smaller portion from a varied selection. On Thursday evenings, there's a set menu only which includes a glass of wine; on Fridays, Fish Deals are on offer; and on Saturdays, it's the turn of steaks to be served at advantageous prices. Then on Sunday, there's a popular Carvery - booking is essential for both Saturday and Sunday. Food is served from noon until 2.30pm; and from 5.30pm to 9pm, Monday to Friday; from noon until 9.30pm on Saturday; and from noon until 8.30pm on Sunday with the Carvery available from noon until 2.30pm.

Lovers of real ale will be delighted to find a choice of 5 different brews - Timothy Taylor Landlord, Black Sheep, Tetley Bitter and Tetley Dark Mild and John Smiths Smooth.. In good weather, customers can enjoy their drinks in the spacious beer garden at the rear where there is also a children's play area.

The inn accepts all major credit cards; there's a large car park, and good disabled access throughout as well as a baby-changing area.

107 THE FOX INN

Stockton-on-the-Forest, York,
North Yorkshire YO32 9UW
Tel: 01904 400359
e-mail: peteandflo@yahoo.com

The picturesque village of Stockton-on-the-Forest lies just off the A64, north-east of York. It's well worth seeking out in order to pay a visit to **The Fox Inn,** a former farmhouse dating back in parts to the 1700s and now an outstanding hostelry. Mine hosts, Flo and Pete Challis, took over here in the spring of 2007 and quickly established a reputation for great hospitality.

Food is taken seriously here with different menus for lunchtimes and evenings. At lunchtime, the choice includes appetising dishes such as the fresh Whitby Haddock, as well as a selection of salads, hot and cold sandwiches and a vegetarian option. From Monday to Thursday, there's an Early Birds Menu, available from 6pm to 7pm. The main evening menu offers grills, and wholesome dishes such as the Stir Fry Chilli Beef,

Pork Normandy, and Poached Chicken with Cream and Spring Onion. To accompany your meal, The Fox's well-stocked bar offers a comprehensive choice that includes 3 real ales. Such is the popularity of the restaurant, booking is strongly advised at weekends.

The Fox hosts occasional quizzes and live entertainment, and also has a rear patio and a converted barn which can cater for functions of up to 100 people.

109 SUTTON PARK

Sutton-on-the-Forest, York,
North Yorkshire YO6 1DP
Tel01347 810249
e-mail: info@statelyhome.co.uk
website: www.suttonpark.co.uk

Sutton Park is a charming lived-in house, built of mellow brick in 1730 by Thomas Atkinson. The house contains beautiful eighteenth century furniture, paintings mostly from Buckingham House, now Buckingham Palace, and an important collection of porcelain. Magnificent plaster-work by Cortese is also in evidence.

The House is a fine example of early Georgian architecture overlooking beautiful parkland. It is filled with a rich collection of 18th century treasures all put together with great style to make a most grand but inviting lived-in stately home.

Silver Gilt winner 2005 Yorkshire in Bloom for Best Tourist & Visitor Attraction, the gardens attract visitors from both home and

abroad and have been featured in many prestigious publications. Herbaceous and rose borders are full of rare and interesting plants, laid out with great care over the past forty years.

In the grounds are a walled pond garden, Edwardian fernery, Georgian Icehouse, Woodland Walks and Children's Adventure Playground.

108 THE BLACK HORSE

Newton Road, Tollerton, York,
North Yorkshire, YO61 1QT
Tel: 01347 838280
e-mail: info@blackhorse-tollerton.co.uk
website: www.blackhorse-tollerton.co.uk

The only pub in the village of Tollerton, **The Black Horse** is one of the few remaining pubs with a traditional 'Tap Room' as well as Lounge Bar, Pool Room, and an intimate Dining Room. The pub dates back to the mid 18th century, when it was a coaching inn on the main toll road from York to the North. Travellers paid a toll to buy protection on their route through the Forest of Galtres, which was inhabited by rascals, wild boar, and other wild things.

Judi and Dave Duff took over as leaseholders in April 2006 as their first venture into this type of business. Since being here their reputation for hospitality, quality food and well kept ales has steadily grown, and The Black Horse is now very popular.

The quality 'olde world' interior gives the pub a relaxing atmosphere, allowing guests to enjoy an extensive menu of quality food, a few drinks, or an evening of fun! A professional chef is employed and brings with him his well known menu and cooking style which includes a range of

'Platter' dishes, two of which are the Texas Feast Platter and Indian Feast Platter, but on Sundays Judi takes over for their popular Traditional Carvery. It's an advantage for parties over 6 to book.

The pub is in a prime village location, and is not far from the Tollerton Caravan Park, Chombeys Farm House B&B and local fishing ponds. Many tourist attractions are within easy reach from The Black Horse, such as Helmsley Castle, Byland Abbey, Fountains Abbey, Aldwark Manor Hotel, Castle Howard, Benningborough Hall, and the James Herriot Centre in Thirsk. The North Yorkshire Moors and Dales are also in easy reach from Tollerton.

The children's playground, quality rear patio area and 'Stable Yard' beer garden make it a very family-friendly atmosphere. Christmas, Halloween and New Years are fun-filled events at The Black Horse, and a quiz is held fortnightly on a Tuesday (phone to check for dates) for charity. Of course everyone is invited to show off their pub-quiz skills!

John Smiths and Timothy Taylor Landlord are the two regular real ales, plus the occasional locally brewed guest ale. Open Mondays (5-11pm) Tuesday – Friday (12.00-2.00pm and 5-11pm), and Sat/Sun (12pm-close). Food is served 5.30-9pm daily.

Dave and Judi hope "you will come and enjoy the friendly village atmosphere in the Black Horse. You will certainly receive a warm welcome from us and the regular customers. We cater for every age group".

110 THE BLUEBELL COUNTRY INN

Main Street, Alne, York,
North Yorkshire YO61 1RR
Tel: 01347 838331
website: www.bluebellalne.co.uk

The quiet and secluded village of Alne, set beside the River Kyle, is located just 11 miles northeast of York, off the A19. It is well worth seeking out as it boasts one of Yorkshire's finest hostelries, **The Bluebell Country Inn**. A former farmhouse, the inn was acquired by Michael and Annette Anson in the spring of 2002. They worked extremely hard on refurbishment, opening only in the evenings for drinks for the local customers, and re-opened fully on the 19th April, 2002. Michael was formerly the Chef at the Fauconberg Arms in Coxwold, having been at the Carpenters Arms, Felixkirk after that - an excellent pedigree! Annete worked for her parents at the Coxwold tea rooms until their retirement.

Michael's menus change regularly but typically would include a Black Pudding Tower, a Goat's Cheese Salad and a home-made soup served with locally baked bread. For the main course, how about Beef Wellington, Lamb Strudel with Gremolata, or a traditional Steak & Ale cooked with local mushrooms? Annette creates the starters and the wonderful desserts such as Lemon & Lime Crunch, Panacotta and Berries, and a hearty Bread & Butter Pudding. Food is served from 6 - 9 Tuesday - Saturday and noon until 7pm on Sunday. The Inn is closed on a Monday. The Stables Restaurant also offers an early evening meal from 6pm to 7pm, Tuesday to Friday.

To accompany your meal, the bar can offer you hand pulled beers courtesy of Timothy Taylors and John Smith, together with Guinness, plus lagers from Kronenburg and Fosters. There's also an excellent variety of bottled beers. Spirits are across the range, with lots of variety and the inn also offers blackboard "special" drinks - Weston's Special Vintage Cider, perhaps.

A popular amenity at The Bluebell is its well-maintained gardens to both the front and rear, ideal for a peaceful drink. A recent addition to the inn's facilities is the accommodation for bed & breakfast guests. There are 2 attractively furnished and decorated bedrooms with bedroom, dressing room and bathroom. They are let as 1 family and 1 double room, and both are available all year round.

111 MOUSEMAN VISITOR CENTRE

Kilburn, North Yorkshire YO61 4AH
Tel: 01347 868218
website: www.robertthompsons.co.uk

From a single acorn to a finished piece of beautifully hand crafted oak furniture. One man's work from start to finish. A simple ethos established by Robert Thompson – The Mouseman of Kilburn.

In perfect reflection of this, the new **Mouseman Visitor Centre** will take you on an amazing journey through the life and times of the Mouseman from humble beginnings to furniture legend. Visitors to the centre can pass through rooms set in the 1930s that are full of Robert Thompson's own personal furniture made with his own hands and signed with early examples of the carved mouse symbol. Learn all about the Mouseman of Kilburn from our audio-visual display then browse our Gift shop where you can purchase handcrafted items that we sell today.

Robert Thompson, born in 1876 dedicated his life to the craft of carving and joinery in English Oak. He taught himself to use the traditional tools and by 1919 he was experimenting with his own ideas for producing furniture based on the English styles of the 17th Century.

Now the famous mouse symbol, found on every item crafted by Robert Thompson has an uncertain history. The story told by Robert Thompson himself is that one of his craftsmen remarked that "We all as poor as church mice" whereupon Robert carved a mouse on the church screen he was working on. That particular mouse has never been found but it has continued as a trade mark of quality and dedication to craftsmen ever since.

112 THE YORKSHIRE AIR MUSEUM

Halifax Way, Elvington, York,
North Yorkshire YO41 4AU
Tel: 01904 608595   Fax: 01904 608246

Over the past few years the **Yorkshire Air Museum** has become one of the most fascinating and dynamic Museums of its type in the country. With its unique collection of over 40 internationally recognised aircraft and displays all combined into this historic site, make the Museum a very special place for aviation enthusiasts young and not so young. The aircraft collection covers aviation history from the pioneering 1849 work of the Yorkshire born Sir George Cayley, recognised internationally as the true "Father of Aeronautics", to WWII aircraft and modern military jets. The Museum has one of the largest special events calendars in the North.

The excellent displays house internationally recognised artefacts and in the many original buildings you can explore histories on a varied list of related topics. These include Bames Wallis; Air Gunners;

Airborne Forces and Home Guard as well as observing aircraft restoration workshops and seeing how wartime life was like in the French Officers' Mess or the Airmen's Billet.

The famous NAAFI restaurant is well known for its excellent fare and Museum shop is well stocked for that extra special gift or keepsake. The site is ideal for private functions, corporate events and conferences.

281

113 THE BLACK BULL INN

Main Street, Escrick, York,
North Yorkshire YO19 6JP
Tel: 01904 728245
e-mail: bookings@yorkblackbullinn.com /
davegaze@hotmail.com
website: www.yorkblackbullinn.com

Located just off the A19, in the idyllic village of Escrick, **The Black Bull Inn** is a former coaching inn parts of which date back to the 1700s. It's a traditional cottage style inn with elegant traditional furnishings and a blazing log fire reflecting the warmth and friendly atmosphere of this peaceful village setting.

The heart of The Black Bull Inn is the kitchen where qualified restaurant chefs work hard to make your home-cooked meal tasty, memorable and excellent value for money. For example, amongst the starters you'll find a tasty Creamy Garlic & Blue Cheese Mushrooms on toasted brioche with port syrup. Main course options include perennial favourites such as Battered Haddock, Chips & Mushy Peas, or Steak & Ale Pie, along with grills and salads. At lunchtimes, a selection of hearty sandwiches is available in the bar. There's a special children's menu offering starters such as Fishcakes & Salad, and main courses that include the Chef's Lasagne. All the desserts are home-made and include a wonderful Chocolate Wot Not and variously topped Cheesecake or Crumble. Food is served from noon until 2pm, Monday to Saturday, from noon until 3.30pm on Sunday when roasts and a few other options are available; and in the evenings from 5pm to 9pm, Monday to Wednesday; from 5pm to 9.30pm, Thursday to Saturday; and from 5pm to 8pm on Sunday. Booking is strongly recommended at weekends.

The cosy well-stocked bar offers a range of fine quality wines and a choice of 4 real ales - John Smiths, Theakstons Best, Black Sheep and Theakstons Black Bull.

The inn provides an ideal alternative place to stay, rather than in a city hotel since it is only a short drive from the historic City of York. The accommodation comprises ten 4-star rated en-suite

bedrooms, one of which has a four poster bed. All the rooms have been freshly redecorated with pastel colours and matching furniture, and are equipped with TV, alarm clocks, tea-making facilities and toiletries. The en suite rooms have power showers and, like the rest of the accommodation, are meticulously clean.

The inn accepts all major credit cards; and there is good disabled access to the bar and restaurant, but the guest bedrooms are upstairs.

Bilton-in-Ainsty, nr Wetherby,
North Yorkshire YO26 7NN
Tel: 01423 359637
e-mail: info@thechequersbilton.co.uk
website: www.thechequersbilton.co.uk

The Chequers Inn in Bilton-in-Ainsty is run by the mother and son team of Heather and Alex Main. They arrived here in early 2006 and carried out a complete refurbishment of the premises before opening in May of that year. They added colourful planting and a heated sheltered terrace to the large beautifully maintained beer garden, they also completely renovated the 3 letting bedrooms, making them all en suite with fully tiled shower rooms.

"The ethos behind our pub" they say, "is to serve the very best local produce, freshly cooked. We call it traditional food with a twist". They complemented this cuisine with cask marque quality ales and an extensive selection of wines and spirits.

Alex is a professional chef and his extensive menu offers an enticing choice of wholesome dishes. Starters include Bantry Bay mussels, Yorkshire feta salad and Whitby crab cakes. For your main course, choose from dishes such as fresh Steak & Ale Pie, Yorkshire Lamb Shank, or a Three Bean Chilli. From the grill there's a 28-day aged Yorkshire sirloin steak garni; a Chequers steak or chicken burger, and a thick grilled gammon steak. Many of the dishes are available as a smaller portion for those with a smaller appetite. A variety of salads is available and for lighter appetites the choice includes a mini fish & chips; a charcuterie platter; ploughmans and a selection of sandwiches. Food is served from noon until 2.30pm, Monday to Friday; from noon until 10pm on Saturday, and from noon until 8pm on Sundays when roasts are added to the menu. Booking ahead is strongly recommended at weekends.

To accompany your meal, the bar stocks a wide range of beverages, including 3 real ales - Black Sheep plus 2 rotating guest ales.

The accommodation at Chequers is of a very high standard. In addition to the shower rooms, each of the 3 double bedrooms is equipped with colour TV, DVD player, CD alarm clocks, Wi-Fi access and hospitality tray. A varied breakfast menu is included in the room price or you can stay on a room only basis. Rooms are available all year round.

Children are welcome at Chequers; all credit cards apart from Diners are accepted, and there's ample off road parking.

115 GEORGE & DRAGON

8 High Street, Wetherby, Leeds LS22 6LT
Tel: 01937 582881
e-mail: margaretmayer@sky.com

Located in the heart of this popular town, adjacent to the River Wharfe, the **George and Dragon** is a fine stone-built former coaching inn dating back to the 1700s. Inside, there's lots of charm and character with one room, The Jockey Room, festooned with sporting memorabilia everywhere, including hanging from the ceiling!

Mine hosts here are Martin and Margaret - Martin knows the town very well since he was born here. They took over here in the summer of 2008 and have quickly stamped their friendly characters on the place. The inn is open all day, every day with John Smiths as the regular real ale with a rotating guest ale to be added soon.

Good hearty food is served from 12 noon until 6pm, Monday to Saturday, and from 12 noon until 4pm on Sunday when there's a Carvery with a choice of meats. Martin and Margaret have expansive plans for the future. They hope to have accommodation available during the lifetime of this book and also to host regular entertainment such as Quizzes and live music.

Payment is by cash or cheque only; children are welcome; there's good disabled access throughout and, very important in Wetherby, the inn has its own off road parking.

116 THE FOX AND HOUNDS

Hall Park Road, Walton,
North Yorkshire LS23 7DQ
Tel: 01937 842192
e-mail: basil@thefoxandhoundswalton.com
website: www.thefoxandhoundswalton.com

The Fox & Hounds is a predominantly food led country pub in the village of Walton, although you'll be made just as welcome if you're just popping in for a drink. This 18th century property can be found a short drive east from Wetherby.

All their food is hand made on the premises using only the finest ingredients, locally sourced wherever possible. The Fox & Hounds is an impressive family run independent business. Their philosophy is to take the best ingredients, prepare and present them well, and to deliver friendly and efficient service. The menu is wide and varied and is updated regularly with the season.

The lunch menu has a range of hot and cold sandwiches, salads, and some interesting dishes such as Hoi Sin Duck Pancakes, Thai Salmon Fishcakes and Beer Battered

Haddock. These are also available in the evening, but with a wider choice of hot dishes. Sunday lunch is popular with roasted beef, pork, lamb and chicken available, and a selection of other meals.

They host three real ales (Timothy Taylor Landlord, Black Sheep, and a rotating guest ale), and have a pleasant beer garden with a children's playground. Food is served Mon-Sat (12-2pm and 5.30-9pm) and Sundays (12-3pm and 5-8pm). Advisable to book.

117 THE PACK HORSE INN

Market Place, Old Town,
Bridlington, East Yorkshire YO16 4QJ
Tel: 01262 675701
e-mail: andrew.apa1@google mail.com

Occupying a handsome late 18th century property in the heart of Bridlington's Old Town, **The Pack Horse Inn** is unusual in having no front door - the entrance is

through the arch because the main road used to run along the side of the premises. The welcoming mine hosts

at this outstanding inn, Andy and Sue, offer their customers an excellent choice of appetising, home-cooked food and a selection of 3 real ales. Outside, there's a delightful garden and patio area and on Tuesdays, the inn hosts a Quiz -all are welcome.

118 SEWERBY HALL AND GARDENS

Church Lane, Sewerby, Bridlington,
East Riding of Yorkshire YO15 1EA
Tel: 01262 673769
e-mail: sewerby.hall@eastriding.gov.uk
website: www.eastriding.gov.uk/sewerby/hall

Sewerby Hall is situated 2 miles north of the seaside resort of Bridlington, on the East Yorkshire coast. The grade I listed country house is set in 50 acres of landscaped gardens in a cliff top location on the outskirts of Sewerby village.

The house was built 1714-1720 by John Greame. Bow wings and a portico were added in 1808-1811. Later additions include an Orangery and dining room. These days the magnificent ground floor Orangery and Swinton Rooms provide wonderful settings for civil marriage ceremonies, concerts & piano recitals, meetings, seminars, educational activities, art workshops and tea dances. The Amy Johnson Room is given over to Amy Johnson memorabilia in 1959. This collection was a gift from Amy's father in October 1958, and consists of various souvenirs and mementoes presented to Amy and her husband, Jim Mollison. Since then, additional material received from other sources has further enhanced the Amy Johnson Collection.

The Lovely Gardens of Sewerby extend some 50 acres and offer magnificent views over Bridlington Bay, from Flamborough

headland to the north-east, down to Spurn Point looking south. The gardens are a skilful blend of art and nature, with formal walks, terraces and contrasting woodland. The magnificent monkey puzzle trees of the pleasure gardens are reputed to be amongst the oldest in England, and there are many more fine specimen trees over 200 years old.entrepiece to many of the beds.

120 THE BUCK HOTEL

1 Market Place, Driffield,
East Yorkshire YO25 6AP
Tel: 01377 253748

A fine old traditional hostelry located in the heart of Driffield, **The Buck Hotel** has been run since 1998 by Graham Frazer, a convivial and welcoming host who is also the chef. His menu offers an appetising choice of main meals such as Steak & Ale Pie and Chicken Curry, along with jacket potatoes, hot and cold sandwiches, burgers, vegetarian options and children's meals. In addition to the regular menu, there are daily specials to savour.

Food is served from 11.30am to 2.30pm, Thursday to Sunday, with a traditional roast lunch added to the menu on Sunday. The bar stocks a full range of lagers, cider, stout, wines, spirits and John Smiths real ale. A recent addition to the pub's amenities is a pleasant outdoor patio area. Karaoke fans should make sure they visit on a Saturday when the entertainment starts at 8pm. Children are welcome at The Buck, there is good disabled access throughout, and payment is by cash only.

119 MANOR COURT HOTEL & AZZURRO RESTAURANT

Carnaby, Bridlington,
East Yorkshire, YO16 4UJ
Tel: 01262 606468
e-mail: info@manorcourt.co.uk
website: www.manorcourt.co.uk

Sitting in and surrounded by up to 12 acres of countryside, in the village of Carnaby, the **Manor Court Hotel** is a 'jewel of the coast'. Robert and Lorraine McGivern have been proud owners since March 1990, and have slowly extended and refurbished the premises, recently opening **Azzurro Restaurant** in Spring 2007.

A selection of 13 en-suite bedrooms with stylish décor are available, from singles to large family rooms. One of the rooms has a 6 foot water bed and others have beautiful sitting out areas with views of the orchard and the evening sunsets, where you can have a glass of wine and consider which one of the hotel restaurants to have dinner in. The bedrooms vary in size and style but are all decorated to a high standard and include features such as satellite TV and flat screen televisions with DVD players (in some rooms). Tariff includes breakfast.

Fine dining in the Champagne Restaurant, informal bistro in the orangery and now the new Italian restaurant Azzurro, offer a wide range of menus and prices. Why not dine al fresco at one of the tables in their pretty courtyard setting. Private dining, celebrations and conference meetings of up to 50 guests can be catered for.

Azzurro, a large and contemporary Italian restaurant has gained a superb reputation with locals and visitors alike. It has an extensive authentic menu and offers you the chance to watch your own pizza cooked in the beautiful 'woodstone' pizza oven, by their entertaining pizza chefs. Offering hot and cold starters, popular pasta dishes including Risotto al Pollo and Tagliatelle Bolognese, as well as a variety of pizzas and many other chicken, pork, steak and salmon dishes.

If traditional cuisine is more your style then you will not be disappointed by the traditional bar meals, or the Champagne Restaurant with its European twist. Manor Court Hotel offers fish, game, trendy salads and sublime comfort food.

Having once been a working farm in the previous centuries, the business won awards for its conversion to a hotel in the early eighties and has continued to grow both in size and success due in no small part to the team of chefs led by Lorraine. Very much family-run, a warm welcome is assured. Children are welcome. Cuisine is served Mon-Sat (12-10pm) and Sundays 12-9.30pm. Best to book Fri/Sat evenings and Sunday lunchtime. A good range of keg ales are available, including specialist Italian lager and German Wheatbeer.

Manor Court Hotel is undoubtedly a gem of the East Coast, and whether your visit is to dine, stay or both, it's certainly worth the trip.

121 SLEDMERE HOUSE

Sledmere, Driffield,
East Yorkshire YO25 3XG
Tel: 01377 236637
website: www.driffield.co.uk

There has been a **manor house** at Sledmere since medieval times. The present house was built in 1751 by Sir Christopher Sykes 2nd Baronet. Sir Christopher employed fellow

Yorkshireman Joseph Rose, the most famous English plasterer of his day, to execute the decoration of Sledmere. Rose's magnificent work, unique in his career, and parkland planned by 'Capability Brown', have combined to create one of Yorkshire's hidden treasures.

The gardens and parkland can offer enjoyment for all, from the beautiful 18th Century walled Rose Garden and recently laid

out knot-garden, to the acres of open space and woodland. Enjoy a leisurely stroll, long walk or just a relaxing summer picnic in the grounds along with the grazing deer nearby.

When the need for refreshment arises try something different in the Bistro-Café, anything from a light snack to a delicious meal, before you move on to the Exhibition Centre, Waggoners Museum, the village, Monuments and Church. Sledmere's famous pipe organ is played for Visitors – Wednesday, Friday and Sunday 2.00pm – 4.00pm.

122 THE OLD MILL HOTEL & RESTAURANT

Mill Lane, Langtoft, Driffield,
East Yorkshire, YO25 3BQ
Tel: 01377 267284
e-mail: enquiries@old-mill-hotel.co.uk
website: www.old-mill-hotel.co.uk

A country hotel situated on the Yorkshire Wolds surrounded by open fields and

rolling countryside. **The Old Mill Hotel** has nine luxury en-suite rooms and a restaurant serving meals at lunchtime and evenings. Dating back to the 17th century, the authentic charm has been retained fully whilst at the same time incorporating present day requirements in the form of the A La Carte restaurant, an impressive bar, banqueting facilities and is the setting for a number of social and business functions.

123 THE GAIT INN

Millington, York,
East Yorkshire YO42 1TX
Tel: 01759 302045
website: www.gaitinn.co.uk

Hidden away on the edge of the Yorkshire Wolds, **The Gait Inn** in Millington is as authentic a village hostelry as you could hope to find. Outside, picnic tables set on a grassy bank overlook the quiet main street; to the rear is a superb beer garden that really is a garden, complete with well-tended flower beds and a pond.

Inside, the décor of the 16th century building is traditional, full of character and charm with horse brasses and other decorations adorning the old beams. Owners Stuart and Helen Stephenson, both former farmers took the helm here in August of 2005. Since then they've established a glowing reputation for providing excellent food, drink and hospitality.

Helen is in charge of the kitchen and bases all her dishes on locally sourced produce: the meat, for instance, comes from the local butcher who only buys from nearby farms. The extensive menu offers a wide choice of wholesome and appetising food. Amongst the starters are some wonderful crispy and soft home-made Yorkshire Puddings with onion gravy and breaded garlic mushrooms with a choice of dip. For the main course, choose between a selection of steaks, a honey roast half duckling or home-made offerings such as the Steak Pie or the Lasagne. Also available are a selection of fish dishes, vegetarian options such as Broccoli & Cream Cheese Bake or Veggie Burger, and a range of dishes for children. For lighter appetites, there are salads, ploughman's,

jacket potatoes, omelettes and a choice of sandwiches. Food is served from noon until 2pm, Friday to Sunday; and from 7pm to 9pm, Tuesday to Sunday. On Sundays, a Roast of the Day is added to the menu. Booking is strongly recommended for Friday and Saturday evenings and Sunday lunch.

To accompany your meal, the well-stocked bar offers a comprehensive range of beverages that includes 5 real ales - John Smiths Cask, Theakstons Best, Tetleys, Black Sheep and a changing guest ale.

The inn accepts all major credit cards; there's off road parking, and good disabled access throughout.

124 QUEENS HEAD

I Main Street, Kirkburn, Driffield,
East Yorkshire, YO25 9DU
Tel: 01377 229261

Set in lovely grounds, this top class premises in the village of Kirkburn is a short drive south west of Driffield, just off the A614. Tenants, Yorkshire couple John and Andrea Bayes, have been here 19 months. The **Queens Head** is their first venture into this type of business, but due to Andrea's talents in the kitchen and the superb hospitality they offer, they may just have a success on their hands.

Andrea is a super cook, and every meal is cooked fresh to order. Food is available 12-9pm daily (except Tuesday) from the classic 'pub food' menu, with a range of mouthwatering starters, classic main courses, 4 special dishes from a Grill section, salads and light meals, and of course some sweet and tasty desserts. The ever popular Sunday lunch has a different menu. Local produce is used as far as possible. Best to book on Sundays.

Feel free to dine throughout the premises, either in the bar, comfortable restaurant, or in the gorgeous garden on a nice day.

There is much to see and do in the area but the Wolds has an open and uncommercial feel to it that attracts both the young and the old. The gentle hills make it an ideal area for both walking and cycling. There are magnificent Halls to see such as Burton Agnes Hall, Sledmere House and Burnby Hall with its famous collection of water lilies.

The beautiful, peaceful Yorkshire Wolds stretch leisurely from the chalk cliffs at Flamborough to the Humber Estuary at Hessle. They curve the land in a loving crescent shape and take in a huge

area rich in history, colour, interesting people and beautiful buildings. There are some of the most picturesque villages and lively market towns in the country in this area, some well known, some well off the beaten track.

The Queens Head offers lovely surrounding grounds, a beer garden and patio area, and some of the best home-cooked food around. A large room is available for Wedding Receptions, Birthday Parties and Christenings etc. Open every day, but on Tuesday opens at 4.30pm. Two real ales on offer, John Smiths and a rotating guest ale.

125 THE WICSTUN CAFÉ

63 Market Place, Market Weighton,
York, East Yorkshire YO43 3AJ
Tel: 01430 874142
e-mail: mikeyouhill803@hotmail.com

A delicious aroma of home baking greets you as you enter **The Wicstun Café**, a popular town centre eating place in this busy little place with its 18th century houses and Norman church.

Owners Mike and Linda arrived here in early 2006 and now enjoy a glowing reputation for the wholesome fare they offer.

In addition to the delicious cakes, pies and puddings, all made with fresh local produce wherever possible, the café also serves cooked meals with roast dinners available three times a week. In addition to the regular menu, a daily special is on offer every lunchtime. There is seating for 19 customers downstairs with another 16 places upstairs.

The café is open from 8.30am to 4.30pm, Monday to Saturday. Children are welcome and there is good wheelchair access. Please note that payment at the Wicstun Café is by cash only.

126 THE WOOLPACK INN

37 Westwood Road, Beverley,
East Yorkshire HU17 8EN
Tel: 01482 867095

Located just a short walk from Beverley's elegant town centre, **The Woolpack Inn** is a fine traditional public house with a truly welcoming atmosphere. Mine Host at this friendly hostelry is 21year old Mandy Hurst, the youngest landlady in Yorkshire. Mandy looks after the bar and cellar work with her mother Sue taking care of the kitchen. Mandy and Sue insist on using only the best locally sourced produce, and they even list the names of the farmers that have produced the meat being used that week.

The menu offers traditional old pub favourites such as fresh Fish and home made chunky chips, Home baked steak and ale pie, and bangers and mash as well as dishes such as honey and mustard salmon, lasagne, salads and vegetarian curry. Specials are also available each week. Food is served from 5.30pm to 9pm Thurs - Sat; and Traditional Roast Dinners are served from noon - 4pm on Sunday. On Saturdays, a selection of light bites is available from noon - 3pm. Thursday is Curry and Pint night, Monday is a 'free for all' musicians evening and Mandy has occasional live entertainment on Friday or Saturday evenings. Lovers of real ales will be in their element here as Mandy has doubled the amount of hand pumps to no fewer than 6! The 3 regular ales are Jennings Lakeland ale, Cockerhoop, and Snecklifter, and then there is an offering of 3 extra rotating guest ales. Within Mandy's first 3 months at the Woolpack, she has developed a great relationship with the local CAMRA groups (campaign for real ale).

Well behaved children and dogs are welcome; there's good disabled access throughout; a smoking area to the rear and benches at the front. Payment at the Woolpack is currently by cheque or cash only but Mandy and Sue will soon be accepting credit cards.

127 GINGERS

I Swabys Yard, Beverley,
East Yorkshire HU17 9BZ
Tel: 01482 882919 Mobile: 0776 596 5762
e-mail: gingersbeverley@hotmail.com

Just a stone's throw from historic Beverley's main market place, **Gingers** offers a truly enticing array of home-made cakes and pastries, light lunches, hot and cold sandwiches, afternoon teas and takeaways.

Bev, the baker is renouned for her superb scones and cakes.

Other specialities of the house include a tasty corned beef & leek pie and seasonal desserts. In addition to the regular menu, there are also daily specials. The café is open from 9.30am to 4.30pm, Tuesday to Saturday. Gingers also specialises in outside catering.

129 HALF MOON INN

16 Main Street, Skidby,
East Yorkshire HU16 5TG
Tel: 01482 843403

A former coaching inn, nearly 340 years old, the delightful **Half Moon Inn** is replete with charm and character. Mine host, Roma Wedgewood, took over here in the winter of 2006 and has established a glowing reputation for her appetising cuisine. Served between

noon - 2pm every day, the menu offers a good choice of main meals including Roma's famous home-made Giant Yorkshire Puddings. Sandwiches, jacket potatoes and vegetarian options are also available. On Sundays, a traditional roast is added to the regular menu. The inn's well-stocked bar includes 2 real ales amongst its offerings.

128 THE POPPY SEED

13 North Bar Within, Beverley,
East Yorkshire HU17 8AP
Tel: 01482 871598

Just down the road from Beverley's medieval gateway, **The Poppy Seed** is an outstanding delicatessen and coffee shop serving quality home-cooked food prepared to the highest standards. It is owned and run by the mother and daughter team of Rita Jones and Kate Johnson who came here in 2001 after some years cooking for weddings at a stately home.

In their ground floor delicatessen you'll find an extensive choice of quiches, patisseries, traditional puddings, sandwiches to take away and picnic 'kits'. These are also served in the two restaurant areas along with a variety of other dishes. These include a choice of breakfasts served daily until 11am, an extensive selection of sandwiches and paninis ranging from Rare Roast Beef to Goats Cheese & Beetroot; salads and daily specials such as Aromatic Lamb

Meatballs. The huge choice of drinks includes a dozen different teas; coffees and iced coffees; pure fruit juices, home-made lemonade, and fresh fruit smoothies and milk shakes.

The Poppy Seed is open from 9am to 5pm, Monday to Saturday, and is licensed. Rita and Kate are also happy to provide outside catering - "We can cater for any size, from whole quiches to whole parties!"

East End, Walkington,
East Yorkshire HU17 8RX
Tel: 01482 882665
e-mail: rayclegg@fergusonfawsitt.com
website: www.fergusonfawsitt.co.uk

Set in the picturesque village of Walkington, just three miles from Beverley with its wonderful Minster traditional Market Square and shops. With Beverley racecourse just over 1 mile away, York and the East Coast towns of Hornsea, Bridlington and

Scarborough nearby, there is plenty to see and do in the area.

Whatever the occasion or event, come to **The Ferguson Fawsitt Arms and Country Lodge** for first class food, warm friendly service and excellent facilities. Relax with friends or family and enjoy one of our real ales, a large selection of beers and lagers, or perhaps a glass of one of our 11 different house wines always in stock. Alternatively, why not enjoy a bottle of wine from our fine wine list.

The Ferguson Fawsitt Arms offers a superb carvery of up to 5 different joints, serving a variety of hot and cold food freshly prepared and cooked on the premises. A bar food menu is also available. Meals can be eaten in the Lounge, the Cocktail bar, the Carvery Room or

the Old Bar with its original hand-carved wood panels and open fire.

The oiginal name of the pub was 'The Bay Horse' and the area now known as the 'Cocktail Bar' was originally the village blacksmith's shop which was in use until 1950. The Carvery area was the area the blacksmiths used to repair carriage wheels and shoe the horses.

The newly built lodge, opening September 2008, has ten en-suite bedrooms, all decorated an furnished to the highest standard, with large beds, flat TV screens, internet access, power showers etc. One of these is a honeymoon suite complete with Jacuzzi, and one ground floor room has full disabled facilities. Come on B&B or Dinner and B&B rates. What an asset this lodge will be to the already outstanding premises.

The Function Room can seat up to 80 guests for a Formal Function and up to 120 guests for an evening reception, and has its own bar facilities. They hold a variety of special events throughout the year, the most exciting being their special Christmas dinner dances during December. Wedding receptions are very popular here.

The business has been well-known for its quality cuisine for many years. Open all day, everyday, food is served Mon-Thurs (12-9pm), Fri/Sat (12-9.30pm) and Sundays (12-9pm). A choice of up to four real ales to enjoy, with John Smiths and Courage Directors being the regulars, other ales rotating. Good selection of draught lagers. A patio is available at the rear, as well as a large off-road car park.

131 THE ROSE & CROWN

33 Market Place, Hornsea,
East Riding of Yorkshire HU18 1AN
Tel: 01964 535756
e-mail: matthewburns07@aol.com

Just a short stroll from the beach and coastline, **The Rose & Crown** is a striking building with a distinctive gabled exterior with half-timbering painted in blue and white which gives it a medieval appearance although in fact it is a relatively modern pub, dating back to the early 1900s.

Occupying the site of an earlier public house, this fine inn offers guests a comfortable and pleasant rest stop in which to enjoy a drink or a meal while touring in the area. Leaseholders Lisa-Jane and Matthew have been here since January 2006. They have recently carried out a complete refurbishment to a very high standard, and they have also had a new addition to the family, baby Oliver. This is very much a family-run business with Lisa-Jane's parents Elizabeth and Bernard also involved in the enterprise.

Lisa-Jane is an accomplished cook and her extensive menu ranges from an All Day Breakfast through good old pub favourites such as Bangers & Mash, burgers and Golden Scampi, to vegetarian dishes and meals for kids. You'll also find salads, jacket potatoes, ploughman's, sandwiches and toasties. In addition to the regular menu, daily specials are also available and on Sundays a traditional lunch is served.

The well-stocked bar has a comprehensive choice of beverages, including 2 or 3 real ales with Jennings Lakeland Ale as the regular brew. In good weather, you can enjoy your drinks in the patio area which also has undercover seating.

The Rose & Crown also offers regular entertainment with a Quiz on Thursday evenings; a karaoke on Friday; and a disco on Saturday. The inn welcomes children and dogs; there is good disabled access throughout; plenty of off-road parking. Please note that payment at The Rose & Crown is by cash or cheque only.

132 HORNSEA FOLK MUSEUM 🏛

**11 Newbegin, Hornsea,
East Yorkshire HU18 1AB
Tel: 01964 533443**

Established in 1978, the excellent **Hornsea Folk Museum** occupies a Grade II listed former farmhouse where successive generations of the Burn family lived for 300 years up until 1952. Their way of life, the

personalities and characters who influenced the development of the town or found fame in other ways, are explored in meticulously restored rooms brimming with furniture, decorations, utensils and tools of the Victorian period. The kitchen, parlour, bedroom, have fascinating displays of authentic contemporary artefacts, and the museum complex also includes a laundry, workshop, blacksmith's shop and a barn stocked with vintage agricultural implements.

133 THE BLUE POST 🍴

**79 Main Street, North Frodingham,
Driffield, East Yorkshire YO25 8LG
Tel: 01262 488300**

Located in the heart of the Yorkshire Wolds, North Frodingham is a peaceful little village but well worth seeking out in order to sample the fare on offer at **The Blue Post**. Mine hosts, Andrew and Jilly Bettney, who have between them more than 30 years experience in the hospitality business, took over here in the spring of 2008 and have speedily attracted a loyal clientele. Andrew is a professional chef and his menu, based on fresh Yorkshire produce, offers an appetising selection of dishes. Amongst them you'll find a variety of roasts and steaks, and traditional pub dishes such as Meat & Potato Pie, as well as vegetarian options such as the Veggie Burger. Those with smaller appetites will be pleased to find that most of the dishes can be ordered in small portions. In addition to the regular menu, there are also daily specials listed on the blackboard, and a special 2-course meal at teatime.

To accompany your meal, the bar offers a comprehensive selection of beverages including 2 real ales with John Smiths as the regular brew plus a guest ale. Food is served from 5pm to 9pm, Monday to Friday; from noon until 9pm on Saturday and from noon until 7.30pm on Sunday. The pub itself is open from 4pm. Monday to Friday, and all day on Saturday and Sunday. It is also open at other times for parties, meetings and so on by prior arrangement. Bookings are welcome at all times.

The inn has a pool table and darts, hosts a regular quiz and also live entertainment such as discos and karaoke at weekends. Children are welcome; all major credit cards apart from American Express and Diners are accepted; there's a large off road car park and good disabled access throughout.

Main Street, Brandesburton,
East Yorkshire YO25 8RL
Tel/Fax: 01964 542392
e-mail: anthony.langley@btconnect.com

A captivating village hostelry, **The Dacre Arms** is unusually rich in history. An inn has stood on the present site since the 16th century and in the heyday of stage coach travel the inn became the most important posting station in the East Riding with stabling for 50 horses around a cobbled yard. One small room in the inn housed the local Court of Justices; another, the "Jockey Room" was used for harnessing. Following the custom of the time, the Dacre Arms (named after Lord and Lady Dacre) had its own brewery. The inn also

had its own secret room for which the only access was by way of a trapdoor. It was here that fugitives from the 1745 Jacobite rebellion found sanctuary. After the failure of that uprising, the room was put to good use by local smugglers as a safe storage place for their contraband.

The present structure of the inn dates from 1806 and for more than a century it was owned by the Charter family. During their tenure, on February 28th, 1844, a society was formed here by a horse dealer who was visiting the annual Brandesburton Horse Fair. He had been distressed to hear that a friend could not afford to bury his wife and set up an early form of co-operative insurance, the Franklin Dead Brief. On the death of a member, all the others contribute £1 to the funeral expenses. The society is still functioning and has more than 350 members.

Today, this grand old inn is noted for its excellent cuisine. The extensive menu offers an array of wholesome and appetising food, ranging from a 'Moby Dick' Haddock & Chips, through a traditional Steak & Ale Pie, to grills, vegetarian dishes such as a Roast Vegetable & Brie Quiche, to salads and home-made Yorkshire Puddings with a choice of fillings. For lighter appetites, there's a good choice of jacket potatoes, baguettes and Light Bites. Because of its popularity, booking for the restaurant is advisable at all times.

Aficionados of real ales will be delighted with the Dacre Arms selection of real ales - John Smiths, and Theakstons Best Bitter, XB and Olde Peculier.

Children are welcome at the Dacre Arms; all major credit cards are accepted; and there's ample off road parking.

135 THE RAILWAY

30/34 Westgate, Patrington,
East Riding of Yorkshire HU12 0NB
Tel: 01964 631517
e-mail: bobmech100@aol.co.uk

Patrington is one of the most delightful villages in the East Riding and also boasts a fine old hostelry, **The Railway**. Back in the mid-1800s it was 3 buildings - a pub and two cottages - which were later converted into the present spacious premises.

Mine hosts, Bob and Diane Schilling, arrived here in the spring of 2007 and carried out a complete refurbishment before re-opening in August of that year.

The pub is open all day, every day, and currently food is served from noon until 2pm. However, Bob and Diane have plans to also serve food in the evenings. Their menu offers a good choice of appetising food based on fresh local produce that includes home-made quiche, jacket potatoes, burgers and sandwiches. On Sundays, there's a choice of 3 roasts which are available in either large or small portions, both at very reasonable prices. The well-stocked bar offers a wide selection of beverages, including

at least 3 real ales - Tetleys, Timothy Taylor's Landlord and one or more rotating guest brews. The inn has a separate dining area seating 20 but you can also dine in the lounge bars. In good weather, enjoy your refreshments on the patio at the rear of the inn.

The Railway also hosts a Bingo and Quiz evening on Friday, while on Saturday there's either a disco, karaoke or even a hypnotist! Children are welcome here; there's good disabled access throughout, and payment is by cash only.

136 NUTMEGS

5 Market Place, Hedon,
East Yorkshire HU12 8JA
Tel: 01482 898450

The lovely aroma of home baking greets customers entering **Nutmegs,** a delightful eating place overlooking the Market Place in Hedon. Owner Jayne Hampshire is renowned for her culinary skills which include the creation of some irresistible cakes, pies and puddings. But her menu also includes an extensive selection of hot meals such as lasagne, Quiche, Gammon Steak, omelettes, salads and an All Day Breakfast. For lighter appetites, the choice includes jacket potatoes, hot and cold sandwiches, and light lunches such as Beans on Toast. Amongst the tea-time treats are scones, toasted tea cakes and, of course, those wonderful cakes. There are special meals for children. On Sundays, Roast Beef and Roast Chicken are added to the regular menu. Booking is strongly recommended to avoid disappointment. Diners are welcome to bring their own wine -

there's a nominal charge for corkage. Food is served from 9am to 4pm, Monday to Saturday; 10.30am to 4pm on Sunday, plus some evenings in December. Nutmegs has seating for 24 customers downstairs; a further 28 places upstairs, and in good weather, diners can enjoy their meals in the spacious patio garden at the rear of the café. There's good disabled access downstairs and to the garden; payment is by cash only.

137 THE BARN FARM

Main Road, Thorngumbald, Hull,
East Yorkshire HU12 9NE
Tel: 01964 600100

This gorgeous converted farmhouse was made a licensed premises 10 years ago. Situated adjacent to the A1033 in the village of Thorgumbald, south east of Hull towards Spurn Head. An

extremely popular property with locals and visitors alike, **The Barn Farm** has all the comforts a good village pub should offer. Stunning gardens out front.

Licensees Michelle and Stuart only arrived here February '08, but together they've really got the place buzzing. It's become the hub of the village and is praised far and wide. Their impressive menu has the rare advantage of a Roast of the Day section, with a choice of meats, meaning you don't have to wait for Sunday for

your roast dinner! Despite this, their Sunday Carvery is very popular, with 4 joints of meat available (booking advised) until 6pm. The Main Courses cater for everyone's taste; with a great variety of Traditional, European, New World, and Fish dishes, as well as a Specials Board.

Friday nights are Disco and Kareoke from 9.30, Saturday sees Live Bands performing from 9.30, and everyone is welcome to the Sunday Night Quiz from 9pm. Food is served Mon-Sat (12-9pm) and Sundays (12-7pm). One real ale available, Theakstons, plus draught keg ales.

138 THE DEEP

Hull, East Yorkshire HU1 4DP
Tel: 01482 381000
e-mail: info@thedeep.co.uk
website: www.thedeep.co.uk

Welcome to **The Deep**, one of the most spectacular aquariums in the world. This award-winning Yorkshire family attraction is home to 40 sharks and over 3,500 fish. The dramatic building designed by Sir Terry Farrell is located in Hull on the Humber Estuary, just an hour from York. The Deep is operated as a charity dedicated to increasing enjoyment and understanding of the world's oceans. Behind the scenes a team of dedicated marine biologists care for all of the animals at The Deep as well as carrying out vital research into the marine environment.

It first opened its doors in March 2002 and so far has welcomed over 2 million visitors from the UK and abroad. Using a combination of hands-on interactives, audiovisual presentations and living exhibits it tells the story of the worlds oceans. Visitors will be taken on a journey from the beginning of time through the present day oceans to the icy darkness of a futuristic Deep-Sea research lab, Deep Blue one.

139 THE BLUE BELL

**West Green, Cottingham,
East Yorkshire HU16 4BH
Tel: 01482 847113**

A small locals' pub with a lunch-time restaurant attractively located on its own little village green, **The Blue Bell** in Cottingham offers excellent portions and welcomes children. The inside arrangement is unusual. One end has a very "cafe" atmosphere, especially at lunchtimes; while the other is more traditionally decked out in dark wood and green leatherette.

Situated in the 'West Green' area of Cottingham and found east off the A164 or west off the A1079. Tenants Andrew and Maria only took over a short time ago, but already they've given the place a buzz; locals are returning and visitors are beginning to find it, and be impressed. Andrew's been in the trade 15 years, but it's the first time he's had his own licensed premises.

Between two and four real ales are hosted, with Jennings Cumberland Ale and Marstons Pedigree being the regulars. **Other beers include** Fosters, Stella and Mansfield Smooth, and hot drinks like tea and coffee are also available.

Food is served Mon-Sat (12-2pm and 5-9pm) and Sunday (12-late). Choose from an excellent printed menu, offering tasty Starters (try the Soup of the Day with crusty bread, spiced breaded prawns, or a mixed combo to share), exquisite Mains (including home-made Steak & Ale pie, wholetail Whitby scampi, or the home-made lasagna), delicious Light Bites (with sandwiches, jacket potatoes and omelettes) and a range of side orders. There is also a Specials Board with tempting meals each day. Traditional Sunday Roasts are available every week.

For those of you who fancy yourself as a bit of a rockstar, why not have a go at the Open Mic Night every Wednesday from 9pm. Everyone is welcome and even if you're not one for performing, it's still worth a watch. There are occasional other types of entertainment, please ring for details.

The Blue Bell employs an experienced cook, Kath Rothery, and Maria also does her part for the kitchen. As much as possible of the produce used here is sourced locally. There is a small off-road car park, a heated outdoor area, undercover smoking area and a patio/decking for those sunnier days. Children are welcome, and Under 14s are welcome up to 9pm. It is advisable to book on Wed/Thurs/Sun lunchtimes to avoid disappointment. All major credit cards are taken. Open all day, everyday 11am – 11pm (Fri/Sat 11am – midnight). A full range of facilities for disabled access is also available.

299

140 THE TIGER INN

105 King Street, Cottingham,
East Yorkshire, HU16 5QU
Tel: 01482 622970

A very popular destination for good food, well kept ales, and above all, quality hospitality.* Leaseholders Eric and Sarah Barker have been here 10 years now, and **The Tiger Inn** is as cosy as ever.

Eric does an excellent job with the cooking, so every meal is cooked to order. Fresh fish dishes are a speciality, as well as their delicious Sunday Lunch (12-2.30pm). Special breakfasts are served from 10 - 11.15am, and other meals are served Mon-Fri (11.30-6pm) and Saturdays (11.30-4pm). Choose from the home-made Steak & Ale Pie or Lasagne, or their Chicken & Scampi combo, Double Ranch Burger, Mixed Grill and a range of steaks. A variety of snacks and side

orders are available, as well as hot beverages. Their extensive Specials Board provides vegetarian options, daily specials, and sweets.

Regular entertainment means you definitely won't get bored at The Tiger Inn, with Quiz night from 9.30pm every Monday, Kareoke from 7pm – midnight on Tuesdays, and a Disco from 9pm – close on Sat/ Sunday nights. They also have a pool table. One real ale is available, Bass, plus a good selection of keg ales. Open all day, everyday.

141 THE TIGER INN

The Green, North Newbald,
East Yorkshire YO43 4SA
Tel: 01430 827759 Mobile: 07896 754108
e-mail: kimberley.tiger@unicombox.co.uk

North Newbald is a delightful small village located just off the A1034 about 4 miles south of Market Weighton. It has a spacious village green and, overlooking it, a fine old hostelry, **The Tiger Inn,** parts of which date back to the 1700s. This is very much a family-run pub with Kimberley, her mother Dee and Kimberley's daughter Jasmin all involved in the enterprise.

The pub is well-known locally for its excellent home-cooked food. Dishes are listed on a blackboard and include old pub favourites such as home-made Beef 'n' Ale Pie, Honey Roast Ham & Eggs, and Battered "Whale" & Chips. A second blackboard lists the desserts of the day. Customers can eat throughout

the pub, at picnic tables overlooking the green, or on the patio to the

rear. Food is served from noon until 2pm, Tuesday to Sunday; and from 6pm to 8pm, Tuesday to Saturday. Booking is strongly advised at all times. A wide choice of beverages is available, including 3 real ales.

The Tiger hosts a Pub quiz on Tuesday evenings and also occasional live music. Children are welcome. Payment is by cash or cheque but there is an ATM on the premises.

142 THE WHEATSHEAF

Moor Lane, Sherburn-in-Elmet,
North Yorkshire LS25 6DX
Tel: 01977 682583

Originally built as a farmhouse, **The Wheatsheaf** has been an inn for more than 100 years. This outstanding hostelry, which stands adjacent to Sherburn's railway station on the York to Sheffield line, is well-known for its wholesome home-made food, especially its Yorkshire puddings with various fillings. Also on offer are a tasty Steak Pie, chicken and fish dishes, burgers, jacket potatoes, hot and cold sandwiches, and a

children's menu. The regular menu is supplemented by daily specials. Food is served from noon until 9pm, Monday to Friday, from noon until 6pm on Saturday and Sunday. On Sundays a traditional roast lunch is available.

The fully stocked bar serves a good selection of fine ales, lagers, spirits and wine. Mine hosts, Nigel, Carol and Carol's sister Sandra guarantee customers a very warm welcome and the inn has a cosy, friendly atmosphere. There's a comfortable lounge bar, big screen television and SKY Sports, and outside an attractive beer garden for warmer days. Children and animals are welcome; there's good disabled access throughout; and ample parking.

144 THE ROYAL OAK INN

Main Street, Hirst Courtney,
Nr Selby, East Yorkshire YO8 8QT
Tel: 01757 270633

In the picturesque village of Hirst Courtney this impressive premises, **The Royal Oak Inn**, offers the very best a local or visitor could wish for. With quality accommodation, so close to the M62 for a stop-over, a quality caravan park to the rear, plus well kept ales and super food. Found between the A19 and A1041, south of Selby and a very short drive to either J34 or J35 of the M62.

Dawn Patrick took over this traditional looking inn four months ago and already has a 'hit' on her hands. Delicious food is available at all opening times (open every session), with various menus to choose from. But these special nights offer real value for money: Sunday is their

Carvery (plus Thursday evenings), Tuesday's offer fresh fish dishes, Wednesday is Steak night, and Friday is Curry night.

Two regular real ales are Tetleys and Black Sheep, but you'll also find the occasional guest ale. There are 12 upstairs en-suite rooms (2 single, 3 double, and 7 twins), and the tariff includes a hearty breakfast. There's a patio for those sunny days, and a pool table for when it's raining! Children are welcome and all major credit cards are taken.

301

143 LA ANCHOR BAR & PIZZERIA

Main Street, Hensall,
East Yorkshire DN14 0QZ
Tel: 01977 663026

Sometimes you find a wonderful establishment in a place you wouldn't expect to- **La Anchor Bar & Pizzeria** is one of those. Situated in the village of Hensall, found north off the A645 between Goole and Knottingley.

This family-run premises oozes class in every department. Mr. J Tanei and co have been the owners for nine months, completely refurbishing it, and through their talents and hard work have made it one of the destination premises for fine food and surroundings. The interior décor is something else.

The cosy restaurant looks onto the open kitchen, where you can view your choice of dish being prepared and cooked. The stone bake oven is also in view to enjoy that magical experience of your pizza being cooked. The aroma of the place makes you dream of being on holidays abroad, and the taste is as good, if not better than the smell.

There is a wide range of choice in the menu, from Pasta dishes such as a classic Carbonara (Spaghetti with pancetta, egg, parmesan cheese with cream) and Polpette (Spaghetti with meatballs), to more exquisite dishes with salmon, duck, seabass, and risotto. Homemade pasta dishes include Crab Ravioli and Gnocchi Al Tricolore (cherry tomato, mozzarella, basil in a tomato sauce). In the Antipasti section of the menu, you can expect to find some high quality cuisine, including Calamari Fritti,

Carpaccio di Manzo (sliced beef seasoned with garlic and lemon juice finished in olive oil and shredded parmesan), and Gambero Americano (prawn cocktail). There is also a big variety of ever-popular pizzas.

Fully licensed bar, and an extensive wine list is available, with one to suit just about everyone's palate and pocket! The quality rear garden is perfect for eating out and relaxing on a sunny day, and there's also a children's play area to keep them entertained. Off-road parking is available.

Open every evening except Mondays, from 5.30pm. It is essential to book Friday and Saturday nights and advisable at all other times to avoid disappointment. All major credit cards taken.

146 THE WHEATSHEAF

83 Hailgate, Howden, DN14 7SX
Tel: 01430 432334
e-mail: wheatsheaf.1@btconnect.com
website: www.wheatsheaf.webeden.co.uk

Situated in the heart of popular historic town Howden (located in East Yorkshire), well known for its Minster, **The Wheatsheaf** offers a warm welcome to all customers new and old. Antony and James have been owners of this very impressive traditional public house since summer 2005. Antony has been in the trade nearly 20 years, and it shows with the excellent hospitality received here.

Two real ales are available; John Smiths and Tetleys. Food is available 12-2pm and 5-8pm (except Monday lunchtimes and Friday evenings). Antony is your chef, using as much local produce as he can. The extensive menu caters for a wide range of tastes, including a variety of tasty Starters (try the Prawn Cocktail, Potato Wedges BBQ Dip, or Garlic Bread & Spicy Spirals), quality Main Meals (including home-made lasagna, Whitby Seafood Platter, and Chicken Curry), a very popular 'From the Grill' section includes a range of steaks,

Vegetarian Options, Salads, Jacket Potatoes, Burgers & Sandwiches, Hot Sandwiches, Side Orders, Hot Drinks, Desserts, and a Children's Menu. Tuesday until Saturday lunchtimes are the 'Senior Citizens Lunchtime Specials', with great deals on hearty meals. And of course, there is an ever-popular Sunday Lunch. Why not try the Meal Deal nights (Tues, Weds, Thurs 5-8pm) with amazing offers on good meals; Thursday is 2 8oz sirloin steaks, chips, peas & salad for £15.95, Wednesday is 2 main meals for £9.95, and Thursday is Family Night (for every to paying adults, one child eats free from the Children's Menu).

Children are very welcome and credit cards are taken (except America Express & Diners). There is a quality beer garden to dine or relax in at the rear of the premises. There's also a covered dining/drinking/smoking area outside. Off-road parking is available. Closed Monday until 4pm (excluding Bank Holidays), but are open all day every other day of the week.

Wheatsheaf Catering is also run by Antony & Jamie; whatever your event, The Wheatsheaf's professional outside catering service can bring the best of restaurant dining direct to you. They offer a bespoke service to suit any occasion, catering for your every whim & fancy- for any event large or small, from a garden party to a corporate event.

145 BIZZY LIZZIE LICENSED CAFÉ

44 Pasture Road, Goole,
East Riding of Yorkshire DN14 6EZ
Tel/Fax: 01405 765071
e-mail: dewa@talktalkbusiness.net

Just a very short walk from Goole Railway
Station, the **Bizzy Lizzie Licensed Café** is a
popular eating place offering an extensive
menu of wholesome and appetising fare.

Starting with full
English breakfast,
(served up to 11am)
the choices include
lots of light bites,
both hot & cold
sandwiches, jacket
potatoes and deluxe
salads. There is also
a selection of
traditional 'hot

dinner' lunchtime specials complimented by
marvellous desserts. Tea-time treats include
crumpets, scones, and a wonderful
Celebration Fruit Cake made to a special
recipe. Bizzy Lizzie is open 10am to 3.15pm,
Tues to Sun.

148 THE BRIDGE LOW LANE

Low Lane, Horsforth, Leeds,
West Yorkshire LS18 4DF
Tel: 0113 258 7339
e-mail: rachel.jenkinson@btconnect.com

The Bridge Low Lane looks very inviting
with its white-painted walls and colourful
floral displays. This popular village inn is
noted for its quality food, cooked by mine
host Rachel
Jenkinson
who
worked
here for 8
years before

taking over
as licensee
in January
2008. Her
appetising
menu offers lots of pub favourites as well as
vegetarian options, children's meals and light
bites. Lovers of real ales will find a choice of
4 brews - Tetley's Bitter, Tetley's Mild, Black
Sheep and a rotating guest ale.

147 HENRY MOORE INSTITUTE

74 The Headrow, Leeds,
West Yorkshire LS1 3AH
General Enquiries: 0113 246 7467
Information Line: 0113 234 3158
Fax: 0113 246 1481
website: www.henry-moore-fdn.co.uk

The Henry Moore Institute in Leeds is a unique
resource devoted exclusively to sculpture, with a
programme comprising exhibitions, collections and
research. The centre was established by the Henry
Moore foundation as a partnership with Leeds city
council in 1982. In 1993 it moved from Leeds city
art gallery to the newly converted Henry Moore
institute next door.

Whereas the Henry Moore foundation at
Moore's home in Perry Green in Hertfordshire
devotes its activities exclusively to the work of
Henry Moore himself, in Leeds they are
concerned with the subject of sculpture in
general; both historic and contemporary, and of
any nationality. Though some exhibitions may

travel from elsewhere, most are generated from within, and draw on research activity or collection
development. The content of the collections is substantially British and is designed to represent a
cross section of material which all, in different ways, represents and documents sculptural activity.

149 TEMPLE NEWSAM

Temple Newsam Road, off Selby Road
Leeds, West Yorkshire LS15 0AE
Tel: 0113 264 5535
e-mail: temple.newsam@leeds.gov.uk
website: www.leeds.gov.uk/templenewsam

Temple Newsam is one of the great historic estates in England. Set within over 1500 acres of parkland, woodland and farmland landscaped by Capability Brown in the 18th century, it is a magnificent Tudor–Jacobean mansion. Famous as the birthplace of Lord Darnley and home to the Ingram family for over 300 years, the mansion houses rich collections of works of art. The garden is renowned for its Rhododendron and Azalea walk and features the National Plant Collections of Delphinium, Phlox and Aster novi–belgii. Europe's largest working Rare Breeds Farm, with over 400 animals, is set within the original estate Home Farm.

Temple Newsam hosts many events each year from music festivals to funfairs and there are regular family activities, demonstrations, guided walks or tours taking place throughout the year.

Temple Newsam is managed and maintained by the Parks and Countryside and Museums and Galleries Sections of Learning and Leisure, Leeds City Council.

150 HAPPY BUNNY CAFÉ

27 Commercial Street, Rothwell,
West Yorkshire LS26 0AP
Tel: 0113 288 9742
website: www.happybunnycafe.co.uk

Situated on the corner of Commercial Street in the heart of this regenerated former mining town, the **Happy Bunny Café** is a family-friendly café offering a wide selection of hot and cold snacks, including sandwiches and jacket potatoes.

Owner David Ford's home-made steak pie and quiches are particularly popular. Other hot meals and 3 sizes of full English breakfast are also available. The café is open from 8am to 4pm, Monday to Friday, and from 8am to 2pm on Saturday. Payment at the Happy Bunny is by cash only.

152 NOSH CAFÉ BAR

188 Huddersfield Road, Mirfield,
West Yorkshire WF14 8AT
Tel: 01924 480174
e-mail: noshcafe@btinternet.com
website: www.noshcafe.co.uk

Set on Mirfield's main street, the **Nosh Café Bar** is just the place for a tasty bite to eat in or take out.

There are all day breakfasts, home-made pies and roasts, salads, oven-baked jacket potatoes, paninis, kids meals, daily

specials and a good choice of coffees, teas and soft drinks. Owner Chris Hull has spent more than 20 years in the catering business and his expertise is reflected in the popularity of his bright and cheerful café. The Nosh Café is open from 7.30am to 2.30pm, Monday to Friday; and from 8am to 1pm on Saturday. Payment is by cash only.

151 CAFÉ BOO

**156 Huddersfield Road, Mirfield,
West Yorkshire WF14 8AN
Tel: 01924 499494
website: www.cafeboo.co.uk**

Occupying a striking building and with a stylish modern décor, the **Café Boo** offers an excellent range of wholesome and appetising food. The choice includes piping hot paninis, hot toasties, jacket potatoes,

daily specials and a soup of the day. There are also salads and freshly prepared sandwiches, and for something sweet, scones, pastries, muffins and cookies. The café is fully licensed and offers a choice of wines by the glass and bottle, as well as coffees, teas and soft drinks.

The café is open from 9am to 4.30pm, Monday to Saturday, and also, every other Friday, it hosts a tapas evening from 5.30pm to last orders at 9pm. Such is its popularity, booking is essential.

Already renowned for their coffees and paninis, owners Anne and Bill Holdsworth and their dynamic young team have ambitious plans for the future. "We plan to offer entertainments to the people of Mirfield, bringing a touch of Mediterranean class in a relaxed and informal atmosphere", said Anne.

Please note that payment is by cash only; there is good disabled access to the ground floor dining area.

153 RED HOUSE

**Oxford Road, Gomersal, Cleckheaton,
West Yorkshire BD19 4JP
Tel: 01274 335100**

This delightful house now looks very much as it would have done in Charlotte Bronte's time when she used it as a model for the Briarmains of her novel *Shirley*. **Red House** was the home of her close friend Mary Taylor and Charlotte stayed here often.

Wander around this wool merchant's home where each room brings you closer to the 1830s, from the elegant parlour to the stone-flagged kitchen with its Yorkshire range, jelly moulds and colourful crockery. Then take a stroll through the re-created 19th century garden with its shaped flower beds and decorative ironwork; even the plants and shrubs are in keeping with the period.

Explore Charlotte Bronte's Spen Valley connections and her friendships with Mary Taylor and Ellen Nussey in *The Secret's Out* exhibition in the barn. What did local people say when they discovered that Charlotte had based some of her characters in *Shirley* on them? And how did Charlotte, Mary and Ellen react to society's strict view of 'a woman's place'?

Move along to the 20th Century and the *Spen Valley Stories* exhibition in the restored cartsheds. Relive schooldays, Teddy Boys, dance marathons and street parties through the pictures and mementoes of local residents. The latest audio technology lets them tell their own stories while you browse through historical photos on a user-friendly, touchscreen terminal.

And, before you leave, call in to the museum shop. With its period toys, books, gifts and preserves, you'll be more than tempted to take home a taste of the past!

154 THE DALESWAY HOTEL

1 Leeds Road, Ilkley,
West Yorkshire LS29 8DH
Tel: 01943 605438
e-mail: daleswayhotel@hotmail.co.uk
website: www.hotelilkley.co.uk

A must for visitors to this very popular area, **The Dalesway Hotel** is set in the centre of Ilkley. A traditional pub with guest rooms, it was recently refurbished and now offers the best of classic style and elegance with every modern comfort and convenience. It's well-known for excellent food,

especially its famous Yorkshire puddings with various fillings. Food is served every lunchtime and evening, Monday to Friday, and from noon until 5pm at weekends. On weekdays there's a special offer for senior citizens on a 2-course lunch. On Sundays, a popular Carvery is added to the regular menu. Real ale lovers will find a choice of 3 real ales - Black Sheep, Timothy Taylors Landlord and Theakstons Olde Peculiar.

The hotel also offers exceptionally comfortable accommodation with 9 beautifully furnished rooms available, all with satellite TV and hospitality tray.. Eight of the rooms have en suite facilities, the ninth has its own private bathroom. The hotel is an ideal base for exploring this scenic and historic area, close to the Yorkshire Dales National Park and Brontë Country.

155 THE RED LION

Kirkgate, Otley, West Yorkshire LS21 3HN
Tel: 01943 464217
website: www.theredlionotley.com

Dating back to the late 17th century, **The Red Lion** is a popular town centre inn with a reputation for serving excellent home-

cooked food at honest-to-goodness prices. The chef is Malcolm Hughes, a well-known figure in the area as he hosts a Saturday morning cookery show on Radio Leeds. Malcolm's extensive menu features plenty of old favourites such as the home-made Steak & Ale Pie, Cumberland Sausage with mash and gravy, and fresh Haddock & Chips. But the menu also offers a good choice that includes Chinese dishes, curries, jacket potatoes, omelettes and hot and cold sandwiches. All the dishes are based on fresh local produce and the regular menu is supplemented by daily specials, Seafood Pancake in a Pernod Sauce, perhaps, or home-made beef burger. Several of the dishes are available in children's portions. Food is served from 11am to 4pm, daily.

The Red Lion is noted for its regular live entertainment with a folk music evening, every other Saturday night; Irish music every other Tuesday; and every Friday evening there's an open "Mike Nite" held in the upstairs function room. Please note that payment at The Red Lion is by cash only.

156 PARK TOP HOUSE

I Rawdon Road, Haworth, Keighley,
West Yorkshire BD22 8DX
Tel: 07969203932
e-mail: vannessa@parktophouse.co.uk
website: www.parktophouse.co.uk

Boasting beautiful views over Howarth and Central Park, **Park Top House** is a smart modern building with a 4-star rating from Visit Britain. It's the home of Vannessa and Kenny who offer top quality B&B accommodation in 4 upstairs guest bedrooms. Three of the rooms are en suite; the fourth has its own private bathroom. A truly hearty breakfast with lots of choice is

served from 7.30am to 9.30pm. An ideal base for exploring the attractions of Brontë Country. Importantly for Haworth, Park Top has its own off road parking.

158 THE PUNCH BOWL INN

Bridge Road, Silsden,
West Yorkshire BD20 9ND
Tel: 01535 652360
e-mail: info@punchbowlsilsden.com
website: www.punchbowlsilsden.com

Located in the heart of Silsden, **The Punch Bowl Inn** is a handsome traditional hostelry where David and his staff offer a warm welcome to all. This lively inn is noted for its superb food, served every lunchtime from noon until 2pm, for its well-kept ales, including a real ale, and for its live entertainment every Wednesday night from 9pm. The inn

also has a function room with a wooden dance floor which can cater for up to 50 guests. The inn is run as a family pub with children and dogs most welcome.

157 COBBLES AND CLAY - THE ART CAFÉ

60 Main Street, Haworth,
West Yorkshire BD22 8DP
Tel: 01535 644218
e-mail: info@cobblesandclay.co.uk
website: www.cobblesandclay.co.uk

Cobbles and Clay also offers an appetising selection of home-cooked food based almost entirely on produce sourced within the county. Try a satisfying bowl of completely home made vegetable soup served in a bowl individually painted on the premises or better still paint your own bowl! The café is licensed so you can enjoy a drink with your meal - choose from an extensive range of beers and wines. In good weather, sample your refreshments in the hidden garden at the rear.

The philosophy of Jill Ross, the owner of **Cobbles and Clay - the art café,** is summed up in the thought: "We don't stop playing when we get old - we grow old when we stop playing". At her colourful café on Haworth's famous cobbled main street, you'll find a huge range of raw pottery

waiting for you to bring it alive with colour and personality. Choose from cups, jugs, bowls and plates and many more individual designs, and transform them into personalised and dazzling pieces of art. Jill will then glaze it for you and fire it in her kiln so it can be kept forever. "They also make a great gift" says Jill, "if you can bring yourself to give them away!"

The café is open from 9am to 5pm, daily; evening bookings taken on request.

Main Road, Eastburn, nr Keighley,
West Yorkshire BD20 7SN
Tel: 01535 653000
e-mail: karen@eastburninn.co.uk
website: www.eastburninn.co.uk

One of the most popular, and certainly one of the most sociable hostelries in the whole region is the **Eastburn Inn** in Airedale, off the A629 between Keighley and Skipton. The inn used to be called the White Bear but after a top-to-toe refurbishment in

2005 it was re-named. Mine host, Karen Schofield, continues a long tradition of hospitality, good food and well-kept ales, and there's no mistaking the warmth of the welcome she and her staff provide, whether it's for familiar faces or first-timers. Strangers soon become friends in the relaxing atmosphere of the well-stocked bar.

Karen is an accomplished chef so good food is a priority here. Karen's extensive menu offers a wide choice of wholesome and appetising food. Naturally, a large Yorkshire pudding features amongst the starters and the main courses range from grills, fish and poultry dishes to old favourites such as Sausage & Mash, or Fish & Chips. Also available are all day breakfasts, a roast, salads and a choice of half a dozen different kinds of burgers. For lighter appetites, there's a selection of hot and cold sandwiches, and various tasties on toast. Children have their own menu with an unusually extensive choice of dishes. In addition to the regular menu, there are daily specials and a traditional roast dinner is served daily with a choice of beef or pork. Food is available from noon until 10pm daily, except on Mondays when the kitchen is closed and the pub opens at 5pm.

This lively inn provides plenty of entertainment. There's a pool table, darts, a big screen TV

and a secure children's play area in the garden where there's also a private barbecue area. Every Wednesday, the inn hosts a Quiz; on Thursday evenings there's free pool from 7.30pm, on Friday evenings, a karaoke from 8pm, and also occasional live entertainment at weekends.

If you are looking for accommodation in the area, the Eastburn has 3 comfortable standard rooms, 2 family and 1 single. A hearty full English breakfast is included in the tariff. The inn accepts all major credit cards; there's good disabled access to the ground floor; and there's a large off road car park.

309

159 THE GROVE CAFÉ

Unit 21, Steeton Grove, Steeton, Keighley,
West Yorkshire BD20 6TT
Tel: 01535 656565

The Grove Café, close to the railway station in the village of Steeton in Airedale, is the place to go to for 'The Full Monty' - a huge breakfast suitable for Desperate Dan appetites. This friendly eating place also serves smaller versions, which are available along with hot and cold sandwiches and various hot snacks. Daily specials might include a giant Yorkshire pudding filled with sausages, gammon dishes, or chilli. The café is open from 8am to 2pm, Monday to Friday; and from 9am to 12 noon on Saturday.

162 GILLY'S FRIENDLY CAFÉ

381 Thornton Road, Thornton, Bradford,
West Yorkshire BD13 3JX
Tel: 01274 833258

Gilly's Friendly Café is exactly what it says - a warm and inviting place that has been dispensing good cheer and good food for well over 50 years. The extensive menu includes dishes such as an all day breakfast (very popular), omelettes, tasty things on toast, and a wide range of hot and cold sandwiches. And if there's something you fancy that isn't on the list, if they have the ingredients they will cook it for you. Gilly's is open from 7am to 2pm, Monday to Friday, and from 7am to 11am on Saturday.

161 BOLLING HALL MUSEUM

Bowling Hall Road, Bradford,
West Yorkshire BD4 7LP
Tel: 01274 723057
website: www.bradfordmuseums.org.uk

Bolling Hall offers visitors a fascinating journey through the lives and times of the Bradford families for whom it provided a home over five hundred years. Situated just a mile from Bradford city centre and situated in a quiet, leafy garden,

Bolling Hall was for many years the seat of two important land-owning families, the Bollings and the Tempests. With parts of the building dating from the Medieval, Bolling Hall is a rambling mixture of styles with every nook and cranny packed with history. During the Civil War the household supported the Royalist cause, and the house provided a stronghold during the 'siege of Bradford'. Rooms are furnished and decorated to give an accurate taste of life at

different periods of the house's history, and the fascinating furniture on display includes a superb bed made for Harewood House by Thomas Chippendale.

Bolling Hall has been furnished in keeping with its long and eventful history with a fine

collection of period furniture, including a bed made by Thomas Chippendale for Harewood House. Bedrooms are decorated by period, providing a fascinating insight into the lives of wealthy families of the 16th, 17th and 18th Centuries. A central exhibit of the Civil War room is Cromwell's death mask. Spend some time exploring a different side of Bradford's heritage - but watch out for an appearance by the 'White Lady' in the Ghost Room!

163 BANKFIELD MUSEUM

Akroyd Park Boothtown Road
Halifax, West Yorkshire HX3 6HG
Tel: 01422 354823
e-mail: bankfield.museum@calderdale.gov.uk

Set in a wonderful Victorian millowner's house, Bankfield has a growing reputation as a centre for textiles and contemporary craft. With its internationally important collection of textiles, weird and wonderful objects from around the world, plus commissions by leading makers and a varied programme of exhibtitions and activities, there is much to see and enjoy. Don't miss the Toy Gallery; the

Duke of Wellington's Regimental Museum and the Marble Gallery, a new selling space for contemporary craft. Open: Tuesday to Saturday 10am - 5pm. Sundays 2pm - 5pm Bank Holiday Mondays 10am - 5pm. Free admission.

165 COPA HOUSE

17 Market Street, Hebden Bridge,
West Yorkshire HX7 6EU
Tel: 01422 845524
e-mail: info@copahouserestaurant.co.uk
website: www.copahouserestaurant.co.uk

A stylish restaurant/coffee shop, **Copa House** is owned and run by the mother and daughter team of Cheryl and Amber

Gatehouse. During the day, they offer a café style menu then, from 6pm, Thursday to Saturday, an evening menu featuring imaginative dishes such as venison, red wine and herb sausages with mustard mash, or a vegetarian smoked Brie baked in puff pastry with tomato stew. The restaurant is licensed, with wine available by the glass or bottle. This popular eating place is open from 10am to 4pm, Tuesday and Wednesday; from 10am to 9.30pm, Thursday to Saturday; and from 10am to 4pm on Sunday.

164 WHITE LION HOTEL

Bridge Gate, Hebden Bridge,
West Yorkshire HX7 8EX
Tel: 01422 842197 Fax: 01422 846619
e-mail: enquiries@whitelionhotel.net
website: www.whitelionhotel.net

Believed to be the oldest building in Hebden Bridge, the **White Lion Hotel** dates back to 1657 when it served as a coaching inn. It is set beside the river in the heart of the town and in its time has had some notable guests. The highwayman Dick Turpin was once arrested here and in the 19th century the famous composer Franz Liszt sampled the White Lion's hospitality.

Today, mine hosts, Chris and Sheila, preside over this welcoming traditional inn with its olde worlde warm and friendly atmosphere. The White Lion has a well-deserved reputation for serving good food with a menu that includes lots of old favourites such as beer-

battered haddock and chips and steaks as well as a good choice of other dishes based on fresh locally sourced produce. Devotees of real ales will be happy there with Black Sheep, Flowers IPA, Timothy Taylor Landlord and a rotating guest ale to choose from.

The inn provides an ideal base for visitors to the Calder Valley and Brontë country with 10 comfortable en suite rooms available. Four of them are on the ground floor and two rooms have been adapted for the disabled.

**58 Towngate, Heptonstall, Hebden Bridge,
West Yorkshire HX7 7NB
Tel: 01422 842027 Mobile: 07833 547276**

The ancient village of Heptonstall lies along the ridge of a steeply sloping spur of land, overlooking the Calder Valley and the town of Hebden Bridge. Now a conservation village, Heptonstall's main street is still cobbled and it's in this street you'll find the impressive stone-built **White Lion**. Your friendly host at this popular hostelry is Barry Shaw who was born into the trade - his parents ran a pub - and his expertise in the hospitality trade is extensive. This experience proved useful when Barry took over here in the summer of 2006 as the inn had fallen on hard times. Happily, he has turned things around and the White Lion is now a very popular destination premises.

Contributing to that success is the quality of the food on offer here. The chef is a professional and his menu is based on locally sourced produce, freshly prepared. You'll find a good choice of pub favourites such as steaks, steak & ale pie, fish and chips and gammon and pineapple along with home-made beef burgers, a vegetarian option, and a home-made Italian lasagne. In addition to the regular menu, there's a daily specials board offering dishes such as poached finny haddock or slow-roasted lamb. On Sundays, traditional roasts are served complete with all the trimmings. Half portions at half the price are available for children. Food is served from noon until 3pm, and from 5pm to 9pm, Wednesday to Friday; from noon until 9pm on Saturday, and from noon until 8pm on Sunday. The inn is also happy to cater for small parties and buffets.

To complement your meal, the bar stocks an extensive range of beverages, including 3 real ales. The White Lion also has one guest bedroom available, a double with en suite facilities, TV, fridge and hospitality tray. Also available is a 4 berth static caravan with panoramic views and holiday cottages available. Walkers are made welcome as well as dogs (provided they are on a lead).

If you enjoy Irish music, be sure to visit the White Lion on Tuesday evening when there's a regular session. Another good time to visit Heptonstall is Good Friday when the Pace Egging takes place, in Weavers Square. This ancient tradition involves actors in elaborate costumes recounting the legend of St George. Another interesting feature of Heptonstall is that it is one of few places where the churchyard has two churches in it. Ted Hughes the poet Laureat used to write poems in the pub. There is a foundation named after him at the top of the village. Sylvia Plath, his lady, is buried in the graveyard, which attracts a lot of tourists from abroad. The coiners (a group of counter-fitters) were commited to York Castle in 1769 and were hung, drawn and quartered before being buried in the graveyard.

167 GRAIN FARM

Haworth Old Road, Pecket Well,
Hebden Bridge, West Yorkshire HX7 8RG
Tel: 01422 845674

The Sunderland family have farmed at **Grain Farm** for well over one hundred years. Miles Sunderland was born here and he and his wife Margaret have lived together here since 1971.

Their farmhouse stands amidst breathtaking scenery with spectacular views in all directions. This Pennine haven provides an ideal base for walking in the lovely Hardcastle Crags or for a hike over the wild and beautiful Brontë moors to Haworth and the Brontë Parsonage. This is also one of the best areas in the country for mountain biking. For artists, too - Miles knows the area intimately and can point you in the right direction for finding the most scenic vantage points.

The farmhouse dates back in parts to 1604 and is full of charm and character. There are 3 guest

bedrooms, all beautifully furnished and decorated, and all enjoying glorious views. Breakfast at Grain Farm is definitely something to look forward to - Margaret is an accomplished cook and her hearty breakfasts will set you up for the day. She is also happy to provide evening meals by arrangement. Grain Farm is dog friendly with separate accommodation for your pet available.

168 THE WINDMILL INN

17 Stanage Lane, Shelf, Halifax,
West Yorkshire HX3 7PR
Tel: 01274 67027

The village of Shelf lies just off the A6036 in the countryside near Bradford. It's well worth seeking out to pay a visit to **The Windmill Inn** which enjoys a glowing reputation for its excellent food, real ales and genuine hospitality.

Mine hosts, Jennifer and David Latty took over here in 2004 and have made the inn a popular destination for discerning diners. Jennifer is an inspired cook and her menu offers an enticing range of dishes based on locally-sourced ingredients. They include a traditional fish & chips, home-made pies and lasagne, steaks, salads and vegetarian meals such as home-made Goat's Cheese & Red Onion Tart. Hearty 'Super Sandwiches' are available, and for lighter appetites a selection of sandwiches and hot melts.

Children are favoured with an unusually extensive choice. On Sundays, a traditional roast lunch is served and 2-course specials are available Tuesday to Saturday. Food is served from noon until 2pm and from 5.30pm to 8pm, Tuesday to Saturday; and from noon until 6.30pm on Sunday.

Other amenities at The Windmill include an airy conservatory overlooking the well-tended beer garden where there's also a superb children's play area.

313

169 CAFÉ ETC

14 Victoria Road, Elland,
West Yorkshire HX5 0PU
Tel: 01422 327555
e-mail: info@cafeetc.co.uk
website: www.cafeetc.co.uk

"The name says it all really" says Chris Gates of his popular town centre eating place, **Café Etc.** "We're a café... etc!" It comprises both a 14-seat café and a takeout sandwich shop, and Chris aims to give his customers just that little bit

more. "Whether it's more for your money" he says, "or that friendly smile you weren't expecting, we want you to leave feeling more than satisfied".

The café offers customers the chance to eat in a comfortable and pleasant atmosphere with the addition of child-friendly facilities and, of course, great home-made food. As it says on the menu 'Basically, you can have what you like but to help you, here are some suggestions'. These include a wide choice of paninis, melts, toasties, jacket potatoes, salads, all day breakfasts - and cakes. In

addition to the regular menu, there are daily specials such as lasagne or a creamy fish pie. Food is served from 8am to 3pm, Monday to Friday, and from 9am to

2pm on Saturday. There are bonuses for regular customers and we offer outside catering for all occasions. Payment at Café Etc is by cash or cheque only.

170 THE CLOUGH HOUSE INN

129 Clough Lane, Rastrick,
West Yorkshire HD6 3QL
Tel: 01484 512120

Dating back to the early 1800s, **The Clough House Inn** is a handsome old hostelry in the village of Rastrick in the Calder Valley. Carol and Steve Hargreaves took over here in 2004 and since then have established a fine reputation for the quality of the food on offer and the well-kept ales.

The menu is based on local produce wherever possible and professionally prepared. The choice ranges from a selection of grills, through perennial favourites such as giant beer-battered fish & chips or home-made pies, to paella, lasagne or Lamb Tagine. There's also a vegetarian lasagne and Greek salad. Specialities of the house include Chicken Tikka Masala and Hunters chicken which is known to the locals as Smothered Chicken since it is indeed smothered with barbecue sauce and cheese. Children are unusually well-catered

for with a menu that includes a 4oz Gammon steak, a sausage and tomato pasta, and a childrens portion of fish and chips - these dishes are also available as smaller plates for smaller appetites! In addition to the printed menus, there are always daily specials listed on the blackboard, along with a choice of delicious home-made desserts. At Sunday lunchtime, a choice of roasts is served together with a few favourites from the regular menu.

Food is served every lunchtime and evening except Monday lunchtime unless it's a Bank Holiday. From Tuesday to Saturday, food is available from noon until 2.30pm; and from Monday to Saturday, from 5pm to 8.30pm. On Sundays, food is served from 12 noon until 8pm. Booking at the weekends is strongly recommended.

To accompany your meal, the well-stocked bar offers a wide range of beverages including 3

real ales - Bass, Theakstons Best and a rotating guest ale. In good weather, customers can enjoy their refreshments in the beer garden at the rear of the inn or in front of the roaring log fire which is a popular feature on cold days.

This popular hostelry has a pool room and on Sunday evenings hosts a Pub Quiz from 9pm - entry is free, a free supper is served and everyone is welcome.

The inn accepts all major credit cards apart from American Express; there is good disabled access throughout. A visit to The Clough House Inn is a must, even if it's just to see their award winning flower displays!

1 Green Lane, West Vale, Greetland, Halifax,
West Yorkshire HX4 8AB
Tel: 01422 372037

Conveniently located just a short drive from junction 22 of the M62 and from Halifax, the **Corner Café** in Greetland is a truly hidden gem. It's owned and run by Hayley and Chris Hare, local people who used to run the next door sandwich shop for three years before acquiring the café in 2007. They are ably assisted by Jackie who came in for a cup of tea one day, saw how busy they were and offered to assist with the washing up. She's been here ever since and is Hayley's 'right hand lady'.

The café opens at 7.30am with a wide choice of breakfasts on offer, including a daunting 'Belly Buster Breakfast'. Lunch choices include Gammon & Egg, home-made Steak & Kidney, Minced Beef & Onion, and Cottage Pie. Curry, Chilli, beef burgers and omelettes are also available. There are also daily specials and a selection of dishes for kids. For lighter appetites, there's a huge choice of hot and cold sandwiches. These are all available to take out and deliveries are available on orders over £10. The café is open from 7.30am to 1.30pm, Tuesday to Sunday, later opening hours by appointment. Payment at the Corner Café is by cash only.

172 THE GOLDEN FLEECE

Lindley Road, Blackley, Elland HX5 0TE
Tel: 01422 372704
e-mail: t7lyn@hotmail.com

Only a few minutes drive from the M62, **The Golden Fleece** is located in the pretty village of Blackley and enjoys breathtaking views of unspoilt countryside. Dating back in parts to the mid-16th century, the inn is full of charm and character. A good choice of wholesome food is
served every lunchtime and from 5pm to 9pm, Tuesday to Saturday. Vegetarians and kids are well-catered for, as are
lovers of real ales. Traditional roasts with all the trimmings are served at Sunday lunchtime. The inn accepts all major credit cards apart from American Express and Diners.

173 THE DUKE OF YORK

Stainland Road, Stainland, Halifax,
West Yorkshire HX4 9HF
Tel: 01422 370217

Originally built as 3 cottages in the mid-1700s, **The Duke of York** is a spacious and impressive building. The interior has a striking décor with a mix of traditional and modern elements, including the stone-built bar, exposed brickwork and walls painted a deep red. The dining area has polished wood floors, stylish seating and floor-to-ceiling windows looking out over the small and attractive beer garden to rolling countryside beyond. Mine hosts Maria and James have been here since 2003, bringing their enthusiasm and warm hospitality to making the venture a great success.

Good home-cooked food is a speciality here. Maria is an inspired chef and her dishes, based on top quality produce most of which is sourced locally, have

something to cosset every palate. The appetising choices include superb home-made pies (Steak, Ale & Mushroom for example), Cajun chicken, giant haddock and more. The lunchtime 'lite bite' menu features hearty favourites such as gammon with egg and chips. scampi, and liver & sausage casserole with mash. Food is served from 6pm to 9pm, Monday and Tuesday; noon until 2pm, and 6pm to 9pm, Wednesday to Saturday; and from noon until 9pm on Sunday. Up to 4 real ales are on tap.

174 GRIFFIN INN

57 Stainland Road, Barkisland,
West Yorkshire HX4 0AQ
Tel: 01422 823873
e-mail: liz@griffininn.net
website: www.griffin inn.net

Hidden away in the attractive village of Barkisland, the **Griffin Inn** is very much a family-run hostelry with the mother and daughter team of Liz and Nikki Lindsay, daughter-in-law Jo and Chris the chef all actively involved in the enterprise. "We are passionate about good food" says Liz, "we love the Griffin and the beautiful village of Barkisland with its friendly residents and we are striving to make this pub a venue that the village can be proud of".

Food is served every lunchtime and evening, Tuesday to Thursday, and all day Friday to Sunday. Everything on the menu is home-made and ranges from local farm rump steak to a pan seared chicken breast with a wild mushroom and mustard cream sauce. Vegetarians are particularly well-catered for with dishes

such as homemade herb pancakes with the chef's own filling of the day,

or haloumi cheese with slow roast tomatoes. A popular recent addition to the menu is the cheese board selection with a selection of cheeses hand-made in Yorkshire and vegetarian friendly. Tuesday evening is Pie Night when up to 7 different home-made pies are available. Children and dogs are welcome; all major credit cards are accepted.

175 THE WHARF

31 Wharf Street, Sowerby Bridge,
West Yorkshire HX6 2LA
Tel/Fax: 01422 833316
e-mail: the wharf@btconnect.com

Located in the heart of historic Sowerby Bridge, **The Wharf** is a handsome building dating back to the early 1800s. It has a large outside seating area for 50 people to the front of the pub which will soon be under cover.

The Wharf is a popular eating place with John the chef offering a good choice of appetising dishes. These include perennial favourites such as fish & chips, steaks, chicke, and sausage and mash. For lighter appetites, there are sandwiches, baguettes, omelettes, burgers and

jacket potatoes. Kids have their own menu which includes desserts specially for them. On Sundays a choice of roasts is also available. Food is served every day from noon until 4.30pm but landlord Chris Helm is considering making it available until later in

the evening. The well-stocked bar at The Wharf offers a full range of beverages, including up to two real ales with Tetleys as the regular brew.

The inn is well-known for its entertainment. In addition to the 3 plasma Tvs, John the chef takes on a new role in the evenings as the DJ. On Friday and Saturday evenings, there's a disco from 8pm, and on Sunday, a karaoke session from 4pm.

176 THE ALMA INN

Cotton Stones, Sowerby Bridge,
West Yorkshire HX6 4NS
Tel: 01422 823334 Fax: 01422 825450
e-mail: info@alma inn.com
website: www.alma inn.com

One of Calderdale's finest traditional country hostelries, **The Alma Inn** offers superb home-cooked food, hand-pulled real ales, luxurious accommodation and dramatic rural views. The Alma is roughly 150 years old and visitors are treated to real open fires, stone-flagged floors, exposed oak beams and a traditional Yorkshire warm welcome. High quality cuisine at The Alma is a top priority. Food is served all day from 12 noon until closing time and is split between informal bar meals served in the large lounge bar or in the Mediterranean Woodstones Restaurant that boasts the only wood-burning pizza oven in the region.

Good food goes hand in hand with good drink at The Alma. The bar stocks an extensive range of hand-pulled real ales, nearly 100 bottled Belgium beers, an extensive wine list and a varied choice of soft drinks.

As well as being a fine food and drink establishment, the inn also has 5 luxurious en suite bedrooms available, each individually designed and furnished to an extremely high standard. Three of them enjoy some of the best views you could ever wish to wake up to, while the Presidential Suite has a double Jacuzzi bath. Also available is a large, separate function room.

178 LAST OF THE SUMMER WINE EXHIBITION

30 Huddersfield Road, Holmfirth,
West Yorkshire HD9 2JS
Tel: 01484 681408
website: www.wrinkledstocking.co.uk/
exhibition

Back in the early 1970s, the sleepy Pennine town of Holmfirth was turned head over heels by the introduction of three rascally men, joined over the years by a mix of equally amusing and varied characters. **Last of the Summer Wine** is the longest-running comedy series on television, with fans all over the Globe, particularly the United States, where they have fallen in love with the gentle charm, Yorkshire humour and rolling countryside.

The dramatic beauty of the Pennine moorlands, featuring quaint villages, dry stone walls and beautiful cottages, is an added bonus to the mischievous antics TV viewers have come to expect from the Summer Wine characters. The late Bill Owen, who played the lovable and famous rogue Compo, described himself as an adopted "Holmfirther", for a time living in the town, and lending his name and support to many local worthy and charitable causes.

He was also heavily involved in the creation and design of the Summer Wine Exhibition in conjunction with local Summer Wine photographer Malcolm Howarth. The BBC supported the venture with props and equipment, and Bill was keen to make sure the Exhibition faithfully represented the programme, and provided an interesting and memorable feature for visitors.

The exhibition was officially opened by Compo on Easter Saturday, 1996, the 25th anniversary of the programme.

319

177 THE SANDS HOUSE

Blackmoorfoot Road, Crosland Hill,
Huddersfield, West Yorkshire HD4 7AE
Tel: 01484 654478   Fax: 01484 461282
website: www.thesandshouse.com

Enjoying a lovely countryside location, **The Sands House** stands beside a very ancient drovers road and began life as a coaching inn. The interior is very traditional in style and you will never need to be in any doubt about what time it is - placed around the pub is a collection of around 300 clocks of all types and vintages.

Mine hosts at this friendly and welcoming hostelry are James and Beverley Haigh. James has been here for some 15 years, starting as a barman and working his way up to become leaseholder in the summer of 2008. Beverley also knows the inn well as she also worked here on and off for 5 years.

Since taking over they have built up a glowing reputation for serving quality food, based on local produce wherever possible. Their menu changes every week to make the most of fresh seasonal produce. Typical dishes amongst the starters are smoked sea trout potato cake with spring onion crème fraiche, or Chicken liver and port terrine with a plum chutney and toasted ciabatta. The main course offerings might include Wild mushroom and chestnut mille feuille; Baby leek and roast aubergine shepherds pie; or Braised pheasant. A roast dinner is always available with additional roasts added to the Sunday menu. If you enjoy early dining, an 'Early Bird' special is available every evening between 5pm and 7pm, excluding Sundays. On Thursdays customers can Wine and Dine for Less between 7pm and 9.00pm with 25% off all main courses and 50% off selected wines. The regular menu is served every day from 12 noon until 9pm and until 9.30pm on Friday and Saturday. Booking ahead is strongly recommended at weekends. The inn has seating for 90 diners inside and about double that number in the spacious beer garden overlooking open countryside which also has a large children's play area.

Lovers of real ales will be in their element at the Sands House. No fewer than six traditional cask ales available and an extensive wine list that includes wines from both new and old worlds.

This lively pub hosts a Family Fortunes style quiz with beer prizes on Wednesday, and on Sunday there's a General Knowledge quiz with cash and beer prizes.

179 HERVEY'S WINE BAR

Norridge Bottom, Holmfirth,
West Yorkshire HD9 7BB
Tel: 01484 686925
e-mail: info@herveys.co.uk
website: www.herveyswinebar.com

One of Holmfirth's hidden treasures, **Hervey's Wine Bar** is a charming place - the light and airy interior is very homely and welcoming, with the Aga and copper pots open to view in one corner, pale wood dining tables and a cream-and-green décor.

Run by Jon and Hazel Shaw, who are friendly hosts offering first class service and hospitality, Hervey's is open throughout the day Tuesday to Sunday and Bank Holidays.

The food on offer includes a range of tasty tapas while the lunchtime and evening menus feature a diverse choice of dishes based on locally sourced produce and prepared by Hazel, an accomplished cook. Real ale lovers will find a choice of 4 brews - Black Sheep and 3 from the Copper Dragon Brewery in Skipton.

During the summer months, food is available from noon until 3pm, and from 6pm to 9.30pm; in winter, from 6pm to 9.30pm. In good weather, customers can enjoy their drinks on the superb patio at the rear.

A highlight of the year at Hervey's is the excellent Folk Festival it hosts over the first weekend in May. Children are welcome at Hervey's; all major credit cards are accepted, and there's good disabled access throughout.

181 COOKHOUSE CAFÉ

17 Station Road, Slaithwaite, Huddersfield,
West Yorkshire HD7 5AW
Tel: 01484 842269

The popular **Cookhouse Café** is a welcoming place with a simple Shaker-style décor. Owner Tracey Shone, who arrived here in early 2007, is also an accomplished chef and her specialities include some magnificent breakfasts and

delicious home-made pies with various fillings. On Sundays, traditional roast lunches with all the trimmings are added to the menu. Food is available from 8am to 2pm, Monday to Friday; 8am to 1pm on Saturday; and from 9am to 1pm on Sunday. Children are welcome at the Cookhouse; payment is by cash only.

180 WHARFESIDE INN

**Carr Lane, Slaithwaite, Huddersfield,
West Yorkshire HD7 5AG
Tel: 01484 847333**

Serving fresh food daily, Real Ales and a warm welcome, the **Wharfeside Inn** is situated just off the main A62 in the heart of Slaithwaite. This quality property was once the ground floor of an impressive Co-operative Society building, but its impressive towers have long since been removed, and since then it has been known as the Wharfeside Inn.

Slaithwaite is located 4 miles west of Huddersfield in the picturesque Colne valley. And while it offers the benefit of a rural retreat it also has facilities that any 'townee' could need. It boasts a fine selection of shops, a bank, swimming pool and sports centre, a health centre as well as a fine selection of pubs, and is well placed for walks around the valley.

The current renovation of the Huddersfield Narrow Canal means that it will soon be possible

to sail a canal barge from Huddersfield right through to Ashton-under-Lyne in Greater Manchester. Stopping off in Slaithwaite as you go, of course!

Jason Raper is an experienced licensee, and he and his staff offer a warm welcome to all, and outstanding facilities in all areas of the business. Open all day, everyday and food is served Mon-Fri (12-2pm and 5-8pm) and Sat-Sun (12-7pm). It is advisable to book on Sundays to avoid disappointment. Choose from the classic menu, with a good selection of dishes, or even something from the Specials board. Roast dinners are available everyday, making the Wharfeside Inn popular with both locals and visitors alike. Produce here is sourced locally within the country.

Accommodation is available all year round, with 4 en-suite guest rooms in double/twin size. Rooms are on a Bed & Breakfast or Room Only basis. There is occasional entertainment i.e. live music on some Saturday nights from 9pm (ring for details).

There are 3 Real Ales to enjoy, including two from the Copper Dragon Brewery, and a rotating guest ale. Children welcome. Pay by cash and cheque only. Regarding disabled customers there are no problems if eating or drinking, but accommodation is upstairs.

Slaithwaite is the setting for the Anglian TV series 'Where the Heart is' as well as having scenes from the *'Last of the Summer Wine'* filmed here.

182 THE GREAT WESTERN INN

Manchester Road, Marsden, Huddersfield,
West Yorkshire HD7 6NL
Tel: 01484 844315 Fax: 01484 845078
e-mail: enquiries@greatwesterninn.co.uk
website: www.greatwesterninn.co.uk

The Great Western Inn occupies a stunning location surrounded by thousands of acres of moorland, looking over and toward both Wessenden and Saddleworth Moor. This family-run Free House dates back to 1838 and began life as a coaching inn.

Owners Rachel and Alex took over here in 2005 and have established a glowing reputation for top quality food, well-kept ales and warm hospitality. Rachel does all the cooking, creating mouth-watering dishes in portions so generous they have to be seen to be believed. Dishes change with the seasons but are served at lunch (12-2.30) and dinner (5-9); pensioners' specials are available Tuesday to Friday lunchtime. All produce is locally sourced; specials include the fresh fish every Friday, bought that morning at the fish market. On

Sunday there are no fewer than 12 main courses to choose from. There are always at least three real ales (Black Sheep, Timothy Taylor Golden Best and Timothy Taylor Best are the regulars here) as well as a good choice of lagers, cider, stout, wines, spirits and soft drinks.

If you're thinking of stopping in this beautiful part of the world, it's worth asking about the campsite available locally - please ring for details.

Looking for:
- *Places to Visit?*
- *Places to Stay?*
- *Places to Eat & Drink?*
- *Places to Shop?*

COUNTRY LIVING RURAL GUIDES
HIDDEN INNS
HIDDEN PLACES
COUNTRY Pubs & Inns
off the motorway 3rd edition

www.travelpublishing.co.uk

183 COLNE VALLEY MUSEUM

Cliffe Ash, Golcar,
Huddersfield, HD7 4PY
Tel: 01484 659762

Three nineteenth-century weavers' cottages near Golcar Parish Church are the home of the museum. See the life and work of the 19th century in restored period rooms – the loom chamber with working hand looms and a Spinning Jenny, the weaver's living room of 1850 and a gas-lit clogger's shop of 1910. The museum is run entirely by its members. On two weekends a year a craft and working weekend is held when there are many different crafts being demonstrated. The museum has featured on TV and is recommended by the Good Museum Guide. Open: Sat, Sun and Bank holidays 2pm-5pm except Christmas and New Year. Facilities for schools. Shop and light refreshments. Admission Charge.

323

Oldham Road, Rishworth, Halifax,
West Yorkshire HX6 4RH
Tel: 01422 822789
e-mail: turnpike-inn@btconnect.com

Conveniently located just a few minutes drive from junction 22 of the M62, **The Turnpike Inn** is an outstanding village hostelry with a wide range of amenities. It has a view of the Rishworth Dam and also of the famous farmhouse that stands in proud isolation between the two carriageways of the M62, the result of the owner refusing to sell the farm when the motorway was being constructed.

When business partners Stuart Porter and John Coulter took over the inn in the spring of 2008 it was in sore need of some tender loving care. They have carried out a complete refurbishment and the Turnpike is once again a popular and lively venue.

A major attraction here is the quality food on offer every day and throughout the day. It starts at 7am with breakfast which is served until midday, then the lunch menu is available until 6pm when the dinner menu is on offer until 9pm. The menu offers main courses such as steaks, liver & onions, a home-made Pie of the Day and a meaty lasagne. Vegetarian options include a Three Cheese & Red Onion Pie and a vegetable lasagne. For lighter appetites, the choice includes hot and cold sandwiches, salads and jacket potatoes. Children have their own menu. Such is the popularity of the food, booking is strongly advisable at weekends.

To accompany your meal, the bar stocks a comprehensive range of beverages, amongst them 4 real ales - 2 Moorhouses brews and 2 rotating guest ales. In good weather, customers can enjoy their refreshments in the spacious beer garden.

On Saturday evenings, The Turnpike hosts live music sessions with a variety of bands in performance. The inn also has a pool table and a well-equipped function room which can accommodate up to 80 guests. The facilities include full screen, DVD and an excellent audio system.

The quality accommodation here comprises 6 attractively furnished and decorated guest bedrooms, all of them with en suite facilities. There are 4 double rooms, a family room and a bridal suite.

The Turnpike accepts all major credit cards; there's good disabled access throughout the eating areas; and the inn has ample space for parking.

185 THE STAR INN

Batley Road, Kirkhamgate, Wakefield,
West Yorkshire WF2 0RZ
Tel: 01924 374431

Dating back to the mid-1800s, **The Star Inn** is indeed a star amongst pubs. Known locally as 'Top of Wooders', the inn has a real charm, its interior full of character with gleaming brass and copper ornaments wherever your eye wanders. The Star is a magnet for lovers of good food and ale. Mine hosts, Andrew and Tracie, took over here in early 2008 and are only the fourth licensees to run the pub in the last 80 years. They both have extensive experience in the hospitality business. Andrew, who is a professional chef and a classically trained pastry chef, has spent an impressive 30 years providing his customers with a wide range of wholesome and appetising food made using fresh local produce wherever possible.

At The Star, amongst the starters on offer are a large Yorkshire Pudding served with onion gravy, creamy garlic mushrooms or Mexican Nachos. As a main course, the choice includes a home-made Pie of the Day, home-made lasagne, a roast of the day, traditional favourites such as gammon and eggs or deep fried haddock, as well as a selection of chicken dishes such as Chicken Szechuan and Chicken Jamaican Jerk. Alternatively there are pasta dishes, fresh salads and vegetarian options. For dessert, the choice ranges from a traditional steamed jam roly poly or treacle tart to Janine's Date Sticky Toffee Pudding. At lunchtimes, in addition to the regular menu, large Yorkshire puddings with various fillings, jacket potatoes and open and closed sandwiches are also available. Food is served from noon until 2pm, Monday to Saturday; from 5.30pm to 8.30pm, Monday to Friday; from 5pm to 9pm on Saturday; and on Sundays from noon until 3pm and from 5pm to 8.30pm. For the 3-course Sunday lunch booking is strongly advised. An Early Bird menu offering 2 courses at a special price is available from 5.30pm to 7pm during the week; from 5pm to 6.30pm at weekends.

The Star's well-stocked bar offers a comprehensive choice of beverages, including a rotating guest real ale. In good weather, customers can enjoy their refreshments in the huge beer garden where there's also a children's play area.

Children are welcome at The Star but must be over 12 to dine in the restaurant; all major credit cards apart from American Express and Diners are accepted; and there's good disabled access throughout.

186 THE BOAT PUB & RESTAURANT

Main Street, Allerton Bywater,
Castleford, West Yorkshire WF10 2BX
Tel: 01977 552646 e-mail:
richardjuliefreddie@btinternet.com

The Boat Pub & Restaurant enjoys a superb setting right beside the River Aire with picnic tables placed overlooking the water. Mine hosts at this fine old traditional

inn are Richard and Julie Wilson who took over here in early 2007 and have made the pub a place that's well worth seeking out - and not just for the lovely location.

Good food is a priority here and the menu offers an appetising choice of dishes. Starters range from a traditional Prawn Cocktail to Goats Cheese Bruschetta, Brie Wedges and a King Scallop Kebab. Main courses include perennial favourites such as Steak & Ale Pie or Fish & Chips as well as a good choice of steaks and poultry, pasta and vegetarian

dishes. For dessert, how about a good old fashioned Jam Roly Poly or Treacle Sponge? Food is served from 12 noon until 9pm, Tuesday to Saturday; from 12 noon until 4pm and from 5pm to 8.30pm on Sunday. At Sunday lunchtime, a choice of roasts replaces the regular menu.

Real ale devotees will be happy here - there are 4 authentic brews on offer, including Tetleys and Midnight Bell from the Leeds Brewery.

188 THE FEATHERSTONE HOTEL

Station Lane, Featherstone,
West Yorkshire WF7 6EW
Tel: 01977 791851

Peter and Sue Green have been the welcoming hosts at **The Featherstone Hotel** for more than 20 years and have established a glowing reputation for quality food, a good choice of well-kept ales and warm hospitality. Food is served every lunchtime and evening and the regular menu is supplemented by daily specials and light bites. On Tuesdays and Thursdays, kids eat free from 5.30pm to 8pm. The hotel also has 9 attractively furnished and decorated guest rooms, all with en suite facilities.

187 THE NEW QUEEN

Lower Mickletown, Methley,
West Yorkshire LS26 9AN
Tel: 01977 515382

Located in the picturesque village of Lower Mickletown, **The New Queen** is a welcoming country hostelry with a glowing reputation for the excellence of the food on offer. Built in the early 1900s, the inn has a stylish conservatory to one side and a pleasant beer garden to the rear.

Mine hosts, Richard Revell and Robert Brennan, took over here in the spring of 2008 and have made the New Queen a place to seek out. Robert is the chef and his appetising menu offers a wide choice of dishes based on locally sourced ingredients wherever possible. Amongst the starters you'll find a freshly made soup of the day and the chef's own home-made pâté. For the main course, the options range from steaks to seafood dishes, from chicken choices - Sweet Thai Chilli Chicken,

perhaps - to Stroganoff variations. Also on offer is a selection of curry dishes and an assortment of vegetarian dishes such as a Spinach and Ricotta Cheese Cannelloni. In addition to the regular menu, daily specials are listed on the blackboard. Children have their own menu with a choice that includes Sausage & Mash and a Mini Cajun Chicken. Food is served from 12 noon until 9pm, Monday to Saturday; and from 12 noon until 6pm on Sundays when a Carvery with a choice of meats replaces the regular menu. Booking is strongly recommended for the Carvery. Diners can enjoy their meals either in the elegant conservatory or throughout the inn.

To accompany your meal, the well-stocked bar offers a comprehensive range of beverages including 2 real ales - Greene King IPA and a rotating guest ale.

Throughout the week The New Queen hosts a variety of events. On Monday evening there's a Pub Quiz starting at 9pm - all are welcome. Tuesday is Free Pool Night and on Wednesday there's a Happy Hour from 9pm to 10pm with special prices for various drinks. Thursday is a food themed evening with a special Carvery and on Friday evening there are special food offers from 7pm to 9pm. The week is rounded off with Saturday's disco and karaoke.

Children are welcome at The New Queen; all major credit cards apart from American Express and Diners are accepted; there's good disabled access throughout and ample off road parking.

Market Place, Pontefract,
West Yorkshire WF8 1AX
Tel: 01977 600863 Fax: 01977 780071
e-mail: theliquoricebush@hotmail.co.uk
website: www.theliquoricebush.co.uk

Located in the heart of Pontefract, in the Market Square, **The Liquorice Bush** takes its charming name from the popular annual Liquorice Fair held in the town every July, and from the long association the town has with liquorice, being a centre for production for hundreds of years. The

inn featured recently on BBC-1's *The One Show* when the programme highlighted liquorice, Pontefract and The Liquorice Bush.

Dating back many hundreds of years itself, the inn has always maintained a strong reputation for hospitality. The décor and furnishings are very attractive and comfortable, enhancing the pub's welcoming ambience. Warm woods, exposed beams - the best of traditional and modern comforts meet here in this truly excellent pub. Three real ales are on tap - Timothy Taylor Landlord, Black Sheep and a rotating guest ale - together with a choice of lagers, ciders, stouts, wines, spirits and soft drinks.

Experienced licensees Shaun and Gill White took over at this fine inn in February 2003. They bring a wealth of experience in the hospitality business and a high standard of service and quality to all their guests.

The inn offers an extensive choice of good, wholesome food at remarkably reasonable prices. The choices range from steaks to giant filled Yorkshire puddings, from salads to scampi & chips, from Steak & Ale Pie to a vegetarian Cauliflower Cheese. For lighter appetites, the selection includes sandwiches and jacket potatoes. Special deals include two main courses at a discount price and there are various drink promotions. Food is available at lunchtime (11am to 2.30/3pm), Monday to Saturday, and also on select Sundays such as race days or during the famous Liquorice Festival.

The inn welcomes children when dining; payment is by cash only, and there is good disabled access throughout.

190 THE BLUEBELL INN

Great North Road, Wentbridge, Pontefract,
West Yorkshire WF8 3JP
Tel: 01977 620697

Located in the picturesque village of Wentbridge, **The Bluebell Inn** is a fine old traditional inn with a rich interior décor. The inn is run by the father and son

team, of Sean and Jamie Merrill who took over here in the summer of 2008.

A major attraction here is the quality of the food on offer. Starters range from a traditional Yorkshire pudding served with onion gravy to a 'Bluebell Sunrise' - strips of deep-fried chicken sprinkled with fried garlic, black pepper and sesame seeds. The extensive choice of main courses includes the Chef's special Bluebell Sizzlers and his home-made Pie of the Day; grills, fish, meat and poultry dishes along with

vegetarian options. At lunchtimes, Monday to Saturday, sandwiches, soup and jacket potatoes are also available. And on Tuesday and Thursday evenings a selection of authentic Thai specialities are also on offer. To complement your food, there's an excellent wine list with wines available by the glass or bottle, and a choice of real ales.

The Bluebell also offers comfortable accommodation in 4 upstairs double rooms, all with en suite facilities.

191 THE CATCHPENNY

Lane Ends, Fitzwilliam, Pontefract,
West Yorkshire WF9 5NJ
Tel: 01977 611984

A charming pub dating back to the early 1800s, **The Catchpenny** occupies a handsome four-square building standing in its own grounds with tables outside on the patio overlooking the garden. Mine hosts, Gary and Melissa, are both from the village and they have made this a popular venue for both locals and visitors.

They offer a good selection of home-made fare based on fresh local produce wherever possible with the regular menu supplemented by daily specials. Food is served from noon until 2.30pm, and from 5pm to 8pm, Monday to Friday. There's no food on Saturdays as the inn is a fashionable location for wedding receptions because of its setting and the good food. On Sundays a Carvery is served from noon until 3pm. The

Catchpenny is also popular with lovers of real ale as it offers a choice of three different

brews - Black Sheep, Theakston's Olde Peculier and a guest ale.

And quiz fans should make a date at the Catchpenny for Wednesday and Sunday evenings when the inn hosts a quiz followed by a buffet. Children are welcome here up until 9pm; all major credit cards are accepted apart from American Express and Diner's; and the inn has good disabled access throughout.

329

70 Quarry Hill, Horbury, Wakefield,
West Yorkshire WF4 5NF
Tel: 01924 272523 Fax: 01924 272173
e-mail: quarry256@hotmail.co.uk

Dating back to 1861, the **Quarry Inn** takes its name from a quarry that once existed nearby. The fine old stone building was originally an alehouse with attached

cottages, all of which are now part of the inn. This is a very popular hostelry with both locals and visitors, due no doubt to the friendly and welcoming hosts, Audrey and Joe. Audrey has been in the hospitality business for some 30 years, Joe for 12 and they have been together here since 2003. The inn is open every lunchtime and evening, and all day on Friday, Saturday and Sunday.

A blackboard displays the choice of wholesome home-made food available with the tasty pies enjoying

great popularity. Food is served every session apart from Sunday evening and all day on Mondays. To accompany your meal, the bar stocks a comprehensive range of beverages, including 2 real ales - Cumberland Ale and a rotating guest ale.

The Quarry Inn also offers quality accommodation in 4 attractively furnished and decorated en suite rooms, 2 of which are downstairs. Other amenities at the inn include a covered patio area; karaoke on Thursday nights and live entertainment once a month.

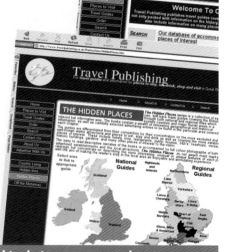

193 THE BREWERS PRIDE

Low Mill Road, Healey Road, Ossett,
West Yorkshire WF5 8ND
Tel: 01924 273865
e-mail: sally@brewers-pride.co.uk
website: www.brewers-pride.co.uk

"Proud to be Independent" says the sign outside **The Brewers Pride** in Ossett. This is indeed a truly independent free house with "real ales, real fires and real food". Mine hosts, Sally and Jon, arrived here in 1998 and have established a glowing reputation for the quality food, well-kept ales and professional entertainment they provide.

First, the food. As a starter, how about Portabella Mushroom flavoured with garlic oil and topped with a brunoise of vegetables and spinach coated with a cream sauce? Or Seafood Roulade, Pork and Sage Terrine or a traditional Prawn Cocktail. For the main course, there's a choice of half a dozen different roasts, as well as fish dishes and a vegetarian Roasted Red & Green Peppers. Daily specials are also available. And you won't want to pass on the delicious desserts - Fresh Fruit Crumble, perhaps, a selection of sliced fruits glazed with a white wine and egg yolk sauce. At lunchtime, from noon until 3pm, Monday to Saturday, a choice of light snacks is also available which includes home-made soup, Cumberland Sausage, beef burger and jacket potato. In addition to the lunchtime session, food is also served from 7pm to 9pm, Tuesday to Thursday. On Wednesday evenings, there's an alternating themed menu - Fish Night, Pie Night and Curry Night.

Lovers of real ales will be very happy here since the bar stocks no fewer than 9 authentic brews. Red Lion Ales are brewed locally (as there is also an Ossett Brewery!) and are supplemented by an ever-changing choice of guest ales. In good weather, you can enjoy your refreshments in the pleasant beer garden which also has a smoking area.

Monday evening at the Brewers Pride is Quiz Night, to get the old grey cells going, with a free supper as reward. Regular live music sessions take place on the 1st and 3rd Sunday of the month, together with Bluegrass evenings on the 2nd and last Tuesday of the month, to which all guest pickers are welcome. The summer months see a programme of live entertainment from local bands, culminating with the inn's Annual Beer Festival over the August Bank Holiday.

Children are welcome at the Brewers Pride up until 7pm; all major credit cards are accepted; and there's good disabled access throughout.

29 Wakefield Road,
Grange Moor, West Yorkshire WF4 4BG
Tel: 01924 848385
website: www.thekayearms.com

Located in the heart of the Yorkshire countryside, **The Kaye Arms** is a former coaching inn with a wealth of charm and character. Owners Paul and Helen Andrews-Garth arrived here early in 2008, bringing with them some 20 years experience of the hospitality trade. Good food is a top priority with them - excellent quality food is professionally served in a welcoming and homely atmosphere, They pride themselves on their traditional fresh seasonal menus and extensive wine lists. Dishes are based on fresh locally sourced ingredients with 90% of the produce used coming from within the county.

Some typical dishes include home-made Bressolla served with poached pears, rocket and parmesan; Wild Mushroom and Truffle Oil Risotto, and French Onion Soup with gruyere croutons amongst the starters. As a main course, how about Confit of Duck with French style peas and dauphinoise potatoes; Grilled Fillet of Seabass with roasted Provençal vegetables, pesto and tapenade, or Fillet Steak served with fondant potato, celeriac purée, baby carrots and a red wine jus. In addition to the regular menu, daily specials are listed on the blackboard. Food is served every lunchtime and evening with last orders around 9.30pm. On Sunday lunchtimes, a choice of roasts replaces the regular menu. To accompany your meal, there's an excellent selection of wines from around the world and the Andrews-Garth are currently preparing to introduce real ales. Such is the popularity of the restaurant, it is strongly recommended that you book

ahead at all times. Service at the Kaye Arms is exemplary with you the customer wanting for nothing during your time there.

Children are welcome here; all major credit cards are accepted apart from American Express and Diners; there's good disabled access and a disabled toilet will be available from August 2008. There's also a large car park.

The Kaye Arms is situated between Huddersfield and Wakefield on the A642, about half a mile from the junction with the A637 going towards Wakefield.

195 BISHOPS' HOUSE

Norton Lees Lane, Sheffield,
South Yorkshire S8 9BE
Tel: 0114 278 2600
website: www.sheffieldgalleries.org.uk

Bishops' House is the best preserved timber-framed house in Sheffield. It was built around 1500 and is tucked away at the top of Meersbrook Park. Bishops' House typifies the development of the smaller English domestic house in the 16th and 17th centuries. Inside, the house retains many of its original features and looks just as it would have done in the 17th century, giving a tantalising flavour of Stuart England.

Many different families have lived in the house over the years, but the first owners remain a mystery. There is a story that the house was built for two brothers, John and Geoffrey Blythe who went on to become Bishops, but there is no evidence that Bishops' House was their home. The first known resident of Bishops' House was William Blythe, a Yeoman farmer and scythe manufacturer whose initials, and the date 1627, are carved in the oak panelling in the Hall. He made a number of improvements to the house before the outbreak of Civil War in 1642. These included inserting a floor above the hall, installing fireplaces in the parlour and chamber above and adding new windows. Later the building was extended with two more rooms, a cellar and an improved staircase.

The last Blythe to live in Bishops' House was Samuel. After he died in 1753 his son sold the house to William Shore. The house was then let to a tenant farmer and his labourer and the building was divided into two self-contained dwellings. In 1886 the property passed to the Corporation (now Sheffield City Council) and until 1974 Recreation Department employees lived in the house. In 1976 Bishops' House was restored and opened as a museum.

197 THE PHEASANT

Station Lane, Oughtibridge,
Sheffield, South Yorkshire S35 0HS
Tel: 01142 862483

This countryside pub, **The Pheasant,** stands close to the centre of Oughtibridge on Station Lane (the back road to Grenoside). Dating back to the late 19th century, the inn was once called the 'Station Hotel'. It is a good looking building both inside and out, and is open Mon-Thurs from 4pm-close, Fri-Sat 12pm-1am and Sundays 12pm - midnight.

There is one rotating real ale to enjoy, and Sunday lunch is a speciality, well known far and wide. Available between 12.30pm – 2.30pm, it is an advantage to book. Entertainment includes Kareoke on Fridays (from 8.30pm), and a Quiz on Saturdays (from 9.30pm).

196 THE DUKE OF LEEDS

Church Street, Wales,
South Yorkshire S26 5LQ
Tel: 01909 770301
Mobile: 07977 484069

A distinguished and comfortable inn offering great food, drink and hospitality, **The Duke on Leeds** dates back to 1730 and began life under the name of The Cockerel. Much mystery surrounds the reason for its change of name but records show that it was trading under its present designation by the end of the 1700s.

This handsome stone-built hostelry has a very traditional atmosphere with a cosy air although it is in fact very spacious. Mine hosts, Andy and Jill, took over here in the summer of 2008 and, despite it being their first venture into the hospitality business, their enthusiasm and friendliness quickly established the inn as a popular venue. It's open every lunchtime and evening, and all day on Sunday. Devotees of real ales will be pleased to find a choice of 4 or 5 brews with Abbot Ale and Wadsworth 6X as the regulars plus 2 or 3 rotating guest ales. Enjoy your drinks in the well-stocked bar with its horse-racing theme.

Andy is an accomplished chef and his menu is based on fresh, locally produced ingredients as far as possible. There's a good choice of dishes with something for everyone with char-grilled dishes as a speciality of the house. On Sundays, the regular menu is replaced by a choice of roasts and a few options. Food is served from 12 noon until 2pm, and from 5pm to 9pm, Monday to Saturday; and from 12 noon until 6pm on Sunday. The dining area seats up to 40 but to avoid disappointment, it is wise to book ahead at all times. From time to time, Andy arranges themed evenings and there are also plans for regular live entertainment. Every Sunday evening the inn hosts a Pub Quiz starting at 9.15pm - all are welcome.

The Duke of Leeds accepts all major credit cards apart from American Express and Diners; there's good disabled access throughout, and ample off road parking.

198 THE STRINES INN

Bradfield Dale, Sheffield,
South Yorkshire S6 6JE
Tel/Fax: 0114 285 1247

Heading northwest out of Sheffield towards the Peak District, you will come across the superb **Strines Inn,** a hidden gem to be found a couple of miles off the A57 just within the Peak National Park. The inn enjoys stunning views and families will be pleased to find an enclosed play area outside where there is also an area for peacocks, geese and chickens. None of the inn's charms is lost during the winter months, as its three open fires create a warm and comfortable atmosphere to help forget about the dreary weather.

The inn is renowned for its good quality traditional English home-made food. The pies are particularly popular and visitors never fail to be impressed as to how 'giant' the 'Giant Yorkshire Puddings' actually are. There's a generous choice of

vegetarian dishes and a special menu for children.

If you are planning to stay in this idyllic spot, the inn has 3 delightful guest bedrooms, each with a 4-poster bed, en suite facilities, colour TV and hospitality tray. Each bedroom has a dining table for two as breakfast is served in your room. All in all, a quite outstanding place.

199 BARNFIELD HOUSE

Loxley Road, Loxley, Sheffield,
South Yorkshire S6 6RW
Tel: 0114 233 6365
e-mail: enquiries@barnfieldhouse.com
website: www.barnfieldhouse.com

Located in the beautiful surroundings of Loxley Valley on the edge of the Peak National Park, **Barnfield House** is an outstanding owner-run guest house with a 4-star Silver Award from the ETB. The house stands in approximately one acre of lovely well-tended grounds and enjoys panoramic views of Loxley Valley, Dam Flask, Strines Moor and the surrounding farmland.

Local history claims that Loxley Valley was where Robin of Loxley, or robin Hood, was born and spent his early years. So owners Helen and Michael Rogers have named their 6 luxurious bedrooms after characters from Robin's band of merry men - and woman, of course, so one room is named after Maid Marian and contains a 4-poster bed. Robin, Friar Tuck and 'Little'

John's rooms are superior double rooms, suitable for

family occupation, while Will Scarlett and Alan-a-Dale's room are doubles. All the rooms are equipped with TV/DVD, alarm clock radio, hairdryer, iron and ironing board, and hospitality tray. A towelling robe and slippers are also supplied.

In the morning, breakfast is based on fresh local produce and the choices include a Full Yorkshire repast with lots of other options.

200 THE ROYAL HOTEL

Main Road, Dungworth, Sheffield,
South Yorkshire S6 6HF
Tel: 0114 285 1213
e-mail: joanne@royal hotel-dungworth.co.uk
website: www.royalhotel-dungworth.co.uk

Set on the edge of the Peak District, high on the moors northwest of Sheffield but only a 20-minute drive from the centre of the city and Meadow Hall shopping centre, the **Royal Hotel** is a welcoming family-run public house with owners David and Linda Lambert and Dave and Joanne Jubb all involved in the enterprise. The hotel was built around 1813 and retains much of its original character. It is divided into 3 areas, all with open fires. There is the snug which overlooks the beautiful countryside; a spacious lounge at the front of the pub; and the 'Dungeon', also at the front of the pub, which is a separate room, ideal for families.

A major attraction at the Royal is Dave and Joanne's quality home-made food - just try one of Dave's Royal

pies, known the world over! Fish, vegetarian and children's meals are also available, along with freshly prepared sandwiches. The Royal also offers comfortable en suite accommodation in 3 centrally heated and double glazed rooms, all equipped with remote control television, hairdryer and hospitality tray.

201 IZABELLA'S COFFEE SHOP & BISTRO

131 Bawtry Road, Wickersley,
South Yorkshire S66 2BW
Tel: 01709 544687

Conveniently located on the A631, **Izabella's Coffee Shop & Bistro** is a popular eating place serving an excellent choice of hot and cold home-made dishes. Owners Barbara and Peter McAndrew took over here in the spring of 2008, although Barbara had been working at the coffee shop for two years before that.

Their menu offers wholesome fare that ranges from a variety of breakfasts (served until 11.30am), through jacket potatoes to ciabattas, paninis and sandwiches. A home-made soup is also available. Tea-time treats include

some wonderful home-made cakes, Danish pastries, fruit scones, and toasted tea cake or muffin. The wide choice of beverages includes wine by the glass or bottle, bottled beers and liqueur coffee. Izabella's is open from 8.30am to 4pm, Monday to Wednesday; 8.30am to 5pm Thursday and Friday; from 9am to 4.30pm on Saturday, and from 9.30am to 1.30pm on Sunday. During the winter months, the café is closed on Sundays and closes at 4pm on Saturday.

Wickersley village is situated 3 miles from Rotherham; access to motorway travel is excellent with junctions for the M1, M18 and A1(M) all close by.

202 CANNON HALL MUSEUM

Cawthorne, Barnsley,
South Yorkshire S75 4AT
Tel: 01226 790270
e-mail: cannonhall@barnsley.gov.uk

Set in 70 acres of historic parkland and gardens, **Cannon Hall Museum** provides an idyllic and tranquil setting for a day out. For two hundred years Cannon Hall was home to the Spencer-Stanhope family. From the 1760s the architect John Carr of York was commissioned to extend and alter the house while the designer Richard Woods was hired to landscape the park and gardens. Over forty varieties of pear trees still grow in the historic walled garden, as well as peaches and nectarines. The famed Cannon Hall vine grows in one of the greenhouses. The park provides an ideal setting for a picnic, outdoor activities and games. Cannon Hall was sold by the family in the early 1950s to Barnsley Council and was first opened as a museum in 1957. The Hall now contains collections of furniture, paintings, glassware and pottery, much of which is displayed in period settings. It also houses 'Charge', the Regimental Museum of the 13th/18th Hussars (QMO).

The Victorian Kitchen Café near the gardens is open each weekend and during the school holidays for home-made light refreshments in the traditional setting of the original kitchens and Servant's Hall. The Museum also has a shop stocking a range of greetings cards, local history books, confectionery and giftware. Off the A635 Barnsley to Huddersfield Road. Easy access from junctions 37 or 38 of the M1.

203 ELSECAR HERITAGE CENTRE

Wath Road, Elsecar, Barnsley,
South Yorkshire S74 8HJ
Tel: 01226 740203
e-mail: elsecarheritagecentre@Barnsley.gov.uk
website: www.Barnsley.gov.uk/leisure

The Elsecar Heritage Centre nestles within the beautiful South Yorkshire countryside and dates from the early 1800's when it was originally owned by the local Earls Fitzwilliam as their main industrial workshops, producing everything needed for their industrial empire. Many of the buildings and facilities have been restored and preserved, with many being used again as workshops for local crafts people, from traditional printers, woodwork shop, to more delicate crafts such as jewellery making and flower arranging.

As well as a large selection of Craft Workshops, the Centre also has an Antiques Centre, a Bottle Museum,

'Playmania' children's activity centre, the Elsecar Preservation Group Steam Railway Line and the world famous Newcomen Beam Engine, the only remaining Beam Engine in its original location. Our on-site 'Brambles Tea-rooms' can provide light refreshments to a full and varied menu of main meals throughout the day.

The Heritage Centre also holds regular special events within its multi-purpose exhibition hall all year round, from concerts, antique fairs, championship dog shows, and natural health festivals to even Japanese Koi Fish shows.

204 ELSECAR PARK CAFÉ

**Armroyd Lane, Elsecar, Barnsley,
South Yorkshire S74 8EY
Tel: 01226 743222
e-mail: alisonbaxter83@yahoo.co.uk**

As the name indicates, the **Elsecar Park Café** is located within Elsecar Park with its many attractions and activities. Alison and Fran (a man) took over here in the autumn of 2007 and because of their hard work and enthusiasm they have made this a very popular establishment.

Their menu is chalked up on the blackboard and includes an all day breakfast that comes in small, large and Xtra large varieties. These are all very popular as are the tasty home-made chips. Also available is a wide choice of hot sarnies, dishes such as chili con carne, soup and a variety of snacks such as sausage rolls. Payment is by cash only.

The café is open from 9am to 7.30pm every day except Wednesday. There's seating for 16 inside, a further 30 at the picnic tables outside, or you can just settle down with your picnic in the park. The many amenities here include pitch and putt and crazy golf, or you can just enjoy the gardens and the surroundings of Elsecar Reservoir.

205 CUSWORTH HALL TEA ROOM

**Cusworth Lane, Cusworth, Doncaster,
South Yorkshire DN5 7TU
Tel: 01302 390959**

Located in the delightful grounds of Cusworth Hall, the **Cusworth Hall Tea Room** occupies the former stables and is replete with old world charm and character. As you enter the tea room with its cobbled floor the ravishing aroma of home baking heralds the treats ahead.

The menu offers customers an extensive choice of delicious home-made hot and cold meals, wonderful cakes and pastries, jacket potatoes, sandwiches, and more, all made with the best of fresh local produce. The regular menu is supplemented by a daily home-made soup, two special main courses and a home-made pudding. The tea room can seat up to 34 people inside, with space for another 32 on the terrace. Opening hours are from 10am to 4pm, every day, but with extended hours during the school summer holidays. Payment is by cash or cheque only; there is good disabled access throughout and a disabled toilet.

Cusworth Hall itself is a magnificent 18th century mansion which has recently re-opened to the public after several years of extensive restoration work. Stunning ceiling paintings in the Italianate Chapel have been revealed and restored, after being hidden under layers of paint for 50 years.

206 THE SCHOOL BOY

High Street, Norton, Doncaster,
South Yorkshire DN6 9EL
Tel: 01302 700264
e-mail: tricia-turner@hotmail.com
website: www.the schoolboy.co.uk

Believed to be the only pub in the country with this name, **The School Boy** pub in the pleasant village of Norton is also rather special in other ways.

Landlady Tricia Turner took over here in the autumn of 2007 and speedily established a reputation for serving good food and well-kept ales. Her menu lists an enticing range of appetising dishes which are supplemented by daily specials. The beautifully furnished and decorated restaurant is separate at the rear of the inn. Food is served from noon until 2pm, and

from 5pm to 8.30pm, Monday to Saturday, and from noon until 3pm on Sundays. A Carvery is also available at lunchtimes from Tuesday to Friday, and at Sunday lunchtime. Tricia also lays on regular food-themed evenings. Thursday is curry night with 4 or 5 choices at special prices; Friday is steak night. And on Wednesday evenings there's a Quiz at which all are welcome.

The inn accepts all major credit cards apart from American Express and Diners; there's good disabled access throughout; and plenty of off road parking.

207 THE OLD GEORGE

Broad Lane, Sykehouse,
South Yorkshire DN14 9AU
Tel: 01405 785635

Tucked away in a small village to the northeast of Doncaster, **The Old George** truly is a hidden gem. Despite its size, Sykehouse claims to be the longest village in England and also boasts this excellent old hostelry which dates back in parts to the mid-1700s. It has a long, low frontage that looks very inviting but step around to the back and you'll find within the 4½-acre site a paradise for children. There's a superb play area and even a swimming pool. It stands at the edge of a spacious patio where parents can keep an eye on their offspring while enjoying their own refreshments.

Inside, there's a pool table for the grown-ups. Owners Paul and Sandra Nelson arrived here in early 2007 and have made the Old George a "destination inn" for lovers of good food, real ales and genuine hospitality. Professional chefs using only the best fresh

local produce create enticing, well-presented dishes, all cooked to order. Food is served from noon until 2pm, and from 5pm to 9pm, Monday to Saturday; and from noon until 6pm on Sundays when a Carvery is laid on. Such is the popularity of the cuisine, it is wise to book ahead at weekends. To accompany your meal, the bar offers a comprehensive range of beverages, including 3 real ales - Tetleys and two rotating guest ales.

The Old George hosts occasional live entertainment; there's good disabled access throughout, and ample parking.

Doncaster Road, Hatfield, Doncaster,
South Yorkshire DN7 6AD
Tel: 01302 840508
e-mail: thehatfieldchace@yahoo.co.uk

Set well back from the A18, close to the M18/M180 interchange, The **Hatfield Chace** is a spacious traditional inn with a well-earned reputation for serving good food. Mine hosts, Claire and Will, are a vivacious couple who took over here in the spring of 2007. They are ably assisted by bar manager, Rick, and his brother Nick who is the Head Chef.

The spacious interior offers something for everyone. The lounge bar provides an excellent drinking and dining area, while the sports bar, decorated with a sporty theme, offers Sky TV, pool and other games. Then there's the large family area where kids can amuse themselves with the range of play apparatus provided. This is very much a family-friendly pub. Claire and Will even open up at 9am on Wednesdays and Fridays so that families with small children can enjoy the play equipment. Beverages and light snacks such as tea-cakes are available.

Diners at the Chace are presented with an extensive choice of dishes, all based on locally sourced ingredients wherever possible. Amongst the starters you'll find dishes such as Creamy Garlic Mushrooms and Thai Beef Salad, while for main courses the choice ranges from an extremely popular Steak & Guinness Pie, through the Landlord's Mixed Grill - "not for the faint-hearted!" warns the menu, to perennial favourites such as steaks, curries and beer-battered cod. Vegetarian options include a tasty Mushroom Carbonara and a Broccoli Cheese Bake. In addition to the regular menu, there's a choice of daily specials listed on the blackboard. For lighter appetites,

there's a good selection of freshly made sandwiches, burgers and freshly oven-baked jacket potatoes. Food is served from noon until 9pm, Monday to Saturday, and from noon until 7pm on Sunday. On Sundays between noon and 4pm, a traditional roast is served with a choice of 3 different joints. To avoid disappointment, booking ahead is recommended at weekends.

To accompany your meal, the well-stocked bar offers a wide range of beverages, including one real ale which changes regularly. The Chace accepts all major credit cards, there's good disabled access throughout; and ample off road parking.

Looking for:

- *Places to Visit?*
- *Places to Stay?*
- *Places to Eat & Drink?*
- *Places to Shop?*

COUNTRY LIVING RURAL GUIDES

HIDDEN INNS

HIDDEN PLACES

COUNTRY Pubs & Inns

off the motorway 3rd edition

www.travelpublishing.co.uk

209 CASTLEGATES COFFEE SHOP & BISTRO

16a Castlegate, Tickhill, Doncaster,
South Yorkshire DN11 9QU
Tel: 01302 751725
website: www.castlegatescoffeeshop.co.uk

Castlegates Coffee Shop & Bistro occupies a traditional stone Yorkshire cottage but with a stylish modern décor inside. The extensive menu offers a good choice of wholesome and appetising food that includes all day breakfasts, ciabattas, sandwiches, toasted sandwiches, paninis, jacket potatoes and salads. In addition to the regular menu there are daily home-made specials, including a home-made soup.

Owners Thomas and Lindsay are also happy to cater for pre-booked private parties of up to 24 people. Castlegates is closed on Sundays; payment is by cash or cheque only.

210 THE BEVERLEY INN AND HOTEL

115-117 Thorne Road, Edenthorpe,
Doncaster, South Yorkshire DN3 2JE
Tel: 01302 882724
e-mail: beverleyinn@hotmail.co.uk
website: www.beverleyinnandhotel.co.uk

The picture perfect front of **The Beverley Inn and Hotel** isn't the only reason it's so appealing. A friendly welcoming abode- a place to rest your head, eat a hearty meal, and quaff fine ales. Situated within the village of Edenthorpe, and found on A18, or off A630, north east of Dancaster.

There's an extensive choice of homemade dishes, all complemented by fresh vegetables. Choose from the 'Pub Tapas' section (starters and light snacks such as Overstuffed Potato Skins, Tikka Sticks, and Smoked Salmon Roulade), Slow Roasting Oven section (including lamb and ribs), The 'Pie Shop', From the Grill, and 'Lady Wellfed's Favourites!' (including BBQ Chicken, Battered Haddock and Thai Green Curry). There's also a variety of dishes on the Specials Board.

Food is served Mon-Thurs 12-2.30pm and 5-8.30pm and Fri/Sat 12-2.30pm and 5-9pm. The popular Sunday Carvery is served 12-3pm.

A range of quality wines and champagnes are also on offer. Three real ales available, with John Smiths cask the regular, plus two rotating guest ales. Good amount of entertainment- Saturday night from 9.30pm they have a singer, and Monday night is the Quiz from 9.30pm, everyone is welcome.

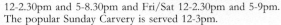

The superb accommodation is available all year round, 14 en-suite rooms all located upstairs and the tariff includes breakfast. Children are welcome.

Thorne Road, Sandtoft,
North Lincolnshire, DN8 5SZ
Tel: 01724 710774

Superb, outstanding, excellent – just a few words used to describe **The Reindeer**, an inn with classy décor, extensive menus, and great atmosphere. Hidden away in the hamlet of Sandtoft, just a stone's throw from the Yorkshire boarder and found off the A18, A614, or A161.

After a complete refurbishment the premises opened again in July '08, making the inn even more welcoming than before. The restaurant is now very classy, and murals around the walls illustrate the locations history. Quality décor and furnishings throughout capture a lovely ambiance. The locals are coming back in their droves and already can't get

enough of the place! The Reindeer has three different menus; A La Carte on Fri/Saturday evenings in their stylish restaurant, Sunday lunch menu, and a bar menu- all of which have some exquisite dishes. Why not try their Caribbean Chicken, Roasted Fillet of Seabass or their Pan-fried Duck Breast, or for those who love the classics choose from quality steaks, pies, 'bangers & mash', and other well known pub meals.

Open every session and from Weds-Sun open all day. Open Mon-Tues from 4pm. Two real ales are available – Black Sheep and a rotating guest ale. Quality beer garden and off-road parking available. Children welcome.

HIDDEN PLACES GUIDES

Explore Britain and Ireland with *Hidden Places* guides - a fascinating series of national and local travel guides.

Packed with easy to read information on hundreds of places of interest as well as places to stay, eat and drink.

Available from both high street and internet booksellers

For more information on the full range of *Hidden Places* guides and other titles published by Travel Publishing visit our website on

www.travelpublishing.co.uk
or ask for our leaflet by phoning **01752 276660** or emailing **info@travelpublishing.co.uk**

THE HIDDEN PLACES OF
THE LAKE DISTRICT AND CUMBRIA

THE HIDDEN PLACES OF
THE PEAK DISTRICT AND DERBYSHIRE

THE HIDDEN PLACES OF
DEVON

212 THE HAXEY GATE INN

Haxey Road, Misterton, Doncaster,
South Yorkshire DN10 4BA
Tel: 01427 890746
website: www.thehaxeygate.co.uk

Occupying an idyllic position beside an ancient bridge over the River Idle, **The Haxey Gate Inn** is a well run, friendly local specialising in good wholesome, reasonably priced food and well kept beer. Because of its location beside the river, the inn is popular with anglers; golfers like it too since there's a golf course just across the bridge. The inn has a large patio and decking area, a spacious conservatory and terrace overlooking the river. Parts of the white-painted building date back to the 16th century and possibly even earlier.

Owners Mark and Lynne Mason took over here in winter 2007 and have made the inn a popular venue for locals and visitors alike. It is open all day, every day, with food based on fresh local produce served from noon until 8.30pm. The menu presents a good choice of main courses that includes Sizzling Steaks and dishes such as Butterfly Chicken, Battered Haddock and various salads. Vegetarians are well catered for and children too have their own menu. A Lite Bite selection is also available until 6pm with smaller portions of popular dishes. Booking is essential for Sunday

lunchtime and advisable at other times. Diners can enjoy their refreshments throughout the inn but the front-facing dining room is popular and seats up to 40. A second small dining room seating up to 12 people is also available. Lovers of real ales will find a choice of 3 - Batemans XB, a seasonal brew from Batemans and a rotating guest ale. The bar also stocks a comprehensive range of beverages.

If you are planning to stay in this pleasant corner of the county, the inn has 8 attractively furnished and decorated guest bedrooms, all with en suite facilities. They are located in a separate building across from the inn. All the rooms are on the ground floor and 1 room has been adapted for the disabled. The tariff includes a hearty breakfast.

Children are welcome; all major credit cards apart from American Express and Diners are accepted; there's good disabled access to the main building; and ample off road parking.

Incidentally, Mark and Lynne also run the Crooked Billet inn at Owston Ferry, just a short drive away.

**Barnsley Road, Marr, Doncaster,
South Yorkshire DN5 7AX
Tel: 01302 390355 Fax: 01302 391750**

Conveniently located close to junction 37 of the A1(M) on the A635 going towards Barnsley, **Marr Lodge** stands in its own grounds with a large and peaceful beer garden at the rear. Nick and Lucy Finlay took over here in the summer of 2007, bringing with them a wealth of experience in the hospitality business.

Nick has been in the trade for some 18 years and is a qualified chef with a passion for good food. His extensive menu of traditional home-cooked food is based on the best, locally-sourced produce. All the meat used here is British and wherever possible is acquired from South Yorkshire farmers. The beef is hung for at least 21 days to ensure it is tender and succulent.

The main menu offers amongst the starters dishes such as home-made soup, Bruschetta topped with tomato and basil, and a tapas portion of four of the most traditional Yorkshire dishes. Main course dishes include a traditional Farmhouse Pie, a hearty Mixed Grill, and Honey & Soy Glazed Salmon. Vegetarian options include Mushroom Stroganoff and Oven Roast Stuffed Red Peppers. Food is served from noon until 9pm, Monday to Saturday; and from noon until 7pm on Sunday. From Monday to Saturday, a Carvery is also available from noon until 3pm, on Saturday evenings from 6pm to 9pm, and on Sunday from noon "till it's gone!".

In addition to the regular menu, from Monday to Saturday Lunchtime Specials are available from

noon until 6pm. These include dishes such as Steak & Chips, omelettes and jacket potatoes. For desserts, how about a Treacle Sponge Pudding, Chocolate Truffle Cake or a Caramel Apple Granny? Because of the popularity of the food served here, booking is strongly advised, especially on Sundays.

Marr Lodge has a well-stocked bar that always has one or two real ales on tap, with Black Sheep as the regular brew. The Lodge also has a separate dining room which is available to hire for functions. Children are welcome here; all major credit cards are accepted; there is good disabled access throughout; and ample off road parking.

Tourist Information Centres

AYSGARTH FALLS

Aysgarth Falls National Park Centre, Aysgarth Falls,
Leyburn, North Yorkshire, DL8 3TH
e-mail: aysgarth@ytbtic.co.uk
Tel: 01969 662910

BARNSLEY

Central Library, Shambles Street, Barnsley,
South Yorkshire, S70 2JF
e-mail: barnsley@ytbtic.co.uk
Tel: 01226 206757

BEVERLEY

34 Butcher Row, Beverley, East Yorkshire, HU17 0AB
e-mail: beverley.tic@eastriding.gov.uk
Tel: 01482 391672

BRADFORD

City Hall, Centenary Square, Bradford,
West Yorkshire, BD1 1HY
e-mail: tourist.information@bradford.gov.uk
Tel: 01274 433678

BRIDLINGTON

25 Prince Street, Bridlington,
East Riding of Yorkshire, YO15 2NP
e-mail: bridlington.tic@eastriding.gov.uk
Tel: 01262 673474

BRIGG

The Buttercross Market Place, Brigg,
North Lincolnshire, DN20 8ER
e-mail: brigg.tic@northlincs.gov.uk
Tel: 01652 657053

CLEETHORPES

42-43 Alexandra Road, Cleethorpes,
North East Lincolnshire, DN35 8LE
e-mail: cleethorpes@ytbtic04.freeserve.co.uk
Tel: 01472 323111

DANBY

The Moors Centre, Danby Lodge, Lodge Lane, Danby,
Whitby, North Yorkshire, YO21 2NB
e-mail: moorscentre@northyorkmoors-npa.gov.uk
Tel: 01439 772737

DONCASTER

38-40 High Street, Doncaster, South Yorkshire, DN1 1DE
e-mail: tourist.information@doncaster.gov.uk
Tel: 01302 734309

FILEY

The Evron Centre, John Street, Filey,
North Yorkshire, YO14 9DW
e-mail: fileytic@scarborough.gov.uk
Tel: 01723 383637

GRASSINGTON

National Park Centre, Colvend, Hebden Road,
Grassington, North Yorkshire, BD23 5LB
e-mail: grassington@ytbtic.co.uk
Tel: 01756 752774

HALIFAX

Address:Piece Hall, Halifax, West Yorkshire, HX1 1RE
e-mail: halifax@ytbtic.co.uk
Tel: 01422 368725

HARROGATE

Royal Baths, Crescent Road, Harrogate,
North Yorkshire, HG1 2RR
e-mail: tic@harrogate.gov.uk
Tel: 0845 389 3223

HAWES

Dales Countryside Museum, Station Yard, Hawes,
North Yorkshire,DL8 3NT
e-mail: hawes@ytbtic.co.uk
Tel: 01969 666210

HAWORTH

2/4 West Lane, Haworth, Near Keighley,
West Yorkshire, BD22 8EF
e-mail: haworth@ytbtic.co.uk
Tel: 01535 642329

HEBDEN BRIDGE

Visitor and Canal Centre, New Road, Hebden Bridge,
West Yorkshire, HX7 8AF
e-mail: hebdenbridge@ytbtic.co.uk
Tel: 01422 843831

TOURIST INFORMATION CENTRES

HOLMFIRTH

49-51 Huddersfield Road, Holmfirth,
West Yorkshire, HD9 3JP
e-mail: holmfirth.tic@kirklees.gov.uk
Tel: 01484 222444

HORNSEA

120 Newbegin, Hornsea, East Yorkshire, HU18 1PB
e-mail: hornsea.tic@eastriding.gov.uk
Tel: 01964 536404

HORTON-IN-RIBBLESDALE

Pen-y-ghent Cafe, Horton-in-Ribblesdale, Settle,
North Yorkshire, BD24 0HE
e-mail: horton@ytbtic.co.uk
Tel: 01729 860333

HUDDERSFIELD

3 Albion Street, Huddersfield, West Yorkshire, HD1 2NW
e-mail: huddersfield.tic@kirklees.gov.uk
Tel: 01484 223200

HULL

1 Paragon Street, Hull, East Yorkshire, HU1 3NA
e-mail: tourist.information@hullcc.gov.uk
Tel: 01482 223559

HUMBER BRIDGE

North Bank Viewing Area, Ferriby Road, Hessle,
East Yorkshire, HU13 OLN
e-mail: humberbridge.tic@eastriding.gov.uk
Tel: 01482 640852

ILKLEY

Town Hall, Station Rd, Ilkley, West Yorkshire, LS29 8HB
e-mail: ilkley@ytbtic.c.uk
Tel: 01943 602319

INGLETON

The Community Centre Car Park, Ingleton,
North Yorkshire, LA6 3HG
e-mail: ingleton@ytbtic.co.uk
Tel: 015242 41049

KNARESBOROUGH

9 Castle Courtyard, Market Place, Knaresborough,
North Yorkshire, HG5 8AE
e-mail: kntic@harrogate.gov.uk
Tel: 0845 389 0177

LEEDS

Gateway Yorkshire, PO Box 244, The Arcade,
City Station, Leeds, West Yorkshire, LS1 1PL
e-mail: tourinfo@leeds.gov.uk
Tel: 0113 242 5242

LEEMING BAR

The Yorkshire Maid, The Great North Road,
Leeming Bar, Bedale, North Yorkshire, DL8 1DT
e-mail: leeming@ytbtic.co.uk
Tel: 01677 424262

LEYBURN

4 Central Chambers, Railway Street, Leyburn,
North Yorkshire, DL8 5BB
e-mail: TIC.Leyburn@Richmondshire.gov.uk
Tel: 01748 828747

MALHAM

National Park Centre, Malham, Skipton,
North Yorkshire, BD23 4DA
e-mail: malham@ytbtic.co.uk
Tel: 01969 652380

MALTON

58 Market Place, Malton, North Yorkshire, YO17 7LW
e-mail: maltontic@btconnect.com
Tel: 01653 600048

OTLEY

Otley Library & Tourist Information, Nelson Street,
Otley, West Yorkshire, LS21 1EZ
e-mail: otleytic@leedslearning.net
Tel: 0113 247 7707

PATELEY BRIDGE

18 High Street, Pateley Bridge,
North Yorkshire, HG3 5AW
e-mail: pbtic@harrogate.gov.uk
Tel: 0845 389 0179

PICKERING

Ropery House, The Ropery, Pickering,
North Yorkshire, YO18 8DY
e-mail: pickering@ytbtic.co.uk
Tel: 01751 473791

REETH

Hudson House, The Green Reeth, Richmond,
North Yorkshire, DL11 6TB
e-mail: reeth@ytbtic.co.uk
Tel: 01748 884059

RICHMOND

Friary Gardens, Victoria Road, Richmond,
North Yorkshire, DL10 4AJ
e-mail: richmond@ytbtic.co.uk
Tel: 01748 850252

RIPON

Minster Road, Ripon, North Yorkshire, HG4 1QT
e-mail: ripontic@harrogate.gov.uk
Tel: 0845 389 0178

ROTHERHAM

40 Bridgegate, Rotherham, South Yorkshire, S60 1PQ
e-mail: tic@rotherham.gov.uk
Tel: 01709 835904

SCARBOROUGH

Brunswick Shopping Centre, Westborough, Scarborough,
North Yorkshire, YO11 1UE
e-mail: tourismbureau@scarborough.gov.uk
Tel: 01723 383636

SCARBOROUGH HARBOURSIDE

Harbourside TIC, Sandside, Scarborough,
North Yorkshire, YO11 1PP
e-mail: harboursidetic@scarborough.gov.uk
Tel: 01723 383636

SCUNTHORPE

Scunthorpe Central Library, Carlton Street, Scunthorpe,
North Lincolnshire, DN15 6TX
e-mail: brigg.tic@northlincs.gov.uk
Tel: 01724 297354

SELBY

Visitor Information Centre, 52 Micklegate, Selby,
North Yorkshire, YO8 4EQ
e-mail: selby@ytbtic.co.uk
Tel: 01757 212181

SETTLE

Town Hall, Cheapside, Settle, North Yorkshire, BD24 9EJ
e-mail: settle@ytbtic.co.uk
Tel: 01729 825192

SHEFFIELD

Visitor Information Point, 14 Norfolk Row,
Sheffield, S1 2PA
e-mail: visitor@sheffield.gov.uk
Tel: 0114 2211900

SKIPTON

35 Coach Street, Skipton, North Yorkshire, BD23 1LQ
e-mail: skipton@ytbtic.co.uk
Tel: 01756 792809

THE DE GREY ROOMS

Exhibition Square, York, North Yorkshire, YO1 7HB
e-mail: tic@york-tourism.co.uk
Tel: 01904 550099

THIRSK

Thirsk Tourist Information Centre, 49 Market Place,
Thirsk, North Yorkshire, YO7 1HA
e-mail: thirsktic@hambleton.gov.uk
Tel: 01845 522755

TODMORDEN

15 Burnley Road, Todmorden, West Yorkshire, OL14 7BU
e-mail: todmorden@ytbtic.co.uk
Tel: 01706 818181

WAKEFIELD

9 The Bull Ring, Wakefield, West Yorkshire, WF1 1HB
e-mail: tic@wakefield.gov.uk
Tel: 0845 601 8353

WETHERBY

Wetherby Library & Tourist Info. Centre, 17 Westgate,
Wetherby, West Yorkshire, LS22 6LL
e-mail: wetherbytic@leedslearning.net
Tel: 01937 582151

WHITBY

Langborne Road, Whitby, North Yorkshire, YO21 1YN
e-mail: whitbytic@scarborough.gov.uk
Tel: 01723 383636

WITHERNSEA

131 Queen Street, Withernsea, HU19 2DJ
e-mail: withernsea.tic@eastriding.gov.uk
Tel: 01964 615683

YORK (RAILWAY STATION)

Outer Concourse, Railway Station, Station Road, York,
North Yorkshire, YO24 1AY
e-mail: kg@ytbyork.swiftserve.net
Tel: 01904 550099

Towns, Villages and Places of Interest

TRAVEL PUBLISHING ORDER FORM

To order any of our publications just fill in the payment details below and complete the order form. For orders of less than 4 copies please add £1.00 per book for postage and packing. Orders over 4 copies are P & P free.

Name:

Address:

Tel no:

Please Complete Either:

I enclose a cheque for £ _____ made payable to Travel Publishing Ltd

Or:

Card No: Expiry Date:

Signature:

Please either send, telephone, fax or e-mail your order to:

Travel Publishing Ltd, Airport Business Centre, 10 Thornbury Road, Estover, Plymouth, Devon PL6 7PP
Tel: 01752 687280   Fax: 01752 697299   e-mail: info@travelpublishing.co.uk

	Price	Quantity		Price	Quantity
HIDDEN PLACES REGIONAL TITLES			**COUNTRY LIVING RURAL GUIDES**		
Cornwall	£8.99	....	East Anglia	£10.99	....
Devon	£8.99	....	Heart of England	£10.99	....
Dorset, Hants & Isle of Wight	£8.99	....	Ireland	£11.99	....
East Anglia	£8.99	....	North East	£10.99	....
Lake District & Cumbria	£8.99	....	North West	£10.99	....
Northumberland & Durham	£8.99	....	Scotland	£11.99	....
Peak District and Derbyshire	£8.99	....	South of England	£10.99	....
Yorkshire	£8.99	....	South East of England	£10.99	....
HIDDEN PLACES NATIONAL TITLES			Wales	£11.99	....
			West Country	£10.99	....
England	£11.99	....	**OTHER TITLES**		
Ireland	£11.99	....			
Scotland	£11.99	....	Off the Motorway	£11.99	....
Wales	£11.99	....	Garden Centres & Nurseries	£11.99	....
COUNTRY PUBS AND INNS					
Cornwall	£5.99	....			
Devon	£7.99	....	**TOTAL QUANTITY:**		
Sussex	£5.99	....			
Wales	£8.99	....	**POST & PACKING:**		
Yorkshire	£7.99	....			
			TOTAL VALUE:		

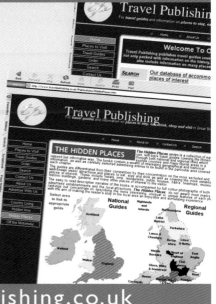

READER REACTION FORM

The *Travel Publishing* research team would like to receive reader's comments on any visitor attractions or places reviewed in the book and also recommendations for suitable entries to be included in the next edition. This will help ensure that the *Hidden Places Series of Guides* continues to provide its readers with useful information on the more interesting, unusual or unique features of each attraction or place ensuring that their visit to the local area is an enjoyable and stimulating experience. To provide your comments or recommendations would you please complete the forms below and overleaf as indicated and send to:

**The Research Department, Travel Publishing Ltd, Airport Business Centre,
10 Thornbury Road, Estover, Plymouth, Devon PL6 7PP**

Your Name:

Your Address:

Your Telephone Number:

Please tick as appropriate:

Comments ☐   Recommendation ☐

Name of Establishment:

Address:

Telephone Number:

Name of Contact:

READER REACTION FORM

COMMENT OR REASON FOR RECOMMENDATION:

....

....

....

....

....

....

....

....

....

....

....

....

....

....

....

....

....

....

READER REACTION FORM

The *Travel Publishing* research team would like to receive reader's comments on any visitor attractions or places reviewed in the book and also recommendations for suitable entries to be included in the next edition. This will help ensure that the *Hidden Places Series of Guides* continues to provide its readers with useful information on the more interesting, unusual or unique features of each attraction or place ensuring that their visit to the local area is an enjoyable and stimulating experience. To provide your comments or recommendations would you please complete the forms below and overleaf as indicated and send to:

The Research Department, Travel Publishing Ltd, Airport Business Centre, 10 Thornbury Road, Estover, Plymouth, Devon PL6 7PP

Your Name:

Your Address:

Your Telephone Number:

Please tick as appropriate:

Comments ☐   Recommendation ☐

Name of Establishment:

Address:

Telephone Number:

Name of Contact:

READER REACTION FORM

COMMENT OR REASON FOR RECOMMENDATION:

....

....

....

....

....

....

....

....

....

....

....

....

....

....

....

....

....

....

READER REACTION FORM

The *Travel Publishing* research team would like to receive reader's comments on any visitor attractions or places reviewed in the book and also recommendations for suitable entries to be included in the next edition. This will help ensure that the *Hidden Places Series of Guides* continues to provide its readers with useful information on the more interesting, unusual or unique features of each attraction or place ensuring that their visit to the local area is an enjoyable and stimulating experience. To provide your comments or recommendations would you please complete the forms below and overleaf as indicated and send to:

The Research Department, Travel Publishing Ltd, Airport Business Centre, 10 Thornbury Road, Estover, Plymouth, Devon PL6 7PP

Your Name:

Your Address:

Your Telephone Number:

Please tick as appropriate:

Comments ☐   Recommendation ☐

Name of Establishment:

Address:

Telephone Number:

Name of Contact:

READER REACTION FORM

COMMENT OR REASON FOR RECOMMENDATION:

....
....
....
....
....
....
....
....
....
....
....
....
....
....
....
....
....
....
....

Index of Advertisers

INDEX OF ADVERTISERS

PLACES OF INTEREST